Israel

the Bradt Travel Guide

Samantha Wilson

www.bradtguides.com

Bradt Travel Guides Ltd, UK
The Globe Pequot Press Inc, USA

edition
I

SYRIA

LEBANON

MEDITERRANEAN

SEA

Dead Sea

Sea of Galilee

Jordan

Yehudiya NR

Jordan River Crossing

King Hussein Bridge/Allenby Crossing

Qumran NP

Tel Meggido NP

Beit She'an NP

Carmel National Park

Mt Hermon 2224m

Golan Heights

Katzrin

Ramot

Kiryat Shmona

Tiberias

Tzfat

Mt Meron 1200m

Nahariya

Akko

HAIFA

Zichron Yaakov

Hadera

Netanya

Herzliya

TEL AVIV-JAFFA

Ashdod

Ashkelon

GAZA

Jezreel Valley

Nazareth

Jenin

Shechem (Nablus)

Ramallah

Bethlehem

Hebron

JERUSALEM

Jericho

KEY
- Capital city
- Other city
- Main town
- Urban area
- Airport
- Main road
- Other road
- Railway
- International boundary
- Palestinian settlement boundary
- Palestinian settlement area of West Bank
- UN separation line
- National park
- Crater
- Archaeological/historic site

Based on mapping by Carta, Jerusalem

Masada
page 226

Ramon Crater Nature Reserve
page 242

Eilat
page 260

Bradt

N

D · E · A · D

Desert

Masada

Arad

Small
Crater

Dimona

Big Crater

Sde Boker

Beer Sheva

Negev
Desert

Mitzpe
Ramon

Ramon Crater

Desert

Arava

EILAT

Yitzhak Rabin Crossing

Taba Crossing

E G Y P T

0   20km
0   20 miles

Israel

Don't miss...

Tel Aviv
People watching
from a chic café
(IGTO) page 97

The Dead Sea
Floating in the
therapeutic waters
(IGTO) page 245

Sea of Galilee
Stepping back into
biblical times
(PZ) page 178

above left   **The Dome of the Rock forms the centrepiece of Jerusalem's holiest Islamic site, the Temple Mount** (SW) page 83

above   **Soldier praying at the Western Wall** (PZ) page 80

left   **Spice stand at the Souk Khan es Zeit (Muslim Quarter souk)** (NS) page 84

below   **Mount of Olives** (PZ) page 87

above **The main street in the Mea Shearim neighbourhood, Jerusalem** (PZ) page 68

below left **Pilgrims walking the Via Dolorosa** (IGTO) pages 76-7

below right **Inside the Church of the Holy Sepulchre** (PZ) page 71 left   Confectionery stand in the Muslim Quarter, Jerusalem (IGTO) page 83

below   Spices and dried vegetables on sale (PZ)

bottom   Souk HaCarmel is Tel Aviv's busiest fruit and vegetable market (IGTO) page 119

AUTHOR

Samantha Wilson found herself in Israel quite by chance. After completing a degree in archaeology at Exeter University she embarked on a trip to south and central America that saw her wind up in the Middle East a year later. There she spent several years travelling to every corner of Israel's little land, rescuing countless stray animals and writing for a variety of publications including *Transitions Abroad* and a regular column on animal and wildlife topics. In 2006, she made the move to Beijing, China, where she wrote, and contributed to, several guidebooks including *Explorer Beijing*, *Streetwise Guide Beijing* and *Sichuan, The Spice of Life*. Whilst writing this book she became a regular face on El Al flights between Beijing and Tel Aviv, jumping at any chance to escape the freezing temperatures of Asia for the mild climes of the Middle East.

AUTHOR STORY

I arrived in Israel quite by chance. After completing my archaeology degree at Exeter University I set off on a trip bound for South and Central America and found myself a year later living in the heart of the Middle East, a region I have grown to love for so many reasons. Perhaps it is its unconventionality, passion, staggering beauty or perhaps even its drama; I couldn't say for sure. Friends and acquaintances would ask me why I lived in such a politically sensitive and volatile country, to me a sad opening question about life in Israel. There is so much more to this small yet incredibly fascinating place and I was driven by this to share my intrigue and discoveries with others. And so I embarked on a thorough (and thoroughly enjoyable) exploration of every corner of Israel, from its snow-capped mountain peaks to its Red Sea coast and every kibbutz in between. Along the way, my project and I were greeted with an enthusiasm, gratitude and assistance I could never have predicted, the people of Israel desperate for others to share in the country of which they are so fiercely proud. In this way, while I may have put pen to paper, this is truly the work of so many who share a common love of this vibrant and colourful little land.

PUBLISHER'S FOREWORD   *Hilary Bradt*

The first Bradt travel guide was written in 1974 by George and Hilary Bradt on a river barge floating down a tributary of the Amazon. In the 1980s and 1990s the focus shifted away from hiking to broader-based guides covering new destinations – usually the first to be published about these places. In the 21st century Bradt continues to publish such ground-breaking guides, as well as others to established holiday destinations, incorporating in-depth information on culture and natural history with the nuts and bolts of where to stay and what to see.

Bradt authors support responsible travel, and provide advice not only on minimum impact but also on how to give something back through local charities. In this way a true synergy is achieved between the traveller and local communities.

First published January 2009

Bradt Travel Guides Ltd, 23 High Street, Chalfont St Peter,
Bucks SL9 9QE, England
www.bradtguides.com

Published in the USA by The Globe Pequot Press Inc,
246 Goose Lane, PO Box 480, Guilford,
Connecticut 06437-0480

Text copyright © 2009 Samantha Wilson
Maps copyright © 2009 Bradt Travel Guides Ltd
Where indicated, maps based on sources provided by © Carta, Jerusalem
Photographs © 2009 individual photographers (see below)

ISBN-13: 978 1 84162 271 2

British Library Cataloguing in Publication Data
A catalogue record for this book is available from the British Library

Photographs Hugo Canabi/Alamy (HC/Alamy), Israel Government Tourist Office (IGTO), Niv Silberman (NS), PhotoZion.com/John Theodor (PZ), Samantha Wilson (SW)
Front cover Judean desert, near Masada (HC/Alamy)
Back cover Jerusalem Old City (PZ), Floating in the Dead Sea (IGTO)
Title page Rock formations in Timna Park (PZ), Jaffa's Old Port (IGTO), Nubian Ibex (PZ)

Maps Alan Whitaker (who dedicates his work on this guide to the memory of Mrs Frances Goddard, who died as he started the drawing)

Typeset from the author's disk by Dorchester Typesetting Group
Printed and bound in India by Nutech Photolithographers

Acknowledgements

A book like this doesn't come together without the help of many people to whom I shall always be grateful. My sincere thanks go out to the whole Silberman family for their wonderful hospitality and countless late-night airport pick-ups, and to Ami Dorfman and his lovely family for sharing their home, and passion and knowledge of Galilee with me. I would like to extend my admiration and appreciation to the Israel Nature and National Parks Protection Authority staff for their dedication and enthusiasm to preserving the country's finest sites, to Guy Brandon for his expert advice and recommendations, and to Zella Philips for posing the right kinds of questions. Special thanks go to Anat Sayag, Inbar Carmeli, Yonatan Bental, Khamis Arbid and Vera Arbid for their help and recommendations and to Ido Bar-Nir, Dror and Zohar Golan, Yotam Shacham, Maya Amit and Allison Gosney for their advice and wonderful company. I would like to extend enormous thanks to my loving friends and family, especially my parents, for supporting and encouraging me throughout the difficult days, late nights and hours on the road. Without you, it just wouldn't have been as much fun. Lastly, my eternal and heartfelt gratitude goes to Niv Silberman without whom, quite simply, this book wouldn't have happened. Your selfless and never-ending help, encouragement and enthusiasm were my inspiration.

FEEDBACK REQUEST

Israel is a modern country with a fast-paced way of living and as such things tend to change quickly in this little stretch of land. The trendiest bar or café today is obsolete tomorrow, hotel prices fluctuate with the political situation, profound archaeological discoveries occur on a daily basis and public transport continues to improve and grow at a rate of knots. Everyone sees Israel in a different way and I would love to hear from readers about their own experiences in the Holy Land, something that would help me to prepare for the next edition of this book. If you come across something that you feel should be included, a hotel that has lost its charm or a fantastic little restaurant nestled away somewhere then please get in touch, be it good or bad it all goes towards making the next edition that much better. Write to me care of Bradt Guides (23 High Street, Chalfont St Peter, Bucks SL9 9QE; www.bradtguides.com).

Contents

LIST OF MAPS

Location Middle East

Neighbouring countries Lebanon, Syria, Jordan, Egypt (Palestinian territories of the West Bank and Gaza Strip)

Area 20,330km^2 (22,145km^2 including the West Bank and Gaza Strip)

Climate Varies according to latitude: temperate in central and northern regions; hot and dry in the south

Status Parliamentary democracy

Population 7,282,000 (Central Bureau of Statistics May 2008 census)

Life expectancy Women 81.7 years, men 79.6 years

Capital Jerusalem (although most countries retain embassies in Tel Aviv)

Other main towns Tel Aviv, Haifa, Eilat, Nazareth, Tiberias, Tzfat, Netanya, Beer Sheva, Hadera, Ashdod

Economy Cut diamonds, high-technology and agricultural products are the major exports

GDP Purchasing power parity US$184.9 billion; per capita US$28,800

Languages Hebrew and Arabic are official languages. English is widely spoken.

Religion Judaism, Islam, Christianity, Druze, Bahai

Currency New Israeli Shekel (NIS)

Exchange rate US$1 = 3.5NIS; €1 = 7NIS; £1 = 5.5NIS

National airline El Al

National airport Ben Gurion International Airport

International telephone code +972

Time GMT +2

Electrical voltage 220V/50Hz

Weights and measures Metric

Flag White and blue with the Star of David in the centre

National anthem Hatikvah

National emblem Menorah

National sport Football (soccer)

Public holidays Rosh Hashanah (September), Yom Kippur (September/October), Succot (September/October), Hannukah (December), Purim (February/March), Passover (March/April), Holocaust Memorial Day (April/May), National Memorial Day (April/May), Independence Day (April/May), Shavuot (May/June), Tisha Bav (July/August). Dates vary according to the Jewish calendar.

Introduction

Israel is a land of dramatic and poignant contrasts, a land whose tumultuous existence often forms a shadow over the rich and vibrant life that beats beneath it, a land of incredible beauty, variety and character. Upon this soil have walked some of the greatest figures of our past, a ground that has seen the birth of world religions and the passionate battles that ensued to protect them.

It is a sad yet realistic state of affairs that the word 'Israel' has today become synonymous with conflict, religious tension and political debate, yet historically this tiny stretch of land has formed the gladiatorial arena where empires and faiths have risen and fallen, a fact that remains as true today as it did 2,000 years ago.

Yet behind the television cameras and glare of the international limelight, Israel's tourist appeal is simply enormous. From the snow-capped peaks that straddle the northern border with Syria, to its barren and eerily beautiful expanse of rock deserts that form the gateway to Egypt and Africa beyond, the country leaves few landscapes unrepresented. As a meeting point between the cold steppes of Europe and the desert lands of the Syrian-African Rift Valley, Israel is a country geographically (and politically) divided. The swirl of green valleys, tree-studded hills and trickling streams that form the northern region are dotted with towns that have stood the tests of time, their inhabitants displaying a vibrant mesh of beliefs, traditions and cultures that remain proud and strong. In contrast are the arid lands of the south, vast craters, tiny isolated settlements and the inhospitable beauty of the Dead Sea swallowed up in their midst. The lively, cosmopolitan hub of Tel Aviv takes pleasure in its role as the country's economic, commercial and diplomatic centre, its wild beaches and secular way of life providing Jerusalem's diametric opposite. Jerusalem: few, if any cities on this planet can attest to the life that this incredible city has lived, its willpower, determination and passion to survive having seen it rise above all else that has come its way. Forming the cross on the map where the world's three biggest religions converge, it is a place like no other, one that leaves even the most religiously apathetic of visitors in awe.

Israel is a modern country that has created, thanks to its millions of immigrants, countless faiths and numberless cultures, a charm and uniqueness like nowhere else on earth. Combine this with its rich historic, geological and natural treasures and it is instantly apparent why so many have fought for so long to keep it.

KEY TO SYMBOLS

—·—·—	International boundary	✡	Synagogue
—····—	Palestinian enclave boundary	☾	Mosque
▬▬▬	UN Demilitarised zone boundary	✝	Church/chapel/cathedral
	National park/protected area	🕎 ☾ ✚	Cemetery (Jewish/Muslim/Christian)
	National forest park/reserve	🏛	Tomb
✈ ✈	Airport (international/domestic)	$	Bank/bureau de change
---◆---	Ferry (pedestrian)	🛉	Statue or monument
═══	Motorway/main road	∴	Archaeological/historic site
═══ = = =	Other road/4x4 track	▲	Summit (height in metres)
▥▥▥	Pedestrianised town street	❀	Garden
‖‖‖‖‖	Stepped ways (paths)	🌾	Windmill
▭▬▭	Railway	⛺	Campsite
= = = = =	Underground railway/subway	🚗	Car hire
▭—○—▭	Cable car	⚲	Cycle hire
VI · · · V	The Stations of the Cross route	🐫	Camel riding
···········	National trail/footpath		Urban park
🚌	Bus station etc	⬚⬚	Urban market
🅿	Car park		Shopping centre/mall
⌂	Hotel, inn etc		Defined "old town" area
☆	Nightclub/casino	⛴	Cruiseships
✕	Restaurant	⌐····┐	Airport runway
♈	Bar		Built-up area
⌸	Café		Coral reef
ⓔ	Internet access	❋	Viewpoint
❸	Embassy	🗼	Lighthouse
ⓘ	Tourist information	○	Hot Springs
⊠	Post office	⌇	Waterfall
✚	Hospital/clinic	⌂	Cave/grotto
✛	Pharmacy/surgery/dentist		Crater edge
🏺	Museum or art gallery		Salt lake or pan
♻	Theatre/cinema	lO	Industrial complex
🏛	Important/historic building	⟨⟩	Beach
🏰	Castle/fort	⤳	Bird-watching area
🏯	Ancient city gate	🎿	Skiing
⚲	City wall		

Part One

GENERAL INFORMATION

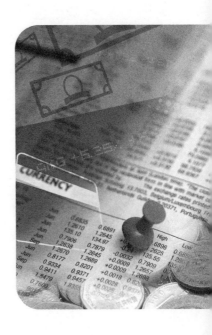

I

Background Information

GEOGRAPHY AND CONSERVATION

Israel is located in the western fringes of the Middle East. The long, narrow strip of land is almost diamond shaped, coming to a point at the Red Sea in the south. It borders Lebanon and Syria in the north, Jordan in the east and Egypt in the southwest, with the eastern coast fringing the Mediterranean Sea. Measuring just 470km in length and 135km at its widest point, the country is unique in that it has three highly contrasting geographical regions. In the west is the fertile coastal plain, home to major cities such as Tel Aviv and Haifa and the most densely populated region of the country. The forests, valleys, mountains and rivers that make up the north and east of the country incorporate the verdant Galilee region and the wild stretch of the Golan Heights, as well as the freshwater Sea of Galilee, Jordan River and Israel's highest peak, Mount Hermon (2,224m). More than half of Israel is desert, stretching all the way down to the Red Sea and the southern city of Eilat. The Dead Sea forms the eastern border with Jordan and stands as the world's lowest point at 400m below sea level. Sitting in the vast Syrian-African Rift Valley, its extreme salinity does not support any living organisms, the freshwater oases that dot the desert the only source of life to the flora and fauna of the region. Comprising the rocky Negev, Arava and Judean deserts, Israel's south is sparsely populated and transport links are few and far between.

NATIONAL PARKS Israel is today home to over 65 national parks and 150 nature reserves, which are under the management of the Israel Nature and National Parks Protection Authority (INPA) (*www.parks.co.il*). In contrast to many other countries where the term 'national park' implies vast areas of open, protected land, in Israel the term is used to denote any protected area, be it a small archaeological site, vast canyon or landscaped hot spring park. Castles and fortresses, churches and synagogues, desert oases, caves, rivers, waterfalls and wildlife reserves grace the list of the country's national parks. Almost all parks charge an entry fee that goes towards continued conservation and management efforts. Discount cards can be bought at any of the park offices for 250NIS per person (or 275NIS for two people) and are valid for one year and provide access or discounts to most national parks and nature reserves in the country.

FLORA The Bible describes the Holy Land as 'a land of wheat and barley, of vines and fig trees and pomegranates, a land of olive trees and honey'. This wealth of plant life not seen in other Middle Eastern countries is down to its varied climate and geology and geographical positioning. A total of 2,380 species of flora have been recorded, many endangered or endemic to Israel. The Mediterranean region supports the densest concentrations, where alpine species thrive mainly along the Carmel Mountain ridge, in the Jezreel Valley and in the Galilee region. Plant life in the desert is sparse with the exception of small pockets of dense vegetation in

About 8% of Israel's population lives in rural areas, divided between small towns, villages and two types of co-operative frameworks unique to the country. These co-operative frameworks, the *moshav* and the *kibbutz*, started appearing in the early part of the 20th century and today remain a key feature of the landscape and social structure of the country.

KIBBUTZ The word 'kibbutz' in Hebrew means 'gathering', and is used to describe a collective, self-contained farm settlement whereby members make decisions together for the good of the community, and wealth and property is shared out. The kibbutz appeared in Israel at the turn of the last century, created by Jewish settlers in Palestine, the first being Kibbutz Deganya Alef just south of the Sea of Galilee (see page 181). For decades, the idealistic community living attracted non-Jews who came to volunteer and live within the enclosed settlements. Parents lived in separate quarters to children, meals were eaten communally and homes were owned by the community not the individual. These days, however, the original concept has been lost and while kibbutz communities are still famously tight-knit where children and dogs run freely through the settlement, many meals continue to be eaten in the communal dining room and a kibbutz-run business remains in each, members in most *kibbutzim* (the plural of kibbutz) are allowed to purchase their own homes, go out to work and live more independent lives. Today 1.7% of the population lives in kibbutzim, their main economies centring on agriculture, tourism, industry and services (many kibbutzim have set up exotic wedding venues).

MOSHAV Created in the early 1900s, the moshav settlement was a collective village based on agriculture. Each family maintained its own farm and household, and land was divided up between family members. Today there are 451 *moshavim* (the plural of moshav) housing 3.4% of the population, and while farming businesses still form the backbone of much of Israel's agriculture (in particular cattle rearing, dairy and poultry), families maintain a more independent lifestyle and generally work outside of the settlement. The safe, homely, family-orientated environment that abounds on these settlements is today much sought after and, as such, property rarely comes onto the market. Children of members of the moshav are entitled to land when they come of age and often choose to remain and raise their own families. In many parts of the country, the incredible popularity of *zimmers* (see page 46), luxury, privately run rural accommodation has seen tourism begin to play an important part in the economies of the moshavim and has made them yet more sought after.

oases such as Ein Gedi and Ein Avdat. In its accreditations, Israel is famed as being the northernmost limit for species such as the papyrus reed, the southernmost limit for plants such as the red coral peony and the only place where the Euphrates poplar still grows. The famed Madonna lily and Gilboa iris, rare Kermes oak trees and gnarled, ancient olive trees decorate the fertile northern terrain while towering date palms flourish in the arid, sub-Saharan soils of the desert.

WILDLIFE
Mammals Israel is home to 116 species of mammal which, compared with the 100 species recorded in the whole of Europe, is vast. The country forms the crossroads for animals originating in the alpine European region to the north and those

arriving from the desert regions of Arabia and Africa in the south. The largest inhabitants are mountain gazelles, wild boar, foxes, Nubian ibex and the rarely seen leopards, hyenas, jackals, wolves and onagers. A large conservation effort is in play to reintroduce many biblical creatures long since hunted to disappearance to their natural lands. Jerusalem's Biblical Zoo (see page 94) and the Hai Bar nature reserves are at the centre of this scheme (see below).

Birds Sitting on the main migratory thoroughfare, Israel's skies and valleys seasonally fill with hundreds of species of birds who rest on their long journey south or north. A total of 510 bird species have been recorded, birdwatching reserves such as those in the Hula Valley and Eilat being prime places to see the splendid array of species that include cranes, honey buzzards and pelicans. Of those who make their home in Israel are the highly endangered griffon and Egyptian vultures and imperial and spotted eagles. The Gamla and Yehudiya national parks are the best places to see wild vultures soaring in the skies above

WALKING IN THE HOOFPRINTS OF ISRAEL'S BIBLICAL ANIMALS

Hai Bar is a nationwide organisation whose principal objective is to preserve the country's endangered animals and reintroduce indigenous species long since hunted to disappearance back to their previous habitats. Lions, cheetahs, bears and crocodiles, some of Israel's more ferocious ancient inhabitants are not, for obvious reasons, a part of this scheme, but more mild-mannered species such as fallow and roe deer, Arabian oryx, Ethiopian ostrich and the onager (a type of wild ass) are being reintroduced to the delicate ecosystem. Two herds of onager were recently released into the arid wilderness of the Arava Desert, with the Arabian oryx, whose impressive horns make them easily recognisable in the landscape, being another success story for the desert terrains. The **Yotvata Hai Bar Reserve** is home to many species who still roam the savanna-like lands of the south and a delightful safari and small conservation zoo makes a highly recommended trip to see the desert as it once may have looked. Hyenas, caracals, leopards, wolves, gazelle, sand- and fennec foxes, desert hedgehogs and many birds and reptiles have all now been placed significantly lower down the endangered list thanks to ongoing efforts.

The last native roe deer was shot in the Carmel forest in 1912 and an intensive project has been underway to return them, and fallow deer, to their original habitat. In a time when Israel held better alliances with Iran, a small herd of Persian fallow deer were brought to the country with the objective of breeding and reintroducing them to the wild. Today, the **Carmel Hai Bar Wildlife Reserve** (04 9841750/2; ☉ 08.00–16.00; admission adult/child 18/8NIS) is home to the biggest population of fallow deer in the world, many of whom have been successfully released. Wild sheep and goats, griffon and Egyptian vultures and Bonelli's eagles are also bred at the reserve, which is located 300m south of Haifa University's main entrance on route 672. It isn't always open during 'opening' hours so it's advisable to call ahead. Another important griffon vulture sanctuary is located next to the hilltop fortress of **Kochav Hayarden** (see page 182).

Visitors are invited to enter the reserves to appreciate up close these biblical animals, the entry fees providing invaluable contributions to their continuing success. Many species, including the more fearsome contenders, can also been seen at the **Biblical Zoo** in Jerusalem, which is closely involved with the conservation efforts (see page 94).

while the Israel Nature and National Parks Protection Authority has a research station and shelter next to Kochav HaYarden in the Lower Galilee.

Reptiles There are 97 species of reptile and seven species of amphibian in the country, most having disappeared along with urban and agricultural expansion and a loss of habitat. Scorpions are still prevalent in the desert while several snake species can be found across the country. Green turtles nest almost exclusively in Israel, Cyprus and Turkey, and researchers believe there are fewer than 1,000 females alive today.

The more common loggerhead turtles, most populous in Greece, Cyprus and Turkey, also nest in Israel, Syria and north Africa, although numbers are dwindling.

Marine life Eilat's Red Sea coast is home to several species of tropical marine life although the once-flourishing coral reefs have been overexploited and are now well past their prime. However dolphins, octopuses, countless fish species and extremely occasionally whale sharks can be seen in the waters off Israel's southern coast.

CLIMATE Israel has a 'Mediterranean', subtropical climate with hot summers and mild winters. Summer months are from April through October with temperatures peaking in July and August. Climatic conditions do, however, vary considerably. The Mediterranean coast suffers hot, humid summers and wet, mild winters, while the hilly regions of the north and east (including Jerusalem) are less humid in summer but have moderately cold winters and occasional snow. Mount Hermon is snow-capped almost year-round but snowfall has been significantly less in recent years. The desert is hot year-round, with exceptionally arid conditions. Rare flash floods can occur during heavy rains as water runs across the surface of the impermeable rock desert. Additional information and weather reports are available at the Israel Meteorological Service (✆ 03 9682121).

CLIMATE CHART

	Tzfat	Haifa	Tiberias	Tel Aviv	Jerusalem	Eilat
Mean temp Jan °C	4–9	9–17	9–18	10–17	6–12	10–21
Mean temp Aug °C	19–29	24–31	23–38	24–30	19–29	26–40
Days' rainfall per annum	58	51	47	46	44	5
Annual rainfall (mm)	712	540	407	524	553	32

HISTORY

IN THE BEGINNING... 'In the beginning God created the heavens and the earth.' And if you asked any observant Jew where Israel's history begins, it would be around this time. Historically, the land that is modern-day Israel has always stood on a great world crossroads, where empires, religions and cultures clashed or convened. In the 24th century, it formed the cultural bull's-eye between Egypt, Assyria, Mesopotamia and Asia Minor and in the 2nd millennium BCE (Before Common Era, term used in lieu of BC in non-Christian regions) various tribes began an invasion of the country, which, at the time was inhabited by the Canaanites. Around the 19th/20th century BCE, the Hebrew Bible's *Book of Genesis* records the appearance of three Jewish patriarchs: Abraham, Isaac and Jacob, the last of whom was also known as Israel. The Bible tells how Abraham was sent to Canaan to create a great nation and bring blessing to others. When famine ravaged the land, the Israelites relocated to Egypt where, according to biblical sources they spent 400 years in slavery. Led by Moses they escaped to freedom and spent the following 40 years wandering the desert before resettling in Canaan. Every year the Jewish holiday of Pesach (Passover) is celebrated in honour of the Exodus.

THE ISRAELITES AND THE IRON AGE (1200–586BCE)

Throughout the next two centuries the Israelites conquered the land, a time known as the Period of Judges. During this time of fierce wars people made allegiances with many of the 'judges', who emerged as leaders at that time. The divided armies were weak and suffering from incursions from the Philistines, a tribe descended from Asia Minor who had settled along the southern coast. In 1020BCE, the Israelites received the gift of unification in the form of King Saul, the Jewish people's first monarch. Upon Saul's defeat against the Philistines, David ascended the throne and it was under his reign that Jerusalem was conquered (vanquishing the Jebusites) and declared capital of the realm. David was succeeded by his son Solomon in 965BCE who not only massively expanded the kingdom, but also commissioned the building of the First Temple. After Solomon's death civil unrest led to the division of the monarchy and the emergence of two kingdoms: Israel in the north, governed by ten tribes; and Judah in the south, led by two tribes. In 721BCE, the Assyrians conquered the Kingdom of Israel and its ten tribes were forcibly taken into exile. In 586BCE, the Kingdom of Judah suffered a similar fate at the hands of the Babylonians who destroyed Jerusalem and sacked the First Temple.

THE PERSIANS, ALEXANDER THE GREAT AND THE HASMONEANS (538–63BCE)

The Persians conquered Babylon in 538BCE and the tribe of Judah was granted permission by the Persian king Cyrus to return to Jerusalem. There, towards the end of the 6th century BCE, they constructed the Second Temple. Throughout the Persian period the Jews prospered and strengthened, the Knesset Hagedolah (Great Assembly – see page 15) owing its origins to this time. In 332BCE, however, Persian rule came to an end with the conquest of Alexander the Great. His death in 323BCE was succeeded by battles over his legacy and right to the throne, a battle that was eventually won by Seleucus I who founded the Syrian-based Seleucid dynasty. This period is characterised in history as the Hellenistic, whereby the remaining descendants of Alexander's Greek kingdom and its merging with the Persians resulted in the emergence of a distinctly Greek cultural phase, even under Seleucid rule. By this time synagogues had become the centre of the Jewish community and when the Seleucid rulers began suppressing the Jewish religion, imposing upon the population the Greek-oriented culture, language and beliefs, the Jews rose in a revolt in 166BCE led by the Maccabees, a Jewish family of patriots (an event celebrated today with the festival of Hanukkah). This in turn led to the establishment of the Jewish Hasmoneans, who eventually ousted the Seleucids and imposed their own religion on the land. It was during this period of Jewish rule that religious tensions caused breakaway groups to emerge, most notably the Essenes who are the believed authors of the Dead Sea Scrolls found at Qumran (see page 250).

JESUS AND THE ROMANS (63BCE–CE212)

In 63BCE, Pompeii captured Jerusalem replacing the Seleucids as the region's great power, and demoting the Hasmonean king, Hyrcanus II, to acting king under Roman rule. The Jewish population was hostile to the new regime and rebellions eventually led to the final demise of the Hasmoneans, and Roman rule over the Land of Judea. In 37BCE, Herod the Great was appointed king, becoming one of the Roman Empire's most powerful leaders.

Under him the great coastal city of Caesarea exploded on to the scene as one of the world's most crucial seaports, the palace of Masada (see page 252) was built as his luxury playground and the temple was given a magnificent makeover. Despite (or perhaps in spite) of these achievements the Jews were displeased, and revolts led to the destruction of the Second Temple under Titus. A last attempt in CE123 (Common Era, used in lieu of AD) to claim Jewish liberation failed after an ambitious but unsuccessful uprising led by Shimon Bar Kochba. According to Josephus Flavius, a 1st-century historian, hundreds of thousands of Jews were exiled and dispersed across the empire, an event known as the Jewish Diaspora. Jerusalem was razed to the ground and on it built a wholly Roman city named Aelia Capitolina. Judea thereafter became known as Syria-Palaestina.

Jesus of Nazareth was born in the early years of Roman rule. However, it would be a further 300 years until Christianity was legitimised by the Romans and became the official religion. Details of Jesus's life – especially his early years – are taken primarily from the Gospels, telling of his descent from the blood line of King David, his mother Mary's Immaculate Conception and his birth in Bethlehem following a move made by Mary and Joseph in compliance with King Herod's census. The Gospels however mention nothing of Jesus between from the age of 12 years until he began his public ministry 18 years later, following his baptism by John the Baptist (see page 182).

For the Jews, the remainder of the Roman period is characterised by the survival of their communities, now scattered across the land and beyond. The supreme legislative and judicial body, known as the Sanhedrin (successor to the Knesset Hagedolah) reconvened in CE70 in Tiberias, reinforced over time by returning exiles. During these exiled years the great texts of Judaism were scribed, the *Mishnah* (a book on Jewish oral law) in the 3rd century CE by Rabbi Judah HaNassi, and the *Talmud* (a commentary on the *Mishnah*) in the 4th century CE.

THE BYZANTINES (CE313–636)
In CE313, Constantine the Great founded the Byzantine Empire and legalised Christianity. An influx of pilgrims and a huge building phase got underway with churches and monasteries appearing all over the country, a total of over 450 ecclesiastical buildings having been dated to this time. In 614, the Persians invaded Palaestina, aided by the Jews who as a sign of gratitude were granted permission to once again rule Jerusalem. But it was to be a short victory as three years later the Byzantine army ousted the Persians and once again expelled the Jewish inhabitants.

ARAB RULE (636–1099)
Four years after the death of the Prophet Muhammad in 632 the caliphate (Arab Islamic Empire) conquered Jerusalem under the caliph Omar along with the lands of Mesopotamia, Syria, Palaestina, and Egypt. According to Muslim tradition, Muhammad ascended to Heaven from Jerusalem and, as such, it is considered Islam's third holiest city. In 638, Caliph Omar built the first mosque on the site of the destroyed Second Temple, which was enhanced by the construction of the Dome of the Rock in 691 by the ninth caliph Abd al-Malik. In the first years of Arab rule, Christians (and Jews) were allowed to enter Jerusalem, but this was stopped in the 11th century, prompting Pope Urban II to call for the crusade to free the Holy City from Muslim rule.

THE CRUSADES AND SALADIN (1099–1291)
In the 200 years that followed, the country was dominated by waves of Crusades that arrived from western Europe with the aim of returning the land to Christendom. The brutal and relentless First Crusade ended in 1099 with the capture of Jerusalem and the massacre of most of the city's Jewish and Muslim residents. Throughout the succeeding decades the

Crusaders extended their power across the country either by diplomacy or, more often than not, brute force directed from their fortresses and castles that formed a fortified network across the land. The result was the founding of the Latin Kingdom of Jerusalem, first under Godfrey of Bouillon and then his brother Baldwin.

In 1187, Saladin, the Muslim sultan of Egypt, recaptured Jerusalem after victory at the mighty Battle of Hittin. Although his death four years later allowed the Crusades to gain another foothold in the country, they remained limited to their castles and fortifications, suffering countless incursions that ended with their defeat at Akko, their last stronghold, against the Mamluks.

THE MAMLUKS AND OTTOMANS (1291–1917) Throughout Mamluk rule the country descended into a dark era; governed from Damascus it became a peripheral province. The once-thriving port cities of Akko and Jaffa were closed through fear of more Crusades and the economy suffered. By the end of the Middle Ages towns were dilapidated, Jerusalem was all but abandoned and the small Jewish, Christian and Muslim communities that remained were poverty stricken, the dire situation not aided by violent earthquakes and a devastating plague. Sources estimate that there were but 200,000 people left in the land by the time the Ottoman period began in 1517.

The Ottoman Turks governed Palestine for the succeeding 400 years, until the onset of World War I, from their centre of power in Istanbul. Constantinople erected a framework of orderly government and his successor Suleiman the Magnificent is attributed with having constructed the great walls around Jerusalem. The small Jewish population that existed in Palestine when the Ottomans arrived expanded quickly as immigrants from north Africa and Europe began to arrive, Tzfat becoming a major centre for Jewish learning (see page 189). However, after Suleiman's death in 1566, things took a turn for the worse and the country fell once more into decline.

ZIONISM Zionism refers to the movement of Jews in the 19th century to establish a Jewish homeland. As the dark Ottoman years were finally consigned to the past, signs of progress emerged: Western powers took an interest in Palestine, opening consulates in Jerusalem; trade links reopened; the Jerusalem to Jaffa highway was constructed; and the land once again became a continental crossroads. Subsequently Jewish numbers in the four holy cities of Jerusalem, Tzfat, Hebron and Tiberias increased, with growing anti-Semitism displayed towards Jews in European countries and the pogroms of Russia. French Baron Edmond de Rothschild (see page 155) ploughed money into Jewish settlements founding Deganya, the first kibbutz. Hebrew was revived amidst the Jewish population, Jerusalem's new city was founded and modern Tel Aviv grew outside of Jaffa. In 1897, Theodor Herzl initiated a Zionist movement at the World Zionist Conference in Basle, Switzerland. This was aided by the signing of the Balfour Treaty in 1917, which saw the British foreign secretary Lord Balfour approve the establishment in Palestine of a 'national home for the Jewish people' provided it did not prejudice the religious and civil rights of the non-Jews who lived there.

BRITISH RULE AND JEWISH IMMIGRATION (1918–48) In World War I, Turkey allied itself with Germany. Having already signed the Balfour Treaty, the British were at the same time allying themselves with the Arabs, pledging to support Arab independence in exchange for them waging war against the Ottomans. In 1916, the Arab Revolt, aided by T E Lawrence (of Arabia) declared war on the Ottomans. When, in 1917, General Allenby entered Jerusalem to a warm Arab welcome, little did they know that France, Britain and Russia had signed the secret Sykes–Picot Agreement to divide up the Middle East. France administered Lebanon and Syria while Britain administered Iraq and Transjordan. Palestine remained under international administration until after World War I when the new League of Nations entrusted Britain with the Mandate for Palestine. As the area east of the Jordan River was not to be included in the new Jewish homeland, Transjordan eventually became the Hashemite Kingdom of Jordan.

The British Mandate Authorities granted the Jews – and, to a far lesser degree, the Arabs – the right to administer their own internal affairs. In 1922, as stipulated in the Mandate, the Jewish Agency was formed. Throughout this period Jewish culture flourished and Hebrew was recognised as an official language alongside English and Arabic, much to the discontent of the Arab population, which was increasingly losing its land. Arab unrest culminated in the Jaffa Riots and the subsequent issuing of a White Paper whereby the British imposed restrictions on the numbers of Jews allowed to immigrate. By this time the country had seen two *aliyah* ('moving up' or large-scale Jewish immigration) in the early 1920s from Russia and in the late 1920s from Poland. The last major wave of immigration (some 165,000 people) before the onset of World War II occurred in the 1930s when Hitler rose to power in Germany.

PARTITION, DECLARATION AND WAR Following the Holocaust, which saw the genocide of over six million Jews and subsequent mass immigration to Palestine, the British intensified their restrictions. Between 1945 and 1948, however, underground Jewish militias smuggled in an estimated 85,000 people in spite of naval blockades and border patrols. As a result of increasing friction between both the Jews and Arabs, and revolts from both sides against the British, the British government turned to the UN. On 29 November 1947, they proposed a partition whereby the land would be divided into one Jewish and one Arab country, with Jerusalem governed by the UN. The Jews reluctantly agreed to the partition but the Palestinian Arab leaders, and leaders of neighbouring Arab countries rejected it.

On 14 May 1948, the same day the British Mandate in Palestine came to an end, Israel declared its independence. Within hours Palestinian Arabs were joined by forces from Egypt, Jordan, Syria, Lebanon and Iraq who retaliated against the declaration, and so began the 1948 Arab–Israeli War. Although Israel successfully defended most of its new country, it submitted to the Egyptians in Gaza and the Jordanians in the West Bank and half of Jerusalem, the latter being absorbed into Jordan. Thousands of Palestinians stormed into these Arab-controlled areas, creating crowded refugee camps. Today, the 1948 Arab–Israeli War is referred to as *al-Nakba* or The Catastrophe, an estimated 15,000 Palestinians losing their lives and a further 700,000 becoming refugees. Despite Israel's ultimate victory, it came at a cost and over 6,000 Israelis died in the war.

THE STATE OF ISRAEL AND THE SUEZ–SINAI WAR After the war Israel set about building a state: the Knesset, Israel's government, was founded, it became the 59th member of the UN, David Ben-Gurion was democratically elected as the first prime minister and between 1949 and 1951 some 700,000 Jews immigrated to Israel. In early 1949, armistice agreements between all warring countries except Iraq confirmed the situation reached at the end of the war, whereby Jordan controlled half of Jerusalem and the West Bank.

The armistice failed, however, to reach lasting peace and security issues in Israel heightened. In 1956, Egypt's Prime Minister, Gamal Abdel Nasser, retaliated against the US and British after they withdrew funding from his Aswan High Dam project following Nasser's association with the Soviet Union. In his retaliation he nationalised the Suez Canal, ousting French and British owners from its management. Blockades on Israeli-bound cargo, massively increasing military preparations in the Sinai Peninsula, blockades in the Straits of Tiran and the signing of a tripartite military alliance between Egypt, Syria and Jordan resulted in the Israel Defence Force (IDF), allied by France and Britain, initiating the Suez–Sinai War. In the course of an eight-day campaign the IDF succeeded in capturing the Gaza Strip and the entire Sinai Peninsula, stopping just 16km short of the Suez Canal. On 30 October, as planned, Britain and France issued an ultimatum demanding Israel and Egypt relinquish control of the Suez Canal. Egypt refused and on 31 October Britain and France responded by bombing Egyptian military bases, an act that put them back in charge of the canal. An urgent ceasefire demand issued by both the US and Soviet Union forced British, French and Israeli forces to relent.

THE SIX DAY WAR (1967) Enraged by the losses he suffered during the Suez–Sinai War, Nasser encouraged the Palestine Liberation Organization (PLO) to continue its raids on Jewish settlements and formed an alliance of Arab states that began preparations for war. This, combined with persistent Syrian artillery attacks in the north and the re-imposition of the Tiran Straits blockade, resulted in Israel making a pre-emptive strike against Egypt on 5 June 1967, decimating the Egyptian air force. King Hussein of Jordan was next to attack but within two days the Israelis had taken Jerusalem. The following day saw the IDF once again reach the Suez Canal and the Egyptians pushed back, essentially now out of the war. That in hand, attentions were turned to Syria who had seen the destruction of two-thirds of its air force at the hands of IDF planes. Israeli forces penetrated the Golan Heights and on 10 June Israel and Syria signed a ceasefire agreement. The result of the Six Day War was a need to redraw the map of the Middle East. Judea, Samaria, Gaza, the Sinai Peninsula and the Golan Heights were now under Israeli control and Jerusalem was once again reunited.

THE PLO After the Six Day War the Palestinian refugee situation worsened and peace in the Middle East was very far away. The UN was not comfortable with the land gained by Israel and urged them to return it. Israel refused, agreeing only to consider returning the land in the cause of a comprehensive peace plan. The Arab states were calling for the destruction of Israel and peace talks were by no means on any agenda. Putting their support behind the PLO (formed in 1964 at a summit meeting of the Arab League in order to provide a more organised form of Palestinian nationalism than that offered by the scattered fedayeen or guerrilla forces, primarily Fatah), they urged them to continue their spate of terrorist attacks on Israel, attacks that were made from bases in Lebanon, Jordan, Syria, the West Bank and Gaza Strip. In 1969, Fatah leader Yasser Arafat was elected chairman of the PLO. The raids on Israel executed from within Jordan were not only straining the fledgling secret peace talks between King Hussein and Israel, but the Palestinians had managed to create a state within a state that was becoming a threat to Jordan. In 1970, a short, bloody war between the Jordanian army and the PLO's fedayeen resulted in the latter fleeing to Lebanon. The heavy losses incurred by the Palestinians have come to be known as Black September.

THE WAR OF ATTRITION (1969) In early 1969, skirmishes between Egyptian and Israeli forces erupted along the Suez Canal, which soon turned into the all-out War of Attrition. Backed by heavy military equipment from the Soviet Union the humiliated Egyptian army sought revenge for the Six Day War and undertook a campaign that inflicted maximum casualties on Israeli troops. In response, Israel's new prime minister Golda Meir retaliated with even more force. The following year Anwar Sadat succeeded Nasser and hostilities ceased, the war-weary Egyptians looking towards the possibility of a pull-out from the Sinai Peninsula.

THE YOM KIPPUR WAR (RAMADAN WAR) (1973)
Peace after the War of Attrition was not to be, however, and the Egyptians, Syrians (backed by Soviet weaponry) and the Israelis (backed by military funding from the US) started to prepare their armies once again. On Yom Kippur, 6 October 1973, Judaism's holiest day, Egypt and Syria executed a surprise attack on Israeli forces along the east bank of the Suez Canal and in the Golan Heights. By mid-October, however, despite heavy losses, the Israelis had pushed the Syrians back out of the Golan Heights and had come within 40km of Damascus. A similar scene was playing out in Suez, whereby Israeli forces had re-crossed the canal and were now stationed a mere 100km from Cairo. Soviet leader Leonid Brezhnev, fearing the decimation of the encircled Egyptian Third Army would have dire consequences on the stability of the country, issued a veiled warning to the US to get Israel to back off or reap the repercussions of a Soviet intervention. US Secretary of State Henry Kissinger subsequently received President Nixon's permission to put the country on nuclear alert. The head to head quickly diffused and on 25 October a fragile ceasefire agreement was signed.

CAMP DAVID ACCORDS AND THE DISENGAGEMENT
For two years after the war Kissinger travelled between Israel and the Arab states looking to achieve a peace accord. Egypt was seeking to reclaim the Sinai Peninsula and was starting to open to the idea of peace talks. In the Geneva Peace Conference in December 1973 the US, Soviet Union, Israel, Egypt, Jordan and Syria signed an accord agreeing to relinquish parts of Sinai. Back in Israel, however, Israelis were angered by Prime Minister Golda Meir's disengagement decision and continued to settle in great numbers in the occupied lands. In May of the following year much of Sinai was turned over to the Egyptians, the Golan Heights border was redrawn to the pre-1967 line and Golda Meir was forced to resign. In her place, Yitzhak Rabin (Labour Party) managed to halt settlement but his successor, Menachem Begin (Likud), funded and encouraged it.

By the late 1970s, Egypt's President Sadat was ready to talk peace and reclaim the remaining strip of Sinai coast still under Israeli control. Sadat journeyed to Jerusalem and in what became known as the Camp David Accords, an Egyptian–Israeli peace treaty was signed in 1979. The Sinai coast was returned to Egypt and normal diplomatic relations ensued. But the rosy picture was soon to turn dark as the Arab League expelled Egypt and in 1981 Sadat was assassinated by Islamist fundamentalists (although relations did continue even after Sadat's death).

THE FIRST LEBANON WAR (1982)
The Camp David Accords, while finally achieving peace between the Egyptians and Israelis, did nothing for the situation with Syria and the PLO. The PLO continued relentless terrorist activity from within Lebanon and in June 1982 Israel, under then Minister of Defence Ariel Sharon, invaded the south of the country. Throughout what was known in Israel as Operation Peace for Galilee the Israeli troops eventually occupied Beirut and drove out the bulk of the PLO who fled to Tunisia. In 1985, Israel finally withdrew from Lebanon leaving itself a small security zone in the south, one that it would hold for the next 18 years.

THE INTIFADA AND THE GULF WAR
In December 1987, the first intifada ('shaking off' in Arabic) occurred when Palestinians in the West Bank and the Gaza

Strip launched violent riots against Israel's occupation. The world once again turned its attentions to the Palestinian situation and demanded a solution. In the meantime, following Iraq's invasion of Kuwait, the Gulf War erupted. An allied coalition of Western and Arab countries led by the US managed to expel Iraq from Kuwait but in an attempt to gain support from the Arab states Iraq launched 39 Scud missiles at Israel, encouraged by Yasser Arafat and the Palestinians.

THE MADRID AND OSLO ACCORDS AND THE ASSASSINATION OF YITZHAK RABIN
Following the Gulf War, what looked to be a glimmer of light in the dark clouds materialised when, in July 1991, Syria, Israel (under an agreement that this did not include the PLO), the US, Soviet Union, Lebanon, Egypt and Jordan convened at the Madrid Conference to openly discuss peace. Negotiations soon broke down, however, with the fate of Jerusalem proving to be the breaking point. In 1993, a breakthrough was finally made when Israel – once again under Yitzhak Rabin – and the Palestinians managed to come to a secret agreement known as the Oslo Accords. The accords set the way for the newly formed Palestinian National Authority (with Yasser Arafat as its president) to take over administrative control of the Gaza Strip and West Bank. At the same time, despite opposition from other Arab countries, Jordan's King Hussein opted to sign a peace treaty with Israel, one that has remained the most stable and lasting.

The Israeli–Palestinian agreement was not well received by everyone, however, and militant extremist groups on both sides undertook a series of terrorist activities. Hamas continued attacks on Israeli civilians and, in the midst of an Israeli peace rally in Tel Aviv, Yitzhak Rabin was assassinated by Yigal Amir, an Israeli student opposed to the peace process. His death is seen by many in the country as one of the darkest events in Israel's history, most notably because he was killed by a Jew.

PEACE TALKS THROUGH THE 1990s
Following Rabin's shocking assassination, Benjamin Netanyahu (Likud) ascended to the position of prime minister and peace talks took a nose dive. The tentative negotiations that had been sparked between Israel and Syria at the Madrid Accords dissolved and, despite withdrawing Jewish settlers from Hebron as part of the Oslo Accords, Netanyahu angered Arabs by encouraging settlement in Arab East Jerusalem. In turn, terrorist attacks on Israeli civilians were relentless and peace talks once again came to an abrupt end. Netanyahu, pressured both from some home sectors (there are many who strongly oppose a land-for-peace accord) and abroad, agreed to withdraw from more of the West Bank in return for cessation of terrorist attacks. Although this went through, negotiations broke down soon after and early elections saw Ehud Barak (Labour) rise to become prime minister.

THE NEW MILLENNIUM
Despite continuing friction between Jews and Arabs, Christian pilgrims continued to flock to the Holy Land, and in 2000 Pope John Paul II made a historic visit. In the same year Israel withdrew its forces from the security zone in southern Lebanon. Controversy arose, however, over the disputed 'Shebaa Farms' a 22km^2 area of land that both countries lay claim to. Almost as soon as the Israelis withdrew, Hezbollah, an Islamic fundamentalist group moved in, the Lebanese failing to assert their rule over the area.

In September of that year Ariel Sharon caused outrage when he visited the Temple Mount (see page 83), sparking the second (or Al Aqsa) intifada (although Israel claims the violence was pre-planned and his visit used as a scapegoat). Amidst a rapidly deteriorating Israeli–Palestinian situation, Barak called for elections, only to lose to Ariel Sharon.

ARAFAT'S DEATH AND ISRAEL'S DISENGAGEMENT FROM GAZA In 2001,
Sharon announced that, although he considered Arafat to be a hindrance to the
peace process, he planned to execute a full withdrawal from the Gaza Strip. Later
that year, following months of heavy terrorist activity, Sharon instigated the
construction of a wall around the West Bank and the IDF surrounded Arafat's
Ramallah home, in effect putting him under house arrest. It wasn't until 2004,
shortly before his death, that he was allowed to leave to seek medical treatment in
France. In November 2004, Mahmoud Abbas stepped in as leader of the PNA. In
the months leading up to the 2005 Gaza disengagement Israel found itself divided,
with many residents strongly opposed. That summer the world watched as
unarmed IDF soldiers dragged Israelis from Jewish settlements in Gaza and parts
of the West Bank.

THE SECOND LEBANON WAR In 2005, Sharon left Likud and formed the Kadima
Party which, after Sharon's stroke, went on to win elections in 2006 headed by
Ehud Olmert. The following year saw continued skirmishes on the border with
Gaza, which erupted into full-scale war when Hamas entered Israeli territory,
killing two soldiers and kidnapping a third. In the two months that followed, Israel
bombarded Gaza with heavy forces, killing in excess of 200 Palestinians and
decimating the infrastructure. At around the same time, Hezbollah militants from
south Lebanon also crossed the border to kidnap two IDF soldiers, killing others

HISTORY IN HOLLYWOOD

The poignant, devastating and dramatic events that have taken place on the tiny
stretch of land officially known today as the State of Israel have given rise to
several acclaimed motion pictures that depict their stories on the glittering silver
screen. The following movies in particular will help to put into perspective some
of the major events of the past.

Exodus (1960) – Tells the story of Palestine under the British Mandate and the
immigration of the Jews.

Mivtsa Yonatan (1977) – Re-enactment of the rescue operation undertaken by
the IDF following the hijacking of a flight from Tel Aviv to Paris that was forced to
land in Entebbe, Uganda.

The Impossible Spy (1987) – Chronicles the life of Eli Cohen, Israel's most
acclaimed spy.

Schindler's List (1993) – Deals with the Holocaust in Europe and the story of
Oscar Schindler who saved his Jewish workers from death camps.

Kippur (2000) – Israeli-produced movie depicting the Yom Kippur War.

Syrian Bride (2004) – Tells the story of a young Druze bride from the Golan
Heights who is sent to Syria for an arranged marriage, never to return or see her
family again.

Munich (2005) – Depicts the massacre of Israeli athletes at the 1972 Munich
Olympics at the hands of Palestinian Black September militants.

Paradise Now (2005) – A story of suicide bombings as seen through the eyes
of two young Palestinian men.

Kingdom of Heaven (2005) – Focuses on the Crusades and the Kingdom of
Jerusalem.

One Night with the King (2006) – Tells the story of Queen Esther for whom
the Jewish holiday of Purim is celebrated.

Beaufort (2007) – Israeli-produced movie depicting Israel's withdrawal from
southern Lebanon after 18 years.

and shelling northern Israeli towns and villages. An attack on southern Lebanon ensued that soon escalated, drawing condemnation from the international community who accused Israel of excessive force. Approximately 1,200 Lebanese civilians lost their lives and thousands more were displaced. Residents of northern Israel spent the summer in bunkers as rockets rained down, most concentrated on Haifa (see page 147). In August 2006, the UN orchestrated a ceasefire and stepped in to man southern Lebanon until such time as the Lebanese army is equipped to do so itself.

THE CURRENT SITUATION If history has taught us anything it's that peace in the Middle East is, at best, tenuous. In 2006, Hamas won Palestinian elections by a wide margin, and, at the time of writing, an Israeli-imposed blockade on Gaza in response to continued rocket fire at southern towns is in play, to much condemnation from across the world. While Israel has received negative press over the years for being a danger zone, and countries often warn their citizens against travel there, the increase in international terrorism has seen tourists look at the country in a new light. Israel's extreme security measures and experience with terrorist attacks has seen tourism numbers rocket. With obvious exceptions throughout the Second Lebanon War, the country has seen a steady influx of tourists and pilgrims coming not only to Jerusalem and the holy sights but to take advantage of the natural and archaeological sites, health resorts, spas and beach holidays and with home football games against England and Ireland and top musicians such as Roger Waters and Phil Collins making appearances, tourism is on the up and up.

GOVERNMENT AND POLITICS

The State of Israel was declared on 14 May 1948 as a parliamentary democracy. The state is headed by the president, whose role is essentially symbolic, but is in effect managed by three authorities: the legislative authority (the Knesset), the executive authority (the government), and the judiciary. Although portrayed as a secular government, issues of religion and politics often find themselves tightly interwoven, the Jewish and Palestinian and Israeli Arab conflict constantly giving rise to internal as well as external political tensions.

THE KNESSET AND GOVERNMENT The Knesset is the country's unicameral legislative body that took its name and declared its membership as 120 based on the Knesset Hagedolah (Great Assembly), the Jewish council that convened in Jerusalem in the 5th century bce. The Knesset members, who represent a wide range of political parties, are chosen every four years through a nationwide election. Voters (aged 18 and over) cast ballots for political parties and not individual members (although the winning party is headed by the country's prime minister) and the entire country forms one electoral constituency. Election Day is a national holiday, and Israel has seen statistics of 77% to 90% of registered voters casting ballots, a testament to the interest taken by most citizens in the running of their country. Israel's main parties, Likud, Labour and the newly formed Kadima, often dominate the votes, but smaller parties representing different opinions on religion, security concerns and social issues have been making more impact in recent elections. Kadima was formed by Ariel Sharon in 2005 after he left the Likud Party and bases itself on a centrist theory whose concerns centre on civil and secular issues. Following Ariel Sharon's stroke in January 2006, Ehud Olmert ascended to prime minister and following an election Kadima extended an invitation to Labour to form a coalition. This act saw Amir Perez, the first Mizrahi Jew to lead a major party, become defence minister.

Biblical times 17th–6th centuries BCE (Before the Common Era)

c17th century	Abraham, Isaac and Jacob settle in Canaan. Famine forces the Israelites to flee to Egypt.
13th–12th century	Israelites are led from Egypt by Moses and settle in Canaan
c1020	King Saul becomes the first Jewish monarch
c1000	Jerusalem becomes capital of King David's kingdom
c960	First Temple built by King Solomon
721	Israel falls to the Assyrians (Northern Kingdom)
586	Judea falls to Babylon (Southern Kingdom). Jerusalem and the First Temple destroyed.
538–142	**Persian and Hellenistic periods**
515	Jerusalem's Temple rebuilt
332	Alexander the Great conquers Persia. Hellenistic period begins.
166	Jewish revolt against the Seleucid dynasty and beginning of the Hasmonean period
63	Jerusalem captured by the Roman general Pompeii
63BCE–CE313	**Roman period**
37BCE	Herod the Great appointed King of Judea
c8BCE	Jesus born
cCE26	Jesus begins his ministry after being baptised by John the Baptist
c30	Jesus crucified
66	Jewish revolt against the Romans
70	Destruction of Jerusalem and the Second Temple
132–135	Shimon Bar Kochba leads the Jews in what becomes known as the Bar Kochba uprising against the Romans
200	New Testament fixed in current form
c210	*Mishnah* (book on Jewish oral law) completed
313–636	**Byzantine period**
c390	*Talmud* (commentary on the *Mishnah*) completed
614	Persian invasion
636–1099	**Arab period**
691	Dome of the Rock built by Caliph Abd al-Malik
1099–1291	**Crusades (Latin Kingdom of Jerusalem)**
1187–93	**Ayyubid period under Saladin following Battle of Hittin**
1291–1516	**Mamluk period**
1517–1917	**Ottoman period**
1537	Suleiman the Magnificent grandly rebuilds Jerusalem's walls
1897	Zionist Organisation founded by Theodor Herzl
1909	Tel Aviv founded. Deganya becomes the first kibbutz.
1917	British issue Balfour Declaration to establish a 'national home' for the Jews in Palestine
1918–48	**British rule**
1922	British granted Mandate for Palestine by League of Nations
1936–39	Arab Revolt

1939	Jewish immigration limited by British White Paper
1939–45	World War II. Holocaust in Europe.
1947	UN proposes Arab and Jewish states
1948	
14 May	End of British Mandate
14 May	State of Israel declared
15 May	Beginning of Arab–Israeli War following attack by Egypt, Syria, Jordan, Iraq and Lebanon
1948–52	Huge immigration from Europe and Arab countries
1949–2006	
July 1949	Armistice agreements signed with Egypt, Jordan, Syria and Lebanon. Jerusalem divided between Israel and Jordan. Israel enters UN.
1956	Suez–Sinai War
1964	PLO (Palestine Liberation Organization) formed
1967	Six Day War. Israel conquers and occupies Gaza, Sinai, West Bank, Golan Heights and Jordanian-controlled Jerusalem.
1969	War of Attrition
1970	Jordan expels PLO who re-settle in Lebanon
1973	Yom Kippur War
1979	Peace treaty signed between Israel and Egypt
1982	First Lebanon War
1987	First intifada (violence) between Israelis and Palestinians
1994	Israel–Jordan peace treaty signed
1995	Palestinian Authority established. Israel and PLO agree to mutual recognition (Oslo Declaration of Principles). Oslo Interim Agreement signed. Israeli prime minister Yitzhak Rabin assassinated by right-wing Jewish fanatic Yigal Amir.
2000	Israel withdraws from southern Lebanon. Second intifada.
2001	Ariel Sharon (Likud Party) elected prime minister
2002	Israel constructs wall around West Bank following series of suicide bombings
2004	Palestinian Authority president Yasser Arafat dies
2005	Israel carries out Disengagement Plan and withdraws Jewish settlers from Gaza and parts of West Bank
2006	
January	Ariel Sharon suffers a stroke. Ehud Olmert becomes prime minister with new Kadima Party.
26 January	Radical Islamist Hamas movement win election in Palestinian territories
12 July–14 August	Second Lebanon War
2007–2008	
February	Hamas and Fatah agree to share power in Palestinian Unity Agreement
June	Hamas ousts Fatah from Gaza
February 2008	Hezbollah member Imad Moughniyeh killed by car bomb in Damascus

THE IDF The Israeli Defence Force (IDF), often referred to simply as the Israeli Army (*tzahal*) comprises conscripts, reserve and career service personnel, the bulk of which is formed by reservists. Conscription is mandatory for men and women of 18 years old, men serving three years and women 21 months. Those undertaking higher education courses in high demand by the IDF may defer entry but will serve after qualification. After completing their service men complete 39 days a year of reserve training until the age of 51, employers and higher education institutions under law to honour positions and not penalise workers and students for missed time. Because of the long periods of compulsory conscription, the army plays a huge part in the lives of most Israelis and service is regarded as heroic and honourable. There are, however, some highly controversial exemptions from conscription that include Orthodox Jews, Israeli-Arabs, new immigrants and Bedouin. Given the choice, Druze residents (see pages 20 and 25) often opt to enter the IDF as do increasing numbers of Bedouin.

Military spending forms a considerable chunk of the country's outgoings, approximately 16.5% of government expenditure, with the United States providing in the region of US$2.4 billion per year in security assistance.

ECONOMY

Since its declaration of independence in 1948 Israel has struggled to cope with several major economic challenges thrown its way: security and the IDF, the immigration of two million Jews according to the country's Law of Returns and the need to establish modern infrastructure and public services. In its earlier years, heavy financial aid from Jewish organisations across the world as well as foreign governments (principally the US) supported the country's massively expanding population and increased security issues. Despite these pressures, Israel has managed in recent years to create a stable economic foundation through extensive privatisation as well as its free-trade agreements, and today its major industrial sectors are based on the production of metal products, electronic and biomedical equipment, processed foods, chemicals, transport equipment and software development. Two other principal exports are cut and polished diamonds (in which it is the world's leading country) and agricultural products, namely fruit and vegetables, its total exports exceeding US$56 billion. In recent years tourism has begun to play an important role, which, despite wars and conflict, recovers rapidly. In 2006, Israel's GDP reached US$195 billion, with a per-capita figure of US$31,767, putting it on a par with European countries such as France and Italy and ranking it 22nd in the OECD (Organization for Economic Co-operation and Development) while its economic growth rate of 5% is faster than that of any other Western nation. Following both the Israeli–Palestinian conflict in 2001 and 2002 and the Second Lebanon War in 2006, the country's GDP growth took a nose dive but managed to get back on course and recover quickly.

PEOPLE

Despite being founded as a Jewish state, Israel comprises a jigsaw puzzle of religions, cultures and traditions. Today the country's more than seven million-strong population is divided into 76.2% Jews, 15.5% Muslims, 2% Christians (mostly Arabs), 1.6% Druze and 3.6% not classified by religion (mostly from the former USSR). Within this varied framework each religion is granted judicial right over its people as well as administration of its own holy sites. Another interesting characteristic of Israel's diverse population is its incredible growth rate, highly unusual for a developed country. Long before Israel declared independence in 1948

Jews had been immigrating to the country, and following the declaration this increased tenfold. In the last 60 years the Jewish population has grown from 650,000 to over five million.

Culturally, the country is a melting pot of different traditions where immigration has led to the emergence of strong communities even within different religious groups. European Jews or Ashkenazi, Jews of Arab descent or Sephardi, Russians, Ethiopians, Druze and Bedouin live within one country, yet retain their strong cultural traditions, language and way of life. For most of the Jewish population, third- or fourth-generation descendants of post-World War II immigrants, their cultural affiliation is most certainly Israeli, and while each is proud of their heritage there is an undeniable feel of nationalism and patriotism.

JEWS Since Israel's declaration of independence (and long before it) waves of immigration, known in Hebrew as *aliyah* or 'ascent', saw the country's Jewish population expand enormously. Between 1948 and 1952 the Jewish population more than doubled, Holocaust survivors and refugees from Arab countries forming a large percentage of this. Subsequent major waves of *aliyah* occurred in the mid 1950s and early 1960s from north Africa and Romania (350,000 people), in the 1990s from the former USSR (900,000 people) and in 1984 and 1991 when virtually all of Ethiopia's Jews were extracted and relocated to Israel.

Today the percentage of Israeli-born Jews (Tsabar) has reached 65%, and while there are still pockets of strong culturally independent communities, intermarriage and cultural assimilation have blended the differences, whereby 'Israeli' culture most certainly prevails. Within the Jewish community levels of religious observance form the biggest separation, and communities of like-minded residents have emerged. Orthodox form 12% of Israel's Jews, religious 10%, traditional 35% and secular 43%.

Israel's Jewish background reaches the far-flung corners of the globe but the following form the greatest numbers of the population:

Ashkenazi This relates to Jews of northern or eastern European descent as well as North America, Australia and South Africa.

Sephardi This relates to Jews of north African or Mediterranean countries, mainly Spain and Portugal in the 15th century. After their expulsion they spread across the Mediterranean.

Mizrahi This is used to loosely define Jews of Arabic descent (mainly countries such as Yemen, Iraq and Iran) although often Sephardi is used instead.

Beta Israel of Ethiopia Ethiopian Jews today number over 100,000 in Israel, brought from their famine-ravaged country in two huge operations: Operation Moses in 1984 and Operation Solomon in 1991 that saw over 22,000 Ethiopian Jews airlifted to Israel. The term Beta Israel (meaning 'House of Israel') was a self-designated term used when they inhabited Ethiopia, preferred to the derogative Falasha, meaning exiles or stranger used by many non-Jewish Ethiopians. Since arriving in Israel, the term Ethiopian Jews has become more politically correct in recognition of their equality. Their exact ancestral link to Judaism is unknown but many believe them to be descended from the biblical Queen of Sheba and King Solomon.

ARABS The largest non-Jewish population in Israel is Arab and communities vary considerably in heritage, religious practice and cultural traditions.

Muslim Arabs Not counting Bedouin Arabs, Muslims (Sunni) make up about 70% of Israel's Arab population. Many hold close family ties with Palestinian Arabs in the West Bank and Gaza Strip and as such classify themselves as Palestinian Arabs (although they are referred to as Israeli Arabs by the Jewish community of Israel). They do not undertake military service in the IDF and live mostly in homogenous communities in villages, towns and cities around the Galilee, eastern coastal plain and the northern Negev. There are also large communities in cities such as Haifa, Akko and Jerusalem.

Christian Arabs Christian Arabs comprise about 9% of Israel's Arab population, the largest concentration living in the Galilean city of Nazareth. Despite their differences in religion many Christian Arabs still consider themselves closely affiliated to the Palestinian people and as such rarely enlist in the IDF. However, personalities such as Salim Jubran, the first non-Jewish Arab judge to preside over Israel's Supreme Court demonstrate a certain degree of cohesiveness between them and Jewish members of society.

Druze Druze (see also *Religion*, page 25) communities are spread mainly across the mountainous areas of Lebanon, Syria and Israel, in the last being concentrated in the northern Golan Heights and towns and villages across the Carmel Mountain range, notably Carmel City (better known as Isfiya and Daliat al-Carmel). In Israel the Druze community (which today numbers some 104,000 people) is officially recognised as a separate religious entity and although their culture and language are both Arabic, their religious beliefs and affiliation to Israel (most serving in the IDF) separate them from the nationalism of other Arab communities. It is an integral part of the Druze faith to serve the country in which they reside, a fact that has seen families separated by Israel's capture of the Golan Heights in 1967 fight for opposing countries (see *Shouting Hill*, page 227). Their loyalty to Israel, peaceful way of life and renowned hospitality has awarded them great respect amongst Jewish members of society, a fact compounded by their presence in political, public and military positions.

Bedouin The term 'Bedouin' generally applies to any member of an Arabic-speaking community of desert nomads in the Middle East. Historically these communities would migrate with the seasons, herding their cattle, sheep, goats and camels to the desert regions during the rainy season. After World War II, however, most Middle Eastern countries, Israel included, prevented this movement by consolidating their borders. Following Israel's declaration of independence and the war that ensued, most Bedouin fled or were expelled from the country, approximately 11,000 of an estimated 65,000–90,000 remaining. In the 1950s and 1960s, the Israeli government relocated almost all of the Negev's Bedouin population to an area known as the *siyag* or closure, a relatively infertile area in the north of the Negev Desert. Despite legally being ordered to live in assigned towns, many Bedouin still preferred to live in makeshift villages, often having permanent structures torn down. The Israeli government also imposed mandatory school attendance on Bedouin children which led to a rise in literacy. The offshoot of this, however, was that unemployment rose and poverty and crime in Bedouin towns increased. However the Bedouin in Israel have benefited from the developed medical care in the country, often serve in the IDF (renowned for their tracking skills), retain strong cultural traditions and have one of the highest birth rates in the world. There are currently an estimated 120,000 Bedouin living in the Negev.

CIRCASSIANS There are approximately 3,000 Circassians (or Cherkessians) living in Israel, all concentrated in the two Galilean villages of Kafr Kama and Reyhaniye. Although their religious affiliation is Sunni Muslim, the Circassians descend from the northwestern Caucasus (today's western Ukraine) and are not

Arabs. Following the Russian–Circassian War, which lasted from 1763 to 1864, large numbers of Circassians were deported to the Ottoman Empire while others settled in Russia. In the Middle East, the largest communities are found in Jordan and Syria, and throughout the French Mandate of then Syria's Golan Heights the members of the town of Quneitra (see page 222) sought a national homeland for themselves in the area (it was not granted). Like the Druze, Circassian leaders have asked to be included in mandatory IDF conscription (although only for men), have strong cultural traditions and are officially recognised as a separate religious entity.

SAMARITANS (See *Religion*, page 26)

LANGUAGE

Hebrew and Arabic are the official languages of Israel. English is compulsory at school which, combined with the lack of international television dubbing, means most Israelis speak at least some English, most to a high level. As a result of the huge waves of immigration over the years French, Spanish, Russian, Yiddish (a pre-World War II European variation of Hebrew), Polish, Hungarian and German are still widely spoken. For more information see *Appendix 1, Language*, page 269.

RELIGION

JUDAISM Judaism is one of the world's oldest existing religions (see *History*, page 6), the foundations of which are based upon monotheism; specific laws and practices; ethnic and territorial identity; Messianism and its belief in a special covenant with God. It began as the ancient religion of a small nation of Hebrews, and through thousands of years of suffering, persecution, diaspora and the occasional victory, has continued to be significantly influential both as a religion and a culture. Today Judaism has approximately 14 million adherents, half of whom live in Israel, the Jewish homeland.

The core belief of Judaism is that there is only one God, something that was unusual for the time the religion was born. According to tradition, God revealed this to Abraham, the founder of the Jewish people. Jewish identity arises primarily from belonging to an ancient people and an upholding of its ancient traditions, today seen as much as a culture as a religion. The following is a designed to provide a brief overview of the practices and beliefs of Jewish religion and culture but it is important to note that rituals and practices vary within different Jewish groups (Reform, who generally have a liberal view of Judaism; Conservative, devout interpretation of Judaism; and Orthodox, rigid and fervent interpretation of Judaism, often having a negative view of modern society).

Theology
Sacred texts Textual tradition in Judaism is rich and old, the *Torah* (the *Old Testament* in Christianity) forming the core of this. In addition is the *Talmud,* (the body of Jewish civil and religious law, including commentaries on the *Torah*) which is divided into two parts: the *Mishnah* (the codification of laws) and the *Gemara* (a commentary on the *Mishnah*).

The Covenant One of the major concepts in Judaism is that of the covenant, or agreement, between God and the Jewish people. The agreement states that the Jewish people acknowledge God as their one and only king, and he, in return, will acknowledge the Jews as his 'chosen people' and take special care of them.

The Messiah One of the principal goals of Judaism is the patient wait for the Messiah, who will free the Jews and restore justice and peace to the world.

Rituals

Circumcision At eight days old Jewish boys are circumcised by a Rabbi as a symbol of belonging to the covenant between God and Abraham (who self-circumcised at age 99).

Upsherin This is the ritual first haircut for three-year-old boys held on the festival of Lag Ba'omer (Orthodox only). Their hair is cut short with the exception of two pieces at the temples known as *peyot*.

Bar and Bat Mitzvah At age 13 boys and girls celebrate their entering of adulthood (Orthodox Jews do not celebrate this).

Daily prayer Jews pray three-times daily: *shaharith* in the morning, *minhah* in the afternoon and *maarib* in the evening. In Conservative and Orthodox groups synagogue prayer is attended daily.

Head coverings Jewish men and boys (in Conservative or Orthodox groups) wear a skull cap known as a *kippah* or *yarmulke* in order to demonstrate their submission to a higher being, God.

Tefillin This is a ritual practised by men only and usually only by Orthodox members. The tefillin consists of two small boxes containing Biblical scriptures which are strapped to the forehead and left arm during weekday morning prayer.

Shabbat See page 33.

Kosher See page 47.

Major religious holidays

Yom Kippur This is the Day of Atonement when most Jews fast and attend the synagogue. It is considered the last day upon which to repent any wrongdoings and change God's judgement for the upcoming year.

Rosh Hashanah This is the Jewish New Year celebrated as a day of remembrance, not celebration. On this day it is common to hear the *shofar* or horn being blown 100 times in accordance with biblical traditions.

Pesach (Passover) and Sukkot These festivals celebrate the Exodus, when Moses freed the enslaved Jews from Egypt and the subsequent 40 years of wandering in the desert. Passover is celebrated by a meal (or *seder*) during which symbolic food is consumed and recitations from the *Haggadah* (book telling the story of the Exodus) are carried out. To commemorate the suffering of the Jews in Egypt no leaven (bread or cake) may be consumed and, as such, *matzah* (unleavened bread) is a major feature.

Hanukkah This festival is post-biblical and commemorates the victory of the Maccabees over the Seleucid rulers of Jerusalem (see page 7). It is celebrated by lighting eight candles, one on each day of the festival.

Purim This is the jolliest of Jewish festivals, celebrated in the name of Esther (see page 200). On this day people dress in costume, partake in a joyous meal, drink alcohol freely and often give gifts.

Holy places The **Western Wall** is the single holiest place in Judaism (see page 80) and stands as the last remaining remnant of the Second Temple, destroyed by the Romans. The second holiest place is the tomb of Abraham in Hebron (today's West Bank). Abraham's son Ishmael is considered the ancestor of Islam making this also a sacred site to Muslims. There are many other holy sites in Israel including the tombs of prominent rabbi's and sages in Tiberias (see page 171), Beit She'arim (see page 169), Tzfat (see page 189), Meron (see page 199) and the Mount of Olives (see page 87).

CHRISTIANITY Christianity is the world's largest religion with an estimated two billion followers. Founded in the 1st century AD (CE), it has at its core the teachings, miracles, Crucifixion and Resurrection of Jesus of Nazareth and, in effect, started as a Messianic orientation of Judaism. The principal texts in Christianity are the Old and New Testaments, of which the first four books are known as the Gospels, written 20 to 100 years after the death and Resurrection of Jesus. He is believed in Christian tradition to be the Messiah, the son of God, the 12 apostles appointed by him during his ministry being the first to believe this.

Jesus was arrested, tried and crucified in Jerusalem (see page 7) by the Roman leader Pontius Pilate, because he was seen as a threat to Judaism and Roman rule in the city. Today the Church of the Holy Sepulchre in Jerusalem's Old City is revered as the holiest site in Christianity, this being the place of Jesus's Crucifixion, burial and Resurrection (Golgotha in the New Testament). The Via Dolorosa (see page 76) marks the traditional route taken by Jesus as he carried the cross on his back to Golgotha and has been a site of pilgrimage for hundreds of years. Other holy sites include Bethlehem (in today's West Bank) where Jesus is believed to have been born, Nazareth (see page 164) where his mother Mary received news of the Immaculate Conception, and several sites around the Sea of Galilee (see page 178).

While the core principles remain the same, Christianity has branched off into many different sects, the three principal ones being Roman Catholicism, Eastern Orthodoxy and Protestantism.

Roman Catholicism Perceived by many as the 'original' Christian denomination, it is seen today as separate thanks to the emergence (and later acceptance) of other denominations such as Eastern Orthodoxy and Protestantism. Roman Catholicism has the largest number of adherents (more than one billion) and is centred on the Vatican City in Rome. Today the most significant difference between Roman Catholicism and other later denominations is its appointment of a pope as leader of the Church, the belief that saints can intercede on behalf of believers and the concept of Purgatory (a place of purification before being allowed to enter Heaven). With respect to ritualistic practices, Roman Catholicism tends to be stricter than Protestantism, with the Eucharist (also known as mass, communion or the Last Supper) one of the central rites (celebrated at least weekly), where transubstantiation (the changing of bread and wine into the body and blood of Jesus) is believed. Catholic nuns, monks and priests take vows of poverty, chastity and obedience, and rosary beads (prayer beads), crosses and the worship of saints are other distinctive features of the denomination. Monastic orders within Roman Catholicism include Jesuits, Dominicans, Franciscans and Augustinians.

Protestantism With an estimated 500 million followers, Protestantism is the second-largest Christian denomination. Because of its numerous, wide-ranging denominations it is difficult to classify as a single religious thought. In essence, the denominations differ in the amount with which they denounce Roman Catholicism, ranging from conservative to very liberal. Most Protestant Churches adhere to two of the biblical sacraments, baptism and communion (as opposed to seven in Roman Catholicism). Throughout history different Protestant Churches have appeared, most in the 16th century. Presbyterians owe their origins to John Calvin, John Knox and the Church of Scotland; the Church of England to King Henry VIII; the Baptists to John Smyth and the Separatists; the Anglicans and Episcopalians to the Church of England; Evangelism and Methodism to a 17th-century Protestant movement; and Lutheranism to Martin Luther.

Eastern Orthodoxy Also known as Orthodox Christianity, it began in the Byzantine Empire (see page 8) and today numbers some 225 million adherents living predominantly in Greece, Turkey and Russia. The separation formed in the 11th century when a divide between Western and Eastern Christian churches materialised, Roman emperor Constantine moving the Roman capital to Constantinople. The main differences lay in opinions relating to political, religious and cultural matters, with the use of icons and the date of Easter just two of the stumbling blocks. Despite the glimmer of reconciliation between the Eastern and Roman Catholic churches during the Crusades (see page 8) there has long since been tensions between the two. Since the 1960s, however, attempts have been made to recognise and respect each other's Churches and beliefs.

Major Eastern Orthodox denominations include the Greek, Russian, Romanian and Bulgarian Orthodox churches, the Church of Alexandria, the Church of Jerusalem and the Church of America. In contrast to Roman Catholicism and Protestantism, Eastern Orthodoxy's religious authority is the scriptures as interpreted by the Seven Ecumenical Councils, and theology and philosophical thought play a bigger role. In Israel, and particularly Jerusalem, Eastern Orthodox architecture is renowned for its beauty and ornate décor.

ISLAM Islam is the world's second-largest religion with over one billion adherents. It is based on the teachings of the Prophet Muhammad, a camel herder who, in the 7th century in Saudi Arabia, was approached by the angel Gabriel. Gabriel delivered to Muhammad a message from God, which he spent the rest of his life. Three decades after his death, Muhammad's life teachings were recorded in what became the spiritual text of Islam, the Koran. Islam, which means 'submission' is based on a submission to God's will and centres on the Five Pillars of Islam: confession of faith; daily prayer; fasting during Ramadan; pilgrimage and charity.

The three most sacred sites in Islam centre on the activities of Muhammad. The holiest site in Islam is the Kaaba in Mecca (Saudi Arabia), which tradition dictates is the mosque built by Abraham. Muhammad declared Mecca Islam's holiest site and that it should be towards this place that all prayers should be directed (*qibla*). Performing the once-in-a-lifetime pilgrimage (*hajj*) to Mecca is one of the Five Pillars of Islam and every year thousands of Muslims congregate here. The second holiest site is Medina or 'City of the Prophet' in Saudi Arabia and marks the place where Muhammad fled when he was exiled from Mecca and the place where his first followers joined him. Jerusalem, or more precisely Al-Haram ash-Sharif (the Noble Sanctuary, or Temple Mount to Jews), comes into the equation as third in spiritual significance and, until Mecca was declared as *qibla*, it was to the mosque here that Muslims directed their prayers. Islamic tradition states that this is where Muhammad ascended to Heaven following the Night Journey, and that the rock housed within the Dome of the Rock bears his last footprint. The stone is also considered holy to Jews, who believe it was the site upon which Abraham prepared to sacrifice his son Isaac to God, and over which the two temples were built.

Sunni and Shi'a When Muhammad died, a battle for the leadership of Islam ensued, a battle that rages to this day and forms a fierce divide between the two sects that emerged. The dispute of who would become *kalifa* or leader was between those who believed that Muhammad had chosen Ali, his cousin and brother-in-law, and those who claimed allegiance to Abu Bakr, Muhammad's father-in-law and good friend. Ultimately Abu Bakr became the first of four caliphs (the anglicised version of *kalifa*) who are attributed with the great spread of Islam in the 7th century (see pages 8–9). Today the vast majority of Muslims are Sunnis, the name associated with those who followed Abu Bakr, while those who pledged allegiance to Ali are known as Shi'ites, of which there are an estimated 120 million adherents. In contrast to the denominations in Christianity and Judaism, Sunni and Shi'ite Muslims are seen more as sects, each refusing to acknowledge the other, a fact that to this day causes a rift across the Islamic Middle East.

DRUZE The Druze (see also *People*, page 20) originated from the Ismaili sect of Shi'a Islam in the 11th century and today call themselves *muwahhidun*, or monotheists for their profound belief in the one God. The Druze religion is based on the belief that al-Hakim, a caliph of the Fatimid dynasty of Egypt, was the incarnation of God. While most Muslims believe al-Hakim died in 1021, the Druze believe he merely disappeared and is waiting to return to the world in the golden age for true believers. It is these beliefs that set the Druze aside from other Muslims (compounded by the fact that the Koran does not seem to play a role in their religious life) and it is apparent that the religion was strongly influenced by Gnostic elements from Judaism, Christianity, Hindu and Greek belief. Although the new religion was proselytised after its creation in the 11th century, this was short-lived and from 1050 has been closed to outsiders, the religion kept to this day a well-guarded secret.

The Druze believe in many prophets who they consider embody the spirit of monotheism: Adam, Muhammad, Abraham, Noah, John the Baptist, Jesus and Solomon as well as in the philosophies of Socrates, Plato, Pythagoras, Aristotle and Alexander the Great. Despite their acknowledgement of all three monotheistic religions they believe that the performing of rituals and ceremonies has caused followers to move away from what they consider the 'pure faith'. They, therefore, do not (with the exception of fasting during the Islamic Ramadan) undertake any ceremonies, rituals, sanctification of physical places or organised prayer sessions, believing one should pray to God at all times. That said, popular gathering places have emerged whereby members will convene to discuss matters relating to the community. In Israel there are several such places, one of the most important being Jethro's Tomb (Nebi Shu'eib) at the Horns of Hittin (see page 177), where the Druze gather on 25 April. According to tradition, on the eve of the great battle between Saladin and the Crusaders, the former had a dream in which an angel assured him, that in the case of victory, he would find Nebi Shu'eib's burial site. When the dream was realised, the Druze built a tomb at the site.

In keeping with the air of secrecy surrounding the Druze religion, the community itself is divided into two groups; the *al-Uqq'l* or 'knowers', and *al-Juhh'l* or 'ignorant ones'. The *al-Juhh'l*, who form about 80% of the population, do not have access to the religious literature and generally occupy political, military or administrative roles. The *al-Uqq'l* on the other hand are the keepers of the religion, and men and women are considered equal with their rights to become *al-Uqq'l*. Under Druze tradition it is forbidden to eat pork and smoking and drinking alcohol are prohibited.

BAHA'I FAITH The Baha'i Faith was founded in 19th-century Persia from Babism (a religion that developed out of the Shi'a branch of Islam). It is a monotheistic religion that believes in one God and, although Baha'is emphasise that God is ultimately unknowable, human knowledge of God can be achieved through his messengers. In 1844, Mirza Ali Muhammad declared himself Bab, the guide to divine truth, also declaring that 19 years later an even greater manifestation would come. In 1863, Mirza Hussayn Ali Nuri, who after Bab's death in 1850 took the name Baha'u'llah, declared himself as this manifestation. Not long after, the Persians began persecuting the Babi (followers of Bab), Baha'u'llah and some of his followers being spared from death and imprisoned (to this day Baha'i followers in Iran suffer considerable persecution). Sent by the Ottomans to Akko in Palestine (modern-day Israel) he remained under house arrest until his death. After his death, however, it was Baha'u'llah's son Abdu l-Baha' who, after being released from imprisonment in 1908, travelled extensively spreading the Baha'i word. Baha'u'llah is perceived as the last in a line of messengers that include Buddha, Jesus, Krishna and Muhammad.

Today there are around five million Baha'is worldwide, most residing in non-Muslim Third-World countries. The faith has no priesthood and spiritual authority rests with elected councils known as 'Spiritual Assemblies'. The ultimate authority, however, rests with the Universal House of Justice in Haifa, Israel, therefore, being the centre of this far-reaching religion. Taking pride of place in the country's third-largest city, Haifa's breathtakingly beautiful Shrine of the Bab and Persian Gardens (see page 146) is not only a site of pilgrimage for Baha'is but attracts admirers from all religions. While this may be the grandest Baha'i shrine, the most sacred is the Shrine of Baha'u'llah just outside Akko (see page 136).

Baha'i claims to be a universal religion based on unity. Its key principles are unity of God, religion and mankind, harmony between races and religions, equality of the sexes, world peace, the elimination of prejudice, a universal language, education for all and the elimination of extremes of wealth and poverty. Gambling, gossip, alcohol, homosexuality and sexual relations outside marriage are forbidden and members over the age of 15 should pray daily. It is claimed that the Baha'i Faith is the second most widespread religion, is established in 247 countries and has religious texts translated into hundreds of languages. To find out more visit the official website of the Baha'i Faith (*www.bahai.org*).

SAMARITANS The Samaritans are a small religious group who claim descent from the ancient Kingdom of Israel. While figures once numbered the Samaritans at over one million people in the 4th and 5th centuries, forced conversion to Islam and Christianity as well as persecution have led to approximately just 600 left today. Of these, half live in Kiryat Luza, close to Mount Gerizim, just south of Nablus in the West Bank, the remainder residing in the Holon district near Tel Aviv. Mount Gerizim is the holiest site in the Samaritan faith and the site of their 6th-century BCE temple, which was constructed following their break from Judaism. The Samaritans broadly practise a religion similar to that of the biblical Jews, with some elements of Islam added in. They write and speak in ancient Hebrew, abide by thousands-of-years-old traditions, recognise Moses as the one prophet and have one holy book, the *Pentateuch* (handed down by Moses).

EDUCATION

The Israeli workforce is well educated, having received many trained professionals through immigration, and today has a literacy rate of 97.1%. Its citizens enjoy a high standard of living with an unemployment rate of 7.6%. Despite this, the level of education in the country has resulted in disproportionate demographics and after Israel stopped Palestinian workers entering the country found itself short of manual labourers. In recent years it has begun recruiting thousands of workers from China, Thailand, the Philippines and eastern Europe to fill the labour void.

School attendance is mandatory from age five to 16 and free until the age of 18. The school system in Israel has created its own solution to the problems of differing social and religious backgrounds by forming different institutions to suit each group: state schools, which are attended by the majority; state religious schools, which emphasise Jewish studies and observance; Arab and Druze schools with classes in Arabic; and private schools. Israel has many higher education institutions attended by over 200,000 students at any one time. Higher education tends to start much later than in most other Western countries on account of the prolonged time spent in the army (and subsequent year abroad that most Israelis undertake afterwards), with men often not beginning studies until their mid to late twenties.

CULTURE AND ENTERTAINMENT

ART Organised art in Israel can be traced back to 1906 and the Bulgarian professor Boris Schatz, who established the Bezalel Academy of Arts and Crafts in Jerusalem, years before Israel's declaration of independence. It encouraged talented Jewish artists to immigrate to the country and proved to be instrumental in the development of the rich artistic culture seen in the country today. To this day artist colonies such as **Ein Hod** and **Rosh Pina** flourish, the artists ranging from painters, sculptors, photographers and ceramicists to those specialising in more unusual crafts such as weaving, glassblowing and calligraphy. Israel's art museums are world class, Jerusalem's **Israel Museum** (see page 115) and **Tel Aviv's Art Museum** (see page 113) holding the highest esteem internationally. Israel's multiculturalism has once more provided for a range of styles, genres and traditions few other countries can attest to.

MUSIC With weekly sell-out performances and record-breaking season-ticket holders, the **Israeli Philharmonic Orchestra** needs little introduction. It was founded in 1936 and often plays host to guest conductors and musicians from around the world. Its home is surprisingly not in Jerusalem as one would expect but in Tel Aviv's Mann Auditorium (see page 110). The **Jerusalem Symphony Orchestra**, while not quite on a par with the Israeli Philharmonic Orchestra, is still highly regarded and its concerts are broadcast on Israel's classical music stations. Other esteemed orchestras include the Haifa Symphony Orchestra, the Ramat Gan Orchestra, the Beer Sheva Simfonetta, and the Israeli Chamber Orchestra. The Israeli Opera Company performs in the Merkaz le-Omanuyot ha-Bama near the Tel Aviv Museum and its repertoire includes classical compositions and modern operas.

Modern music is also big business and many young Israelis have a rather deep passion for heavy trance. Rock, jazz and classic 1970s and 1980s hits also make their way into bars and clubs (with the odd Christmas song thrown in during July for good measure). For more information about music events see *Chapter 4, Entertainment and nightlife*, page 107.

THEATRE Israeli theatre comprises both large and small theatre troupes, the **Habima Theatre** in Tel Aviv forming the national core of theatrical performances (see page 109). The mesh of cultures that immigrated to the country in the early 20th century formed a unique blend of theatre that has lasted to this day. Jerusalem and Tel Aviv play host to the most number of theatres and productions (many of which provide English translation) whose styles and genres span a vast range.

DANCE Dance is gaining in popularity and over the last decade institutions such as the **Suzanne Dellal Centre**, **Bat Sheva Dance Troupe** and the **Israeli Ballet**

have become household names. However, they are still nowhere near as well established as theatre and classical music and as such performances are less frequent (see page 110).

Cinema Israeli cinema is more developed than most would imagine and several have made their way along the red carpets of the Cannes Film Festival and even received Academy Award nominations as best international films. Cinematographic topics tend to centre on issues close to the hearts of Israelis and Jews, such as the Holocaust, the Israeli–Palestinian situation and the IDF. The enormous **Jerusalem Cinematheque** (*www.jer.cine.org.il*) is the best place for film aficionados to start, with its wealth of information, eclectic mixture of showings and educational courses, while the **Spielberg Film Archive** (*www.spielbergfilmarchive.org.il*) at the Hebrew University of Jerusalem is the world's largest centre for Jewish and Israeli film material.

SPORT

If you look at Israel's medal-winning record in international events, you'd be forgiven for thinking that sport doesn't feature very highly in the country. That is, however, wrong and, despite their lack of presence in any sport other than

THE DARKEST DAY IN OLYMPIC HISTORY

On 5 September 1972, the Munich Olympics were well underway when gunmen from the Palestinian terrorist group Black September stormed the athletes' village, killing two Israelis outright and taking hostage a further nine. Just 27 years after the Holocaust, Israeli participation in the event was seen as a significant and important step towards rebuilding the Jewish morale and attempting to repair relations with Germany, yet the event was to be marred for ever, and seen as one of the darkest days in Israel's history. The terrorists demanded the release of over 200 Palestinian prisoners from Israeli jails and free passage for themselves out of Germany, throwing the body of wrestling coach Moshe Weinburg out of the building as grim evidence of their intentions should their demands not be met.

The Tunisian ambassador and members of the Arab League offered their help to the German authorities in negotiating with the terrorists, but it was to minimal avail, Israel standing firm on its policy of not negotiating with terrorists. At one stage in the negotiations, German officials offered to personally take the places of the Israeli athletes, such was their distress and horror that harm might come to the Jewish captives in their country so soon after the end of World War II. After more than 12 hours, the terrorists requested to leave the Olympic Village and were taken by helicopter to a military airport, handcuffed to the hostages. It was around this time that mounting pressure on the International Olympic Committee finally succeeded in getting the games halted, which, until then, had continued, seemingly oblivious to the events unfolding. At the airport, as the terrorists and their hostages walked across the runway to a waiting aircraft, German snipers attempted unsuccessfully to pick them off, an act that was to go horribly wrong and see the immediate murder of the Israeli athletes as the terrorists turned their guns on them. The remaining hostages were inadvertently killed when a German grenade was thrown into the helicopter in which they were waiting. At the end of the shocking and tragic day 11 Israeli athletes had lost their lives. In a move seen in Israel and many countries across the world as insensitive and disrespectful, just 24 hours after the shocking day had ended, the Olympics resumed.

basketball, Israelis love sport, most notably extreme sports. Basketball, and in particular Maccabi Tel Aviv, is very successful and during a game is the quietest the streets ever get. Israel received its first (and to date only) Olympic gold medal in windsurfing in 2004 (interestingly the medal was inadvertently stolen in a run-of-the-mill house break-in and was later found discarded in woodland and returned to the athlete). Football (soccer), judo and tennis also feature highly whilst sky diving, scuba diving, parasailing and kite surfing are the new 'in' extreme sports. Golf is limited to the Caesarea golf course (see page 161) while, rather surprisingly, Mount Hermon has a semi-decent ski slope (although in recent years has been somewhat lacking in snow, see page 225).

In the same style as the Olympics and Commonwealth Games, every four years Israel hosts the **Maccabiah Games**, where Israeli and Jewish athletes from across the world compete in the country's biggest sporting event. The games were founded in 1932 and by 2005 had 7,700 participants from across the globe.

2

Practical Information

WHEN TO VISIT

Israel's mild winter climate and brilliant sunshine means that visiting the Holy Land is possible at any time. However, the extreme summer heat that permeates the entire country can often make sightseeing hard and exhausting work, so if you don't plan to spend a lot of your time on the beach then spring and autumn are prime tourist times (see *Climate*, page 6). It is important to note that while getting the opportunity to experience Israel's national holidays (in particular Yom Kippur – see below) as a wonderful insight into the culture of the country, the collection of holidays that fall around the end of September and into October see the country barely open to business. Between the holidays and Shabbat working days during that time can be very limited and many shops, restaurants, museums, national parks and sites of interest may be closed.

PUBLIC HOLIDAYS AND FESTIVALS

The dates of Israel's national holidays change yearly according to the Jewish calendar. The following table provides the dates for the forthcoming years. It is important to note that holidays run from sunset to sunset, so the dates listed below will, in fact, begin the evening before. Holidays' eves are considered the same as Fridays (see page 32) with respect to all opening hours listed in the guide, while holidays will correspond to Saturdays.

	2009	2010	2011
Rosh Hashanah	19–20 September	9–10 September	29–30 September
Yom Kippur	28 September	18 September	8 October
Sukkot	3 October	23 September	13 October
Simchat Torah	10 October	30 September	20 October
Hannukah	12 December	2 December	21 December
Purim	10 March	28 February	20 March
Passover (Pesach)	9 October	30 March	19 April
Holocaust Memorial Day	21 April	11 April	1 May
National Memorial Day	28 April	18 April	8 May
Independence Day	29 April	19 April	9 May
Shavuot	29 May	19 May	8 June
Tisha Bav	30 July	20 July	9 August

Religious and national holidays in Israel are an emotional time, where raw passions of sorrow, celebration, faith and pride emerge. Of these, there are two times of the year particularly when visitors can see Israeli patriotism and the resilience of the Jewish people come to light: the holy festival of Yom Kippur and the week in which Holocaust Memorial Day, National Memorial Day and Independence Day are celebrated. Yom Kippur, or the Day of Atonement, is the holiest day in Judaism, marking the end of the 'Ten Days of Repentance'. It is a day of fasting and prayer, for many secular Jews the only day of the year they attend the synagogue. Like a scene from a movie it is a fascinating sight to behold as not a single vehicle moves, children ride bicycles down the great motorways, the sounds of pigeons flap through the normally manic streets of Tel Aviv and the television and radio station shuts down.

In contrast to the country's most religious day, Holocaust Memorial Day and, exactly one week later, National Memorial Day are times of great sorrow, where the raw pain of the world's worst genocide and the loss of the soldiers who have died in Israel's many wars comes bubbling up. Television stations play reels of the fallen's faces, families attend memorials and the country collectively mourns. Yet come 20.00 on the eve of National Memorial Day the country erupts into an almighty celebration of independence, relief from the pain of the previous week lifted from heavy hearts. Jerusalem, Tel Aviv and towns across the country explode into a vibrant party of fireworks, folk dancing, beer swilling, dancing and raucous, family fun.

TOUR OPERATORS

For those who want hassle-free, well-organised excursions around Israel, there are copious amounts of extremely good (and plenty of extremely bad) tour companies offering a plethora of trips. In addition you can find hundreds of private licensed tour guides at *www.israel-guides.net*.

Desert Eco Tours ℡ 052 2765753/052 5394469; e angela@desertecotours.com; www.desertecotours.com. Based in Eilat, they offer a multitude of trips around the country as well as to Jordan & Egypt. Well known for their adventure excursions.

Egged Tours ℡ 03 9203919; e israel-4-u@ eggedtours.co.il; www.egged.co.il. In addition to their city tours they also arrange fantastic, reasonably priced tours around the country that depart from Jerusalem & Tel Aviv.

Mazada Tours ℡ 02 6235777; e mazada@ mazada.co.il; www.mazada.co.il. Arrange tours & transport to Jordan & Egypt. There are daily buses to Amman (300NIS) & Cairo (400NIS) & a range of tours around Israel.

Society for the Protection of Nature in Israel (SPNI) ℡ 03 6388688; e bela@spni.org.il; www.teva.org.il. Offer trips ranging from 1–5 days that centre on hiking, environmentally friendly outdoor activities & guided tours to sites of interest.

United Tours ℡ 02 6252187; e united1@ netvision.net.il; www.unitedtours.co.il. One of the biggest tour companies in Israel offering a wide range of coach tours.

Yambateva Travel and Tour Operator ℡ 08 6323002/03 5430000; e info@yambateva.com; www.yam-bateva.com. Arrange tours within Israel departing from Tel Aviv, Jerusalem & Eilat as well as trips to Jordan from Eilat. Specialist tours include pilgrimage tours, desert adventures & archaeological tours. They can also book car rental & hotels.

Zel Tours ℡ 02 5630611; e zel@zeltours.com; www.zeltours.com. Accredited, knowledgeable, native English-speaking guide Zed Lederman offers tailor-made trips to sites around the country.

With the exception of Yom Kippur, Shabbat, or the Sabbath, is the holiest day in Judaism and, as it comes around every seven days, there are a lot of them. According to the Ten Commandments and the *Old Testament* it was on this day that God rested during his creation of the world, and so man, too, must rest. Shabbat is seen as one of the great Jewish institutions and even the most secular of Israelis will greet each other with '*Shabbat Shalom*', meaning 'peace on the Sabbath'. In the Jewish calendar days begin not at midnight but at sunset, and each week Shabbat begins as the sun sets on Friday evening until one hour past sundown on Saturday. Shabbat practices vary considerably. Religious Jews abstain from most activities, including work, travel, switching electricity on or off (hence automatic elevators in some hotels), cooking or answering the telephone. For observant Jews it is a day of rest, most of which is spent praying. For the secular members of society it still entails a day off work and as public transport, offices and many businesses are closed this limits movement. In cities such as the eternally secular Tel Aviv, the dawn of Shabbat sees the bars, cafés and beaches fill to bursting as Israelis take advantage of their free time in a country that works five-and-a-half-day weeks. Jerusalem, on the other hand, sees the city all but shut down. While there are still non-Shabbat observant restaurants and bars, a large majority abide by the day of rest, and as the sun sets on Friday a calm settles over the normally bustling streets. Needless to say, in Arab communities, life continues as normal, the Muslim holy day being Friday when many services and businesses close and residents attend mosque prayer services.

RED TAPE

Citizens from the following countries will be issued with a tourist visa at their port of entry, valid for up to three months (a passport valid for six months from the date of entry will need to be provided).

Europe Austria, Belgium, Croatia, Cyprus, Czech Republic, Denmark, Finland, France, Germany, Gibraltar, Greece, Holland, Hungary, Iceland, Ireland, Italy, Latvia, Lichtenstein, Lithuania, Luxembourg, Malta, Monaco, Norway, Poland, Portugal, San Marino, Slovak Republic, Slovenia, Spain, Sweden, Switzerland, United Kingdom.

Asia and Australasia Australia, Fiji, Hong Kong, Japan, Micronesia, Mongolia, New Zealand, Philippines, South Korea, Vanuatu.

Africa Africa Central African Republic, Lesotho, Malawi, Mauritius, South Africa, Swaziland.

The Americas Argentina, Bahamas, Barbados, Bolivia, Brazil, Canada, Chile, Colombia, Costa Rica, Dominican Republic, Ecuador, El Salvador, Guatemala, Haiti, Jamaica, Mexico, Panama, Paraguay, St Kitts and Nevis, Surinam, Trinidad and Tobago, United States, Uruguay.

Citizens of all other countries should contact their local Israeli consulate or Israel's Ministry of the Interior (*www.mfa.gov.il*).

ISRAELI STAMP Israel does not hold diplomatic relations with most Arab and predominantly Muslim countries and, therefore, Israeli citizens are not permitted to travel to such countries. More than that, however, foreign nationals who have an Israeli visa stamp inside their passports will be refused entry into many of these countries. As such, it is a good idea to ask that the Israeli stamp not appear on your passport if you are planning travel to any countries where this may be a problem (Egypt and Jordan are notable exceptions). You can request this of the passport control officer when you arrive but their compliance is purely discretional.

EXTENDING VISAS Most tourist visas are issued for three months but can be extended at the Ministry of the Interior.

Jerusalem 24 Hillel St; ✆ 02 6294726
Tel Aviv 125 Menachem Begin St; ✆ 03 5193305;
Ben Gurion Airport; ✆ 03 9774200
Haifa 15 Pal Yam St; ✆ 04 863333

Eilat 2nd Floor, City Centre Mall, HaTemarin St; ✆ 08 6381333
Tiberias 23 Zaki Elkhadif St; ✆ 04 6729111

Ⓔ EMBASSIES

FOREIGN EMBASSIES IN ISRAEL Since 1967 when Israel captured East Jerusalem (and the West Bank and Gaza Strip), the UN and much of the international community is unwilling to recognise all of Jerusalem as Israel's capital. Almost all countries therefore maintain embassies and consulates in Tel Aviv, although a few have now got consulate offices in Jerusalem.

Australia 4th Floor, Europe Hse, 37 Shaul HaMelech St, Tel Aviv; ✆ 03 6950451; e telaviv.embassy@dfat.gov.au; www.australianembassy.org.il; ⊕ 08.00–12.00 & 13.00–16.30 Mon–Thu
Canada Hasapanut Hse, 3 Nirim St, Tel Aviv; ✆ 03 6363300; e enqserv@dfait-maeci.gc.ca; www.dfait-maeci.gc.ca/telaviv; ⊕ 08.00–16.30 Mon–Thu, 09.00–13.30 Fri
Egypt 54 Basel St, Tel Aviv; ✆ 03 5464151; f 03 5441615; ⊕ 09.00–12.00 Sun–Thu; **Consulate** 68 Afroni St, Eilat; ✆ 08 5976115; ⊕ 09.00–15.00 Sun–Thu
France 112 Herbert Samuel St, Tel Aviv; ✆ 03 5208300; f 03 5208340; www.ambafrance-il.org; ⊕ 09.00–12.00 Mon–Fri; **Consulate** 5 Paul Emil Botta, Jerusalem; ✆ 02 6259481; www.consulfrance-jerusalem.org; ⊕ 09.00–12.00 Mon–Fri
Germany 3 Daniel Frish St, Tel Aviv, ✆ 03 6931313; f 03 6969217; e ger_emb@netvision.net.il; www.germanemb.org.il; ⊕ 08.00–16.00 Mon–Thu, 08.00–12.30 Fri
Ireland 3 Daniel Frish St, Tel Aviv; ✆ 03 6964166; f 03 6964160; ⊕ 08.00–13.00 & 14.00–16.00 Mon–Thu, 08.00–13.00 Fri
Jordan 14 Aba Hilel St, Ramat Gan, Tel Aviv; ✆ 03 7517722; f 03 7517712; ⊕ 09.00–15.00 Sun–Thu

Netherlands 14 Aba Hillel St, Ramat Gan; ✆ 03 6957377; e info@holland-israel.com; www.netherlands-embassy.co.il; ⊕ 08.00–15.00 Mon–Thu, 08.00–13.00 Fri
South Africa Top Tower, Dizengoff Centre, Tel Aviv; ✆ 03 5252566; e diplomatie@ambafrance-il.org; www.safis.co.il; ⊕ 09.00–11.30 Mon–Fri, 09.00–11.30 & 14.00–15.00 Wed
United Kingdom 192 HaYarkon St, Tel Aviv; ✆ 03 5249171; f 03 5243313; ⊕ 08.00–16.00 Mon–Thu, 08.00–13.30 Fri **Consulate** 1 Ben Yehuda St; ✆ 03 5100166; e webmaster.telaviv@fco.gov.uk; www.britemb.org.il; ⊕ 08.00–13.00 Mon–Thu, 08.00–12.30 Fri; **Consulate** 19 Nashashibi St, Jerusalem; ✆ 02 5322368; e Britain.Jerusalem@fco.gov.uk; www.britishconsulate.org; ⊕ 07.30–15.30 Mon–Thu
USA 71 HaYarkon St, Tel Aviv; ✆ 03 5197575; f 03 5102444; ⊕ 08.00–16.00 Mon–Thu, 08.00–13.00 Fri **Consulate** 1 Ben Yehuda St; ✆ 03 5175151; e nivtelaviv@state.gov; www.telaviv.usembassy.gov; ⊕ 08.00–16.30 Mon–Fri; **Consulate** 18 Agron Rd, Jerusalem; ✆ 02 6227230; e jerusalemvisa@state.gov; www.jerusalem.usconsulate.gov; ⊕ 08.00–16.30 Mon–Thu

ISRAELI EMBASSIES ABROAD
Australia 6 Turrana St, Yarralumla, Canberra; ✆ +61 2 6215 4500; e info@canberra.mfa.gov.il; www.canberra.mfa.gov.il; ⊕ 09.30–13.30 Mon–Fri

Canada 1155 Rene Levesque, Montreal; ✆ +1 514 940 8500; e info@montreal.mfa.gov.il; www.montreal.mfa.gov.il; ⊕ 10.30–12.30 Mon–Fri;

Suite 1005, 50 Ocoonor St, Ottawa; ✆ +1 613
567 6450; e info@ottawa.mfa.gov.il;
www.ottawa.mfa.gov.il; ⏰ 10.00–12.00 Mon–Fri
Egypt 6 Sharia Ibn-el Maleck; ✆ +20 2 3332
1500; e info@cairo.mfa.gov.il; www.cairo.mfa.gov.il;
⏰ 10.00–12.30 Sun–Thu
France 3 Rue Rabelais, Paris; ✆ +33 1 40 76 55
00; e info@paris.mfa.gov.il; www.paris.mfa.gov.il;
⏰ 09.30–12.30 Mon–Thu; 146 Rue Paradis,
Marseilles; ✆ +33 4 91 53 39 90;
e info@marseilles.mfa.gov.il; ⏰ 10.00–12.00
Mon–Fri
Germany 74–75 Auguste Victoria, Berlin; ✆ +49 30
8904 5500; e info@berlin.mfa.gov.il;
www.berlin.mfa.gov.il; ⏰ 09.30–13.00 Mon–Thu,
09.00–12.30 Fri
Ireland 122 Pembroke Rd, Dublin; ✆ +353 1 230
9400; e info@dublin.mfa.gov.il;
www.dublin.mfa.gov.il; ⏰ 10.00–13.30 Mon–Fri

Jordan 47 Maysaloun St Rabiya, Amman; ✆ +962 6
550 3500; e info@amman.mfa.gov.il;
www.amman.mfa.gov.il
⏰ 09.00–13.00 & 14.00–16.00 Sun–Thu
South Africa 428 Kings Highway, Pretoria; ✆ +27
12 470 3500; e info@pretoria.mfa.gov.il;
www.pretoria.mfa.gov.il; ⏰ 09.00–13.00 Mon–Thu,
09.00–12.00 Fri
United Kingdom 2 Palace Green, London; ✆ +44 20
7957 9500; e info@london.mfa.gov.il;
www.london.mfa.gov.il; ⏰ 10.00–13.00 Mon–Thu,
10.00–12.00 Fri
United States 800 Second Av, New York; ✆ +1 212
499 5400; e consular@newyork.mfa.gov.il;
www.israelfm.org; 3514 International Drive,
Washington; ✆ +1 202 364 5500; e
info@washington.mfa.gov.il; www.israelemb.org;
⏰ 09.30–13.00 Mon–Fri

GETTING THERE AND AWAY

✈ **BY AIR** Ben Gurion International Airport (TLV) (✆ 03 9755555; www.ben-gurion-airport.co.il) is Israel's only international airport (with the exception of the odd few charter flights that go into Ovda Airport near Eilat). The velvet ropes came down in 2004 to reveal a plush, new terminal that Israelis are rightly proud of. There are good bus and train transport links with Tel Aviv (see pages 98–99) and Jerusalem (see pages 56–57) and car-rental counters can be found on the first floor of the East Gallery in the arrivals terminal (⏰ 24hrs) (see page 100).

Israel's national airline is **El Al** (✆ 03 9716854; www.elal.co.il; code LY) and it operates regular flights to destinations all around the world. While in-flight service has improved considerably, the stringent security measures (see the box, Flying with El Al, see page 36) mean prices are high compared with other airlines. It is important to note that El Al does not fly on Shabbat and all meals are kosher (Glatt kosher can be ordered in advance).

Tickets Most airlines offer online ticket purchasing or tickets can be booked over the phone. Alternatively, travel agencies such as ISSTA (see pages 70 and 112) or Ophir Tours (see pages 70 and 112) offer good budget deals and last-minute flights. In 2007, the budget airline Thomsonfly started offering regular flights to and from Manchester and London Luton, **UK** which are considerably lower than British Airways or El Al (860NIS one way). Travellers coming from **Australasia** and **South America** (or countries that do not have diplomatic relations with Israel) will need to change in Asia or Europe. El Al offers regular flights from **Hong Kong**, **Beijing** and **Bangkok** (approx 4,000NIS return). Delta, El Al, Israir and American Airlines run regular flights between Tel Aviv and **New York** as well as **Los Angeles** and other major airports in the **United States** and **Canada**. Air France, Iberia, Lufthansa, KLM and Alitalia offer fairly pricey tickets from **western Europe** and are the most commonly used connections to **South America**. Apart from **Jordan** and **Egypt** (which does not operate flights to Tel Aviv), **Turkey** is the only other Middle Eastern country with relations with Israel. As a top Israeli tourist destination flights to **Istanbul** and **Marmaris** can be bought relatively cheaply, as can tickets to the Greek Islands and Cyprus.

El Al is Israel's national airline and flying with this famously security-conscious company is certainly an interesting experience. Since its conception in 1949 when it flew Israel's first president Chaim Weizmann home from Switzerland on its maiden voyage, it has had security at the forefront of its management. Post 9/11, El Al has become a model for other airlines looking to improve their security standards and while El Al flights are considerably pricier than their competitors, they most certainly give you peace of mind. They are so confident of their security measures in fact, that after you have gone through their rigorous security checks they provide passengers with metal cutlery as a reward.

Embarking on a flight with El Al, however, needs some preparation, as even the most seasoned flyers will find things work a little differently. Firstly, check-in. In most airports across the world, El Al's check-in can be found at the furthest end of the terminal, cordoned off by barriers and surrounded by a selection of burly, heavily armed airport police. Only passengers may approach the cordoned-off area and passports and tickets must be shown to even get in line. At this point an Israeli El Al staff member, clip-board in hand will approach and begin to ask rather a lot of questions. Who do you know in Israel? Why are you going there? Plus the standard did you pack your own bag? questions. With the interrogation over you will then proceed to the enormous x-ray machine into which you will heave your suitcases. More often than not, your suitcase will then undergo an intensive search and rub down with a long, wand-looking object (which is, in fact, an explosive detector). After checking-in comes phase two. As you approach the heart-sinkingly long line to go through security you will suddenly be ushered down a different, El Al-only (and, therefore, considerably shorter) channel. Once through, there is another long walk to the gate, again the furthest the airport has to offer where you will finally board the plane. Most flights go by uneventfully unless you have yet to experience often large groups of Orthodox men praying fervently in the aisles, tefillin affixed to their heads and arms (see page 22). While Israelis are notorious amongst airline staff for not abiding by seatbelt signs, as the wheels of the plane touch down a round of applause normally erupts in recognition of the pilot.

Airlines

Air Canada ℡ 03 6072111; www.aircanada.co.il

Air France ℡ 03 7555050; www.airfrance.com

Alitalia ℡ 03 7960760; www.alitalia.com

American Airlines ℡ 03 7952122; www.aa.com

Arkia ℡ 03 6903712; www.arkia.com

Austrian Airlines ℡ 03 5115111; www.aua.com

British Airways ℡ 03 6061555; www.ba.com

Cathay Pacific ℡ 03 7952111; www.cathaypacific.com

Continental Airlines ℡ 03 5116777; www.continental.com

Delta ℡ +1 800 241 4141; www.delta.com

Iberia ℡ 03 5163239; www.iberia.com

Israir ℡ +1 700 505 777; www.israirairlines.com

KLM ℡ 03 7967999; www.klm.com

Lufthansa ℡ 1800 9371937; www.lufthansa.com

Royal Jordanian Airlines ℡ 03 5165566; www.rj.com

South African Airways ℡ 03 5102828; www.flysaa.com

Thomsonfly www.thomsonfly.com. Budget airline operating flights to Manchester and London Luton, UK.

Turkish Airlines ℡ 03 5172333; www.turkishairlines.com

BY LAND Of Israel's neighbours it only has diplomatic relations with Jordan and Egypt and, therefore, it is only possible to travel overland (or by any other means for that matter) between these countries. While getting to either country under your own steam is perfectly achievable, **Mazada Tours** (see page 32) arranges buses to Amman and Cairo from both Tel Aviv and Jerusalem.

Egypt Despite several border crossings with Egypt, only the **Taba Border Crossing** (↘ 08 6660999) in the south of the country near Eilat is open to tourists (the **Rafah Border** is closed to foreign travellers for the foreseeable future owing to its proximity to Gaza). To travel to Sinai you don't need to apply for a visa in advance but can instead obtain one at the border crossing (£30) which is open 24 hours. There is also a 68NIS exit fee from Israel. If you plan on continuing to the Egyptian mainland you will need to apply for a visa at the Egyptian consulates in Tel Aviv (see page 34) or Eilat (see page 34). It is a modern and well-run crossing with streams of Israelis and tourists crossing daily. Rental cars cannot be taken into Egypt.

Jordan There are three border crossings to Jordan and, with the exception of the King Hussein/Allenby Border Crossing, visas can be obtained at the border (45NIS). Those using the Allenby Border will need to apply for a visa from the Jordanian embassy in Tel Aviv beforehand (see page 34). Your passport must be valid for at least six months.

Yitzhak Rabin Border Crossing (*Eilat;* ↘ *08 6300555;* ⊕ *06.30–20.00 Sun–Thu, 08.00–18.00 Fri/Sat*) This was the first border between the two countries and is used mainly for day trips to Petra and Wadi Rum. While there is a lot of toing and froing, passport stamping, photographing and form filling it is a relatively easy crossing. Exit tax is 68NIS. There are no buses from Eilat but it is a short taxi ride. On the way back, ask the Israeli guard at the gate to call you a taxi. There are a few taxis on the Jordanian side that will take you to Aqaba.

Allenby Border Crossing/King Hussein Bridge (↘ *02 5482600;* ⊕ *08.00–18.00 Sun–Thu, 08.00–14.00 Fri/Sat*) This border is used mainly for traffic to and from Amman and Jerusalem (1hr from Jerusalem). Buses on both sides are regular and will take you to the capital cities. Exit tax is 130NIS. Note that opening times on the Jordanian side differ (*06.30–22.00 Sun–Thu, 08.00–20.00 Fri/Sat*).

Jordan River Crossing (*Beit She'an;* ↘ *04 6480018;* ⊕ *08.00–22.00 daily*) This border is convenient if you're travelling in the Galilee or coming from Jerusalem and Haifa. There is a 2km no-man's-land between the two terminals so either hitch a lift or walk. There are buses to the border from Beit She'an. Exit tax is 70NIS.

BY SEA Ferry lines have been closed due to lack of traffic for several years but it is still possible to get on one of the increasingly popular cruises departing from Haifa's port. Cruises to and from Turkey, the Greek Islands and Italy can be arranged through **Mano Tours** (*2 Paliam St, Haifa;* ↘ *04 8606666;* f *04 8667666; www.mano.co.il*) or **Caspi Shipping** (*76 Ha'atzmaut St, Haifa;* ↘ *04 8674444;* e *lea@caspi-sapanut.co.il; www.caspitours.co.il*) and leave from the rather nice **Maritime Passenger Terminal** (↘ *04 8518245; www.haifaport.co.il*).

✚ HEALTH

Israel is a modern, developed country with Western standards of health, hygiene and medical facilities. Visitors do not need to have any vaccinations to enter the country although it is advisable to be up to date on tetanus, diphtheria and polio, which comes as an all-in-one vaccine (Revaxis) that lasts 10 years. It is also advisable to get children vaccinated against measles as outbreaks have occurred primarily in Orthodox neighbourhoods of Jerusalem where vaccination is opted against. Those working in medical settings are advised to be vaccinated against Hepatitis B. Israel is home to several highly reputable and internationally renowned hospitals, in particular Ichilov in Tel

Aviv, the Hadassah Ein Kerem in Jerusalem and Soroka in Beer Sheva (see the relevant chapters for details). Pharmacies are commonplace, well stocked with most Western-brand medicines and have pharmacists who speak a high level of English. Superpharm is the most widely distributed chain and most cities have several branches.

HEALTH TOURISM With the increasing international popularity and awareness of the medicinal effects of the Dead Sea and its products, health tourism in Israel is growing by the year. Health clinics and spas that centre on natural resources such as the Dead Sea or hot springs have been known to help heal a whole host of ailments (see page 250).

INSURANCE As with all sensible travel, insurance is most certainly a requirement. However, many policies do not cover injuries sustained through acts of terrorism so be sure to check the small print of your insurance provider. Most insurance companies only provide emergency dental treatment so, if you have any concerns, get your teeth checked before leaving home. While Israel has good dental clinics, they come at a rather hefty price.

WATER Tap water is generally safe to drink in Israel and poses no health risks. It can occasionally have a rather chlorine-like taste so if your palate doesn't approve, bottled water is widely available and inexpensive.

HEALTH RISKS

Heat-related sicknesses Israel in general doesn't pose many health risks, with the exception of travel in the desert. Temperatures can reach as high as 45°C, which combined with the intense sunshine and arid conditions, poses **dehydration** risks. Be sure to always carry plenty of water when venturing into the southern desert region and stay hydrated. A hat, strong sunscreen and sunglasses are also important to minimise the effects of the relentless sun, both in winter and summer. For more details on safety around the Dead Sea, see page 245.

Mosquitoes and sand flies Israel does not suffer from malaria so no antimalarial drugs are necessary. In summer, however, mosquitoes are out in their millions and can cause infections and irritations so be sure to use strong mosquito repellent, such as those containing around 50–55% DEET. Likewise, sand flies along coastal regions can leave sore, itchy bites so be sure to apply repellent regularly.

Stray animals and rabies Stray cats are a major problem in Israel and although most are not tame enough to be touched, some (mainly kittens) have got used to people and beg for food in outdoor restaurants. Despite their heartbreaking plight it is best not to touch them as a variety of pests, infections and funguses can be transferred to you. Rabies is also present in Israel although contained almost wholly in rural areas so be attentive when camping and do not touch stray animals. Pre-exposure rabies vaccinations are advised and are particularly important for those intending to have contact with animals and/or likely to be more than 24 hours from medical help.

Jellyfish While Israel's jellyfish do not cause any lasting harm and are not poisonous, they can leave you with a rather painful sting and red, whip-like mark. In general those that wash onto the shores of the Mediterranean do so in waves between the months of June and August and, for the most part, the coast is clear. The small jellyfish that occasionally appear along Eilat's Red Sea coast, however, are sting-less and can be moved gently aside so as not to harm them while swimming.

Scorpions and snakes Scorpions are found in the desert and can provide a nasty, painful bite. In general the black scorpion bites are not life threatening but those inflicted by the yellow scorpion can be much more severe. Either way, seek medical advice if you get bitten. Be aware when moving rocks or stones and keep shoes on, especially at night. Israel is home to several species of venomous snakes but bites are rare. Don't stick your arms or hands into cracks, crevices or under rocks and if you're camping make sure you keep the tent flaps zipped closed at all times. If you do get bitten by a snake, keep calm – most snakes are harmless and even venomous species only dispense poison in about half their bites. Prevent movement of the limb by applying a splint, keep the limb below heart level and apply a bandage to the whole limb. Seek medical help as soon as possible.

WOMEN'S HEALTH As in any country, women travelling in areas with below-average sanitation levels should be aware of the possibility of contracting urinary tract, bladder or yeast infections, and should take necessary medication with them. Loose-fitting clothing, drinking plenty of fluids and carrying toilet paper with you are preventative measures that can be taken to avoid these complications. If you do develop a gynaecological problem, over-the-counter medications are widely available and most hospitals have women's health departments. Tampons, sanitary towels and condoms are available in all supermarkets, mini-markets and pharmacies, although not all brands are stocked so if you use something specific be sure to take enough with you. Contraceptive pills differ from country to country so take a supply sufficient to last you your trip.

SAFETY

In general visitors to Israel encounter few problems. **Crime** levels are low and while petty theft and pickpocketing do occur, violent crimes are extremely rare. The most worrying safety threat for most people considering a trip to Israel is terrorism which, despite considerable improvements over recent years, is unfortunately a part of life in the country. As the security situation in Israel and the Palestinian Territories can change rapidly it is important to check with your country's foreign office (see the following list) before setting off.

Australia www.smartraveller.gov.au
Canada www.voyage.gc.ca
Germany www.auswaertiges-amt.de
Ireland www.dfa.ie

New Zealand www.safetravel.govt.nz
South Africa www.dfa.gov.za
United Kingdom www.fco.gov.uk
United States http://travel.state.gov

TERRORISM Compared with many countries, Israel has a high risk of terrorism. At the time of writing there had been three terrorist attacks in the previous year: suicide bombings in a shopping mall in Eilat and in Dimona, and a shooting in a religious college in Jerusalem. The majority of terrorist attacks in Israel have been in the form of indiscriminate suicide bombings that target crowded areas such as transport terminals, shopping centres, restaurants, markets and nightclubs. It is important to be vigilant and stay away from establishments that do not have security guards outside (it is common to be checked with a metal detector and be asked to open bags before entering most places). As situations can change quickly it is a good idea to monitor media outlets and always follow the instructions of Israeli authorities. It is highly recommended to register at your country's consulate upon arrival as they will be able to inform you of any changes to security issues.

BORDERS It is advisable not to travel to the **Shebaa Farms area** and **Ghajar** along Israel's northern border with Lebanon because of ongoing military operations over the highly disputed land. At the time of writing all but essential travel to within 12km of the border with the **Gaza Strip** was strongly warned against by Israeli and foreign authorities due to the firing of rockets by Hamas members. Because of a breach in the Gazan/Egyptian border in March 2008, **route 10** running along the Egyptian/Israeli border is closed to civilian traffic until further notice. Live **minefields** along some border areas with Lebanon, the West Bank and Gaza remain in place so it is important not to venture off marked roads or tracks. The Golan Heights too sees a number of live mine areas, remnants of past wars, and it is therefore imperative to stick to designated paths (see page 215).

NATURAL DISASTERS Israel is located along an active earthquake zone and while most tremors go undetected (and it has been several hundred years since the last major earthquake), scientists and meteorologists have said the country may experience larger quakes in the future. Sandstorms and flash floods in winter months can become serious dangers in the desert regions so it is important to check with local national park authorities and meteorological stations before venturing off-road (see page 231).

DRIVING Statistically you are considerably more likely to come to harm driving down Israel's fast and furious motorways than in a terrorist attack, and it is important to be aware of the somewhat haphazard driving techniques many Israelis have adopted. The idea that road traffic rules only apply to others combined with aggressive driving techniques and high speeds sadly result in hundreds of deaths a year. Tiredness on the long, straight, monotonous roads in the desert can also lead to accidents so be sure to pull over and rest if you feel yourself start to tire.

CULTURAL CONCERNS Religious observances can often be the cause of serious negativity so it is important to be aware of religious and cultural taboos and respect them. Serious issues include the following:

- Being inappropriately dressed in religious neighbourhoods. When entering ultra-Orthodox Jewish neighbourhoods it is important to dress conservatively. This includes women not wearing trousers. Violent reactions towards those dressed or not behaving in accordance with Orthodox Jewish traditions have been reported.
- Inappropriate conduct in religious neighbourhoods. Shabbat is devoutly observed and therefore no cars should be driven through ultra-Orthodox neighbourhoods during these hours (see page 90). The stoning of vehicles not abiding by this is commonplace. Likewise, these neighbourhoods are best avoided during the holy day of Yom Kippur.
- Public displays of affection in religious sites. This applies to Jewish and Muslim religious sites as well as ultra-Orthodox neighbourhoods, and applies to both heterosexual and (considerably more so) to homosexual couples. Appropriate dress in any religious site should be adhered to (see page 70).
- Public conduct on religious holidays. Fasting during both the Muslim holiday of Ramadan and the Jewish holiday of Yom Kippur is strictly followed and you should abstain from eating or drinking alcohol (and in the case of Muslim areas during Ramadan, smoking) in public areas during these times.
- Taking photos of military or police installations. This is prohibited and enforced for security reasons.

WOMEN TRAVELLERS As with any country, women travelling alone can incur unwanted attention and face additional security risks. On the whole Israel is a relatively safe country for women and violent crimes are rare. However, sensible precautions should be taken to ensure you have a hassle-free trip. Wearing a

Israelis love children and having a large family is common practice, and as such your little ones will be welcomed into most venues with open arms. What many foreign parents often find a little disconcerting to begin with, however, is the tendency of complete strangers to come up and pinch cheeks, pick up, cuddle or play with their children, something not accepted in many, more conservative Western countries. While obvious precautions should always be taken with regards to your children, do not be alarmed by these acts as they are almost always offered in the most tender way and are purely an outpouring of affection that most Israelis, men and women alike, hold for babies and young children. Being stopped in the street and given 'helpful' advice as to whether your child should be wearing a hat, be given more water or needs a nap are also common, and while few parents appreciate advice from strangers, this is again not meant to offend.

wedding ring, dressing modestly, not accepting hitch-hiking lifts, staying in well-lit areas at night, letting someone know where you are going, carrying cash on you for a taxi or phone call, staying in women-only dormitories and ignoring male advances can all help avoid unwanted confrontations.

SECURITY CHECKLIST

The following are recommendations as to how best to minimise potential problems whilst travelling in Israel:

- Organise a variety of ways to obtain money, for example credit cards, cash, travellers cheques, etc.
- Make two copies of your documents (passports, insurance details, credit cards, etc). Give one set to a relative or friend at home and keep the other set with you but separate from the originals.
- Leave expensive jewellery behind to minimise the risk of theft.
- Steer clear of political demonstrations which can occasionally turn violent.
- Be vigilant in crowded areas (see page 39).
- Register with your consulate upon arrival.
- Be prepared to undergo lengthy questioning and bag searches on arrival into and departure from Israel.
- Abide by cultural and religious traditions in certain areas (see above).
- Avoid travel to within a 12km radius of the border with the Gaza Strip.
- Check foreign office warnings before leaving home.
- Do not venture off marked roads and footpaths to avoid live minefields and army training zones.
- Beware of flash floods in desert regions. Abide by ranger instructions, avoid ravines, narrow gorges and caves and monitor weather conditions before setting off.

WHAT TO TAKE

While there are few things that you cannot buy in Israel, prices for many products are equal to, if not more expensive, than other Western countries, and considerably more expensive than in developing countries. Shopping malls, big chain stores and vast supermarkets generally stock all the necessities you may have forgotten, but while camping and outdoor shops are well stocked, they are expensive and you're best buying any equipment before leaving home. Summers are hot so bring lightweight clothing and some long-sleeved shirts and trousers for entering religious sites. Sunscreen, sunglasses and a hat are essential items whatever time of year, especially if you're travelling into the desert region. A wet-weather jacket is a good idea during the autumn, winter and even spring months when rain is likely. Electricity is 220 volts and while most power sockets have three pin holes, they will usually work with standard European two-pin plugs. Plug adapters are cheap and most mini-markets and pharmacies will stock them.

$ MONEY, CURRENCY AND BANKING

Israel's official currency is the New Israeli Shekel (NIS), referred to simply as shekels; anything under a shekel is known as an *'agora'* (plural *agorot*). There are coins of five, ten and 50 agorot and one, five and ten shekels as well as notes of 20, 50, 100 and 200 shekels (you can see the notes at *www.bankisrael.gov.il/catal/cataloge*). Standard exchange rates are usually around 3.5NIS to US$1, 5.5NIS to £1 and 7NIS to €1 but vary according to current exchange rates. Most major credit cards are widely accepted in stores, tour agencies, restaurants, hotels, etc, and ATMs are commonplace.

CHANGING MONEY AND TRAVELLERS' CHEQUES There is no limit on the amount of money allowed into Israel, be it in cash, travellers' cheques or credit cards. Most major currencies and travellers' cheques can be exchanged for shekels at the airport, banks, post offices, many hotels or licensed exchange booths dotted around most towns and cities. To exchange travellers' cheques you will need to show your passport. Exchange rates vary and you will often get the best rate from the exchange booths in city centres, but it is a good idea to shop around a little, especially if you are changing large sums. All public services such as banks and post offices are closed on Shabbat so be sure to arrange your finances before Friday evening. At the end of your trip it is possible to change money from shekels only at the airport. A maximum of US$500 (or equivalent in other currencies) can be changed, or up to US$5,000 if you have the receipt original conversion.

TIPPING AND BARGAINING In a country that tends to complain loudly about most things, it is a surprising fact that bad service is rarely reported and tips are still given to sullen staff. It is customary to tip about 12% in restaurants, cafés and sit-down bars as well as bellboys and other service providers. In general, taxi drivers are not tipped, although it is common to tell the driver to round up the fare to the nearest appropriate round number (for example a 18NIS fare would be rounded to 20NIS). Taxi drivers are required by law to run the meter and those who refuse are highly likely to be overcharging you. Bargaining is standard procedure only in open markets.

BUDGETING

Israel isn't a cheap country in which to travel and you'll find that without keeping a close eye on your expenditures, money can fly out of your pocket at a rate of knots. One of the biggest expenses is ultimately accommodation which, outside the big cities is limited to luxury rural zimmers or camping (see *Accommodation*, page 45). Food is less of a problem if you're travelling on a tighter or shoestring budget as Israeli/Arabic fast food is healthy, widely available, extremely cheap, filling and delicious (see *Eating and drinking*, page 46) so you won't be reduced to the likes of McDonald's. Public transport is reasonably priced and if you plan on doing a lot of travelling then it is worth considering purchasing an **Egged Israbus** card (see page 43), which is a good money saver. If you're renting a car then petrol, not the rental itself, will be your biggest expenditure as prices are around 6.10NIS per litre. Alcohol in bars and pubs is also expensive in Israel so you're best off opting for the perfectly good local Goldstar or Maccabee beers (22–25NIS for half a litre) than imported brands. Spirits are also pricey, a single shot of Baileys for example setting you back 40NIS.

Many of Israel's top archaeological and natural sites are managed by the **Israel Nature and National Parks Protection Authority** who offer a season ticket that can save you huge amounts of money on entry. They can be purchased for 250NIS per person (or 275NIS for two people) at any park ticket office and are valid for one year. Likewise, the Tel Aviv and Jerusalem city municipalities offer free guided tours around their cities which are a good and cost-effective way to dig deeper into the history and culture. Students and senior citizens can get discounts on entry to most sites of interest as well as on public transport (see the following section) by showing an international student card or identification respectively.

GETTING AROUND

Israel is wonderfully compact, making travel relatively easy, affordable and free of draining, long-distance journeys. It is in fact possible to drive from Israel's northernmost point in the Golan Heights to the southernmost tip of Eilat on the Red Sea in about eight hours. While public transport is good in most urban regions, travelling around areas such as the Golan Heights and Negev and Arava deserts can be arduous and time consuming without your own wheels, so renting a car is highly recommended to get the most out of your time in these beautiful, wild and remote regions. It is important to note that, with the exception of some services in Haifa (see page 140), none of Israel's public transport runs on Shabbat or religious holidays.

BY BUS Buses are the most commonly used form of public transport in Israel, and both inter- and intra-city networks are very developed. Egged provides the bulk of bus lines, although some areas have their own inter-city companies. Conditions are good, and although inter-city buses can get crowded, all are air conditioned, clean and comfortable (in particular long-distance coaches for which seats need to be reserved). Tickets can be purchased either at ticket booths inside bus stations or from the driver. Discounts for students and senior citizens are available. Egged offers foreign tourists the chance to buy **Israbus** tickets valid for seven, 14, 21 or 30 days on all Egged lines that can save a lot of money if you plan on doing a lot of travelling. Tickets can be purchased at branches of Egged Tours or their website (❈ *03 96948888 or ★2800 from landlines; www.egged.co.il*).

BY TRAIN Although still in its fledgling stage, Israel's rail networks are gradually improving and now serve mainly the coastal region between Tel Aviv, Haifa, Akko and Nahariya as well as connecting with Jerusalem, Ben Gurion Airport and Beer Sheva. Owing to heavy traffic congestion along these routes, trains are a recommended way of getting around. Tickets can be purchased at either ticket booths or automated vending machines (also in English) at all train stations. Discounts for students and senior citizens are available.

BY SUBWAY Israel's one and only subway system is located in Haifa, the country's third-largest city. Designed to help residents navigate the steep geography of the city, it has five stops running between Paris Square near the port and the Central Carmel area (see page 141).

BY TAXI All major towns and cities have copious amounts of taxis, which can either be hailed from the street, telephoned for or found at taxi ranks. Rates start at 9.10NIS and an average inter-city ride costs around 20NIS. An additional 2.90NIS will be added for each suitcase and 3.50NIS if you telephone order. Rates increase by 25% during Shabbat and between 21.01 and 05.29. Taxi drivers almost always try to negotiate a price with foreigners and are reluctant to run the meter. Insist they use the meter or find another taxi. There is no need to tip taxi drivers although a rounding-up change is common.

BY SHARED TAXI (SHERUT) Shared taxis, known as *sherut*, run along the main intra- and inter-city bus routes and consist of small minibuses that generally only depart when full. Their appeal is that apart from being marginally cheaper, they can be stopped anywhere along the route and often run on Shabbat. The number of the bus route they correspond to is normally posted in the front window and fares are paid to the driver once the journey is underway (normally passed down the bus via the other passengers).

BY DOMESTIC FLIGHTS The country's diminutive size means that internal flights are often unnecessary and almost always more expensive than other forms of transport. Some companies do, however, offer special deals at certain times of the year so it is worth asking if you're pushed for time. It is really only worth flying between Eilat and Tel Aviv or Haifa. The following companies offer internal flights between Tel Aviv (Sde Dov and Ben Gurion airports) and Eilat and between Haifa and Eilat.

✈ **Arkia** ✆ 03 6902222; www.arkia.co.il. Offer flights only between Eilat and Haifa.

✈ **Israir** ✆ 03 7955777; www.israirairlines.com
✈ **El Al** ✆ 03 9716111; www.elal.co.il

BY CAR If your budget runs to it, renting a car is the best way to get the most out of your trip to Israel, especially in regions where public transport is sparser. Most

ISRAEL NATIONAL TRAIL

Stretching from Kibbutz Dan in the far north of the country to Eilat in the south, the Israel National Trail (Shvil Yisrael) was created to incorporate some of the most stunning natural landscapes, pristine countryside and national treasures that Israel has to offer. The entire trail is approximately 940km in length and winds its way through varied terrains, where verdant, green hills roll down to the Sea of Galilee, where the sandy Mediterranean coast sweeps through the metropolitan cities, which, in turn, explode into the vast, barren beauty of the Negev Desert. To undertake the entire trail takes seasoned hikers between 30 and 50 days, and is undoubtedly one of the most challenging and rewarding activities Israel has to offer. Cutting the Israel National Trail down into bite-sized chunks is a more realistic choice and offers hikers the opportunity to experience some of the best sections. The trail is clearly marked by tri-colour markers (orange, blue and white) but good hiking maps are an essential piece of kit to have in your backpack before embarking on long sections. Unfortunately, English literature on the trail is limited but in progress so be sure to check with the **Israel National Trail Committee** (✆ 03 6388719). There is currently a set of 16 maps that, although in Hebrew, are still usable for non-speakers and cost around US$20 per map. There is also a new book *Shvil Yisrael* that details places to stay, what to look for and a wealth of other information that is, again, in Hebrew but in the process of being translated.

ISRAEL NATIONAL TRAIL

0 ———— 30km
0 ———— 30 miles
Based on mapping by Carta, Jerusalem

international and national rental companies have offices at Ben Gurion Airport (see page 35), and in major towns and cities (see the relevant chapters). To rent a car you must be over 21 years of age and be in possession of an international driving licence. Driving in Israel is on the right-hand side of the road and most signs are in Hebrew, Arabic and English (although the continuity of English spelling can vary drastically and be a bit confusing at times, a classic example being Tzfat which can be seen on road signs spelt Safed, Tsfat and Zefat). It is the law to wear seatbelts and talking on mobile phones whilst driving is strictly illegal and subject to fines of 500NIS (some car-rental companies offer hands-free sets). Carta (*www.carta.co.il*) have produced a good English-language road map designed especially for tourists, which can be bought in any branch of Steimatsky bookshops or from their website.

BY SEA Israel's ferry links are sadly not what they used to be and at the time of writing there are no passenger ferries into and out of Israel. However, it is possible to get to Turkey, Italy and Greece aboard cruises that depart from Haifa (see page 140).

ACCOMMODATION

While it may appear that Israel has more than its fair share of hotels, statistics released by the government have revealed that the country is close to bursting with respect to availability of rooms versus the number of visitors. Needless to say, booking ahead in the height of summer and national holidays is highly recommended, especially in Jerusalem, Tel Aviv and Eilat. Other areas are slightly less pressured so you are more likely to find somewhere at the last minute. In general, however, the higher-end establishments seem to fill up fastest.

Israel has a sweeping array of accommodation types, but as it has yet to establish itself on the backpacker route, budget hostels are less well represented than luxury hotels, cabins and resorts. **Note** In this book, **price codes** are used. For the prices represented by each band, **see inside front cover**.

CAMPING Camping is an extremely popular activity in Israel, both with youngsters and families who pitch giant tents, set up the compulsory barbecue and settle in for a long weekend. There are many campsites dotted around the country that range from lovely grassed areas inside national parks to the beaches of the Sea of Galilee, Dead Sea and Mediterranean to Bedouin-style encampments in the desert. Some beaches, particularly in Eilat and along the Mediterranean where turtles nest, do not allow camping, but these will be signposted. While Israelis love being pampered, they are essentially outdoor types and all big towns and cities have camping shops aplenty and equipment is easy to come across. Safety issues arise when pitching tents outside designated campsites, which while it is possible and legal, needs to be approached with caution. Beware of army training zones (in the desert and Golan Heights) and minefields (in the Golan Heights) which pose obvious dangers. Rabies and poisonous snakes exist in Israel, which are important safety considerations when camping (see page 38).

HOSTELS Israel is still somewhat lacking in this department and hostels can be few and far between. Those that do exist however can be divided into those belonging to **Hostelling International** (HI) (✆ *02 6558400; www.iyha.org.il*) and privately run establishments. HI hostels can be somewhat sterile and attract large groups of teenagers on organised trips but do offer good value for money and are undoubtedly clean. A 50NIS membership card needs to be purchased from any hostel to be able to stay. Private hostels are more hit and miss but on the whole are full of character, reasonably priced and friendly.

ZIMMER Israel has, over recent years, been overtaken by zimmer fever. The zimmer (based on the German word for room and pronounced 'tzimeh') is essentially a luxury rural cabin built in the owner's back garden or on their land. There are quite literally thousands of them found in every part of the country and while some can be slightly questionable, most are beautifully decorated, set in stunning locations and run by friendly owners as a little side earner. One of the main features are the jacuzzi baths and no self-respecting Israeli would pay for one without such a feature. Prices can range between 300NIS per night for a standard zimmer up to 800NIS (or more) for something more luxurious during peak season. It is important to note that prices quoted in this guide are based on weekend rates, which during the week are up to 200NIS less per night.

HOTELS Hotel standards in Israel are high and most major international chains are represented. National chains such as Fattal, Dan and Isrotel also have numerous high-quality hotels dotted around the country. In addition, spa resorts have become big business in the Holy Land, especially along the Dead Sea, as well as 'boutique hotels' found mainly in Tel Aviv that blend modern Art Deco with classy (if sometimes a little pretentious) service.

✗ EATING AND DRINKING

FOOD With such a diverse population, there is not really such a thing as 'Israeli food'. Culinary styles have blended together from all across the world to leave a rather eclectic mix of cuisines. Apart from the insuppressibly popular Middle Eastern fast foods such as hummus and falafel (see the box, page 48), both kosher and non-kosher restaurants are well and equally represented. Tel Aviv is undoubtedly the culinary centre of the country, and is home to the bulk of non-kosher restaurants. Seafood, fish and French-style gourmet is found alongside traditional Indian food, steakhouses and Japanese sushi bars. That isn't to say that Jerusalem doesn't offer good food, as it most certainly does. While it may be considered a little more conservative than experimental, secular Tel Aviv, it has a wonderful mixture of cuisines, including some creative vegetarian places. Haifa too has benefited from its varied population make-up and offers a wealth of great eateries. For rustic country food, juicy, succulent steaks and age-old traditional Druze dishes the wilds of the Golan Heights, with its cattle ranches, farming communities and sweeping lands is the best bet, while Eilat offers the complete opposite with themed restaurants, beach bars and all things glitzy. **Note** In this book, **price codes** are used to indicate what to expect from your restaurant bill. For the prices represented by each band, **see inside front cover**.

DRINKS Israelis love their coffee so you are likely to find cafés in the most unlikely of places. Apart from the European brews, be sure to try the strong, aromatic Arabic coffee that is hugely popular in Israel. A word of warning, however; be sure not to drink the entire contents of the cup as a thick layer of coffee sediment sits at the bottom, which is rather unpleasant to swallow. In the height of the sweaty summer fruit-juice bars will freshly squeeze you your own fruity concoction and most kiosks sell inexpensive, creamy iced coffee. While Israelis aren't particularly big drinkers they love the whole bar scene and most alcohols are represented. The local beers are Goldstar and the more famous but less popular Maccabi, which are both more than respectable.

KOSHER When asked the reason behind kosher laws most Jews will reply that it is for health issues. While several of the laws do indeed seem to have positive health effects, there are others that do not appear to have relevance. In fact, the reason behind kosher laws (or *kashrut*) is that the *Torah* says it should be so. It doesn't, however, elaborate as to reasons why these laws were put in place, but for devout Jews there doesn't need to be. Kosher is upheld to varying levels of strictness in Israel, the secular barely abiding by it al all, or simply eliminating pork from their diet. There is no law in Israel that restaurants need to be kosher and, as such, a large proportion of those in secular cities such as Tel Aviv choose the 'not' option. While seafood and meat and dairy dishes are widely available on non-kosher menus, pork is the lasting taboo and doesn't often feature in Israel.

General rules:
- Certain animals cannot be eaten. Of mammals, only those that chew their cud and have cloven hooves are considered kosher. Pigs, camels and rabbits are not kosher. Marine life must have fins and scales, therefore shellfish is not kashrut. The *Torah* mentions only birds of prey as not being edible along with rodents, reptiles, amphibians and insects.
- Of permitted animals, they must be slaughtered in accordance with kashrut. This includes not consuming animals that died of natural causes.
- No blood of any animal must be consumed. Slaughtered animals must be drained of blood so as to ensure none of the animal's spirit is left.
- Certain parts of an animal may not be eaten including certain fats and nerves.
- Meat and dairy must be separated. Not only can they not be eaten together but they cannot be cooked or come into any contact with each other. A time period of three to six hours must elapse between consuming the two foods.
- Cooking utensils must be kept kosher. This involves reserving one set for cooking with dairy ingredients and another for preparing meat. Kitchen work surfaces, towels and even dishwashers are included in this rule.
- Wine must be made only by Shabbat-observant male Jews and all preparatory instruments must be kept kosher.

MCFALAFEL – FAST FOOD, MIDDLE EASTERN STYLE

Israel is a virtual casserole dish of cultures, traditions, culinary styles, religions and nationalities yet if you were to pinpoint the single unifying ingredient, one that has become the unofficial national symbol it would undoubtedly be the modest chickpea or, more specifically, hummus and falafel. Israelis eat these two inexpensive, fast food-style dishes by the bucket load and there is unlikely to be a fridge in the country that doesn't have an emergency pot of hummus inside. The good news for visitors is that the country's cheapest food is also some of its best and no trip would be complete without several helpings of creamy hummus, puffy pita, moist falafel, crunchy salad, crisp aubergine, roasted lamb meat or seasoned goat's cheese. Below is a guide to the best of Israel's fast-food dishes:

Hummus A thick, creamy mixture of chickpeas, tahini, oil, lemon juice and garlic served with pita. It can be eaten hot or cold, lumpy or smooth, and with a variety of toppings.

Falafel Ground, spiced chickpea balls deep fried and served piping hot in fresh pita with hummus, tahini and a selection of salads.

Sabich Believed to have come to Israel with Iraqi Jews, it is a big favourite, more so in Israel than any other Middle Eastern country. Pita is stuffed with fried aubergine, a hard-boiled egg, hummus, tahini and a variety of salads.

Shawarma Known in other countries as doner kebab, gyros and a whole host of other names it consists of slow-roasted, spiced lamb meat on a large skewer, finely sliced and eaten in pita with a choice of sauces and salads.

Burekas and sambusak Thin pastry parcels stuffed with a variety of fillings such as spinach, potato, cheese, mushroom or meat. *Sambusak* are in effect big *burekas*.

Labane Soured, creamed goat's cheese usually eaten by scooping with pita alongside salad, hummus and chips.

Tahini A thick sauce made from sesame seeds that is a crucial ingredient of hummus. It can also be eaten on its own with pita.

Shakshooka While not exactly considered fast food, this cheap, filling dish is a big Israeli favourite and was brought to the country by Sephardic Jews from north Africa. It involves a big mash of eggs, tomatoes, onions, green and red pepper and garlic cooked in a frying pan and eaten by scooping it onto bread.

SHOPPING

One of the favourite Israeli pastimes is shopping, and more specifically shopping in malls. In fact, Israel has one of the highest mall-to-population ratios in the world. Malls and high-street shops are comparable to any western European country and you can find pretty much anything you can at home, with many major international brands represented, particularly in Jerusalem and Tel Aviv. For many tourists, however, the vibrant markets are one of the main shopping appeals, where bargaining, noise, hustle and bustle and Middle Eastern charm are the main draws.

⨍ MEDIA AND COMMUNICATIONS

POST The Israel Post Office has several branches in all major cities and towns, which are denoted by their red sign with the white logo of a gazelle inside. While branches do differ slightly, most are open 08.00–12.00 and 15.30–18.30 Sunday, Tuesday and Thursday, 08.30–12.30 Wednesday and 08.00–12.00 Friday (the last includes the eve of holidays). Postal services include express, registered mail and

EMS. EMS is a quick, international service that allows for tracking of parcels and includes insurance. All post offices in Israel offer a Poste Restante service to tourists for up to three months. They will hold post for up to 30 days and identification needs to be shown to collect mail.

TELEPHONE Telephone connections in Israel are reliable, convenient and modern and international calls can be made with ease. Most hotel rooms come with direct-dial telephones, but be aware that prices can be grossly overinflated. Public phones can be found widely distributed in towns and cities and operate with telephone cards that can be purchased in post offices, kiosks and supermarkets. Alternatively, many kiosks offer coin-operated phones or pay after you use-style phones, but these are normally more expensive than the pre-paid cards. Mobile phones are big business in Israel and you are unlikely to find an Israeli, young or old who doesn't have one. Pelephone, Cellcom and Orange mobile phone companies will rent you phones for the duration of your stay (their rental offices are located in the airport).

INTERNET AND FAX Most businesses and homes are connected to the internet and, as such, internet cafés are fairly easy to come across, offering inexpensive, fast connection (you will pay more for fancy cafés offering drinks and snacks so if it's just the internet you're after look for somewhere less glitzy as it will certainly cost less). In more rural areas internet connection is generally limited to hotels. Faxes can be sent from the post office, hotels or internet cafés for the price of an international call.

MEDIA In a country with such a tumultuous existence it is perhaps unsurprising that most Israelis are fanatical about reading, watching, listening to and talking about current affairs and the news. Because of the country's wide-ranging cultural and linguistic differences, television and newspapers offer a plethora of languages and topics to suit the eclectic mix of the population. There are currently seven daily **newspapers** published in Hebrew, the one with the highest circulation being *Yediot Aharanot*, comprising approximately two-thirds of all newspaper readers in the country. *Ha'aretz*, which is published also in English, is the country's oldest daily, founded in 1919 and enjoys a wide circulation. In addition there are several publications printed in Russian and French as well as the internationally renowned *Jerusalem Post* (formerly the *Palestine Post*), which is published in English in Israel and North America, and French in western Europe. *Al-Ittihad* is the main Arabic-language daily and there are also several periodicals.

Despite the sweeping popularity of cable **television**, which has found its way into over 70% of Israeli homes, the two Israeli television channels still enjoy high viewing statistics and cover a wide range of topics from news broadcasts to entertainment to Arabic- and English-language programmes, to Latin American soap operas, children's programmes and live sporting events. Likewise, **radio** is an integral part of Israeli life and Kol Yisrael (Voice of Israel) is responsible for eight stations, broadcasting in countless languages and covering a wide range of genres. One of the most popular stations is Gal Galatz, a predominantly music and news headline station run and hosted by the IDF.

While freedom of the press is an important institution in Israel, there is a military censorship in place that deals with stories considered a threat to national security and which, therefore, must undergo governmental screening before release.

GIVING SOMETHING BACK

MEIR PANI (*www.meirpanim.org*) Israel's ongoing conflict and political problems and the cost of supporting the IDF has led to government cuts in social welfare, payments, health and education and, as such, the lowest-paid and unemployed members of society suffer most. Meir Manim is a national organisation dedicated to providing a range of welfare care, including food handouts, free kitchens, meals on wheels to elderly members of the community, youth clubs, vocational training, homes for abused women and centres for the elderly. Volunteers are always needed to help prepare and hand out food at one of the 30 free restaurants dotted around the country as well as donations.

SOS CHILDREN'S VILLAGES (*www.soschildrensvillages.org.uk* or *www.sosisr.co.il*) This UK-based global organisation has created over 400 villages for orphaned or homeless children and teenagers across 131 countries. In Israel there are two such homes, Neradim near Arad in the Negev Desert and Megadim near Nazareth in the Lower Galilee. Children live in a wholesome family environment with a 'mother' assigned to each house containing up to nine children. The two villages in Israel are home to over 150 children who receive state education, recreational facilities, vocational training, emotional support and a loving environment. Donations can be made via the website or it is possible to sponsor a child for US$40 per month.

CAT WELFARE SOCIETY OF ISRAEL (*www.cats.org.il*) Feral street cats are a major problem in Israel's cities and their numbers increase exponentially every year. The CWSI is one of the biggest animal welfare institutions in the country committed to educating, rescuing, neutering and caring for feral or unwanted cats. In 2004, during Israel's disengagement from Gaza and parts of the West Bank, thousands of street cats that survived on handouts or scavenging in rubbish bins were left in the blistering summer sun as Jewish settlers moved out. The CWSI (with help from other organisations) managed to lobby against the government for access to the closed Gaza Strip and went in to capture hundreds of the animals. Today they reside in a huge, purpose-built shelter in Hadera, and as most cannot be re-homed will remain there, cared for and happy. Visitors to Israel can choose to volunteer their time at the shelter, raise awareness in their home countries, donate blankets and equipment or sponsor a cat for US$25 per month. They have a small internet shop where you can buy a 'I helped save a Holy Cat!' T-shirt or alternatively a link to Amazon.com whereby 15% of your purchase will be donated to CWSI.

SAFE HAVEN FOR DONKEYS (*www.safehaven4donkeys.org*) In many rural areas of Israel working donkeys are still very much a part of life. Yet because of their cheap purchase price, those that get sick or old are just abandoned, many to suffer considerably. British-born Lucy Fensom arrived in Israel many years ago and vowed to do something to help these 'beasts of burden'. Today she runs an enormous shelter for abused and abandoned donkeys, which is home to over 100 animals. The enormous costs of running the shelter, located between Netanya and Hadera, are difficult to maintain and donations are always needed.

Part Two

THE GUIDE

JERUSALEM
Environs

MOUNT SCOPUS

500m
500yds

Hebrew University

MOUNT OF OLIVES

Mt of Olives Cemetery

JERICHO ROAD

see page 88

N

Bradt

Based on mapping by Carta, Jerusalem

EAST JERUSALEM

Ambassador Hotel

Jerusalem Hotel

NABLUS ROAD

SULEIMAN ST

OLD CITY

KIDRON VALLEY

YERUSHALAYIM ST

see pages 72–73

HATZANHANIM

Hebrew University

MEA SHEARIM ST

MEA SHEARIM

HANEVIIM STREET

STREET

MOUNT ZION

HA TATE

Jerusalem Cinematheque

St Andrew's Guesthouse

Khan Theatre

DAVID

HEBRON ROAD

REMEZ ST

German Colony

YEMIN MOSHE

AGRON ST

KING DAVID STREET

GERSHON ST

see pages 58–59

Independence Park

KING GEORGE

V ST

GAZA STREET

REHAVIA

USSISHKIN ST

see pages 58–59

EMEK REFAIM ST

Museum of Islamic Art

HAPALMACH STREET

MALCHEI YISRAEL ST

JAFFA STREET

AGGRIPAS ST

KING

BEN ZVI ROAD

YITZHAK RABIN BD

RUPPIN ROAD

Central Bus Station

The Knesset

Israel Museum

Monastery of the Cross

Rehavia Park

HA'ARI

HERZOG

Malha Mall (Shop)

Mt Herzl Museum, Yad Vashem Museum

MENACHEM BEGIN BOULEVARD

Malha Mall (Shop)

52

3

Jerusalem

As the sun sets over Jerusalem's white-stone buildings, it is impossible to imagine the millions of people who have stood and witnessed the very same event. For centuries Jerusalem has stood as the single most revered, contested and loved city in the world, its many different inhabitants having given it a cultural and religious make-up like no other place on earth, a place to which pilgrims flock and residents defend to the bitter end. To define the city is impossible, as it is, above all else, a city of contrasts. A city where Judaism, Christianity and Islam meet; where ancient neighbourhoods tumble into shiny new ones; where the devout and the secular find their own place and where modern and traditional somehow flourish together.

At its core sits the Old City, a remarkable and awe-inspiring area that has come to define the Holy Land's capital. Yet despite its historic, archaeological and religious treasures, its centuries of turmoil and conflict, and its political tensions, Jerusalem is first and foremost a vibrant, living city. Outside its walls, Jerusalem is a mesh of modern neighbourhoods, efficient transport networks, bustling souks, world-famous museums and high-class universities. Jewish Orthodox, secular and Arabic neighbourhoods each emanate their own traditions, for the most part respecting each other's day-to-day lives.

Visitors to the city find they leave changed. For the spiritually minded, the almost overwhelming wealth of holy sites is humbling and moving, while the more religiously apathetic find themselves stirred, a history that seemed so distant now as real as the present. For Jerusalem has always marked the final battle for the land, a fact that reigns as true today as it did thousands of years ago. The stumbling block over which peace negotiations fall, Jerusalem sits unwittingly in the midst of an international drama, the world watching every move out of the corner of its eye. Yet for those who live there, and for those who get the chance to visit, the tensions and turmoil are put to the back of the mind as you witness first hand the reason so many want to call it home.

HISTORY

THE CANAANITES AND THE ISRAELITES Although evidence points to occupation in the Stone Age, by c4000BCE the more technologically advanced Canaanites had taken over the area we now know as Jerusalem. In the 15th century the Egyptians conquered, ruling until the Israelites took control of the region in 1250BCE. While they managed to capture most of the realm, the fortified Jerusalem didn't fall for another 200 years. During this time David was declared the first King of Israel and in 1004BCE finally stormed the city, declaring it capital of his kingdom and renaming it the City of David.

THE FIRST TEMPLE PERIOD (1006–586BCE) Following David's conquest, the city soon became the political, religious and cultural centre of the kingdom. He

53

constructed a great palace, installing in it the sacred 'Ark of the Covenant'. The construction of the First Temple is attributed to Solomon, David's son, who at the same time enlarged the city. Soon after Solomon's death the kingdom split in two, the northern Kingdom of Israel forming a new capital, while the southern Kingdom of Judah retaining Jerusalem as their centre. In 586BCE, however, Jerusalem fell to the Babylonians who exiled the Jews and destroyed the temple.

THE SECOND TEMPLE PERIOD (536BCE–CE70) Shortly after, the Persians came to rule and the Jews were once more allowed to return. During the following years they constructed the Second Temple and reignited the religious and spiritual fervour that had been flourishing before the Babylonian incursion. When Alexander the Great conquered the Persian Empire and in 333BCE Jerusalem with it, the city entered a period of Greek and Hellenic cultural influence. Upon Alexander's death a fervent battle for rule over the great city took place, the Syrian ruler Antiochus IV emerging as victor and installing Seleucid rule over the land. Subjugation of the Jews and the destruction of the Second Temple instigated a great revolt under the leadership of the Maccabees, a Jewish family of patriots. This in turn led to the establishment of the Hasmoneans, who eventually ousted the Seleucids, beginning an 80-year period of Jewish independence.

THE ROMANS AND THE HERODIAN ERA (63BCE–CE96) In 63BCE, Roman general Pompeii conquered Jerusalem and in 37BCE Herod ascended as king. His reign saw the city expand northwards and a massive phase of building get underway. Herod constructed the second wall of the temple, today part of which is the Western Wall. He is also attributed with giving the temple a magnificent makeover and constructing the Antonia Fortress, Citadel, numerous palaces, markets, a theatre and a hippodrome.

It was during this time that Jesus of Nazareth was also active. After gathering support and naming his apostles in the Galilee, Jesus made his way to Jerusalem where, according to the **New Testament**, he was tried and crucified by Pontius Pilate as a rebel to Roman rule. Herod's death and the subsequent iron-fisted rule of the Romans led to a Jewish revolt, which ended in Roman victory. The Jewish residents were once again expelled, the Second Temple destroyed and Jerusalem burnt to the ground.

THE ROMAN BYZANTINE PERIOD (CE135–638) In CE135, Emperor Hadrian named his new conquest Aelia Capitolina, a new city layout was installed (the main streets of which still form the central cross-section through the Old City), Roman buildings erupted, Paganism prevailed, Jerusalem became a backwater city and Jews and early Christians were forbidden to enter. Until, that is, Constantine assumed power in CE303. Constantine was the first Roman ruler (by this time Byzantine after the break-up of the western Roman Empire) to be converted to Christianity, and throughout his rule Jerusalem exploded onto the scene as a pilgrimage destination, with hundreds of churches, including the Church of the Holy Sepulchre, owing their origins to this time. Over the next three centuries Christianity became the official religion of the Byzantine Empire, marking a crucial chapter in Jerusalem's history. In 614, Jerusalem fell to the Persians who massacred the city's inhabitants and decimated many of the holy sites. Although the Emperor Heraclius managed to reclaim the city six years later, it was not to last and Jerusalem fell once again, this time to the rising force of the Arab Islamic Empire.

THE EARLY MUSLIM PERIOD (CE638–1099) In CE638, Jerusalem came under Muslim rule following Calpih Omar's conquest of the kingdom. Although the

Koran does not mention Jerusalem by name, the *hadith* (a collection of sayings and traditions of Muhammad) specify that it was from here that the Prophet ascended to Heaven in the Night Journey. The conquest was bloodless and Christians and Jews were granted permission to continue practising their faiths unhindered. By the end of the 7th century Jerusalem was recognised as the third holiest site in Islam (after Mecca and Medina), and shortly after Abd Al-Malik built the Dome of the Rock above the stone said to be both where Muhammad ascended to Heaven, and the site of the former First and Second Temples. A short distance away the grand Al-Aqsa Mosque was also built.

THE CRUSADES AND SALADIN (ce1099–1250)

The 11th century saw the city come under the harsh rule of the Turkish Seljuks, an event that saw Pope Urban II call for the Crusades. Led by Godfrey of Bouillon, European Christians travelled to Jerusalem with the aim of liberating it from Islamic control. In 1099, they captured the city, naming it the capital of the Latin Kingdom of Jerusalem. It was a vicious and bloody conquest and most of Jerusalem's Jewish and Muslim residents were slaughtered. Jerusalem entered a new cultural phase whereby European customs and language became commonplace and where Christianity prevailed. Churches were restored and the holy sites on the Temple Mount (see page 83) became Christian, the Knights Templar (an order of monastic knights) installing their headquarters there. Even though the Kingdom of Jerusalem lasted until 1291, the capital fell to Saladin, a powerful Islamic hero, in 1187. Saladin allowed the worship of all religions and during this time many exiled Jews returned. Despite attempts by Richard the Lionheart to recapture the city in the Third Crusade, it remained under Saladin's control until the Mamluk conquest in 1260.

THE MAMLUKS AND OTTOMANS (1250–1917)

Somewhat of a peripheral city, Jerusalem fell into a period of decline and poverty. A respite from the dire situation was offered when the city was incorporated into the Ottoman Empire and Sultan Suleiman took the reins. Under his rule the great Old City walls were erected along with gates and an aqueduct. Following his death, however, things took a turn for the worse and the succeeding 300 years are seen a dark era in Jerusalem's history. Poverty, neglect and a static population riddled the once great city and it wasn't until exiled Jews fled to the land in the 15th and 16th centuries that things began to improve. By the 19th century, as the Ottoman Empire weakened, Jerusalem was taking on a more Europeanized outlook. Foreign consulates were established, trade links flourished, the population exploded and neighbourhoods burst out of the Old City walls. The population at the time was divided into four major communities; Jewish, Christian, Muslim, and Armenian (see pages 80, 71, 83 and 78), each living around the concentration of their respective religious shrines.

THE BRITISH MANDATE, THE ARAB–ISRAELI WAR AND A CITY DIVIDED (1917–1948)

Towards the end of World War I and the collapse of the Ottoman Empire, Jerusalem surrendered to British forces and on 11 December 1917 General Allenby marched through Jaffa Gate on foot as a sign of respect to the holy city. By this time the patchwork of cultures and religions dotted across the Old and New cities had expanded considerably, but was lacking any sort of planning. With the advent of the 1922 Mandate granted to the British by the League of Nations, they set about developing plans for its growth. The use of the white sandstone façades that are today one of the city's most endearing features was made law, while buildings such as the Hadassah Medical Centre, Hebrew University, King David Hotel and Jewish Agency headquarters owe their origins to this period. Yet as the city expanded, the separation between Jews and Palestinian Arabs once observed in the Old City again began to materialise. The struggle for religious and political control began to escalate and tensions heightened. Tensions culminated in the 1920s riots and the Arab Revolt of 1936–39. Following the departure of the British (and the dissolution of the Partition Plan), Israel declared independence on 14 May 1948. Less than 24 hours later, neighbouring Arab nations invaded the fledgling country and so ensued the 1948 Arab–Israeli War. The end of the war found the city divided: Jordan had control of East Jerusalem and the Old City, Israel of West Jerusalem. From this time until the Six Day War in 1967 fences and land mines separated the two halves of the city.

A UNITED CITY OF DIVIDED PEOPLE The 1967 Six Day War saw Israel capture the Jordanian-controlled half of Jerusalem and in 1980 the Knesset officially declaring the united city its capital, a declaration highly contested by the UN and international community to this day. The Moroccan area of the Old City was demolished, and in its place the Western Wall Plaza was built. The Waqf (the Supreme Muslim Religious Council) was granted administration of the Temple Mount and Jews forbidden (both by Israel and the Waqf) from praying there (see page 83). Over time clear divisions appeared between West and East Jerusalem, both culturally and economically. Money was poured into West Jerusalem and the Old City given a makeover, yet East Jerusalem, now populated by almost equal numbers of Jews and Arabs, was suffering. To this day the UN and much of the international community do not recognise the annexation of East Jerusalem (and the West Bank and Gaza Strip) and nearly all countries maintain embassies in Tel Aviv.

JERUSALEM TODAY Under Israeli control, members of most religions are granted access to their holy sites, the exceptions being those Palestinians living in the West Bank and Gaza Strip. Jews are also forbidden to pray or study inside the Temple Mount although entrance is permitted. Inside this fragile and highly sensitive city, where political and religious tensions sit upon a knife edge, conflicts do arise. Events such as the arson attack on the Al-Aqsa Mosque in 1969 by a Christian fundamentalist, rioting following the digging of an exit to the Western Wall tunnels in the Muslim Quarter, Jewish opposition to the Waqf's excavations inside the Temple Mount and the igniting of the Second Intifada by Ariel Sharon's visit to the Islamic holy site in 2000 being but some examples. Jerusalem has always been the stumbling block over which any form of peace negotiations break: Israel lays claim to the entire city; the Palestinians to at least the eastern half including the Old City. As the conflict continues with little sign of a solution on the horizon, it must be said that for travellers, the Old City at least displays a remarkable aura of calm. While this cannot be classified as unity, day-to-day tolerance of one another is a good enough step for now.

GETTING THERE

BUS AND SHARED TAXI (SHERUT) Jerusalem's new **central bus station** (*Jaffa St;* ⊕ *06.00–21.30 Sun–Thu, 06.15–15.45 Fri*) has buses running to all over the country.

TRAIN The new **Jerusalem Malha Train Station** (*Itzhak Modai;* ✆ *02 5774000; www.israrail.org.il*) is located in the southwest of the city near the Jerusalem Mall. Western Israel's train network is still in its fledgling stage and you, therefore, need to change once in Beit Shemesh before arriving in Tel Aviv's Arlosorov Train Station. Trains depart hourly (1hr 30mins/19.5NIS). There is also a station at the Biblical Zoo a few minutes from the main station. Bus 6 stops outside.

To	Frequency	Bus number	Duration	Price
Tel Aviv	10mins	480	1hr	23NIS
Haifa	30mins	947/940	2hrs	39NIS
Tiberias	hourly	961/962	3hrs	42NIS
Nazareth	16.00/18.00	955	2hrs 15mins	35NIS
Kiryat Shmona	06.30/10.30/ 13.30/23.30	963	4hrs	55NIS
Beer Sheva	30mins	446/470	1hr 45mins	39NIS
Ein Gedi (Dead Sea)	7 daily	486/421/487	1hr 20mins	32NIS
Ben Gurion Airport	30mins	947	40mins	20NIS
Eilat	07.00/10.00 14.00/17.00	444	5hrs	65NIS
Katzrin	08.45/17.15	966	4hrs	51NIS

AIR Jerusalem is one of the few capital cities in the world that hasn't got its own international airport. That said, Tel Aviv's Ben Gurion Airport (see page 35) is located in between the two cities and can be accessed easily from the capital (approximately 30mins by car or bus).

CAR RENTAL Most of the car-rental agencies can be found along King David Street and there are offices of most major national and international companies based at Ben Gurion Airport (see page 100). Parking in the city can be difficult and expensive and parking illegally will result in your car being towed away. Cars are not an ideal way to get around the city but by far the best option for exploring the country at large. You must be over 21 to rent a car anywhere in Israel.

Car rental companies

🚗 **AVIS** 22 King David St; ☏ 02 6249001/2; www.avis.com; ⏰ 08.00–18.00 Sun–Thu, 08.00–14.00 Fri

🚗 **Budget** King David Hotel, 23 King David St; ☏ 02 6248991; f 02 6259456; www.budget.co.il; ⏰ 08.00–18.00 Sun–Thu, 08.00–14.00 Fri

🚗 **Eldan** Eldan Hotel, 24 King David St; ☏ 02 6252151/2; e jer_hotel@eldan.com; www.eldan.co.il; ⏰ 08.00–18.00 Sun–Thu, 08.00–13.00 Fri

🚗 **Hertz** 18 King David St; ☏ 02 6231351; www.hertz.co.il; e hertzjerusalem@hertz.co.il; ⏰ 08.00–18.00 Sun–Thu, 08.00–14.00 Fri

🚗 **Sixt** 8 King David St; ☏ 02 6250833; www.sixt.com; ⏰ 08.00–18.00 Mon–Fri, 08.00–18.00 Sun

TAXIS Taxi fares are calculated by a meter which drivers are obliged by law to run. If they refuse, get out and look for another one as they will no doubt try to overcharge you.

Taxi companies

🚗 **Gilo** ☏ 02 6765888
🚗 **Israel** ☏ 02 6252333

🚗 **Mount of Olives** ☏ 02 6272711
🚗 **Ram Hakirya** ☏ 02 5388744

GETTING AROUND

BUS The Holy City has yet to see the influx of underground trains, trams or metros and buses connect Jerusalem's mountainous, higgledy-piggledy neighbourhoods quite efficiently. A one-way ticket to anywhere costs 5.50NIS or two rides (within 1hr) costs 6.30NIS. Useful bus routes are as follows:

#1 Runs from the central bus station along Sarei Yisrael, down Malchei Yisrael and past Mea Shearim before running clockwise around the walls of the Old City and returning to the central bus station.

#4 & #4a Runs from Malha along Yohanan Ben Zakai, Emek Refa'im in the German Colony and onto King David where it then proceeds to Keren Hayesod, King George V, Nathan Strauss, Yehezkel and then continues to French Hill. The 4a continues to Mt Scopus.

#6 Runs from French Hill, along Bar Lev Boulevard to the New Gate. From there it heads down Jaffa Street, along Herzl Boulevard, Shmuel Beyt and onto Herzog (for the Israel Museum). It terminates at Malha Train Station.

#18 Runs from the central bus station along Jaffa Street stopping at the New Gate of the Old City and then heading down the German Colony.

#19 Runs from Ein Kerem along Malcha, Harav Herzog and Gaza before heading along King George V, Yehekel, Hativat Har'el and onto Levi Eshkol (for Ammunition Hill). It terminates at Mt Scopus before turning back.

#20 Starts in Yemin Moshe and runs past Jaffa Gate, along Jaffa Street to the central bus station and then continues to Herzl Junction (for Yad Vashem and Mt Herzl).

#27 Runs between the central bus station and Ein Kerem.

SHERUTS *Sheruts* (see page 44) generally follow the lines of the major bus routes but can be hailed from anywhere along those routes. They cost marginally less than the buses and are a convenient option on Shabbat when the buses stop running. *Sheruts* to Tel Aviv, Haifa, Eilat and all the stops along the way leave from the central bus station.

TOURIST INFORMATION

TOURIST INFORMATION CENTRES

Christian Information Centre Jaffa Gate; ☎ 02 6272692; www.cicts.org; ◐ 08.30–13.00 Mon–Sat. Offers information on Christian sites in & around the Old City. Located opposite the Citadel.

Jaffa Gate Tourist Information Office Jaffa Gate; ☎ 02 6271422; f 02 6271362; www.tourism.gov.il; ◐ 08.00–17.00 Sun–Thu. Offers a wealth of information including free maps, hotel reservations & tour guide recommendations. You can also buy a **Holy Pass** (*adult/child 99/50NIS*), which is a cost-effective way of visiting many of the religious sites in the Old City as well as obtaining restaurant discounts.

Other tourist information There are some good web resources you can check out before setting off: the **Ministry of Tourism** (*www.tourism.gov.il*) and the **Municipality of Jerusalem** (*www.jerusalem.muni.il*), which also has a 24-hour hotline 106 (from land lines). The *Jerusalem Post* is an English-language newspaper that has lots of practical information and entertainment listings about Jerusalem and Tel Aviv for tourists and foreign residents. *Haaretz*, Israel's leading newspaper, is also printed in English daily. Another good publication to pick up is the *Tours and Sites* booklet produced by the Municipality of Jerusalem Tourism Department.

Local tour operators The sheer volume of things to see in Jerusalem and its wide-ranging history means that taking guided tours is a good way to get your orientation and learn that much more. Apart from those listed below, the Tourist Information Office (see page 33) can supply a list of licensed tour guides. The **Jerusalem Municipality** offers three-hour free themed tours on Saturdays starting from the main entrance to the Russian Compound (*32 Jaffa St; tours begin* *at 10.00*). Tours change on a weekly basis so for more information call 02 5314600 or visit *www.jerusalem.muni.il*. They also have a great website (*www.jerusalemp3.co.il*) that allows you to download guided tours and maps and upload them to your MP3. For national tour operators, see page 32.

AVIS (see *Getting around* above for contact details) Very good free audio driving tour & map provided with all car rentals.

Egged City Tour ✎ 050 8422473/ landline*2800; www.city-tour.co.il. Run by Egged Bus Company. Red, open-top double-deck buses do a circuit of Jerusalem's major sites (*2hrs; adult/child 65/56NIS*) or you can hop on & off. There are 4 buses daily (Sun–Thu) & tickets can be purchased on board. Buses stop at the Jaffa Gate at 09.45, 11.45, 14.15 & 16.30. Commentary in 8 languages via headphones.

Knesset Guided Tours (see page 92)

Mazada Tours Pearl Hotel, 15 Jaffa St; ✎ 02 6235777; e mazada@mazada.co.il;

www.mazada.co.il; ⊕ 09.00–17.00 Sun–Thu, 09.00–14.00 Fri. Arrange tours & transport to Jordan & Egypt. There are daily buses to Amman (300NIS) & Cairo (400NIS) & a range of tours around Israel. They can also book flights & hotels.

Zion Walking Tours Jaffa Gate; ✎ 02 6277588/6713543; e zionwt@dsites1.co.il; ⊕ 09.00–14.00 Sun–Fri. Zion are 30-year veterans of tours around the Old City. Don't let the dusty little shop put you off – these guys know their way around. 3hr tours cost 100NIS pp & leave at 09.00, 11.00 & 14.00 daily. They also offer tours to the Mount of Olives (09.00 Mon & Wed), Judean Desert (book in advance) & Western Wall Tunnels (14.00 Mon & Wed).

WHERE TO STAY

CITY CENTRE

🏠 **David Citadel Hotel** (384 rooms) 7 King David St; ✎ 02 6211003; e reservations@tdchotel.com; www.thedavidcitadel.com. One of Jerusalem's hotel greats it is second in line to the throne after the King David Hotel. It combines Old City views, traditional Jerusalem architecture, plush, modern facilities (including a swimming pool) & fresh, contemporary décor. **$$$$$**

🏠 **King Solomon Hotel** (148 rooms) 32 King David St; ✎ 02 5695555; e reservationjeru@ kingsolomon-hotel.com; www.kingsolomon-hotel.com. A Jerusalem hotel veteran. While the décor could do with modernising it does add a certain refined age to the place. Attractive features include a rooftop pool, views towards the Old City, a Glatt kosher dining room & Shabbat elevators. **$$$$**

🏠 **St Andrew's Scottish Guesthouse** (19 rooms) 1 David Remez St; ✎ 02 6732401; e info@ scotsguesthouse.com; www.scotsguesthouse.com. One of the few buildings constructed by the British during the Mandate period, St Andrew's Church stands on the Valley of Hinnom & is a beautiful, castle-like building offering refined elegance & a taste of classic Jerusalem. **$$$$**

🏠 **Agron Guesthouse (HI)** (55 rooms) 6 Gershron Agron St; ✎ 02 6217555; e agron@iyha.org.il; www.iyha.org.il. Located on the corner of Gershron Agron & Keren Hayesod sts this huge hostel offers

the high standard of quality demonstrated by all Hostelling International (HI) establishments. Large, comfortable beds & AC in all rooms & kosher breakfast included. Reception closed during Shabbat hours. *Single-sex dorms available (132NIS).* **$$$**

🏠 **Montefiore Hotel** (48 rooms) 7 Shatz St; ✎ 02 6221111; e info@montefiorehotel.com; www.montefiorehotel.com. While the rooms are perfectly pleasant (the beds are delightfully comfortable) it is the hotel's great central location that makes this a good choice. **$$$**

🏠 **Allenby B&B** (9 rooms) 2 Allenby Sq; ✎ 052 2578493/02 5344113; e nmr@netvision.net.il; www.bnb.co.il/allenby. Perfectly located near the central bus station & within easy walking distance of the Israel Museum & Mahne Yehuda Market, this traditional Jerusalem house offers a great little balcony & garden, kitchen, TV lounge, bicycle rental & tours. **$$**

🏠 **Mount of Olives Hotel** (61 rooms) 53 Mount of Olives Rd; ✎ 02 6284877; f 02 6264427; www.mtolives.com. Its proximity to the Christian sites on the Mount of Olives has made this simple but comfortable family-run hotel a favourite with small pilgrim groups. It offers great views over the Mount & Old City. **$$**

🏠 **The Jerusalem Hostel** (14 rooms) 44 Jaffa Rd, Zion Sq; ✎ 02 6236102; e reservation@ jerusalem-hostel.com; www.jerusalem-hostel.com.

What the rooms lack in character the hostel makes up for in cleanliness & great location. Well-equipped kitchen, roof terrace & internet access. *Dorms available (50NIS).* $

EAST JERUSALEM

🏠 **American Colony Hotel** (92 rooms) 23 Nablus Rd; ✆ 02 6279777; e reserve@amcol.co.il; www.americancolony.com. The breathtakingly beautiful building & grounds exemplify the elegant, classic charm that Jerusalem stands for. Its long history has seen it rise in the ranks of prestige from the home of a Turkish *pasha* to today acting as the temporary home of visiting diplomats, journalists & UN officers. It was from this building that the 'white flag' today housed in London's Imperial War Museum was flown, an act signifying Jerusalem's surrender in World War I. The epitome of elegance, service & top-of-the-range facilities. $$$$$

🏠 **Jerusalem Hotel** (14 rooms) Nablus Rd; ✆ 02 6283282; ✆ toll-free USA +1 800 657 9401; UK 0800 328 2393; e raed@jrshotel.com; www.jrshotel.com. Run by the same family since 1960 & rebuilt following its devastation in 1967, this traditional Arabic mansion hotel has retained its age-old Palestinian charm & character. Decorated with Islamic & Andalucian furniture & antiques throughout & boasts an indoor dining room & beautiful garden restaurant. Facilities include AC, balconies, TV, Wi-Fi, travel arrangements & classical Arabic music evenings. $$$$$

🏠 **Ambassador Hotel** (120 rooms) Nablus Rd; ✆ 02 5412222; e amb@netvision.net.il; www.jerusalemambassador.com. Bright, spacious rooms with AC, TV, minibar, hairdryer & telephone. The hotel is well located in the vibrant East Jerusalem neighbourhood 15mins' walk from the Old City. $$$$

🏠 **Faisal Hostel** (5 rooms) 4 Haniviim St; ✆ 02 6287502; e faisalsam@hotmail.com. Although a little rough around the edges, this is a great place to chill out with a *sheesha*, game of backgammon & black coffee. Located a few mins' walk from Damascus Gate. Staff can help arrange trips to sites around Israel & the Palestinian Territories. *Dorms (40NIS) & simple private rooms available.* $

OLD CITY

🏠 **Gloria Hotel** (100 rooms) 33 Latin Patriarchate St; ✆ 02 6282431/2; e gloriahl@netvision.net.il. Opened in 1957, it has retained all its Old-City charm combined with modern facilities. A rustic, stone-arched lounge & bar is an ideal place to rest after a day of sightseeing. Rooms have AC & TV. $$$

🏠 **Austrian Hospice** (34 rooms) 37 Via Dolorosa; ✆ 02 6265800; e office@austrianhospice.com; www.austrianhospice.com. Beautiful building in the beating heart of the Muslim Quarter. Impressive collection of modern & classical art plus high ceilings, a rich history & antique furniture. There is also a lovely café (see *Where to eat* below), garden

A ROYAL HOTEL

The King David (23 *King David St;* ✆ *02 6208888;* e *kingdavid@danhotels.com; www.danhotels.co.il;* $$$$$) stands as Israel's most prestigious and luxurious hotel, frequented by politicians and royalty from across the globe. With five restaurants, a fitness centre, swimming pool, tennis courts and flawless, elegant rooms it doesn't get much better than this. More than just a hotel however, the King David is a Jerusalem landmark, with a tumultuous and dramatic history. The hotel was founded in 1931 and afforded asylum to King Alfonso VIII of Spain, Emperor Haile Selassie of Ethiopia and King George II of Greece who were all exiled from their countries. The British Mandate period saw the King David act as the headquarters of British rule in Palestine until it was violently bombed by the Irgun Zionist group in July 1946. Throughout the 1948 Arab–Israeli War the hotel became a Jewish stronghold, only to find itself poignantly isolated between Israeli- and Jordanian-controlled lands. When Israel recaptured Jerusalem in 1967, the hotel was restored to its former grandeur and elegance and has since stood as the jewel in Jerusalem's royal crown.

& great view from the roof terrace. Rooms are simple but enormous & the breakfasts (included) are wonderful. *Dorm beds available (88NIS).* $$

 Citadel Youth Hostel (60 beds) 20 St Marks St; ☎ 02 6285253/6284494; e admin@citadelhostel.com; www.citadelhostel.com. Located in a 700-year-old building full of charm & originality. Free internet, movie nights, barbecue area & luggage storage. Roof terrace open for sleeping on. Bicycle & mobile-phone rental, kitchen & TV room. *Dorms available (50NIS).* $$

 Hashimi Hotel & Hostel (65 beds) 73 Souq Khan es Zeit St; ☎ 02 6284410; e hashimihotel@hotmail.com; www.hashimihotel.com. Nestled in the Muslim Quarter markets, it offers single-sex dorms with fans & private rooms with AC. There is a TV lounge, internet access, money-changing facilities & rooftop restaurant. The hotel abides by Islamic law where unmarried couples are not permitted to share rooms & no alcohol is permitted on the premises. *Single-sex dorms available (30NIS).* $$

 Petra Hostel (40 rooms) Omar Bin Khatab St; ☎ 02 6286618; e petrahtl@netvision.net.il. Bohemian backpacker hostel in the Christian Quarter market. Dorms are good value for money with small balconies overlooking the Old City although private rooms are a bit shabby. Located upstairs past a money-change kiosk as you enter the market street from Jaffa Gate. *Single-sex or mixed dorms available (45NIS).* $

✖ WHERE TO EAT

Israelis love to eat out and the country is awash with fabulous restaurants serving more cuisines than you'd find at a UN dinner party. Whilst Tel Aviv is accepted as Israel's culinary centre, Jerusalem does its best to keep up. In contrast to its secular neighbour, Jerusalem's restaurants are generally kosher and abide by Shabbat opening hours (see page 33), although it is possible to find plenty that are open during this time, notably in East Jerusalem and the Muslim Quarter of the Old City. Outside Shabbat, restaurants, cafés and fast-food joints stay open until the small hours and serve a myriad international styles. Restaurants tend to cluster in certain areas and neighbourhoods so the following have been divided into broad geographical zones. The nationally renowned *www.e-rest.co.il* website provides a comprehensive list of the country's dining options and is a good resource to check out.

CITY CENTRE

✖ **Jacksi** 1 Shlomizion Hamalka St; ☎ 02 6222527; ⏰ 12.00–01.00 daily. Trendy lounge-style restaurant with a fascinating selection of exuberant French dishes. $$$$$

✖ **Adom** 31 Yaffo St; ☎ 02 6246242; ⏰ 18.30–02.00 daily. Elegant yet unpretentious French-style bistro set in a beautiful stone building. The gourmet menu includes dishes such as lamb in red wine risotto, crab bisqué with scallops & entrecôte in mustard & cream sauce. $$$$

✖ **Foccacia Bar** 4 Rabbi Akiva St; ☎ 02 6256428; ⏰ 09.00–02.00 daily. Italian-influenced food & ambience. Housed in a stone cottage with a lovely garden, its *pièce de résistance* is its oven-baked pizzas & breads. Calamari, quails' eggs & goose breast have all made their way onto the menu alongside more traditional dishes. As the sun goes down this is a great place to chill out with a glass of wine & good music. $$$

✖ **Little Jerusalem Restaurant at Ticho House** Abraham Ticho St; ☎ 02 6244186; ⏰ 10.00–00.00 Sun–Thu, 10.00–14.00 Fri, end of Shabbat–23.45 Sat. Vegetarian café set inside the delightful Ticho House (see page 86). Sandwiches, baked potatoes, soups & a creative selection of salads make a great light lunch while pastas, mushroom strudel or grilled fish are more filling. They also have a wonderful breakfast menu. $$$

✖ **Osho** 3 Shlomizion Hamalka St; ☎ 02 6251666; ⏰ 19.00–late Sun–Fri, 12.30–late Sat. Trendy, modern fusion restaurant known for its quality meats, fresh fish & seafood. As the sun goes down it turns into a rather swanky wine bar. $$$

✖ **Village Green** 33 Yaffo St; ☎ 02 6251464; ⏰ 09.00–22.00 Sun–Thu, 11.30–15.00 Fri; kosher. Green is the magic word here with all food fresh, homemade & vegetarian. Menu includes quiches, soups, pies, lasagne, stuffed vegetables & salads & are extremely well priced. $$

✖ **Pinati** 13 King George St; ☎ 02 6254540; ⏰ 08.00–20.00 Sun–Thu, 08.00–15.00 Fri; kosher. Considered one of, if not the, best falafel joints in Jerusalem as attested to by the queues of salivating customers lining the street outside. $

GERMAN COLONY

✖ Masaryk 31 Emek Refaim St; ✆ 02 5636418; ⏰ 07.30–midnight Sun–Thu, 07.30–Shabbat Fri, end of Shabbat–02.00 Sat; kosher. Cosy, unpretentious restaurant specialising in Mediterranean-style fresh fish & pastas. The regulars come time & again for the huge breakfast menu (around 40NIS). $$$$

✖ Olive 36 Emek Refaim St; ✆ 02 5611102; ⏰ 12.00–midnight Sun–Thu, end of Shabbat–midnight Sat; kosher. Eclectic mix of meat dishes ranging from kebabs to chicken in pineapple to grilled lamb chops. Vegetable noodles are a good vegetarian option. $$$$

✖ Caffit 35 Emek Refaim St; ✆ 02 5635284; ⏰ 07.00–01.00 Sun–Thu, 07.00–14.00 Fri, end of Shabbat–01.00 Sat; kosher. Although it may appear under the title 'café' this is a great option for a relaxed meal (the breakfasts are particularly good).

The menu includes fresh sandwiches, pies, salads, grilled fish & gooey desserts & there is a breezy little terrace on which to enjoy them. $$$

✖ Joy 24 Emek Refaim St; ✆ 02 5630033; ⏰ 12.00–late Sun–Thu, 12.00–Shabbat Fri, end of Shabbat–late Sat; kosher. Housed in a typical 19th-century German-Colony stone building this is a delightful place to enjoy some prime, juicy meat with an oriental twist. Renowned for its steaks & beefburgers. $$$

Yo ja 25 Emek Refaim St; ✆ 02 5611344; ⏰ 12.00–23.00 Sun–Thu, 12.00–15.00 Fri, end of Shabbat–23.00 Sat; kosher. Noodles served with a variation of Asian sauces can be vegetarian or with chicken or beef. Chinese spicy Szechuan dishes are a big favourite & Peking duck can be ordered in advance. $$$

MAHANE YEHUDA MARKET

✖ Azura Inside the Iraqi Market section; ✆ 02 6235204; ⏰ 09.00–17.00 Sun–Thu; kosher. Situated in the delightful Iraqi area of the market, where old men while away the hours playing backgammon, this is a true local joint where you are unlikely to get a seat & even more unlikely to get one with your companions. Kube (see next entry), hummus, stuffed vegetables & lentil dishes are cheap & authentic. $$

✖ HaKubi'a 18 10 Beit Ya'akov St; ✆ 02 6235225; ⏰ 12.00–late Sun–Thu, 12.30–15.00 Fri; kosher.

Authentic Iraqi & Kurdiah dishes specialising in kube (semolina dumpling stuffed with meat & often served in soup). $$

✖ Ima 189 Agripas St; ✆ 02 6246860; ⏰ 11.00–23.00 Sun–Thu, 10.00–16.00 Fri; kosher. Ima translates as 'mother', & this is exactly the sort of hearty food Jewish mama's cook up for their off-spring; salads, soups, stuffed vegetables & a variety of meat dishes. Big portions of Israeli/Middle Eastern food at really decent prices. $$

YEMIN MOSHE

✖ El Marakesh 4 King David St; ✆ 02 6257577; ⏰ 13.00–16.00 & 18.00–midnight Sun–Thu, end of Shabbat–midnight Sat; kosher. Sizzling, aromatic Moroccan restaurant with vibrant, traditional décor straight out of Marrakesh's medina. $$$$

✖ Te'enim 12 Paul Emil Botta St; ✆ 02 5630048; ⏰ 09.00–23.00 Sun–Thu, 09.00–14.30 Fri; kosher.

Unique vegetarian restaurant with wonderful views of the Old City walls. The French owner/chef has created colourful dishes influenced by styles from across the globe. Cosy, unpretentious restaurant in an old 3-storey stone building behind the King David Hotel. $$$

EAST JERUSALEM

✖ Ambassador Hotel Restaurant 23 Nablus Rd; ✆ 02 5412213; ⏰ 11.00–23.00 daily (tent 20.00–23.30). Found in the charming Ambassador Hotel (see page 60), you can choose from European-style food in a sleek, indoor setting or an enchanting garden Bedouin tent complete with water pipes, thick red cushions & sizzling Middle Eastern dishes. Live music on Thu & Sat nights. $$$$$

✖ Blue Dolphin 7 Shimon HaTzadik St; ✆ 02 5322001; ⏰ 12.00–midnight daily. Lebanese-influenced Mediterranean restaurant renowned for its incredible fresh fish. Local catches such as St Peter's fish, sea bream, sea bass & mullet are particularly good. $$$$

About 20 minutes' drive from Jerusalem, located just off route 1, is the little town of Abu Ghosh, best known across Israel for its Middle Eastern restaurants. One of the best is **Lebanese Restaurant** (*88 HaShalom St; Abu Ghosh;* \ *02 5702397;* ⊕ *09.00–23.00 daily; $$*), the queues of people waiting for a seat in the enormous, rustic restaurant are testament to its incredible popularity. This most certainly isn't a quiet meal in the countryside, as children race about, the chatter reaches high decibels, running waiters fling piles of fresh hummus, pita, salads, grilled skewered meats and ice-cold lemonade onto tables, and pans clatter in the busy, open kitchen. Yet it is most certainly a wonderful expression of Israeli life, where Jewish families and local Arabs clamour for their succulent weekend meal amidst an atmosphere of relaxed, high-spirited entertainment.

OLD CITY The Old City specialises in traditional, home-cooked food that reflects the origins of those who make and serve it. Smells of warm, fresh hummus, falafel, *shwarma*, spices, nuts, aromatic coffee and sticky pastries waft down the narrow streets of the **Muslim Quarter souks**, while the Jewish Quarter sports the more sedate cafés and bakeries along the leafy **Tiferet Yisrael Boulevard**. There are also some cheap eateries around **Muristan Square** in the Christian Quarter.

✕ **Papa Andrea's** 64 Aftemeos St; \ 02 6284433; ⊕ 08.00–midnight daily. Open-air terrace on the 3rd floor (well signposted). While the service leaves a lot to be desired, the view across the rooftops of the Old City is spectacular. $$$

✕ **Viennese Café** Austrian Hospice, 37 Via Dolorosa; \ 02 6265800; ⊕ 07.00–22.00 daily. Take afternoon tea away from the hubbub of the Muslim Quarter in the tranquil gardens of the Austrian Hospice. Traditional, delicate Viennese cakes, teas, coffees & liquors are all home baked & superb. $$$

✕ **Armenian Tavern** 79 Armenian Orthodox Patriarchate St; \ 02 6273854; ⊕ 11.00–22.30 Tue–Sun. One of the most atmospheric places to enjoy a meal in the Old City. Housed inside a Crusader-era cellar with rustically elegant décor,

traditional Armenian dishes & comfortable ambience. $$

✕ **Quarter Café** 11 Tiferet Yisrael St; \ 02 6261336; ⊕ 09.00–19.00 Sun–Thu, 09.00–15.00 Fri; kosher. Wonderful view over the Western Wall & Dome of the Rock. $$

✕ **Abu Shukri** 63 Al Wad Rd; \ 02 6271538; ⊕ 08.30–16.30 daily. Located where the Via Dolorosa crosses Al Wad Rd this is one of, if not the, best, hummus joints in the city. It is easy to spot by the throngs of people queuing for their turn on the little plastic tables inside. Twinned with the magical ambience of the Old City this will be a plate of mashed chickpeas to remember. $

✕ **Bonkers Bagels** 2 Tiferet Yisrael St; \ 02 6272590; ⊕ 09.00–18.00 Sun–Thu, 09.00–Shabbat Fri; kosher. Wide range of fresh bagels & fillings. $

EIN KEREM
✕ **Pundak Ein Kerem** 13 Hamaayan St; \ 02 6431840; ⊕ 10.30–late Sun–Thu, 10.00–late Fri/Sat. Serves a mixture of French- and Italian-style hearty meals including pasta, entrecôte, grilled

fish & pizza. The delightful ambience of the old stone building and views over the quaint neighbourhood are the best reasons to go. $$$

ENTERTAINMENT AND NIGHTLIFE

BARS Jerusalem's bars are not quite on a par with its naughty neighbour Tel Aviv, but then again, they don't try to be. Watering holes tend to be more refined and less

3

rowdy, attracting those who want to enjoy some sociable drinks with friends in pleasant surroundings. There are, however, several places where you can let your hair down to live music, have one too many and enjoy a good dance.

♀ **Bolinat** 6 Dorot Rishonim St; ☎ 02 6249733; ⏰ 24hrs daily. Animated, energetic bar & restaurant that attracts the 20-something Jerusalemites. Music varies but you are unlikely to hear Abba here. Their rich, feel-good meals are another big draw.

♀ **Cellar Bar** 23 Nablus Rd; ☎ 02 6279777; ⏰ 19.00–midnight daily. Housed within the famous American Colony Hotel, this is a favourite watering hole of foreign journalists. The intimate, charming ambience is perfect for sipping a glass of smoky red wine & discussing the current situation in the Middle East.

♀ **Constantine** 3 Hahistadrut St; ☎ 02 6221155; ⏰ 21.00–late Sat–Tue & Thu. Opened in late 2007, this is the new 'in' place in Jerusalem's city centre. The enormous bar/club has been decked out in flashy modern décor & offers live performers, a huge drinks menu & a selection of bar food.

♀ **Egon** 9 Nahalat Shiva St; ☎ 02 6222458; ⏰ 24hrs daily. Relaxed, cosy Bohemian haunt where Indian prints hang from the walls & ceilings, a mish-mash of bottom-friendly seating is scattered across the floor & an open-air courtyard allows for dancing under the stars.

♀ **Grappa** 7 Ben Shetach St; ☎ 02 6235001; ⏰ 12.00–02.00 daily. Cosy, intimate bar & restaurant that has an extensive drinks menu & serves some authentic French-style dishes. The music gets going around midnight until which time the place is quiet & laidback. Unpretentiously classy.

♀ **Mona** 8 Shmuel HaNagid St; ☎ 02 624523; ⏰ 19.00–midnight Sat–Thu. Mona's is predominantly a restaurant specialising in fish & meat but its rustic charm & wide bar has seen it become popular as a comfortable place to enjoy a cool beer. Popular with journalists & Jerusalem personalities. Located inside the Jerusalem Artists' House.

♀ **Osho** (see *Where to eat* page 61)

Shanti 4 Nahlat Shiva St; ☎ 02 6243434; ⏰ 19.00–late daily. This chilled, Bohemian-feeling bistro bar prides itself on its relaxed, carefree atmosphere, atmospheric surroundings, funky live jazz music & varied menu.

♀ **Yehoshua** 3 Ben Sira St; ☎ 02 6246076; ⏰ 20.00–late Mon–Sat. A more refined watering hole, Yehoshua's elegant interior & modern décor tends to attract a slightly older crowd of Jerusalemites in their 20s & 30s.

LIVE MUSIC

Dublin 4 Shamai St; ☎ 02 6223612; ⏰ 17.00–03.00 Sat–Thu, 17.00–05.00 Fri. Friendly, relaxed Irish-style pub. Modern Hebrew & Irish music, rock performances & DJ nights every night of the week.

Mike's Place 37 Jaffa St; ☎ 054 9292551; www.mikesplacebars.com; ⏰ 16.00–late daily. This quintessential British pub has branches in Jerusalem & Tel Aviv & has managed to remain firmly popular over its years of existence. Live rock, jazz,

blues & acoustic performances & open mic nights on every night of the week.

Yellow Submarine 13 HaRechivim Rd, Talpiot; ☎ 02 6794040; www.yellowsubmarine.org.il; shows get going late (after 22.00) & finish early; admission 30–90NIS. Known across the country for its live rock, punk, jazz & acoustic performances, this is Jerusalem's hottest spot to catch up-and-coming artists (despite its rather inconvenient location in the Talpiot Industrial District).

FESTIVALS

Israel Festival (May–June) Theatre, dance and classical music performances in theatres and concert halls around Jerusalem.

Jerusalem Film Festival (July) International, avant-garde, Israeli directed and modern films and documentaries shown in theatres and cinemas around the city.

Taste Festival (Te'ami) (During Sukkot; Old Train Station, German Colony) The city's best restaurants lay out their finest meals for 20NIS per dish. It is a great way to taste the best of the city's cuisine.

Gay Pride (June) In total contrast to the event in Tel Aviv, Jerusalem's gay pride parade is fraught with controversy and animosity, and following the stabbing of two participants by Haredi Orthodox members in 2005 was moved into the confines of the football stadium.

International Puppet Festival (August; Train Theatre) Jerusalem has become the international centre for puppetry and this week-long festival is the culmination of the most colourful performances of this rare art form.

PERFORMING ARTS Israel has long been high in the world rankings of classical music, churning out a continuous stream of top-class musicians and orchestras. The arts remain incredibly popular and getting tickets to many of the concerts and theatre performances can be difficult (see page 112 for box offices).

Jerusalem Performing Arts Centre (*20 David Marcus St, German Colony;* ✆ *02 5605755; www.jerusalem-theatre.co.il*) houses the Jerusalem Theatre, Henry Crown Auditorium and Rebecca Crown Hall that show a collection of Israeli plays, Hebrew translations of classic plays and concerts by the **Jerusalem Symphony Orchestra**, the **Israel Chamber Ensemble**, and occasionally the world-renowned **Israel Philharmonic Orchestra** whose permanent home is in Tel Aviv.

Khan Theatre (*2 David Remez Sq;* ✆ *02 6718281; www.khan.co.il*) is one of the most popular venues for new Hebrew theatre performances ranging from Israeli pieces to translations of international classics. There are also regular chamber and jazz concerts, Israeli folklore nights and occasional English performances.

Habima Theatre (*Floor 4, 4 Yad Harozim St;* ✆ *02 6254463; www.habima.org.il*) shows avant-garde and experimental pieces in the small studio. Performances are in Hebrew only.

Jerusalem Cinematheque (*11 Hebron Rd;* ✆ *02 6724131; www.jer.cine.org.il*) shows a mixture of classical, avant-garde, Hollywood and experimental films. For more mainstream films your best bets are the grandiose cinema complexes of **Rav Chen** (*19 Ha'uman St;* ✆ *02 6792799*) and **Gil** (*Jerusalem Mall, Malha St;* ✆ *02 6788448*).

Ticho House (see page 86) has regular music performances, art exhibitions and poetry readings. There is a jazz, wine and cheese night every Wednesday at 20.00.

YMCA (*26 King David St;* ✆ *02 5692692*) has a regular stream of Israeli music concerts and folk dancing performances. Seats cannot be reserved in advance so get there early.

Train Theater (*Liberty Bell Park;* ✆ *02 5618514; www.traintheater.co.il*) is the home of the world puppetry centre and has regular performances (see *Festivals* above).

Sultan's Pool (*between Jaffa Gate & Mt Zion*) often acts as the beautiful and dramatic setting for modern rock, classical, jazz and theatre performances in the summer months.

SHOPPING

West Jerusalem's modern shops and malls are comparable to those found in western Europe, with their marble-floored glitzy walkways, fashionable clothes shops and plethora of eateries. **Malha Mall**, also referred to as 'the Kanyon', is located in Jerusalem's southern Malha neighbourhood and stands as one of the country's biggest and finest shopping bonanzas. If time is of the essence then you're best advised to give this a miss for there is little to distinguish it from any other mall. **Ben Yehuda Street** in the city centre is a pedestrianised hub of fun, albeit with mainstream commercial activities: bustling cafés; ice-cream parlours; fast-food kiosks; overpriced souvenir and Judaica shops; high street-type chain stores and, come summer evenings, a carnival of festivals and street entertaiment (particularly in Zion Square). The **Ahava Centre** (*5 Ben Yehuda St;* ✆ *02 6252592;* ⊕ *09.00–21.30 Sun–Thu, 09.00–15.00 Fri, end of Shabbat–23.00 Sat*) sells a wide range of often discounted Dead Sea skincare products.

For more cultural shopping experiences you can't beat the colourful **Old City souks** (see pages 78 and 84) and **Mahane Yehuda Market** (see page 80). Despite their obvious tourist appeal they are undoubtedly among the main attractions of the Old City, each quarter selling wares that reflect the ethnic origins of the vendors. The **Cardo** in the Jewish Quarter is one of the best places to buy quality Judaica, jewellery and Israeli art although it is important to note that most Judaica stores do not give refunds so make sure you compare prices first. Bargaining is not the done thing here but you can politely ask for a 'discount'. Other good areas for buying Judaica include **Yochanan Migush Halav Street**, the **Mea Shearim neighbourhood** and for more modern styles, the **German Colony**. The Muslim Quarter souks are known for their vibrant, bustling atmosphere and are certainly more 'alive' than their Christian Quarter counterparts, which cater wholly to tourists. At the bottom of Armenian Patriarchate Road in the Armenian Quarter are some good, little-known-about **craft and pottery stalls** that sell handmade products for a fraction of the price of the Muslim Quarter. To buy the unique turquoise and blue-patterned tiles and ceramics like those adorning the Dome of the Rock look no further than **Armenian Ceramics-Balian** (*14 Nablus Rd;* ✆ *02 6282826; www.armenianceramics.com*) or **Jerusalem Pottery** (*15 Via Dolorosa, Old City;* ✆ *02 6261587; www.jerusalempottery.biz;* ⊕ *09.30–17.00 Mon–Sat*) that specialise in authentic, hand-painted wares in a range of geometric patterns, floral motifs and animals and bird designs. Outside **Damascus Gate** is East Jerusalem's busiest shopping area, where local residents come to buy and sell a wide range of products, from food to home wares to Arabic-style embroidered clothes.

As with the rest of the country, **shopping hours** in West Jerusalem are 08.30–13.00 and 16.00–19.00 Monday to Thursday and 08.30–14.00 Friday. Stores tend to reopen on Saturday evenings after Shabbat. In Muslim areas such as East Jerusalem and the Muslim Quarter of the Old City many shops will be open during Shabbat but will often close or have shorter working hours on Fridays, the Muslim holy day. Likewise shops in the Christian or Armenian quarters will likely close on Sundays. When you are making purchases bear in mind that it may be possible to get a tax refund on items over US$50 so be sure to ask the vendor for a special receipt or voucher that can be submitted upon departure from Israel at Ben Gurion Airport.

BOOKSHOPS

Steimatsky 39 Jaffa St; ✆ 02 6253654; ⊕ 08.30–17.00 Sun–Thu, 08.30–14.00 Fri. This was the original shop in this now incredibly popular nationwide chain & has been open since 1925. Big selection of English novels, non-fiction, maps & travel guides.

Munther's Book Shop Nablus Rd; ✆ 02 6279777; ⊕ 09.00–21.00 daily. Friendly, fascinating little bookshop opposite the American Colony Hotel. Stocks many English books including maps, bestsellers, history & politics.

CAMPING AND OUTDOOR EQUIPMENT

La'metayel 5 Yoel Salomon St; ✆ 02 6233338; ⊕ 10.00–20.00 Sun–Thu, 10.00–14.00 Fri. Big branch of nationwide chain of camping & travel

shops. Good range of outdoor equipment, travel books, road & hiking maps & travel information.

EMERGENCIES

Fire ✆ 102
Ambulance ✆ 101

Police Russian Compound I Cheshin St; ✆ 100 or 02 5391256
Tourist Police Jaffa Gate ✆ 100 or 02 6226222

MONEY Branches of major banks can be found all over the city but should not be your first choice for changing money. Change bureaux – kiosks denoted by the word 'Change' above them – may look shifty but are reputable and offer commission-free currency exchange at pretty much the same rate to each other but at better rates than the banks, have shorter queues than the banks and the post office and are open longer hours. Zion Square, Ben Yehuda St shopping centre and in the Old City (particularly around Jaffa Gate) have concentrations. Travellers' cheques can be changed at most banks and at the post office for no commission.

$ **Bank Hapoalim** 236 Jaffa St; ✆ 03 6532407/ landline*2407; ⏰ 08.30–13.15 Sun, Tue, Wed, 08.30–13.00 & 16.00–18.30 Mon & Thu. There are other useful branches at I Zion Sq, 16 King George St (also ⏰ 08.15–12.30 Fri) & I Malchei Yisrael St.

$ **Bank Leumi** 21 Jaffa St; ✆ 03 9544555/ landline*5522; ⏰ 08.30–14.45 Sun–Thu, 08.30–12.00 Fri. This is the main branch (located next to the Central Post Office) but other convenient branches can be found at 19 King David St, 22 King George St, 4 Hananya St & Nablus Gate, Saladin St.

POST Most major post offices are open 08.30–18.00 Sun–Thu, 08.00–12.00 Fri. The postal authority's website can provide a list of all branches in the city (✆ 03 5385909; www.postil.com). Postal services such as FEDEX (✆ 02 6512693; www.fedex.com), DHL (✆ 03 5573557; www.dhl.com) and UPS (✆ 02 6541880; www.ups.com) are commonplace in Israel and Jerusalem.

✉ **Central post office** 23 Jaffa St; ✆ 02 6290676; ⏰ 08.00–18.00 Sun–Thu, 08.00–12.00 Fri. There are other useful branches at 6 King George St, Jaffa Gate & Klal Bldg, 42 Agrippas St.

MEDICAL

✚ **Hadassah Hospital** Ein Kerem; ✆ 02 6777111
✚ **Shaare Zedek Medical Centre** 12 Beit Shmuel St; ✆ 02 6666666
✚ **Newpharm pharmacy** 27 King George St; ✆ 02 6259999; ⏰ 08.30–19.30 Sun–Thu, 08.30–14.00 Fri
✚ **Superpharm pharmacy** 3 Hahistadrut St; ✆ 02 6246244; ⏰ 08.00–midnight Sun–Thu, 08.00–15.00 Fri

INTERNET Internet cafés are commonplace around Jerusalem and most offer a fast internet service, new computers and refreshments. Prices vary between 10NIS and 25NIS per hour.

🖳 **Café Net** 3rd Floor, new central bus station, 232 Jaffa St; ✆ 02 5379192; www.cafenet.co.il; ⏰ 05.30–midnight daily. 15NIS/hr. Fast internet and an extremely cheap selection of hot and cold drinks and snacks.

🖳 **Jerusalem Internet Café** 31 Jaffa St; ✆ 02 6223377 & I Heleni Hamalka St; ✆ 02 6223375; www.triptouch.co.il; ⏰ 24hrs Sun–Fri; 15NIS/hr.
🖳 **Ali Baba Internet** Via Dolorosa, Old City; ✆ 02 5271959; ⏰ 09.00–23.00 daily; 10NIS/hr.

LAUNDRY

Superclean 16 Hapalmach Rd; ✆ 02 5660367; ⏰ 07.00–19.00 Mon–Thu, 07.00–17.00 Fri, 07.00–14.00 Sat

Jerusalem OTHER PRACTICALITIES

3

TRAVEL AGENCIES

ISSTA 31 Hanevi'im St; ↘ 02 6213600; www.issta.co.il; ⊕ 09.00–18.00 Sun–Thu, 08.30–13.00 Fri. Israel's biggest agency. Specialises in budget travel.

Ophir Tours 42 Agrippas St; ↘ 02 5398666; e henriette_h@ophirtours.co.il; www.ophirtours.co.il; ⊕ 08.30–18.00 Sun–Thu, 09.00–12.30 Fri

BOX OFFICES

Bimot 8 Shamai St; ↘ 02 6237000; www.bimot.co.il
Ben Na'im 38 Jaffa St; ↘ 02 6231273

Klaim 12 Shamai St; ↘ 02 6222333

WHAT TO SEE

OLD CITY In a city of such religious and historic poignancy, Jerusalem's Old City sits like the jewel in the crown. Within the grand city walls, a living, breathing museum of sacred buildings, fervent worshippers, ancient architecture and centuries-old traditions abound. The Old City is but 1km² in size, yet its reach extends across the world, Jews, Christians and Muslims worshipping it with passion and zeal. The Western Wall, Church of the Holy Sepulchre and Temple Mount may stand as the three most ideologically and conceptually opposing religious sites yet are by no means the extent. A jumble of buildings fall into four rough quarters: Christian, Armenian, Jewish and Muslim, forming a decoupage of ornate architectural styles from every corner of the globe, and every century in its long life. Holy men, pilgrims, tourists and street vendors together wander the cobbled alleyways, bazaars and souks, their customs and dress adding yet more colour to this eclectic mini city.

Christian Quarter Located in the northwest quadrant of the Old City, the Christian Quarter is characterised by its ancient churches, bustling bazaars and representation of most Christian denominations. Its centrepiece, the **Church of the Holy Sepulchre**, is the holiest place in Christianity and marks the final stop on the Via Dolorosa pilgrimage walk, an approximation of the footsteps of Jesus on his path to Golgotha. The quarter is accessed by the New and Jaffa gates, the latter being the Old City's busiest visitors' entrance. Of the 4,200 people who reside within the Christian Quarter, the vast majority belong to the Greek Orthodox Church, its architectural and cultural influence clearly visible, while Arabic remains the predominant language.

Jaffa Gate The best-known and busiest of the seven gates that surround the Old City, the Jaffa Gate is located on the border between the Armenian and Christian quarters to the left of the Citadel of David. At the time of its construction it marked the beginning (or end) of the highway leading to the thriving port city of Jaffa. The gate has gone by a plethora of names over the years, notably the Arabic Bab al-Halil (Hebron Gate), named for the road leading from the gate to the city of Hebron. A closer inspection reveals two entrances: the arched L-shaped one and next to it a wider one created in 1898 to allow Kaiser Wilhelm II to enter the city without dismounting his carriage. Today the gate is accessed from the main Jaffa Road, and steps on the left lead up to the beginning of the Ramparts Walk.

Church of the Holy Sepulchre (⊕ *04.30–19.00 daily; see map, page 74*) This awe-inspiring church is the traditional site of Jesus's Crucifixion, burial and Resurrection and is the single most important shrine in Christendom. From the exterior, the church looks rather shabby, its scaffolding a long-lasting remnant of the conflict of ownership between the countless religious sects that have put claim to it. Today, the church is divided amongst the Greek Orthodox, Armenian Orthodox and Roman Catholic denominations, their different ecclesiastical styles and ornate methods of worship forming a fascinatingly beautiful blend within the ancient church.

History Following Constantine the Great's adoption of Christianity, his mother Queen Helena arrived in the Holy Land in search of Jesus's site of Crucifixion and burial. She is attributed with having discovered what is believed to be the rock of Golgotha and nearby tomb, known as Anastasis (Greek for resurrection). Constantine commissioned a shrine above the site in CE330 but none of this early church remains, having been destroyed by the Persians in 614. Most of the building we see today dates to the 12th-century Crusader period as well as later renovations following a series of earthquakes and fires.

The Unction Stone is located immediately inside the entrance and commemorates the preparation of Jesus's body for burial. The ornate lamps that hang over the stone belong to each of the different denominations that are represented within the church.

Calvary (Golgotha) is the traditional site of Jesus's Crucifixion and is accessed by narrow steps to the right of the entrance. It is the most extravagantly decorated part

SHABBAT AND RELIGIOUS HOLIDAYS

Unlike Israel's second city Tel Aviv, Jerusalem strictly abides by Shabbat rules and come Friday afternoon most places in the city shut down. Public institutions, shops, offices and public transportation do not operate during Shabbat hours (Friday sundown to Saturday sundown) and there is a palpable feel of calm during these times. Inside the Old City and more religious neighbourhoods there is a mad dash to get home and settled before the sun goes down, a fascinating experience to witness. Some restaurants, cafés and bars, however, are open during Shabbat particularly in the downtown area, around the Russian Compound and in Ein Kerem (with the exception of Yom Kippur – see page 22). Inside the Old City, different institutions are open depending on their religious connotation. The Muslim holy day is Friday and therefore Saturdays see cafés, religious sites, restaurants and markets open as usual (Friday has more limited opening hours). While Christianity's day of rest is on Sundays, most sites within the Old City are open for prayer services.

THE CHURCH OF THE HOLY SEPULCHRE

(SKETCH MAP)
Scale & layout approximate

N

Bradt

St Helena's Church

Edicule
(Tomb of Christ)
Rock of Calvary
Statue of Mary

Holy
Prison

Rock of
Golgotha

Chapel of the
Nailing to the Cross

Calvary

Entrance Court

Catholicon
(Greek Cathedral)

Chapel of Adam

Unction
Stone

Rotunda

Edicule
(Tomb of Christ)

Tomb of Joseph
of Arimathea

In Memoriam: Frances Goddard

of the church and comprises three parts: the **Chapel of the Nailing of the Cross** (station 11 along the Via Dolorosa) to the left of the altar, the **Statue of Mary** (station 13) marking the spot where Jesus's body was removed from the cross and given to his mother and, next to this, the **Rock of Calvary** (station 12). It was around this rock that the church was built and is today encased in glass, a small hole allowing visitors to touch it.

The Rotunda (**Anastasis**) is the church's *pièce de résistance*, located to the west of the entrance beneath the vast dome. In the centre sits the **edicule**, revered as the tomb of Christ. It is housed within a rather unsightly wooden structure, supported by scaffolding against earthquakes. Inside, the **Chapel of the Holy Sepulchre** (station 14) contains the tomb of Jesus, marked by a marble slab.

Other notable sights within the church include the **Chapel of Adam**, which houses the cracked rock said to have been caused by the earthquake that occurred at the moment of the Crucifixion; the **Holy Prison** where tradition has it Jesus was kept before the Crucifixion; and **St Helena's Church**, a vast underground complex containing the **Chapel of the Finding of the Cross**. Also of note is the small **tomb of Joseph of Arimathea**, whose discovery proved this area was once used as a burial site and, according to Christian tradition, that it was the site of Jesus's death, burial and Crucifixion (although the Garden Tomb is another, later contender – see page 93).

Church of St John the Baptist (*Muristan Sq*) The silver-domed Church of St John the Baptist stands as the oldest in Jerusalem, and is the original 'Hospital of St John' for which the Knights Hospitaller were named. The present church was built on the site of a 5th-century chapel, possibly because of the presence of the relics of St John the Baptist, and belonged to a pilgrim hospice which was founded before the First Crusade. In 1099, Christian knights wounded in the battle for Jerusalem were cared for in the church, many of whom, upon their recovery and subsequent defeat of the Crusaders, dedicated themselves to caring for the sick and protecting pilgrims of the Holy Land. They called themselves the Knights Hospitaller, and so the order was formed. They later developed into the military order that played a crucial role in the defence of the country. The church can be seen from the fountain in the middle of **Muristan Square**, an Arabic word meaning 'hospital'. With the exception of the simple façade and its two bell towers, the church remains as it has for 1,000 years, still managing to hold its own against its glamorous ecclesiastical neighbours (notably the green and gold iconastasis) and is an integral part of Jerusalem's Christian history. The entrance is located along Christian Quarter Street in Muristan Square. It is signposted in Greek only but a small blue painting of St John indicates you are in the right place. The church doesn't keep regular opening hours but you can ask the Greek Orthodox priest who resides in the adjacent monastery to open it for you.

Lutheran Church of the Redeemer (*Muristan Sq;* ✆ *02 627611;* ⊕ *09.00–13.00 & 13.30–15.00 daily; guided tours are available for 10NIS*) The current Protestant church was consecrated by Kaiser Wilhelm II on 31 October 1898, built upon land granted to the German emperor by the Ottomans as a symbol of alliance. It has formed the seat of the Lutheran sect in Jerusalem ever since. While the history of the site is undoubtedly significant, the view from the top of the bell tower (3NIS) is most certainly its most charming feature. Climb the narrow, circular stone steps past the vast bell to the top of the tower for a 360° panoramic view over the Old City. While rather demanding, those who undertake the hike

3

The Via Dolorosa (Way of Sorrow or Suffering) is one of Christianity's most celebrated devotional routes and follows what tradition states was Jesus's path from his condemnation to his Crucifixion in Golgotha. Today the route begins near the Lion's Gate in the Muslim Quarter and ends in the Church of the Holy Sepulchre in the Christian Quarter. Every Friday at 15.00 Christian pilgrims, led by Italian Franciscans, walk the course, which is marked by 14 Stations of the Cross (nine located along the route and four within the Church of the Holy Sepulchre). Stations III, IV, V, VI and VII are open only on Friday afternoons. During Holy Week, thousands of pilgrims join the procession that winds down the narrow alleys of the Old City, a moving and impressive sight to behold.

HISTORY Pilgrims began to trace the route taken by Jesus when open Christian worship became permitted during the Byzantine period. Over the years the route has changed along with the Old City's jumbled façade, and would have looked very different during Jesus's time. From the 14th to 16th centuries, pilgrims followed what was known as the Franciscan route, which began in the Church of the Holy Sepulchre and included eight stations. At the same time, the tradition of 14 stations was emerging in Europe, so as not to disappoint European pilgrims, six more were included. Although members of different denominations follow their own routes, the most widely accepted is that of the early Byzantine Christians. Eight of the 14 stations along the Via Dolorosa are described in scriptures, while the other six are traditional. It is important to note that the stations are not historical sites but commemorate religious events.

STATION I – JESUS IS CONDEMNED TO DEATH

Located on the left, 300m from Lion's Gate is the large courtyard of the **Omariye College** (🕓 14.30–18.00 Mon–Thu & Sat, 14.30–16.00 Fri) that marks the beginning of the Via Dolorosa. The minaret that stands in the distance is traditionally named the 'Antonia Tower' after historian Josephus's description of the ancient Roman fortress where Jesus was condemned to death by Pontius Pilate. The college is still used as a school and can be visited at limited times.

STATION II – JESUS TAKES UP THE CROSS

Across the street in a large courtyard are the **Sanctuaries of the Flagellation and Condemnation** (🕓 08.00–11.45 & 14.00–18.00 daily) where, according to tradition, Roman soldiers flogged Jesus and placed a crown of thorns on his head. A few metres further along is the **Sisters of Zion Convent** where steps lead down to what has long been claimed to be the **Lithostratos (Pavement of Justice)** (🕓 08.30–17.00 daily), the section of paving stones where Pilate condemned Jesus (it has since been dated to the 2nd century CE). A little further on, and spanning the route, is the **Ecce Homo Arch** named for Pilate's words 'Here is the man!' upon Jesus being presented to the crowd. The arch is a traditional symbol, having also been built in the 2nd century CE.

STATION III – JESUS FALLS UNDER THE CROSS FOR THE FIRST TIME

This traditional station is marked by a small 19th-century **chapel** that was funded by Catholic soldiers of the Free Polish Army during World War I. Walk to the corner of

El-Wad Road and turn left. The chapel is immediately on the left with a relief of Jesus falling above the door.

STATION IV – JESUS MEETS HIS MOTHER
The station is marked by a small Armenian Chapel located a few metres along from Station III. Blue iron doors, above which is a bas-relief of the Virgin Mary comforting Jesus, mark the entrance.

STATION V – SIMON OF CYRENE IS FORCED TO CARRY THE CROSS
The event, where Simon of Cyrene (a north African pilgrim) was compelled by Roman soldiers to help Jesus carry the cross, is mentioned in three of the Gospels. The station is marked by a **Franciscan oratory** and is located on the corner of El Wad Road and the Via Dolorosa.

STATION VI – VERONICA WIPES THE SWEAT FROM JESUS'S FACE
The chapel of the **Convent of the Little Sisters of Jesus** is 100m further along. The chapel is the traditional house of Veronica from where she emerged to wipe the sweat from Jesus's face.

STATION VII – JESUS FALLS FOR THE SECOND TIME
This station traditionally marks the place where Jesus passed beneath the Gate of Judgement on his way to Golgotha. Today a large Roman column housed within a **Franciscan chapel** commemorates the event. Walk to the crossroads at the end of the Via Dolorosa. The chapel is located on the northwest corner where Souk Khan es Zeit Street and El Khanqa Street meet.

STATION VIII – JESUS CONSOLES THE WOMEN OF JERUSALEM
A stone embedded on the outer wall of the **Greek Monastery of St Haralambos** commemorates the point where Jesus met the daughters of Jerusalem, who wept over his fate. According to Luke's Gospel he replied: 'Do not weep for me; weep for yourselves and for your children.' In Jesus's time this would have been an open field between the city wall and Golgotha. The monastery is located 30m up El Khanqa Street on the opposite side to Station VII.

STATION IX – JESUS FALLS FOR THE THIRD TIME
Walk back to Souk Khan es Zeit Street and turn right. After 50m a stairway on the right leads to a **Coptic church** within which is a Roman column painted with a Latin cross. This marks the traditional spot where Jesus fell for the third time. A doorway to the left of Station IX leads onto the roof of the Chapel of St Helena, where an Ethiopian church is located.

STATIONS X–IV
The final four stations are located within the Church of the Holy Sepulchre. From the Ethiopian chapel walk down the stairs which will bring you out in the courtyard of the Church of the Holy Sepulchre (see page 71).

will reap the rewards of Jerusalem's best viewpoint. The bell rings daily at 12.00 so visitors (in the interest of preserving their eardrums) cannot ascend between 11.45 and 12:20.

Bazaars *(generally ⊕ 09.00–19.00 Mon–Sat with limited opening on Sun)* In contrast to the Muslim Quarter souks that remain an active part of local daily life, those in the Christian Quarter cater only for the throngs of visitors who pour in through Jaffa Gate. Packed into the narrow, cobbled alleys stores sell an interesting mix of religious items, the vendors happy to promote rosary beads alongside *yarmulkes* with a few novelty T-shirts thrown in for good measure. Handicrafts, jewellery, pottery, Arabic-style home decorations and spice stalls compete for space amidst the crowds that weave through the alleyways and yet somehow, despite its obvious tourist appeal, the souk is a fascinating and lively place to explore. Prices are predictably overinflated so if you wish to buy authentic handicrafts, the Armenian workshops along **En Nebi Dawoud** near the Zion Gate are a better bet. Alternatively, bargain hard! Stores are generally open 09.00–19.00 Monday–Saturday with limited opening on Fridays.

From Jaffa Gate walk straight ahead and enter **David Street**, the busiest Christian Quarter souk. At the end, three streets lead off to the left: **Souk el Lahannin**, **Souk el Attarin** and **Souk el Khawadjat**.

New Gate New Gate was not one of Suleiman's original seven gates (hence the name) but was built in 1887 by Sultan Abdul Hamid to link the houses in the northwest with the Old City. The adjacent Tancred's Tower, named after the Latin Kingdom ruler who is believed to have commissioned it, is built from stones originally prepared for Herod's palace. During the Crusader period, the stones were removed and used to build the tower. The tower is known in Arabic as Qasr Jalud (Goliath's Castle) after a legend that it was near here that David killed Goliath.

Armenian Quarter The Armenian Quarter is the smallest area of the Old City and is today home to some 2,200 residents. The area centres on the ornate Armenian Cathedral and has its own schools, seminary, library and residential areas, all occupying what was once the site of Herod's great palace. The Armenians have formed part of the city's demographic make-up since the 1st century when the Roman emperor Titus brought Armenian traders, artisans and soldiers to the Holy Land. They were the first to adopt Christianity in the 4th century and within 100 years, following an influx of pilgrims, had erected over 70 monasteries in Jerusalem. The Armenians are an ancient people whose history dates back over 4,000 years, their rich cultural value and dramatic history often being overlooked in favour of their more vocal Old City neighbours. As an exiled people who have suffered great persecution and a devastating genocide over the years, the small community in Jerusalem has a strong sense of cultural identity and independence, and has largely managed to avoid the battles and wars that have ravaged the rest of the Old City.

Citadel and Tower of David Museum
History The Tower of David Museum occupies the imposing citadel that forms one of the Old City's most recognisable landmarks. Throughout Jerusalem's tumultuous past, the citadel stood as the main line of defence to the north and west, being reinforced and rebuilt by each generation of invaders. The area was hugely fortified by the Hasmonean kings and, in 24BCE, refortified by King Herod.

Throughout the ages the citadel was used as a garrison for Roman soldiers and, with the adoption of Christianity, a quasi-monastery. It once again resumed its military role throughout the Muslim conquest and Crusader rule, during which time its large moat was constructed. It also became the seat of the Crusader king of Jerusalem. The fortress in its present form dates from the Mamluk period, and later underwent changes during the Ottoman period when a large mosque was built, its towering minaret later dubbed the 'Tower of David' by 19th-century European travellers (which has caused considerable confusion over the years). When the British army entered the city in December 1917, it was on the platform outside the citadel that General Allenby addressed the people of Jerusalem, declaring freedom of worship.

The museum (✆ 02 6265310; *www.towerofdavid.org.il;* ⊕ *10.00–16.00 daily; admission adult/child 30/15NIS*) Today the citadel is home to the Tower of David Museum, one of the city's top attractions and a valuable tool in piecing together Jerusalem's past. Displays are spread throughout the network of guard rooms and cover the 5,000 action-filled years of Jerusalem's history. Exhibits present the city's chronological story through the aid of models, visual aids and multi-media displays. The walls and ramparts of the citadel provide for some fantastic views of both the Old City and modern city.

Tours Every evening (except Fridays) the citadel hosts the **Son et Lumiére** show, a light display depicting the city's history. Free **guided tours** in English leave the main entrance at 11.00 Sunday to Thursday. A multiple-entry ticket is available (*adult/child 80/50NIS*).

St James Cathedral (⊕ *08.00–17.00 daily*) Amidst such an abundance of ecclesiastical buildings within the Old City, St James Cathedral is often sadly overlooked. Tradition has it the cathedral was named after both Jesus's brother and James the Apostle, both of whom are said to be buried within. Jesus's brother is believed to be buried within the central nave, while St James the Apostle rests under the exquisitely decorated shrine behind large wooden doors. Hundreds of gold and silver lanterns hang in the cathedral illuminating the domed ceiling. If possible, try to visit during Armenian Orthodox Mass; it is a fascinating experience. Afternoon mass is signalled by the priest clanging wooden bars in the porch. The entrance to the monastery is located approximately 200m along Armenian Patriarchate Street from Jaffa Gate on the right.

Museum of Armenian Art and History (*Armenian Orthodox Patriarchate St;* ✆ 02 6282331; ⊕ *10.00–16.00 Mon–Sat; admission 5NIS*) Heading south towards the Zion Gate, pass under the narrow bridge and turn left after 30m. The museum is located on the right of a large, 200-year-old courtyard. Displays are simple yet informative, depicting the lives, history, culture and art of the Armenian community in Jerusalem. The most moving and horrifying exhibit depicts the Armenian genocide in Turkey during World War I, a graphic and powerful display of photographs and personal descriptions.

Zion Gate The gate leads out of the Armenian Quarter and provides access to and from Mount Zion. It remains in the original 'L' shape, designed to prevent horse-mounted soldiers from charging, and to slow the battering rams used in attacks during the Ottoman period. Cars slowly weave their way through the awkwardly shaped pass and a resident camel often sits in the corner. The gate bears the scars from the 1948 Arab–Israeli War in the form of bullet marks on its outer edge. It is known in Arabic as Bab el Nabi Daoud (Gate of the Prophet David) because of the traditional site of David's tomb just outside.

Jewish Quarter The Jewish Quarter is undoubtedly the most serene area of the Old City, where Jerusalem's oldest synagogues stand, where bougainvillea flowers creep over brick walls, and where an air of religious learning permeates the quiet cobbled alleys. During Herod's reign, this was the city's most affluent neighbourhood, inhabited mainly by aristocratic and priestly families and also formed the core of the Roman city of Aelia Capitolina with the grand Cardo, the city's main thoroughfare, beginning here. The quaint Hurva Square sits at the centre of the quarter and is fringed by outdoor cafés and bakeries. At the eastern edge of the Jewish Quarter, the vast plaza stretches the length of the Western Wall, the last remaining icon of the Second Temple, and the holiest Jewish site.

Western Wall The Western Wall is the single most sacred site in the Jewish faith. It stands as the last remaining remnant of the Second Temple and has been a site of pilgrimage for Jews from all over the world since the Ottoman period. For centuries, Jews have come here to lament over the loss of their temple, their emotional and sorrowful prayers awarding it the name 'The Wailing Wall'. Today it remains the heart of the Jewish faith and one of the most religious and politically sensitive sites on the planet.

History The wall, or HaKotel, was built by King Herod in 20BCE as part of the Temple Mount complex and is all that remains after the Romans destroyed the Temple in CE70. From the Ottoman period, Jewish pilgrims flocked to the wall, at the time accessed by a narrow alley 3.6m wide and 28m long embedded in the Muslim neighbourhoods around. Throughout the 19th century, conflict hummed around the wall and several prominent Jews, including Baron Rothschild and Sir Moses Montefiore, attempted unsuccessfully to gain control of it. During the British Mandate period there were numerous clashes between Jews and Muslims and from December 1947 Jews were banned from approaching the wall which, following the capitulation of the Jewish Quarter in May 1948, lasted 19 years. After the 1967 Six Day War the wall once again fell into Jewish hands and was greatly expanded to create the vast plaza that we see today.

The wall and tunnels The **Western Wall** lies at the end of the 56m-long, sloping **Western Wall Plaza** and is the principal site of Jewish pilgrimage, where worshippers come to slip prayer notes in between in the ancient stones. The plaza itself is a great place to people watch, especially during religious celebrations or the Shabbat prayer sessions. Inside the men's area the cavern-like **Wilson's Arch** serves as the main place of prayer (particularly in summer when it is air-conditioned) and once formed part of the great bridge linking the upper city and Temple. To the left of the men's prayer area is the beginning of the **Western Wall Tunnels** (✆ *02 6271333; www.thekotel.org;* ⊕ *08.00–last tour booking Sun–Thu, 08.00–12.30 Fri; admission adult/child 25/15NIS*), excavated to reveal buried sections of the original temple wall and stretching as far as the Via Dolorosa. Guided tours (in English, 1 hour, must be booked in advance) are a fascinating insight into the wall's complex layers of history. Tours take visitors along the narrow **Secret Passage** to the **Herodian Wall**, once a beautiful public building. The **Large Hall** leads to the **Largest Stone**, a 570-ton building stone that is the last remaining foundation block and the largest stone to be unearthed in the country. **Warren's Gate** (and the three other ancient gates found along the wall: Wilson's, Barclay's and Robinson's) are so named after prominent 19th-century researchers of

There are three entrances to the plaza, one from the Shlomo Goren (near the Dung Gate), another from the base of the steps leading down from the Burnt House and Western Wall viewing platform and the third from Hakotel Street that leads off Bab el Silsila Street. Modest dress is mandatory and bared shoulders or legs above the knee are forbidden. Shawls are supplied at the entry points. Men are supplied with paper *yarmulke* if needed. Visitors of all faiths are welcome to approach the wall provided they respect religious rules. On the Sabbath, taking photographs, mobile phones and smoking are forbidden inside the plaza.

Jerusalem and leads to a **small alcove** that is part of the wall closest to the temple. Known as 'the holy of holys', it is separated from the foundation stone (located beneath the Dome of the Rock) by a mere 100m. From here the tunnels lead to the **Herodian Wall** which, during temple times was a bustling shopping street, past a **quarry** and **aqueduct** and emerges along the **Via Dolorosa** in the Muslim Quarter. The **Generation Centre** (✆ *02 6271333; www.thekotel.org;* ⏱ *08.00–20.00 Sun–Thu, 08.00–12.00 Fri; admission adult/child 20/10NIS*) is a good accompaniment to the tunnel tour, relating the story of the Jewish people throughout the past 3,500 years using a combination of music, sculpture, archaeology, glass, light effects and holographic images. It was seven years in the making and is a revolutionary museum experience.

The Cardo The Cardo formed the main north–south thoroughfare of Roman Jerusalem, which was modelled on the structure of typical Roman cities. The street was excavated for 200m and today a small section at its southern end has been restored to reveal the parallel columns that ran its length and would have supported a wooden roof. The 22.5m-wide thoroughfare was flanked by shops, but later had a row of buildings erected down the centre. The street now comprises two lanes: Chabad and Hayehudim. The street is bordered by cafés, art galleries and age-old bakeries and is one of the busiest areas of the Jewish Quarter. A section of the Cardo has been rebuilt as a modern shopping area comprising mainly pricey Judaica stores and art galleries and is a far cry from its ancestral shops selling grain, spices and olives, but nevertheless a pleasant place to stroll around.

Synagogues The **Hurva Synagogue** (meaning 'ruins'), was originally commissioned by Rabbi Yehuda HaNassi who arrived in Jerusalem in 1701 with 500 Ashkenazis. Following his death, the synagogue fell into disrepair and wasn't fully rebuilt until 1856. From then, until its destruction during the 1948 war, it acted as the spiritual core of Jerusalem's Ashkenazi Jews. After the Israeli capture of Jerusalem in 1967, plans were discussed to rebuild the ancient synagogue, but weren't put into action until 2006 when its signature arch was dismantled. A budget of US$6.2 million has been awarded to rebuild it to its former neo-Byzantine splendour and is due for completion in 2009.

The **Rambam Synagogue** is named after Rabbi Moshe ben Nachman (the Rambam) who arrived in Jerusalem in 1267 following the decimation of the city in the battle between the Crusaders and the Mamluks. He established a synagogue amidst the destruction, a poignant event seen by Jews as the beginning of the reconstruction of Jerusalem. In the 16th century, the Muslims commandeered the building, and between 1949 and 1967 it was used to house livestock. Only after Israel gained control of the city was it returned to its original purpose. Since then

Jerusalem **WHAT TO SEE**

3

it has superseded the Hurva Synagogue as the most important Jewish house of worship within the Old City. It has been well restored and marks a key point on the Jewish history trail.

The **Four Sephardi Synagogues** (☎ *02 6280592;* ⊕ *09.30–16.00 Sun–Thu, 09.30–12.30 Fri*) is a complex of four Jewish houses of prayer, each representing different histories, religious requirements and prayer practices. Following the arrival of Sephardic Jews expelled from Spain in the 17th century, a new synagogue was built, becoming the first since the Ottoman period. It was named the **Yochanan ben Zakai Synagogue** after the notable sage who is attributed with later establishing the Sanhedrin (Jewish school of biblical studies). Another wave of Sephardic immigrants arrived from Istanbul, Turkey later in the 17th century who constructed the adjacent **Istanbuli Synagogue**. Named after Elijah the Prophet, the third, **Eliyahu Ha'navi Synagogue** was used solely for Torah study. In the centre of the three buildings a courtyard formed, which during the 18th century was converted into the **Emtsai (or Middle) Synagogue**. The complex is also attributed with being the last position held by Jewish defenders before the fall of the Jewish Quarter to the Jordanians in 1948.

The Herodian Quarter During the Second Temple period, the Upper City (the present-day Jewish Quarter) housed the most affluent of Jerusalem's residents and was the last section to be razed to the ground by the Romans in CE70. The **Burnt House** (☎ *02 6287211;* ⊕ *09.00–17.00 Thu–Sun, 09.00–13.00 Fri; admission adult/child 25/12NIS*) stands as a testament to the day the Upper City was burned and those within lost their lives. Finds discovered in the house include that of an arm bone seemingly reaching for a nearby spear, coins and many household objects, including a set of weights inscribed with the name 'Bar Kathros'. This find proved to be the most telling, possibly identifying the occupants as being that of the priestly family known from the **Talmud** to have lived at the time of the Second Temple. Inside the house there is a short film (every 40 minutes) that delves into the history of the site and the Upper City. A visit to the house is more interesting for what it represents than for the finds inside.

The **Wohl Archaeological Museum** (*1 Hakara'im St;* ☎ *02 6283448;* ⊕ *09.00–16.30 Sun–Thu, 09.30–12.30 Fri; admission adult/child 35/15NIS (combined with Burnt House)*) contains remains of Jewish mansions and houses from the affluent Upper City, which was mostly occupied by Jewish Temple priests. On display are luxury relics ranging from mosaic floors to expensive glassware that provide an insight into the Herodian Quarter and its wealthy residents. The quarter lies today 3–7m below street level, a staircase leading up from the submerged museum ending abruptly and providing a clear reminder of the devastation caused by the Roman destruction. The museum contains three sections, the most impressive being the **Palatial Mansion**, the most complete of the Herodian houses on display.

Jerusalem Archaeological Park The park (☎ *02 6277550; www.archpark.org.il;* ⊕ *08.00–17.00 Sun–Thu, 08.00–14.00 Fri; admission adult/child 30/16NIS*) covers the area surrounding the Western Wall Plaza and southern wall of the Temple Mount complex, and has been extensively excavated to reveal substantial remains from the Second Temple period. Jumbled remains from the Byzantine, early Islamic, Crusader and Mamluk periods provide an interesting glimpse into Jerusalem's layers of occupation and are best appreciated by first paying a visit to the Davidson Centre, which displays historic exhibits and virtual reconstructions. A one-hour guided tour of both the centre and park costs 160NIS and must be booked in advance.

Dung Gate The Jewish Quarter is accessed by the Dung Gate located on its southern wall. A bus stop at the top of Shlomo Goren Street that passes through the gate is directly outside the southern entrance to the Western Wall Plaza. It also provides access to the visitors' entrance of the Temple Mount and Jerusalem Archaeological Park. There are conflicting theories as to the origins of the name of the gate, the most plausible being that it was where rubbish was brought out of the city from the 2nd century onwards. The gate is also often referred to as the Gate of Moors because of the north African immigrants who lived in the neighbourhood next to the gate in the 16th century.

Muslim Quarter What the Christian, Jewish and Armenian quarters have in historic buildings, state-of-the-art museums and ecclesiastical marvels, the Muslim Quarter has in vivacity. It is undoubtedly the liveliest of the four quarters, the Damascus and Herod's gates opening into a thriving Arab neighbourhood in the northeast of Jerusalem. Its markets are incomparable; a hub of activity, noise, aromas and traditional Arabic merchandise, a wonderful contrast to the more serene streets elsewhere in the quarter. But the area is not without its historic gems: the vast, walled **Temple Mount** complex occupies the most prized piece of real estate in the country, its majestic golden **Dome of the Rock** forming the centrepiece of the Old City. As the call of the muezzin echoes across the city signalling the beginning of Friday prayer sessions, swarms of worshippers pour down the lanes towards Islam's third holiest site, while from its easternmost gate begins the **Via Dolorosa**, Christianity's holiest processional (see pages 76–77).

Temple Mount (☎ 02 6283292; ☉ 07.30–10.30 & 12.30–13.30 Sun–Thu; admission free) Rising above the city, the golden **Dome of the Rock** forms the centrepiece of Jerusalem's holiest Islamic site, the Temple Mount. Known to Muslims as Haram Es Sharif (Noble Sanctuary) it is believed to be the site from where Muhammad began his Night Journey to Heaven and today ranks as the third holiest Islamic site in the world after Mecca and Medina. To Jews, this is also the pinnacle of holiness, the site where the First and Second Temples stood, where the Foundation Stone upon which the world was built stands, where Adam was created and where Isaac was almost sacrificed by Abraham. In a city that has seen more than its fair share of turmoil and tension, the Temple Mount is today still a raw and sensitive point, often acting as the centre of unrest between Jews and Muslims. For the most part, however, the area is a peaceful and tranquil place of worship and as you wander around the wide, open complex, it is hard to envisage the 3,000 years of turmoil that have surrounded it.

History The history of the Temple Mount spans 3,000 years, seven periods of time, three world religions and five cultures. Upon land bought by King David, Jerusalem's First Temple was built by his son King Solomon and stood until the Babylonians destroyed it in 586BCE. Not long after, Jews returning from exile rebuilt it and so the Second Temple came into being. Following the Roman destruction of the city in CE70, the temple (bar the Western Wall) was left in ruins until the Muslim conquest in 638 when Caliph Omar built the first mosque upon the site. Fifty years later, during the reign of Caliph Abd al-Malik, the Dome of the Rock and **Al-Aqsa Mosque** were erected.

In 1099, the Crusaders captured Jerusalem whereby holy sites on the Temple Mount were declared Christian and the area became the seat of the Knights Templar. In 1187, Saladin put an end to Crusader rule, reconverting churches to mosques.

Safety issues Following the 1948 Arab–Israeli War, Jerusalem remained divided, with the Old City and Temple Mount under Jordanian rule. After Israel captured the city during the 1967 Six Day War, the Waqf was allowed to retain administration of the site on the proviso that non-Muslims be allowed to enter. In order to prevent rioting and religious unrest, the Israeli government has banned any non-Islamic praying on the site. Modest dress is compulsory and open displays of affection are not appreciated. At the time of writing, the Dome of the Rock, Al-Aqsa Mosque and Islamic Museum are closed to all non-Muslims. Some Jews do enter the Temple Mount but often limit themselves to the perimeter wall. During times of political unrest it is best to check government warnings on the advisability of visiting the complex, although entry is generally prohibited if threats arise. During the relatively short opening times, queues for entry can be long so it is best to arrive early.

What to see While the most impressive and alluring structure within the Temple Mount is undoubtedly the Dome of the Rock, the 144,000m² **Al-Aqsa Mosque** is the holiest part of the complex. It was the earliest mosque constructed in Palestine and is today one of Islam's most important houses of prayer, believed to be the place referred to in the Koran as '*al-aqsa*' (the furthermost). Although the mosque has suffered great tragedy over the last century, being amongst other events the site of King Abdullah of Jordan's 1951 assassination, it is today a mostly peaceful and active centre of prayer holding up to 4,000 worshippers at any one time. In the southeast corner of the temple esplanade are the scanty remains of **Solomon's Stables** which, contrary to their title, were not in existence in Solomon's time but acted as stables during the Crusader occupation. Just north of the mosque, the circular **Al Kas Fountain** dates to 709 and is used by Muslims for the ritual washing prior to prayer sessions. Directly ahead lies the octagonal **Dome of the Rock**, crowned by its gold-leafed dome, a million-dollar gift from Saudi Arabia in 1965. It stands as the oldest Islamic shrine in the world dated to 688 and also boasts the world's oldest-surviving *mihrab* (niche indicating the direction of Mecca). Extensive decoration from a variety of periods including mosaics, painted wood, marble, coloured tiles, carpets and carved stone covers both the interior and exterior of the building, most of the blue and gold exterior tiles laid under Suleiman the Magnificent. Muslim pilgrimage to Jerusalem is known as *taqdis* and marks the final destination on the main pilgrimage (*hajj*).

Bazaars (☉ *09.00–19.00 daily*) The Muslim Quarter bazaars are among the most fascinating places to visit in the Old City, a clear demonstration of the thriving Arab communities who call this area (and the neighbourhoods in east Jerusalem) home. Beginning at the swarming Damascus Gate two market streets branch off southwards: **El Wad Street** and **Souk Khan es Zeit**. A third street, **Souk el Qattanin (Cotton Market)** is located at the southern end of El Wad Street, and is probably the most ancient and attractive market, with its stone-arched roof and rudimentary stalls. An atmosphere of effervescent hubbub surrounds the markets where colourful shops, cafés and food stalls squeeze into any available space. Compared with the Virgin Mary statues and Stars of David that abound in the Christian Quarter markets, the Muslim markets form the centre of daily life in the Arab community. Spices, leather goods, Arabic-style clothes, carpets, butchers, bakers and candlestick makers all have their place.

Bargaining is customary in all of the markets so don't be shy or you'll pay over the odds. Expect to pay in the region of three-quarters of the vendor's opening price (you can offer half and go from there). It is a lively and fun activity and a smile goes a long way. You will no doubt get offered strong Arabic coffee or mint tea so take it – it's a great way to get to know the people and a more relaxing way to bargain.

Church of St Anne and the Pools of Bethesda The vast church complex (✆ *02 6283285;* ⊕ *08.00–12.00 & 14.00–17.00 Mon–Sat; admission 7NIS*) is located on the right of Sha'ar Ha'arayot Street 30m from Lion's Gate. Entering through the large wooden gate, the Church of St Anne is located at the rear of a small garden (on the right) and the excavations of the Pool of Bethesda opposite.

Pools of Bethesda The Pools of Bethesda were documented in John's Gospel account as the site where Jesus healed a man who had suffered illness for 38 years (John 5:2). Until 1871, however, proof was based on faith alone, until excavations unearthed remains of a colonnaded pool matching John's description. It is now considered by archaeologists and Christians to be the exact site described in the Gospel. The Pool of Bethesda is today a series of impressive submerged dry relics, but during Jesus's time was a site of healing, where legend had it an angel moved the waters and cured the sick.

Church of St Anne The church and ruins are located within peaceful, quiet gardens that are often cloaked in pilgrims who come to sing hymns in the beautiful 12th-century Crusader church that is renowned for its amazing acoustics. The church was erected over the traditional site of the birthplace of St Anne, the mother of Mary. The Crusader church that stands today was built over an earlier Byzantine church, which was later converted by Saladin into a Muslim theological school (an inscription above the church commemorates this). The church was eventually abandoned until, in 1856, the Ottomans donated it to France who restored it to its former beauty (although most of what you see today is, in fact, original). From within the church stone steps lead down to the cavern, traditionally regarded as St Anne's birthplace.

Zedekiah's Cave (✆ *02 6277550;* ⊕ *09.00–17.00 Sun–Thu*) Located 100m east of Damascus Gate (see below), Zedekiah's Cave (also known as Solomon's Quarries) is believed to be the vast quarry from which the building blocks of the First Temple were unearthed. While there isn't an awful lot to see inside, the cave's interest lies in its history and as the site of ritual ceremonies of the Freemasons, the Order claiming spiritual ancestry from the founders of Jerusalem's Temple. The 225m-long cavern was named after the King of Judea who Jewish tradition holds fled the city through tunnels to Jericho during the Babylonian siege.

Gates
Damascus Gate At the northern end of the main Muslim Quarter souk and leading onto Sultan Suleiman Street, the Damascus Gate is in fact known by three names: the Christians refer to it as 'Damascus' as it marks the beginning of the highway that led through Israel to Syria; it is known in Hebrew as 'Sha'ar (gate of) Shechem' after the biblical city (modern-day Nablus) that was accessed by a road crossing the Damascus route; Arabs refer to it as 'Bab al 'Amud' (Gate of the Pillar) after the remains of the 2nd-century wall discovered beneath. The gate is the main entrance into and out of the Muslim Quarter and a constant buzz of activity surrounds it, where merchants and worshippers stream through on their way to the souk or Al-Aqsa Mosque. There is a great view of the Muslim Quarter from the top of the gate which can be accessed by steps on its eastern side.

Golden Gate (closed) The sealed gate that is today located along the eastern wall of the Old City in the Temple Mount complex dates to CE640 and was built either by the last Byzantine rulers or the first of the Arab conquerors. Jews claim that it is through this gate that the Messiah will pass on his way to the Old City and is said to have been sealed by the Muslims during Suleiman the Magnificent's reign in an attempt to prevent the Messiah from entering. Today the closure of the gate is not seen by most Jews as a sensitive point. Many jokingly claim that if the Messiah can get this far, he will find a way to get in. The **Ophel Promenade** runs along the outside of the east wall of the Old City and passes the gate, also referred to as the Gate of Mercy.

Lion's Gate Tradition states that Sultan Suleiman the Magnificent dreamed of being eaten by lions and that to prevent this, the walls of Jerusalem had to be rebuilt. On either side of the gate are reliefs of leopards that are mistakenly referred to as lions. The gate also goes by the name St Stephen's Gate as, according to tradition, this was the site where the first Christian martyr Stephen was stoned to death. In Arabic the gate is known as Bab Sitti Maryam, Gate of the Virgin Mary. The gate once again entered the history books when, during the Six Day War, Israeli soldiers from the 55th Paratroop Brigade marched through and raised the Israeli flag, signalling the conquest of the Old City.

Herod's Gate Located on the northern side of the city, Herod's Gate faces the vibrant Arab area of East Jerusalem. During the British Mandate period it became the principal entry point to the Old City and had its L-shape removed to allow for an easier flow of traffic. It was called Herod's Gate by 16th- and 17th-century pilgrims who mistakenly believed a house located just inside it was that of Herod Antipas, Herod the Great's son. It was also at Herod's Gate that at midday on 15 July 1099, the Crusaders breached the wall and took Jerusalem, declaring it part of the Latin Kingdom.

Mount Zion Accessed by the towering, bullet-ridden Zion Gate that leads from the Armenian Quarter, Mount Zion's wealth of religious and historic relics sees it incorporated into any tour of the Old City. It is a small, easily navigable area but often crowded with Jewish and Christian tour groups who make the pilgrimage to the holy sites concentrated here.

Dormition Abbey (✆ 02 5655330; ⊕ 08.30–12.00 & 12.40–18.00 Mon–Fri, 08.30–12.00 & 12.40–17.30 Sat, 10.30–11.45 & 12.40–17.30 Sun; information leaflet 1NIS) This beautiful rounded church was commissioned in 1906 by Kaiser Wilhelm II, its robust architecture and conical corner towers evoking thoughts of medieval European castles. According to the Roman Catholic and Eastern and Oriental Orthodox churches, this is the site upon which the Virgin Mary fell asleep and was taken to Heaven (the Assumption of Mary). In the basement of the cavernous church is a statue of the Virgin Mary. The church is frequented by hordes of tour groups so be prepared for a squeeze.

King David's Tomb and the Upper Room These two holy sites, located one above the other, attract vast crowds of quite varying religious backgrounds. To the Jews this is the site of King David's cenotaph, located on the ground floor of the building complex. It is one of the most venerated Jewish sites in the world and high on the pilgrimage list, particularly on Shavuot, the traditional day of David's death. The vast ornate sarcophagus is located within a stone-cut. To Christians, the **Upper Room** (or Coenaculum) (⊕ 08.00–17.00 daily) is the site of Jesus's Last Supper, the establishment of the rite of the Eucharist and the location of his last appearance to the apostles. The room, today accessed by a flight of steps, was once a part of the Crusader Church of Our Lady of Mount Zion but is now located above various Jewish *yeshivas* (schools of Torah study). There isn't a lot to see inside the room bar

Oskar Schindler (28 April 1908–9 October 1974) was a German businessman and member of the Nazi Party who is renowned for saving his Jewish workers from entering concentration camps during the Holocaust. He established a factory as a sub-camp of the Plazow labour camp, employing his Jewish workers and keeping them safe from execution. In 1944, he relocated his factory, opening it under the ruse of manufacturing tank shells. Through contacts and bribery he instead spent his fortune buying medicine and food for his Jewish workers. Following the war, Schindler found himself ostracised from his native homeland and moved to Argentina. In 1962, he was invited to plant a tree in the Avenue of the Righteous in Jerusalem, an act that brought his World War II acts to light and subjected him to abuse and harassment from Nazi sympathisers. He became the only member of the Nazi Party to be recognised as a 'righteous gentile' in Israel and shortly before his death in 1974, he declared his wish to be buried there. He died a poor man in Germany and his remains were transported to the Jewish country where his coffin was carried through the streets and buried in the Catholic Cemetery on Mount Zion. He is attributed with having saved 1,200 Jews from persecution and was venerated in the book *Schindler's Ark* and later Stephen Spielberg's Academy Award-winning movie *Schindler's List* (1993), in which he was portrayed by Liam Neeson.

Today the cemetery appears long forgotten. Overgrown and dishevelled, its tombstones are untended and have fared badly with the passage of time. At the bottom of the cemetery Oskar Schindler's grave stands out, tiny white stones lined along its clean slab. The custom of piling stones dates to biblical times when they were used to mark graves. Today they represent a more permanent symbol than flowers to show love and respect.

some sparse examples of Crusader architecture. Guides direct visitors to one or other of the rooms, managing to successfully ascertain their religious preference by a mere glance.

Montefiore's Windmill Born in Italy, Moses Montefiore (1784–1885) was a British-Jewish businessman, renowned for his Zionist dreams, Jewish philanthropy and establishment of the Yemin Moshe neighbourhood to the west of the Old City walls. Today, the unmistakable **Montefiore's Windmill** is a lasting legacy to his tireless efforts (although it was never actually used on account of a distinct lack of wind in this area).

MOUNT OF OLIVES AND THE KIDRON VALLEY

City of David (✆ 02 6262341; *www.cityofdavid.org.il*; ⊕ 08.30–17.00 Sun–Thu, 08.30–13.00 Fri; admission adult/child 23/12NIS) The City of David referred to in the Bible lies outside the modern day walls in the Kidron Valley. In the area between the Temple Mount and Mount of Olives, excavations have revealed the original capital of Jerusalem, built by King David more than 3,000 years ago to unify the tribes of Israel. For most, the highlight of a trip to the archaeological park is taking a 30-minute wade through the 2,700-year-old **Hezekiah's Tunnel** that leads from the **Gihon Spring** to the **Siloam Pool** further down the valley (although there is a dry route for those less disposed to getting wet). The spring was the principal water source of the city and its waters are mentioned in countless events documented in the Bible. In the 8th century BCE, under Assyrian threat, King

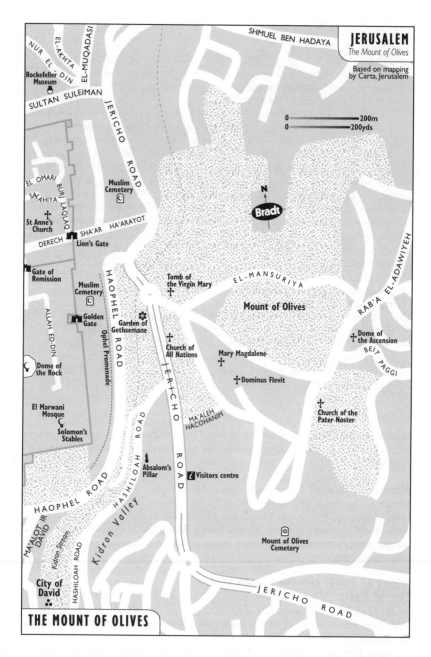

THE MOUNT OF OLIVES

Hezekiah had the water flow diverted underground in an attempt to protect this important life source. Today, the 533m-long tunnel can be traversed (be sure to wear appropriate clothing as water reaches knee height). Other important sites include the extensive **Area G** excavation zone and **Warren's Shaft**, all of which benefit from a guided tour (*in English at 10.00 on Mon, Wed, & Fri; or with a private guide adult/child 50/45NIS*).

Church of All Nations and the Garden of Gethsemane At the foot of the Mount of Olives is the garden (⊕ *08.30–12.00 & 14.00–sunset daily*), known in Christian tradition as the site of Jesus's agony, prayer, betrayal by Judas and subsequent arrest. The name Gethsemane derives from the Hebrew '*gat shemen*' meaning 'oil press', a reference to the ancient olive trees that remain standing to this day, believed by many botanists to predate Christianity. Within the tranquil, shady garden stands the magnificent **Church of All Nations** (also known as the Basilica of the Agony). The church, with its vast fresco adorning the façade, was rebuilt in 1924 on the site of earlier Byzantine and Crusader churches thanks to contributions from Catholic communities all over the world. Inside the church mosaic symbols of each of these communities are represented in the domes. Inside, the **Rock of the Agony** is said to be the stone where Jesus prayed.

Tomb of the Virgin Mary This cavernous church (⊕ *06.00–12.30 & 14.00–18.00 daily*), which dates to the Crusader period, is the traditional burial site of Jesus's mother. While this event is unrecorded in the Bible, belief in this site dates back to the 2nd or 3rd centuries CE. Muslims also worship this spot in the belief that the Prophet Muhammad saw a light shine over Mary's tomb on his Night Journey from Mecca. A wide marble staircase leads down to the eerily beautiful, grotto-like church, the ceiling of which is adorned with hundreds of ornate lanterns. Mary's tomb is located at the bottom of the steps to the right past a Greek Orthodox altar.

THE FINAL RESTING PLACE OF TWO ROYAL NUNS

The elegant golden domes of the **Mary Magdalene Church** (✆ *02 6284371; ⊕ 10.00–12.00 Tue–Thu*) stand as glittering landmarks on Jerusalem's horizon, unmistakable in their position halfway up the Mount of Olives. Yet the church is not just a pretty face. This is the final resting place of two rather prominent royal women: the Grand Duchess Elizabeth Fyodorovna and Queen Alice of Battenberg. The Grand Duchess was the granddaughter of Britain's Queen Victoria and the mother of Tsar Alexander III who built her the church in 1888 in traditional Russian style. Upon the assassination of her husband, Elizabeth retreated into a monastic life, giving away her possessions and dedicating her life to caring for Moscow's needy. In 1918, Elizabeth and her family were exiled and brutally murdered by the Bolsheviks. Her remains were buried in the crypt in the Mary Magdalene Church and she was canonised by the Russian Orthodox Church in 1992.

At around the same time Elizabeth's niece, Princess Alice of Battenberg (the mother of Britain's Prince Philip) married the Prince of Greece and lived in Athens until the royal family's exile in 1917. Alice was born deaf, and in 1930 diagnosed with schizophrenia and institutionalised. After recovering, she separated from her husband and cut off ties with her family and, like her aunt before her, dedicated her life to serving God and the poor. In 1938, Alice returned to Athens and lived in a small, cramped apartment where she helped the poor, serving the Red Cross and risking her life throughout World War II. Upon the Nazi occupation of Athens, Princess Alice was approached by Rachel Cohen and her children, a Jewish family who had helped King George I of Greece in 1913. In return for this help, Alice saved the family and was posthumously honoured as 'Righteous Amongst the Nations' in Jerusalem, a ceremony attended by Prince Philip. The princess finally left Athens in 1967 and moved to Buckingham Palace in England where she died two years later. In accordance with her wishes, her body was interred 20 years later in the Mary Magdalene Church alongside her aunt.

Formed of Jerusalem's oldest neighbourhoods that grew outside the Old City walls, this area is today a fascinating example of the unique atmosphere that characterises the city, where ancient and modern have continued to develop alongside one another. From the ultra-Orthodox neighbourhood of Me'a She'arim where biblical times have stood still, to the vibrancy and noise of the Mahne Yehuda food market, a day's walk leads you through the present and past of the city centre.

Start in the irrepressibly fascinating ultra-Orthodox neighbourhood of **Me'a She'arim,** which was founded in 1875 by eastern European Jews. Easily recognisable in their traditional black clothes, felt hats (*streimel*) and side curls (*peyot*), most speak Yiddish, an old Jewish variant of German, reserving Hebrew only for prayer. Signs plaster the walls surrounding the neighbourhood's entrances requesting those entering to dress appropriately (those who don't heed the warnings often find themselves at the receiving end of verbal abuse and anger). Short sleeves or the baring of legs is not allowed at any time, and photographing the residents is also not permitted. Within the area are numerous synagogues, ritual baths, Talmudic schools and Judaica stores. The neighbourhood is also home to the Neturei Karta, an extreme group that does not recognise the state of Israel as it was not founded by the Messiah.

Leave the neighbourhood and walk down the narrow Ethiopia Street towards Hanevi'im Street. On the left of the narrow road, lined with stone mansions you will find the lovely, circular **Ethiopian church** (⊕ 07.00–18.00 daily). Built in 1896, it is believed to have been a gift to the Ethiopian Queen Sheba from King Solomon. Directly opposite the large church and marked by a plaque on the wall outside is **Ben Yehuda's House**, where he lived and did much of his work on the revival of the Hebrew language.

At the bottom of Ethiopia Street cross Hanevi'im Street and walk down Harav Kook Street. On your left is the **Rothschild Hospital**, today the Hadassah College, which was built in 1888 by funds from the baron (see page 155) and became the first Jewish hospital to be built outside the Old City. Across the street is the delightful **Ticho House** (✆ 6244186; www.go-out.com/ticho; ⊕ 10.00–17.00 Sun/Mon & Wed,

To the right of the tomb is a Muslim prayer arch dating to medieval times. The church is the Greek Orthodox rival to the Dormition Abbey on Mount Zion as the site of Mary's assumption.

Dominus Flevit (⊕ 08.00–12.00 & 14.30–17.00 daily) To find the church, turn left off Jericho Road and then right up the extremely steep and narrow lane that runs along the edge of the cemetery. Continue almost to the top and the entrance to the church is on the left through a large gate. Inside is a small, well-kept garden within which is a teardrop-shaped chapel, designed to represent the tears shed by Jesus as he lamented over the future destruction of Jerusalem.

Dome of the Ascension (*admission 5NIS*) This small octagonal chapel is the traditional site of Jesus's ascension to Heaven. A church once stood on the site but today a mosque covers the rock believed to be indented with Jesus's last footprint, the church taken and destroyed by Saladin in 1187 (Islam recognises Jesus as a prophet although does not accept that the Christian belief that he was the son of God). It is but one of the contenders for Jesus's ascension, the Russian Orthodox Church and the Church of the Pater Noster also in the running. Opening hours vary but access can normally be gained during the mornings (ring the doorbell outside to gain entry).

10.00–22.00 Tue, 10.00–14.00 Fri), one of Jerusalem's earliest buildings outside the walls. It belonged to Dr Avraham Ticho, a German optometrist and his wife Anna who in 1924 opened an eye clinic that operated until she death in 1960. Anna worked as both his assistant and landscape artist until she passed away in 1980. Upon her death, the house was converted into a museum, library, art gallery and café. Walk to the end of Harav Kook Street and turn right onto Yafo Street. Take a mildly strenuous 25-minute uphill walk until you reach the unmistakable **Mahne Yehuda Market**. This covered food market is one of the city's liveliest spots, especially on a Friday before Shabbat when all and sundry come to buy their weekend groceries.

Exit the market at the southern end onto Agrippas Street and turn right onto Eliash Street. Follow the road until you get to Shmuel Hanagid Street (crossing Ben Yehuda Street). Follow it to where it meets Bezalel Street, where you will see the **Ratisbonne Monastery** (⊕ *08.00–16.00 Mon–Thu, 08.00–14.00 Fri*). Founded in 1876 by Father Ratisbonne, a Jewish aristocratic banker turned monk, the monastery was built as a French Catholic monastery and vocational school. Today, the building remains as impressive as when it was first erected, its tower believed to be one of 16 that stretched from Jaffa to Jerusalem, each acting as part of a chain of smoke signals conveying the arrival of merchant ships. Continue walking to the end of Shmuel Hanagid Street and right onto King George V Street. A short distance away, on the left, is the **Heichal Shlomo and Great Synagogue**, the former seat of the Israeli Rabbinate and Supreme Rabinical Court. The magnificent synagogue next door was designed to reflect architectural features of the First Temple. From here continue across **Independence Park (Gan Ha'atzma'ut)**, the eastern part of which is a pre-1948 Muslim cemetery. Graves can still be spotted amongst the shrubbery. Exit onto Shlomitzion Hamalka Street and turn left. At Yafo Street turn left and immediately right onto Cheshin Street. At the top is the **Russian Compound**, whose green-domed cathedral takes pride of place. The compound was built in 1860 to accommodate the thousands of Russian pilgrims flocking to Jerusalem up until World War I. Today most of the buildings are occupied by various government institutions.

Mount of Olives Cemetery The Jewish cemetery that blankets the side of the Mount of Olives resides on some of the country's prime real estate and for good reason. According to Jewish belief, the resurrection of the dead will begin here upon the coming of the Messiah. Although the cemetery dates to the First Temple period, most of the tombs that we see today are from the 15th century. During the Jordanian rule, a road leading to Jericho was built over the graves, many gravestones smashed, destroyed or used in construction. Following the 1967 Six Day War and Israel's conquest of Jerusalem, the government went to great lengths to restore the tombstones to their original positions. The small **visitors' centre** (*Jericho Rd*; ⊕ *09.00–17.00 Sun–Thu, 09.00–13.00 Fri*) at the base of the cemetery provides information on finding some of the most prominent graves (and can provide keys to the locked tombs for a deposit), including amongst many, Eliezer Ben-Yehuda, Shmuel Yosef Agnon (awarded the Nobel Prize for literature) and Menachem Begin.

Tomb of Absalom In past centuries devout Jews, Muslims and Christians would pelt stones at the magnificent stone structure that holds pride of place in the Kidron Valley, a symbol of their contempt for King David's son who rebelled against his father. Today, however, the tomb has been dated to almost a millennium after Absalom and is believed by some to be the tomb of Jehosophat, King of Judah.

A recent hidden inscription has also laid claims that this was the true tomb of the priest Zachariah, father of John the Baptist, although this is hotly contested. Rather confusingly, the rock-cut **tomb of Zachariah** is located a few metres away.

CITY CENTRE

Israel Museum (*Ruppin Rd;* ✆ *02 6708811; www.imj.org.il;* ⊕ *10.00–17.00 Sun/Mon, Wed/Thu & Sat, 16.00–21.00 Tue, 10.00–14.00 Fri; admission adult/child 42/21NIS (free to under 17s 16.00–21.00 Tue & Thu)*) This is Israel's largest, and one of the world's leading, archaeology and art museums. Its exhibits cover a wealth of topics, housed within the vast complex, interconnected pavilions and surrounding gardens. The **Judaica and Jewish Ethnography Wing** consists of the world's largest collection of Jewish religious objects gathered from communities across the globe, each reflecting the local traditions and styles of its origin. There is also a costume exhibit and reconstructions of 17th- and 18th-century synagogues from Italy and Germany. The **Shrine of the Book and Model of Jerusalem** in the Second Temple period is the museum's most famous exhibit, housing the **Dead Sea Scrolls** (see page 250). The onion-shaped roof of the pavilion was designed to reflect the jar in which the scrolls were discovered. On the lower level of the building letters written by Simon Bar-Kochba during the Second Jewish Revolt and artefacts discovered in Masada (see page 251) are displayed. The **Art Pavilion** proudly displays works by artists such as Corot, Monet, Renoir, Degas, Gauguin and Matisse along with the beautifully landscaped Billy Rose Art Garden containing classical and modern European, American and Israeli pieces by, amongst others, Rodin, Picasso, Henry Moore and Chana Orloff. The **archaeological garden**, contains Greco-Roman sculptures, sarcophagi and mosaics, most excavated from sites in Israel. The hugely popular **Archaeology Wing** is currently under renovation and is due to be reopened in 2009–10.

Free tours are arranged in English starting at the **Entrance Pavilion** (✆ *02 6708811; reserve in advance*). Alternatively, free audio guides are available from the entrance. On Saturday or holidays, tickets must be purchased from a local ticket agent outside the main entrance.

Knesset (*Rothschild St;* ✆ *02 6753420; www.knesset.gov.il*) The Knesset is the seat of Israel's parliament, a vast, proud building holding pride of place in Jerusalem's centre. An interesting tour can be arranged illuminating not only the workings of the country's political centre but a fascinating insight into the history, culture and heritage of the Jewish people. Tours include architecture, art, the magnificent menorah (which can be seen standing sentry outside the main complex), divisions of the Knesset, the library, archives and synagogue. Guided tours must be booked in advance (*08.30–14.30 Sun–Thu*), while sessions can be viewed with no need for advance reservation (*16.00 Mon/Tue, 11.00 Wed*). The Knesset operates a strict dress code and no jeans, shorts, skimpy tops and sandals for men are permitted. Passports must be shown on entry.

Museum of Islamic Art (*2 HaPalmach St;* ✆ *02 5661291; www.islamicart.co.il;* ⊕ *10.00–15.00 Sun–Thu, 10.00–14.00 Fri/Sat; admission adult/child 20/10NIS*) This privately owned museum houses a varied selection of Islamic artistry from every corner of the globe and depicts the history and religious beliefs of Islam. Exhibits include weaponry, glass, jewellery, pottery and carpets from the last 1,400 years. Guided tours can be arranged in advance in Hebrew, English and Arabic.

Monastery of the Cross (✆ *02 6790961;* ⊕ *10.00–16.30 Mon–Sat*) This beautiful, castle-like church sits in the middle of what is today referred to as the Valley of the Cross (Rehavia Park) near the Knesset. According to biblical belief, Lot planted branches from pine, fir and cypress trees, which grew into one tree, later used to make the cross upon which Jesus was crucified. The monastery dates to the Byzantine period, built by Greek Orthodox monks with funding from the King of Georgia. Almost all the complex is open to the public, the kitchen in particular providing a rare and insightful view of daily monastic life. The church's dome, frescoes and earlier 5th-century mosaic floor are also worth visiting.

EAST JERUSALEM
Rockefeller Museum (*Sultan Suleiman St;* ✆ *02 6708011; www.imj.org.il;* ☉ *10.00–15.00 Sun/Mon & Wed/Thu, 10.00–14.00 Sat; admission adult/child 26/12NIS*) Located opposite the northeast corner of the Old City's Herod's Gate, the Rockefeller Museum is easily recognisable by its massive, limestone tower. It was commissioned by its namesake John D Rockefeller in 1927 following a growing need for an appropriate home for finds being unearthed throughout Palestine at the time. For those embarking on a trip around the country, the museum is best saved as a finale, where finds from great sites such as Caesarea, Akko, Beit She'an, the Carmel and the Galilee can be envisioned in their original context. Amongst the most impressive exhibits are the relief carving from the Church of the Holy Sepulchre, the 200,000-year-old skull excavated from the Carmel Caves, wooden beams from the Al-Aqsa Mosque and Egyptian and Mesopotamian material unearthed from Beit She'an.

The Garden Tomb (*Conrad Schik St;* ✆ *02 6272745; www.gardentomb.com;* ☉ *08.30–12.00 & 14.00–17.30 Mon–Sat; admission free*) The Garden Tomb is the second contender for the site of Golgotha, and couldn't be further removed from the grand Church of the Holy Sepulchre. Tombs discovered by the British general Charles Gordon in 1883 have led many to believe this is the spot mentioned in the Bible. Some archaeologists, however, date the tombs to Old Testament times. Today the pretty tomb area is a place of quiet, simple prayer and reverence visited predominantly by Protestant pilgrim groups.

GREATER JERUSALEM
Yad Vashem The Holocaust was one of, if not the, most horrific and devastating events in human history. Over six million Jews lost their lives in unthinkable ways and many more suffered unimaginable trauma and loss. In Israel, remembrance of the Holocaust is as raw today as it was post-World War II, and forms the underlying backbone and social unity in the country. The new **Yad Vashem Holocaust Museum** (✆ *02 6443420; www.yadvashem.org;* ☉ *09.00–17.00 Sun–Wed, 09.00–20.00 Thu, 09.00–14.00 Fri; admission free (under 10s not allowed)*) was created to keep alive the memory of those who suffered, and to tell the story through their eyes. The museum, which was inaugurated by Israeli heads of state and attended by those of 40 other nations, depicts the human story behind the Holocaust. The triangular-shaped, concrete hall in which the main museum is located takes visitors on a walk-through of history, each room depicting a different stage in the events leading up to and during the Holocaust. Displays, which include authentic artefacts, testimonies, personal letters, documentary evidence, films, art and, chillingly, mountains of hair and shoes, are pieced together to tell the wider picture through the personal stories that emerged.

At the end of the museum, the **Hall of Names** has been given a new home. The circular hall is covered with the faces of those who perished and is a moving finale. In a separate room, the **Central Database of Shoah** (Holocaust) **Victim's**

Names can be accessed, allowing visitors to search for relatives. It can also be accessed through the website (see above).

Ein Kerem A short 20-minute bus ride from the hustle and bustle of central Jerusalem is the picturesque, tranquil village of Ein Kerem, tucked into the green hills, terraced hillsides and olive groves southwest of the city. Famed in Christian tradition as being the birthplace of John the Baptist, Ein Kerem is home to impressive churches, a burgeoning artists' colony and a few cafés and restaurants. Ein Kerem, whose name literally means 'Spring of the Vineyard', also appears in the Mishnah as being the site from where the stone for the altar of the First Temple was taken.

The Franciscan **Church of St John** (✆ *02 6323000;* ☉ *08.00–12.00 & 14.30–18.00 daily*), is said to have been built over the grotto in which John the Baptist was born to Elizabeth and Zachariah. The church (not to be confused with the Eastern Orthodox church of the same name) was built in the 19th century over the remains of earlier Byzantine and Crusader churches. Inside is the birth cave and well-preserved ancient mosaic. At the far end of the village, the beautifully tended **Church of the Visitation** (☉ *08.30–12.00 & 14.30–18.00 daily*) was originally built by the Crusaders to commemorate the 'visitation', when the pregnant Mary visited her cousin Elizabeth, who was pregnant at the same time with John. On one wall of the church are the words of the *Magnificat*, the hymn Mary traditionally sang at the time, in 62 languages. The gates are closed on Saturdays so ring the bell for entry. Not far from the church is **Mary's Spring**, the traditional site of Mary and Elizabeth's meeting and from which the village received its name.

Ammunition Hill (*Givat Hatachmoshet;* ✆ *02 5828442; www.givathatachmosht.org.il;* ☉ *09.00–18.00 Sun–Thu, 09.00–14.00 Fri; admission adult/child 15/12NIS*) The Ammunition Hill memorial site stands as a long-lasting reminder and tribute to members of the IDF Paratrooper Regiment who fell in one of the Six Day War's bloodiest battles. The hill, a Jordanian army stronghold, was seen as a crucial strategic point in the battle for Jerusalem along the Jerusalem–Ramallah road and, on 6 June 1967 in a battle that lasted four hours, 36 men lost their lives in the capture of the hill. Visitors can join the throngs of young IDF soldiers who frequent the site in exploring the battleground, which includes a tour of the tunnels and bunkers.

Castel National Park Although its history stretches from biblical times to the Crusades, the Castel Fortress (*Mivasseret Zion;* ✆ *02 5330467;* ☉ *08.00–17.00 daily; admission adult/child 12/6NIS*) is most poignantly remembered for its role in the 1948 Arab–Israeli War when the crucial route leading to Jerusalem was being fiercely contested. For five days, Jewish forces fought off attacks from Arab troops, a battle that resulted in the death of Arab commander Abd-el-Qader el-Husseini and, despite drastic and almost total loss of life, the eventual victory by Jewish forces. Models, exhibits and a great view from the fortress's 790-m elevation make it a worthwhile trip. The park is located 15 minutes from the city centre near the village of Mivasseret Zion on route 1.

Biblical Zoo (✆ *02 6750111; www.jerusalemzoo.org.il;* ☉ *09.00–17.00 Sun–Thu, 09.30–16.30 Fri, 10.00–17.00 Sat; admission adult/child 41/33NIS*) Complete with its very own Noah's Ark, the Biblical Zoo aims at preserving endangered and rare animals from across the world. The non-profit zoo concentrates mainly on animals from Israel's past, most especially those mentioned in the Bible.

LATRUN The area of Latrun most likely owes its name to the almost completely dilapidated remains of a **Crusader fortress** 'Le Toron des Chevaliers' (The Tower of the Knights), an integral part of the many battles that took place here during the Crusades. Latrun is an area of the Ayalon Valley that stretches between Tel Aviv and Jerusalem that, for hundreds of years, has formed one of the country's most important strategic routes. Running alongside today's route 1 and 15km outside the capital, there are several attractions worth making a pit stop for. Much of the fortress is still underground and awaiting excavation so tread with care as some areas can be unstable and dangerous. It is located behind the monastery.

The **Latrun Monastery** has, over recent decades, become known for its wine, its thriving vineyards sweeping up the valley to the doorstep of the beautiful building inhabited by monks of the French Trappist order. In 2006, the monastery shot into a different spotlight as the unlikely setting for the much-anticipated Roger Waters concert that attracted thousands of Pink Floyd fans from around the country. Opposite the monastery is the **Armoured Corps Museum** (*Yad La'Shiryon, Latrun;* ` 08 9246722; www.arcm-latrun.org.il;* ⊕ *08.30–16.30 Sun–Thu, 08.30–12.30 Fri, 09.00–16.00 Sat; admission adult/child 30/20NIS*), a British-built police fort used to control the passage between Tel Aviv and Jerusalem. After the British Mandate period, control of the fort passed to Arab forces, an act that resulted in a siege of Jerusalem during the 1948 Arab–Israeli War. After Israel declared independence, forces led by ex-Prime Minister Ariel Sharon stormed the stronghold, suffering two brutal and bloody defeats. Today the police fort and its environs act as a tank museum and memorial site.

Just up from the police station is the **Mini Israel Park** (` 08 9130000/10; www.minisrael.co.il;* ⊕ *summer 10.00–21.00 Sat–Thu; winter 10.00–18.00 Sat–Thu, 10.00–14.00 Fri; admission 69NIS*) where visitors can feel like Gulliver in the Holy Land. Impressive reconstructions of the country's most prolific religious, architectural and geographical places occupy an area designed to resemble the Star of David.

Getting there Buses 433, 434 and 414 from Jerusalem Central Bus Station will stop at the Hativah Sheva junction from which all sites are within walking distance (30mins/15NIS).

SOREQ CAVES The Soreq Stalactite Cave Nature Reserve (*Near Beit Shemesh;* ` 02 9911117; www.parks.org.il;* ⊕ *08.00–17.00 daily; admission adult/child 23/12NIS*) is unique in that its relatively small area (the cave measures 82m by 60m) is home to the vast majority of cave formations known throughout the world. As old as five million years, some of the formations measure up to 4m in length, occasionally meeting up with their stalagmite counterparts rising off the cave floor. A visit to the caves involves a guided tour and slide show. Photography is permitted only on Fridays when there are no tours.

Getting there The caves are located 2km east of Beit Shemesh. From Jerusalem buses 415 and 417 run hourly to Beit Shemesh from where you can take a taxi the final short stretch.

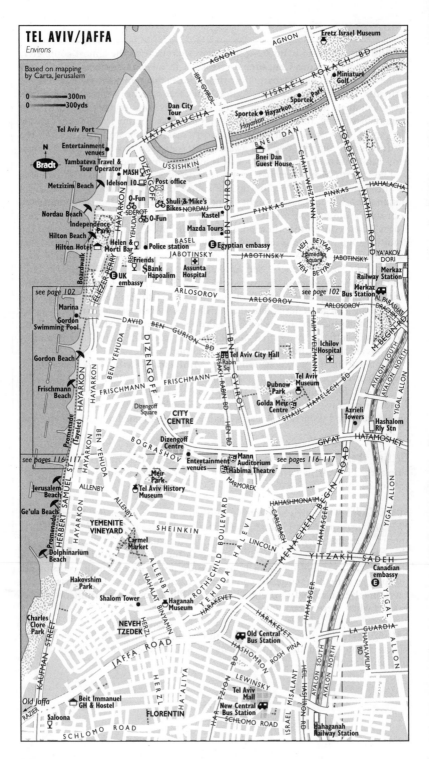

TEL AVIV/JAFFA

Environs

Based on mapping
by Carta, Jerusalem

0 ————300m
0 ————300yds

Eretz Israel Museum

AGNON

AGNON

IBN GVIROL

YISRAEL ROKACH BD

Miniature Golf

HATA'ARUCHA

Dan City Tour

Sportek Park

Sportek

Sportek Hayarkon

Hayarkon

MORDECHAI NAMIR ROAD

HAHALACHA

Tel Aviv Port

BNEI DAN

Entertainment venues

USSISHKIN

CHAIM WEIZMANN

PINKAS

Bnei Dan Guest House

Yambateva Travel & Tour Operator

MASH

DIZENGOFF

Post office

PINKAS

Metzizim Beach

Idelson 10

O-Fun

SDEROT YEHUDA

Shuli & Mike's Bikes

NORDAU

Kastel

IBN GVIROL

BE'IYAR

HEH

YA'AKOV DORI

Nordau Beach

O-Fun

NORDAU

Mazda Tours

HEH

BE'IYAR

Independence Park

BASEL

Hamedina Square

JABOTINSKY

Merkaz Railway Station

Hilton Beach

Helen & Morti Bar

Police station

JABOTINSKY

Egyptian embassy

Hilton Hotel

Friends

JABOTINSKY

Merkaz Bus Station

Boardwalk

ELIEZER PERRY

Bank Hapoalim

Assunta Hospital

AL PARASHAT DRACHIM

UK embassy

ARLOSOROV

ARLOSOROV

see page 102

M-BEGIN RD

see page 102

Marina

DAVID BEN GURION BD

ARLOSOROV

Gordon Swimming Pool

BEN YEHUDA

DIZENGOFF

CHAIM WEIZMANN

Ichilov Hospital

Tel Aviv City Hall

AYALON SOUTH

AYALON NORTH

YIGAL ALLON

Gordon Beach

Rabin Sq

IBN GVIROL

HAYARKON

FRISCHMANN

FRISCHMANN

Dubnow Park

Tel Aviv Museum

Frischmann Beach

FRISCHMANN

YITSHAK-RABIN-BD

Azrieli Towers

Dizengoff Square

CITY CENTRE

HEN-BD

Golda Meir Centre

SHAUL HAMELECH BD

Hashalom Rly Stn

Promenade (Tayelet)

BOGRASHOV

Dizengoff Centre

GIV'AT

HATAMOSHET

see pages 116–117

BEN YEHUDA

Entertainment venues

Mann Auditorium

see pages 116–117

Jerusalem Beach

ALLENBY

Meir Park

Habima Theatre

MARMOREK

HAYARKON

Ge'ula Beach

Tel Aviv History Museum

HASHASHMONA'IM

MENACHEM BEGIN ROAD

YIGAL ALLON

Promenade

HERBERT SAMUEL ST

ALLENBY

YEMENITE VINEYARD

SHEINKIN

ROTHSCHILD BOULEVARD

YEHUDA HALEVI

CARLEBACH

LINCOLN

YITZAKH SADEH

Dolphinarium Beach

Carmel Market

NAHALAT BINYAMIN

Canadian embassy

Hakovshim Park

Shalom Tower

Haganah Museum

YEHUDA HARAKEVET

HAMASGER

YIGAL ALLON

Charles Clore Park

NEVEH TZEDEK

HERZL

HARAKEVET

HARAKEVET

LA GUARDIA

KAUFMAN STREET

JAFFA ROAD

HERZL

Old Central Bus Station

HASHOMRON

ROSH PINA

AYALON SOUTH

AYALON NORTH

HAMA'APILIM BD

HA'ALIYA

LEWINSKY

Tel Aviv Mall

Old Jaffa

RAZIEL

Beit Immanuel GH & Hostel

Saloona

SCHLOMO ROAD

HERZL

FLORENTIN

New Central Bus Station

SCHLOMO ROAD

ISRAEL MISALANT

HEIL HAHANDASA

Hahaganah Railway Station

4

Tel Aviv-Jaffa

The black sheep of the family, **Tel Aviv** is seen as Israel's rebel. In a country of such profound historical importance, passionate religions, political struggles and strict traditions, Tel Aviv stands out and knows it. Where Jerusalem is proud of its biblical history, architectural beauty and devout religiousness, Tel Aviv's pride is found in the opposites. This colourfully loud and vibrant city has an almost hedonistic atmosphere, where the main concerns are what to wear, where to be seen and where to party.

Tel Aviv, whose name translates as 'Spring of Hill', is the second-largest city in Israel with an ever-growing population of currently 390,000. While Jerusalem is the capital, it is not recognised as such by much of the international community, and so Tel Aviv steps in to fill the shoes as the economic, financial and commercial capital. A recent boom in international business has seen the city flourish, a new international airport, seafront overlooked by large five-star hotels, a highly profitable diamond exchange and the emergence of modern high-rise buildings standing as testament to this. While few would describe Tel Aviv as beautiful, a closer look will reveal the world's largest collection of **Bauhaus buildings**, a pre-Nazi German architectural style, granting it UNESCO World Heritage status in 2004.

In a country steeped in centuries-old history, Tel Aviv has managed to make its mark on the country in just six decades. Today it epitomises the average Israeli. The fast-paced, hardworking and fun-loving way of life has drawn people from all over the country and abroad to make money and have plenty of fun spending it. While it may be easy for visitors to overlook Tel Aviv, using it as a gateway to the more traditional sights in Jerusalem, the Dead Sea and Galilee, a trip to Israel would most certainly be a biased one without a stop in this, the most Israeli of Israel's cities.

Merely a few kilometres down the coast from the cosmopolitan hub that is Tel Aviv, sits **Jaffa**, one of the most beautiful, charming and ancient places in Israel. Jaffa's Old City and port form the historic core of this predominantly Arab neighbourhood, its artists' houses, cobbled alleys, breathtaking views and old-worldly atmosphere having become a magnetic draw for visitors to the country. The once-thriving fishing port, in bygone days one of the most crucial seaports in the world, is today a tranquil area where small boats chug in and out of the harbour, old men sit patiently fishing and aromatic smells waft out of the countless restaurants. In 'modern' Jaffa the streets are abuzz with everyday hustle and bustle, the flea market, Middle Eastern eateries, mosques and Arabic culture providing a contrast with Tel Aviv so stark one would be forgiven for thinking they had crossed a border into another country.

While the town is undoubtedly steeped in charisma, crime rates tend to be higher than in neighbouring Tel Aviv so it is important to be aware of pickpocketing, especially at night. Violent crimes are rare but solo women travellers are not advised to wander the streets after dark, especially outside the Old City.

HISTORY

Modern Tel Aviv was officially founded by 66 Jewish families in 1909. The idea was to create a Jewish commuter suburb on the outskirts of Jaffa, the 4,000-year-old fortified port city located approximately 3km from Tel Aviv's centre. Jaffa was mentioned several times in the Bible but flourished during the 19th century when its city walls were built, trade markets established, its main mosque was erected and the great trunk road to Jerusalem constructed. It grew into a major trading port city through the Egyptian and Ottoman rules and after the opening of the Suez Canal in 1869 saw the appearance of vast cargo ships from Europe. The clock tower face was even set to European time so as to aid merchants arriving in the port. Yet it wasn't just trade that disembarked in Jaffa. Scores of early pilgrims trudged up and down the road to Jerusalem's holy sites and German Templar and American colonies were established near the Old City.

By 1914, the population had expanded to 40,000, 15,000 of whom were Jews and the city became the centre for waves of Jewish immigrants moving to the Holy Land until the creation of Tel Aviv. Following near abandonment during World War I Jaffa recovered to become an almost wholly Palestinian city with Tel Aviv housing the majority of the Jewish population. It flourished until the 1936–39 rebellion, which saw the closure of the once-prosperous port in favour of the new one in Tel Aviv. In 1948, Arab forces in Jaffa shelled nearby Tel Aviv, an attack quickly countered by Jewish forces who captured the Old City, poignantly two days before Israel's independence was declared. After Jaffa fell to the Jews in 1948 most of the 65,000 Palestinians left the city and in 1950 Jaffa was incorporated into the Municipality of Tel Aviv.

TOURIST INFORMATION

Tourist information centre Tel Aviv Promenade; 46 Herbert Samuel St (corner of 2 Geula St); ✆ 03 5166188; e tamia@tourism.gov.il; www.visitisrael.gov.il; ⊕ 09.30–17.30 Sun–Thu, 09.30–13.00 Fri; City Hall, 69 Ibn Gvirol St; ✆ 03 5218214 & 7 Mendele St; ✆ 03 5207600; ⊕ 08.00–16.30 Sun–Thu

LOCAL TOUR OPERATORS

For Bauhaus tours, see page 114.

Dan City Tour ✆ 03 6394444; e information@dan.co.il; www.dan.co.il; tickets 45NIS. Runs an open-top tourist sightseeing bus around Tel Aviv & Jaffa taking in the major sights from the port area to Jaffa's Old City. Buses run hourly (*Sun–Fri*) & it is possible to hop & off throughout the day. Audio information is in several languages. The tour begins at the Dan Bus Station on Hata'arucha Street but you can join at any point.
Egged Tours 59 Ben Yehuda St; ✆ 1700 707576; f 03 5272020; www.egged.co.il. Operates a system of well-run tours around Israel ranging from 1 day to over a week.

Mazada Tours 141 Ibn Gvirol St; ✆ 03 5444454; e mazada@mazada.co.il; *www.mazada.co.il* (see page 33).
Yambateva Travel and Tour Operator 305 Hayarkon St; ✆ 03 5430000; e info@yam-bateva.com; www.yam-bateva.com. Arrange tours within Israel departing from Tel Aviv, Jerusalem & Eilat as well as trips to Jordan from Eilat. Specialist tours include pilgrimage trips, desert adventures & archaeological tours. Can also book car rental & hotels.
Yarkon Tours 4 Bograshov St; ✆ 03 5179606; f 03 5176849; www.yarkon.co.il. Specialise in Jewish & Christian pilgrimage tours.

GETTING THERE

Tel Aviv forms the hub of Israel's transport network, with good-quality bus and/or train links to most places in the country.

The Tel Aviv Municipality has set up several free guided tours in English that are a great and cost-effective way to see some of the city's main sights. There is no need to reserve a spot in advance, just show up at the meeting point and join in.

1 Tel Aviv University: Art and Architecture 11.00 Mondays. Meeting point: Dyonon bookstore, university campus entrance at the junction of Haim Levanon and Einstein streets. The tour provides an introduction to the university's Israeli architecture including styles, international influences, history, environmental sculpture and landscape designs.

2 Bauhaus: 'The White City' (See page 114)

3 Tel Aviv by Night 20.00 Tuesdays. Meeting point: on the boulevard where Rothschild Boulevard and Hertzl Street meet. Incorporating a bit of everything, this tour details some of the city's history as well as shedding light on its restaurant, bar and café scene. It centres on the lively and hip southern Rothschild Boulevard and Nahalat Binyamin Street and is a great way to find out what's 'in' and trendy in the city that never sleeps.

4 Old Jaffa 09.30 Wednesdays. Meeting point: Clock tower, Yefet Street, Jaffa. The tour takes in the best of the quaint Old City of Jaffa including the flea market, cobbled alleyways, views of Tel Aviv from Hapigsa Gardens and the area's archaeological sites.

BUS Tel Aviv has two main bus stations: the **central bus station** (*106 Levinsky Rd; 03 6948888*) and **Merkaz Bus Station**, which is adjacent to the train station (both are often referred to as Arlosorov stations). Most buses depart from the central bus station although many of them will also stop at Merkaz Bus Station. Egged and Dan bus companies form the core of bus travel, Egged providing most of the long-distance services.

SHERUT Shared taxis leave from the central bus station to most major cities in the country (following regular bus routes) and will stop anywhere along the way to pick up or drop off passengers. *Sheruts* run on Shabbat.

ROUTES FROM TEL AVIV CENTRAL BUS STATION

To	Frequency	Bus number	Duration	Price
Jerusalem	25mins	405	1hr	17.70NIS
Eilat	1hr 30mins	394	4hrs	65NIS
Haifa HaCarmel	hourly	910	1hr 30mins	23NIS
Nazareth	5 daily	823	2hrs 40mins	36NIS
Kiryat Shmona	20mins	841/842/845	3hrs 30mins	53NIS
Katzrin	16.00	843	3hrs 50mins	51NIS
Tiberias	15mins	830/835/842	2hrs 30mins	44NIS
Tzfat	17.00	846	3hrs 20mins	51NIS
Ben Gurion Airport	20mins	475	30mins	11.70NIS
Golani Junction	15mins	830/835/841	2hrs 15mins	39NIS
Beer Sheva	30mins	370	1hr 30mins	13.70NIS

TRAIN Tel Aviv forms the centre of Israel's fairly limited train network and is an affordable, comfortable and convenient way of avoiding the coastal traffic. The city has four train stations running from south to north: HaHaganah, HaShalom, Merkaz (often referred to as Arlosorov) and Universita. All trains will stop at all stations. There are regular services to Nahariya (1hr 40mins/38NIS) which stops at Atlit (50mins/26NIS), Haifa Hof HaCarmel (55mins/26NIS), Haifa Bat Galim, Haifa Merkaz HaShmona, Haifa Lev HaMifratz, Haifa Hutzot HaMifratz and Akko (1hr 22mins/34NIS) along the way. A shorter line runs as far as Caesarea (which is in Binyamina), stopping at Herzliya (12mins/7.50NIS), Netanya and Hadera (25mins/20NIS). To get to and from Jerusalem (1½hrs/19.50NIS) you need to change in Beit Shemesh. Services south run as far as Beer Sheva (1½hrs/25.50NIS) and Dimona. Trains to Ben Gurion Airport (20mins/12.50NIS) run every half an hour 24 hours a day.

AIR Tel Aviv is home to Israel's only international airport, Ben Gurion (see page 35), which also operates domestic flights to Haifa and Eilat. **Israir** (↘ *03 7955777; www.israirairlines.com*) runs regular flights to both Haifa and Eilat for between 180NIS and 375NIS each way while **Arkia** (↘ *03 6902222; www.arkia.co.il;*) offers flights only to and from Eilat for approximately 200NIS each way.

GETTING AROUND

BUS Dan (*www.dan.co.il*) operates Tel Aviv's intra-city buses and fares around town cost 5.10NIS. The following bus routes run along most major streets and stop at the main attractions:

#4 Runs every five minutes from new central bus station up Allenby and Ben Yehuda streets.

#5 Runs every five minutes from new central bus station up Rothschild and Dizengoff streets to the Dizengoff Centre then turns right and goes down Nordau, Pinkas and Weizmann streets and finishes at the central train station.

#10 Runs every 15 minutes from the central train station along Arlozorov Street, turns left to go down the coast along Ben Yehuda, Herbert Samuel and Kaufman streets to Jaffa. It then weaves back through the Florentine area along Herzl Street to Rothschild Boulevard before turning back.

#11 Runs every 15 minutes down Dizengoff Street turning right onto Ben Gurion Boulevard. It then turns onto Ibn Gvirol Street before turning onto Arlosorov Street and on to the central train station.

CAR RENTAL Most car-rental agencies can be found along Hayarkon Street near the bottom of Frishman and Gordon streets. Parking in the city can be difficult and expensive and your car will be towed in the blink of an eye if you park illegally. Cars are not an ideal way to get around the city but by far the best option for exploring the country at large. You must be over 21 to rent a car anywhere in Israel.

✈ **Avis** 113 Hayarkon St; ↘ 03 5271752; f 03 5223649; www.avis.co.il; ⊕ 08.00–18.00 Sun–Thu, 08.00–14.00 Fri; Ben Gurion Airport; ↘ 03 9712315; ⊕ 24hrs

✈ **Budget** 99 Hayarkon St; ↘ 03 5245233; f 03 5245234; www.budget.co.il; ⊕ 08.00–18.00 Sun–Thu, 08.00–14.00 Fri; Ben Gurion Airport; ↘ 03 9712315; ⊕ 24hrs

✈ **Eldan** 114 Hayarkon St; ↘ 03 5271166; f 03 5271174; www.eldan.co.il; ⊕ 08.00–18.00 Sun–Thu, 08.00–13.00 Fri; Ben Gurion Airport; ↘ 03 9773400; ⊕ 24hrs

✈ **Hertz** 144 Hayarkon St; ↘ 03 5223332; www.hertz.co.il; ⊕ 08.00–18.00 Sun–Thu, 08.00–14.00 Fri; Ben Gurion Airport; ↘ 03 9772444; ⊕ 24hrs

✈ **Sixt** 122 Hayarkon St; ↘ 03 5244935; www.sixt.co.il; ⊕ 08.00–18.00 Sun–Fri; Ben Gurion

Beneath Tel Aviv's cosmopolitan, bustling streets lie the silent heroes of its creation. Almost without exception, the city's street names are dedicated to those who remain close to the hearts of Israelis and Jews the world over. As you explore the city, take the time to notice the street names; it's a great way to put some of the country's complex history into context.

Allenby Sir Edmund Henry Allenby (1861–1936) was a British World War I commander who is best known for his Middle East campaign. He battled the Turks in Palestine, capturing Gaza and Jerusalem in 1917. In 1918, he won the vicious battle on the plain of Meggido and later took Damascus and Aleppo.

Arlozorov Haim Arlozorov (1899–1933) was a Ukrainian-born Zionist who represented the *yishuv* at the League of Nations in Geneva and who rose to become head of the political party of the Jewish Agency. He was assassinated in 1933, two days before he was to negotiate the Ha'avara (transfer) agreement with the Nazi government.

Begin Menachem Begin (1913–92) was Prime Minister of Israel from 1977–83.

Ben-Gurion David Ben-Gurion (1886–1973) was Israel's first prime minister following the formation of an independent state in 1948 (see page 229).

Ben-Yehuda Eliezer Ben-Yehuda (1858–1922) was one of the first Zionists, and was responsible for reintroducing the Hebrew language as the spoken tongue of Israel.

Dizengoff Meir Dizengoff (1861–1936) was the first mayor of Tel Aviv from 1911 until his death in 1936.

Frischmann David Frischmann (1859–1922) was one of the first major writers of modern Hebrew literature. His most famous work is the *Bar Midbar* (1923), a series of fictional biblical tales.

Herzl Theodor Herzl (1860–1904) was the founder and first president of the World Zionist Organisation.

Ibn Gabirol Solomon Ibn Gabirol (1021–58) was a Hebrew poet and Jewish philosopher.

Jabotinsky Vladimir Evgenevich Jabotinsky (1880–1940) led the Revisionist Zionist Party and in 1920 organised and led the Hahaganah, a Jewish militia.

Namir Mordechai Namir (1897–1975) was a Knesset member, government minister, one of the heads of the Labor Zionist Movement and Mayor of Tel Aviv.

Rothschild (see page 155)

Samuel Sir Herbert Samuel (1870–1963) was the British High Commissioner for Palestine from 1920–25. He became the first Jew to govern the land in 2,000 years.

Shaul Hamelech Saul the King was the first king of the ancient Kingdom of Israel as recorded in the Old Testament and Koran. He reigned from c1020–1000BCE.

Weizmann Chaim Weizmann (1874–1952) was the first president of Israel from 1949–52, President of the World Zionist Organisation and founder of the Weizmann Institute of Science.

Rabin (see page 13)

Sadeh Yitzhak Sadeh (1890–1952) was Commander of the Palmach and one of the founding members of the Israel Defence Force.

Tel Aviv-Jaffa **GETTING AROUND**

4

Airport; ☎ 03 5244935; ⊕ 24hrs
🚗 Suncar 134 Hayarkon St; ☎ 03 5237017; f 03

5223828; www.suncar.co.il; ⊕ 08.45–17.30
Sun–Thu, 08.45–13.30 Fri

TAXI Tel Aviv has no shortage of taxis, except on Shabbat when the buses and trains stop and it can take a little longer to hail one. To order a taxi call **Kastel** (☎ *03 6993322*), **Ichilov** (☎ *03 6967070*) or **Hashekem** (☎ *03 5270404*).

SHERUT *Sherut* taxis (see page 44) operate along the main Dan bus routes and will have the same bus number in the front window. The fare is marginally lower than that of the buses and you can get on or off anywhere you choose. Routes 4, 5 and 16 (amongst others) also run on Shabbat. Inter-city *sherut* taxis to Jerusalem, Haifa, Eilat, Nazareth and all stops along the way leave regularly from the central bus station.

BICYCLE There are a few places in the city where you can rent a bicycle. Prices are usually around 40NIS per day but less if you hire them for longer.

O-Fun 245 Dizengoff St; ☎ 03 5442292 & 197 Ben Yehuda St; ☎ 03 5442292

Shuli and Mike Bikes 280 Dizengoff St; ☎ 03 5443392

🏠 WHERE TO STAY

🏠 **David Inter-Continental** (516 rooms) 12 Kaufman St; ☎ 03 7951111; f 03 7951112. . Renowned as being Tel Aviv's most prestigious & luxurious hotel. Located equidistant from Jaffa & central Tel Aviv, beautiful beachfront location & views, immaculate rooms & an indulgent breakfast. There are 3 restaurants in the lobby including the French gourmet **Aubergine** (open 12.00–23.00 Sat–Thu). **$$$$$**

🏠 **Hilton Tel Aviv** (582 rooms) Independence Park; ☎ 03 5202222; f 03 5272711; www1.hilton.com. Great seafront location just north of the marina, outdoor salt-water swimming pool, spa, 2 restaurants & cocktail bar combine with the high standards & service of the international Hilton chain. **$$$$$**

🏠 **Isrotel Tower** (90 rooms) 78 Hayarkon St; ☎ 03 5113636; f 03 5113666; www.isrotel.co.il. This cylindrical 30-storey hotel is one of the most eye-catching buildings in the city. Located in the heart of the city centre it affords great views of the sea & is within walking distance of most attractions. Its rooftop swimming pool is fabulous, but perhaps not if you're not a fan of heights. **$$$$$**

🏠 **Sheraton Moriah** (335 rooms) 155 Hayarkon St; ☎ 03 5216666; www.sheraton.co.il. Classic elegance & considerably better than its sister hotel in Jerusalem. Seafront location on the edge of the marina. Facilities include an outdoor swimming pool, balconies in all rooms, a spa & a 17th-floor restaurant. **$$$$$**

🏠 **Center Hotel** (56 rooms) 2 Zamenhof St; ☎ 03 5266100; e reservations@atlashotels.co.il; www.atlas.co.il. Fashionable & trendy boutique hotel in Bauhaus architecture. Fresh, minimalist décor with each room sporting a different painting by up-and-coming young artists. Located on the southeast corner of Dizengoff Sq opposite the **Cinema Hotel** under the same ownership (although staff there are decidedly less friendly). Breakfast is included & internet & free bicycle rental are offered. **$$$**

🏠 **Deborah Hotel** (63 rooms) 87 Ben Yehuda St; ☎ 03 5278282; e reservation@deborah-hotel.co.il; www.deborah-hotel.co.il. Rooms are spacious, well priced & well equipped, if a little old-fashioned. All rooms come complete with a sea view, AC, bath, TV, safe & fridge & kosher breakfast is included. **$$$**

🏠 **Miguel Hotel and Bistro** (21 rooms) 88 Hayarkon St; ☎ 03 5107744; www.miguel.co.il. Resembling the elegant, family-run hotels of France & Italy, Miguel's abounds in character & finesse. On the seafront, it is 10mins from the centre. Rooms all have AC & TV. A gourmet French-style restaurant & bar (⊕ 12.00–17.00 Sun–Thu) serves fresh fish & meat dishes. **$$$**

🏠 **Prima Tel Aviv** (60 rooms) 105 Hayarkon St; ☎ 03 5206666; e primatlv@prima.co.il; www.prima.co.il. Tel Aviv's representative in this nationwide chain of reputable hotels is located on the seafront in front of Frishman beach, 15mins' walk from the city centre. The recently renovated rooms are elegant, breezy & modern & have the complete range of facilities. Breakfast is included & there is a swish bar & lounge area. $$$

🏠 **Bnei Dan Guest House (HI)** (45 rooms) 36 Bnei Dan St; ✆ 03 5441748; e telaviv@iyha.org.il; www.iyha.org.il. A member of the Hostelling International group this large hostel is located near the Yarkon Park & river. Immaculately clean rooms have AC & bathrooms but lack imagination & character. Kosher breakfast is included. Often frequented by large groups. *Dorms (70NIS) & private rooms available.* $$

🏠 **Gordon Inn Hotel and Guesthouse** (27 rooms) 17 Gordon St; ✆ 03 5238239/052 8666158; e gordonin@gmail.com. A welcoming & friendly little guesthouse located a few mins' walk from the beach. Double rooms (shared bathroom or en suite) have TV, coffee facilities & are pleasantly decorated & extremely clean. Guests receive a 55NIS voucher for a meal at La Mer Restaurant on the beachfront as well as 10% discount in the Gordon Inn pub next door. $$

🏠 **Hayarkon 48 Hostel** (36 rooms) 48 Hayarkon St; ✆ 03 5168989; e info@hayarkon48.com; www.hayarkon48.com. This is undoubtedly Tel Aviv's best hostel & is unsurprisingly often booked to capacity. Located a few mins' walk from the beach, this immaculately clean hostel offers a fabulous array of services & facilities including a well-equipped kitchen, lively lounge complete with pool table & TV, free safe, breakfast & a breezy rooftop balcony overlooking the Mediterranean. *Dorms available (65NIS) with discounts on bookings of over a week.* $$

🏠 **Maxim Hotel** (71 rooms) 86 Hayarkon St; ✆ 03 5173721; f 03 5173726. A rare budget option with sea views, this 3-star hotel has a fantastic location. Comfortable, well-equipped rooms are exceptionally well priced. Israeli breakfast, laundry service & wireless internet in all rooms. $$

🏠 **Mugraby Hostel** (14 rooms) 30 Allenby St; ✆ 03 5102443; e mugraby-hostel.com; www.mugraby-hostel.com. Simple backpacker hostel located above a newly renovated internet café. The hostel is clean but in need of a little tlc. Basic

JAFFA

🏠 **Beit Immanuel Guest House and Hostel** 8 Auerbach St; ✆ 03 6821459; www.beitimmanuel.org. This cosy & family-oriented pilgrim's guesthouse has captured the serenity & atmosphere of Old Jaffa with its leafy garden & sunny balcony. The décor is a little old-fashioned but seems somehow apt for

single-sex & mixed dorms available as well as double rooms with or without en-suite facilities & AC. Facilities include a kitchen, free lockers & lounge. *Single-sex & mixed dorms (65NIS).* $$

🏠 **Sky Hostel** (23 rooms) 34 Ben Yehuda St; ✆ 03 6200044; e sky@sky1hostel.com; www.sky1hostel.com. Great location 10mins' walk from the Dizengoff Centre & 3mins from the beach. Rooms are basic & functional but do the job. A simple breakfast is included in the price & there is a small kitchen. *Dorms available (55NIS).* $$

🏠 **Sun City** (18 rooms) 42 Allenby St; ✆ 03 5177913; e suncity1@netvision.net.il; www.suncity.co.il. Located on the corner of Yona Hanavi St, 10mins' walk from the popular Rothschild Bd. Despite rooms being available for rent on an hourly basis, the hotel is clean & comfortable, if a little plain. Rooms with balconies can be noisy when Allenby St's bars swing into action. $$

🏠 **The Bell Hotel** (23 rooms) 50 Hayarkon St; ✆ 03 5174291; e hotelbell@barak.net.il; www.bellhotel-telaviv.com. The phrase 'don't judge a book by its cover' seems appropriate for the Bell Hotel, one of Tel Aviv's oldest establishments. While the exterior leaves a little to be desired, the inside is charming, modern & tastefully decorated. Rooms are fresh, bright & beautifully furnished & offer fantastic value for money. Balconies with sea views are available but are noisier than those set further back. Breakfast, free internet & laundry services available. $$

🏠 **Sub Kuch Milega** (16 beds) 22 Hamashbir St; ✆ 03 6813412; e sub_kuch_milega@yahoo.com. Attracting the young, bohemian backpacker types this 4-storey guesthouse & restaurant (🕐 12.00–late) is as laidback as they come. Facilities include a bar, gaming area, laundry machine, free internet access, pool table, rooftop lounge & bicycle hire. The Indian cuisine is authentic & filling & interestingly there are no fixed prices – you pay only what you feel it is worth. Big screens & a party atmosphere can be found on the roof terrace in summer. *Dorms (80NIS) & dbl rooms available.* $

this part of the city but rooms are clean & comfortable. *Dorms & private rooms available.* $$

🏠 **Old Jaffa Hostel** (29 rooms) 8 Olei Zion St; ✆ 03 6822370. Oozing Old Jaffa's rich character, the hostel is located within an ancient stone house just mins from the harbour & beach. Facilities include a roof terrace with wonderful views of the sea & cobbled streets below, TV room, cosy kitchen,

internet access & bicycle rental. *Dorms available (55NIS). Studio with kitchenette, TV & AC (300NIS).*

✗ WHERE TO EAT

In recent years Tel Aviv has managed to well and truly insert itself on the international cuisine map and today prides itself on its culinary prowess and thriving restaurant scene. In total contrast to Jerusalem, few restaurants are kosher and all are open straight through Shabbat, which is generally their busiest time. Prices in Tel Aviv seem to increase by the day and you can expect to pay European prices for a meal in any restaurant or indeed café throughout the city. The standard is also very high and you will rarely leave dissatisfied, although the customer service often leaves a little to be desired. Mediterranean-influenced food is the most popular, generally cooked in a gourmet, fusion style, but the Israelis are also big meat-lovers so there are plenty of South American steakhouses too.

The best budget options are the Israeli staples of hummus, falafel, *shawarma* and *sabich* but if you've had enough of chickpeas for a few days there are also plenty of small pizza places (although some are decidedly shabby so choose carefully), sandwich bars, *burekas* bakeries and cheaper-end restaurants. Most bars and pubs also serve cheap snacks for a late-night meal.

✗ **'2C'** 49th floor, Round Azrieli Tower; ☎ 03 6081990; ⏰ 12.00–midnight Sun–Thu; kosher. This rather unimaginatively named restaurant invites you to 'feast at the top of the world', & from the top of the Azrieli Observatory (see page 109) that's exactly how it will feel. While prices are steep, you pay for good Mediterranean gourmet food & an utterly fabulous view (make sure you get a table by the window). The business lunch (79NIS) is a great option for those who can't quite run to the evening prices. $$$$$

✗ **Rafael** 87 HaYarkon St; ☎ 03 5226464; ⏰ 12.00–15.00 & 19.00–late daily. This is often considered Tel Aviv's best restaurant producing food cooked by Israel's best chef. The chic restaurant is located inside the Dan Hotel & sports a rustic French-style menu infused with Moroccan spices & a touch of Middle Eastern. Great sea views so be sure to reserve a seat by the window. $$$$$

✗ **El Gaucho** 20 Rothschild Bd; ☎ 03 5104777; ⏰ 12.00–midnight Sun–Thu, 12.00–15.00 Fri, 20.00–midnight Sat; kosher. Part of a nationwide chain of Argentinian steakhouses that have managed to become commercial without losing quality. The rump steak is highly recommended. $$$$

✗ **Gilly's** Hangar 15, Tel Aviv Port; ☎ 03 6057777; ⏰ 10.00–late daily. The once ultra-trendy Jerusalem restaurant is now the ultra-trendy Tel Aviv restaurant & is one of the most popular port eateries. Their all-day breakfasts are one of the key attractions where 60NIS will get you a choice of

meats, eggs, salads & even seafood. A set lunch (85NIS) is a good way to try some of the fresh seafood, grilled meats & fancy creations if you're on a slightly tighter budget. $$$$

✗ **Max Brenner** 45 Rothschild Bd; ☎ 03 5604570; www.maxbrenner.com; ⏰ 09.00–late Sun–Thu, 08.00–late Fri/Sat. Chocolate is the name of the game at Israel's sweetest restaurant. It has become one of the country's most popular exports, making chocolate waves in the US & Australia. Outlandish, gooey recipes have been created that are rich & calorie-laden but any sweet tooth's dream come true. A good selection of salads, sandwiches, chicken dishes, pasta & crêpes form the savoury menu, but be sure to leave room for dessert. Mains $$$; dessert $$$$

✗ **Pastis** 73 Rothschild Bd; ☎ 03 6202586; ⏰ 12.00–01.00 Sun–Thu, 10.30–01.00 Fri/Sat. Elegant French cuisine served in comfortable, unpretentious surroundings. Fresh fish, juicy meats & rich desserts form the core of the menu. Set lunch meals are fantastic value for money & include 3 courses & drinks. $$$$

✗ **Yakimono** 19 Rothschild Bd; ☎ 03 5175171/2; www.yakimono.com; ⏰ 12.00–01.30 daily. Undoubtedly the plushest, trendiest Japanese restaurant & sushi bar in the city (with the exception of its sister branch located inside the Tel Aviv Hilton). Skilled Japanese chefs show off their slicing skills while preparing fresh sashimi & delicate sushi. The décor is minimalist & there is an impressively stocked bar. The afternoon set menu (12.00–18.00) is a more affordable way to experience this otherwise extremely pricey establishment. $$$$

✖ **Cantina** 71 Rothschild Bd; ✆ 03 6205051; 🕐 12.00–late Mon–Sat, 19.00–late Sun. Traditional, well-priced Italian fare including a big array of pasta dishes, fresh pizzas & pricier fish meals. $$$

✖ **Indira** 4 Shaul Hamelech St; ✆ 03 6954437; 🕐 12.00–midnight daily. Considered Tel Aviv's best Indian restaurant. The menu includes all the traditional, spicy favourites served within funky, Indian décor. $$$

✖ **Miguel Hotel and Bistro** (see page 103)

✖ **Moses** 35 Rothschild Bd; ✆ 03 5664949; 🕐 12.00–04.00 daily. This ultra-trendy restaurant has become one of the 'in' crowd's favourite haunts, & a glimpse at their menu explains why. Described as modern American cuisine, it jazzes up the simple hamburger & gets creative with sandwiches. $$$

✖ **Giraffe Noodle Bar** 49 Ibn Gvirol St; ✆ 03 6916294; 🕐 12.00–01.00 daily. Noodles from all over the world converge in this trendy, laidback, quick-eat bar. They have a range of rice, dumplings & sushi but it's the noodles that give it its reputation. The French-style desserts are also highly recommended. $$

✖ **Orna and Ella** 33 Sheinkin St; ✆ 03 6204753; 🕐 10.00–midnight Sun–Fri, 11.00–midnight Sat. Easy to find by the queues of young Tel Avivians waiting their turn inside one of the city's most well-known & long-lasting café/restaurants. There are plenty of vegetarian options including a selection of quiches & sandwiches, & they serve great coffee. Meals are light so not the place to go for a big slap-up dinner. $$

✖ **Sandwich bars** Ben Gurion Bd, Rothschild Bd (southern end); 🕐 08.00–23.00. Made-to-order sandwiches, cheap sushi, coffee & breakfast bars have popped up along Tel Aviv's wide, leafy boulevards & have become the 'in' place to see & be seen. $$

✖ **Shalvata** Tel Aviv Port; ✆ 03 4551279; 🕐 10.00–late Sun–Thu, 09.00–late Fri/Sat. This relaxed & comfortable café serves a varied selection of light meals, tapas, salads, sandwiches & desserts. Tables, lounge chairs & sun umbrellas have been scattered across the sand allowing for relaxing afternoons, while at night the music is turned up full volume & the place springs to life. $$

✖ **Sub Kuch Milega** (see page 104)

JAFFA

Jaffa's restaurants are known for their freshly caught fish and Middle Eastern-influenced dishes. The port area is teeming with good restaurants of varying price so have an early evening stroll around and see what catches your eye. There are also several small restaurants nestled into the ancient buildings around Kedumim Square which, come summer, lay tables outside.

✖ **Cordelia Restaurant** ✆ 03 5184668; 🕐 12.00–15.00 & 19.00–midnight Mon–Sat. A rustically romantic place housed in a Crusader-era building where chandeliers hang from the vaulted ceiling. The food is presented with as much flair & class as it is cooked with. Along with the Yaffa Bar and Noa Bistro, it is under the direction of nationally famed Israeli TV chef, Nir Zook A real treat & the most luxurious of the 3. $$$$$

✖ **Margaret Tayar's** 4 Retzif Ha'aliya Hashniya, St; ✆ 03 6824741; 🕐 Oct–May 13.00–19.00 Mon–Sat; Jun–Sep 12.00–16.00 & 19.00–midnight Mon–Fri, 12.00–19.00 Sat. This is the quintessential Jaffa fish restaurant. Its freshly caught fish & Middle Eastern-influenced home cooking have seen it rise high in the ranks of Israel's best restaurants. Visiting in summer is particularly recommended as the covered outdoor seating offers fabulous views of Tel Aviv's glittering coast. Margaret Tayar does all the cooking herself & makes sure her guests never go home hungry. $$$$

✖ **Yoe'ezer Wine Bar** 2 Ish Habira St; ✆ 03 6839115; 🕐 13.00–01.00 daily. Fine wines, delicate liquors & rich delicacies are the signatures of this classy yet slightly pretentious wine bar. Nestled in an ancient Crusader building it has a prize-winning wine list with patés, cheese & bread platters, & oysters forming the appetiser menu. Mains include veal tartar with truffles, beef bourguignon & prime rib. Located off Yefet St opposite Clock Tower Sq. $$$$

✖ **Noa Bistro** 14 Hatzorfim St; ✆ 03 5189720; 🕐 09.30–late Sun–Thu, 08.30–late Sat/Sun. More laidback than Cordelia's, with unique décor, an interesting menu and relaxed atmosphere. The breakfast is certainly a highlight. $$$

✖ **Saloona** 17 Tirtza St; ✆ 03 5181719; 🕐 21.00–late daily. Slightly difficult to find down a small road behind a big metal gate — look for the bouncer sitting outside. Funky lounge bar with

unique modern décor. While bar staff are officious & the food mediocre, the overall ambience is cool & trendy & there is a pleasant outside courtyard. $$
✗ **Said el Abu Lafia Bakery** 7 Yeffet St; ☎ 03 6834958; ⊕ 08.00–22.00 Mon–Sat. This was Jaffa's first bakery, opened in 1880 & remains today one of the country's most famous & well-loved snack shops. Arabic-style pizza, pitas, fluffy

burekas, freshly baked breads & sticky *baklava* are cheap, delicious & filling. There are plenty of bakeries around so make sure you find the right one. $
✗ **Yaffa Bar** (*Simchat HaZchuchit, off 30 Yefet St;* ☎ 03 5184668; ⊕ 18.00–late daily) is relaxed & comfortable with big, funky sofas, indoor & outdoor seating areas & a good selection of reasonably priced bar foods & snacks. $

CAFÉS

Café culture is huge in Tel Aviv and come Friday morning every seat in the city will be full with chic Tel Avivians sipping cappuccinos, wearing big sunglasses and soaking up the sun. You don't have to look very far to find a decent café serving good-quality coffee, Israeli breakfast (eggs, salad, bread, muesli, fresh fruit and yoghurt) and a range of salads and sandwiches. The biggest concentrations can be found along the sides of Rabin Square and along Ibn Gvirol Street, down the length of Rothschild Boulevard and along Sheikin and Bograshov streets.

🍽 **Arcafe** 31 Rothschild Bd; ☎ 03 5660259; 35 Basel St; 03 5467001; ⊕ 07.00–midnight daily. Branches of this popular chain are dotted all over the city. Their delicate pastries, fresh baguettes & sweets are what pull the crowds.
🍽 **Café Hillel** 65 Rothschild Bd, ☎ 03 5288666/777; ⊕ 07.00–01.00 Sun–Thu, 07.00–Shabbat Fri, end of Shabbat–01.00 Sat. Ideally situated for people-watching on Rothschild Bd, you'll be lucky to get a seat on weekends. Part of an extremely successful nationwide chain. A selection of sandwiches, pies, quiches & cakes is available for around 25NIS each.
🍽 **Café Jo** 130 Dizengoff St; ☎ 03 5272533; ⊕ 24hrs daily. Located on the corner with Gordon St, this is a great place to sit outside & watch the world go by.
🍽 **Idelson 10** 252 Ben Yehuda St; ☎ 03 5444154; ⊕ 07.30–midnight Sun–Fri. Located on the corner with Yermiahu St, this is the place to enjoy a quiet cup of tea or coffee & some fabulous homemade baked goods. The menu is much simpler than other

cafés but the cakes & chilled ambience are what the regulars come here for.
🍽 **Nina** 29 Shabazi St; ☎ 03 5161767; ⊕ 08.00–midnight Sun–Thu, 08.00–17.00 Fri. Catering to the newest trend in Tel Aviv – organic food – this café is a vegetarian's delight. It's a small & cosy place that attracts the nouveaux bohemian crowd.
🍽 **Suzana** 9 Shabazi St; ☎ 03 5177580; ⊕ 10.30–01.00 daily. Relaxed café in the heart of the Neve Tzedek neighbourhood just along from the Suzanne Dellal Centre. It has a shady terrace out front where you can enjoy the Iraqi-style foods including stuffed vegetables & *kube*.
🍽 **Tika** 41 Sheinkin St; ☎ 03 5284997; ⊕ 07.30–midnight Sun–Thu, 07.30–20.00 Fri. Rustic & comfortable, this is one of the most fashionable cafés along Sheinkin St without the pretention of some of its neighbours. A small wooden balcony provides the perfect stance for people-watching while you enjoy an iced coffee & sandwich.

ENTERTAINMENT AND NIGHTLIFE

FESTIVALS

Taste of the City (Ta'am Ha'ir) (May), Hayarkon Exhibition Centre. The city's best restaurants cook up and serve their finest dishes for 20NIS each in this festival of food. A true culinary bonanza.

Gay Pride Parade Rabin Square. With markedly more success than the Jerusalem event, Tel Aviv's gay pride is a fun and raucous procession attended by thousands.

BARS While in most countries it is easy to differentiate between a bar and a nightclub, in Tel Aviv the line seems to have become a little blurry. Come 01.00

Hummus and falafel are a godsend to those on a budget or those who simply want to savour the staple foods of the Middle East. Tel Aviv is teeming with small, cheap restaurants and kiosks selling freshly cooked falafel, pita, hummus, salads, *shwarma* and *sabich* but the following are particularly recommended:

✖ **Humus Shlomo** HaCarmel Market; ⏱ 08.00–14.30 Sun–Fri. Age-old hummus hideaway in the depths of the HaCarmel Market – ask any vendor to point you in the right direction. $$

✖ **Abu Hassan (Ali Karavan)** 1 Dolphin St; ☏ 03 6820387 & 14 Shivtai St; ☏ 03 6828355 ⏱ 07.45–14.45 Sun–Fri. Renowned as the best hummus in the Tel Aviv area, these rudimentary eateries are packed day in & day out. Hummus is the extent of the menu, but that's all you need. $

✖ **Falafel HaKosem (The Wizard)** 174 HaNevi'im St; ☏ 03 5252033; ⏱ 10.00–20.00 Sun–Thu, 10.00–15.00 Fri. This is the best falafel you will find in Tel Aviv. Be prepared to queue but expect rare customer service from the lively owner. *Shawarma*, schnitzel & *sabich* also served. Falafel $

✖ **Haj Kahil Shawarma** Clock Tower Sq, Jaffa; ⏱ 09.00–midnight daily. Turkey, beef & lamb *shawarma* you can eat safe in the knowledge they haven't been sitting there all week. Great fillings to go on top. $

✖ **Mashwesha** 40 Pinsker St; ☏ 03 6293796; ⏱ 11.00–23.00 Sun–Thu, 10.30–17.00 Fri, 12.00–23.00 Sat. Rudimentary little eatery just off Bograshov St; get there early before the hot, chunky hummus runs out. $

✖ **Shuk Bezalel Falafel** Bezalel Market, King George St; ⏱ 08.00–20.00 Sun–Thu, 08.00–16.00 Fri. Located in the grotty Bezalel Market, this is one of the oldest falafel stalls in town & has had plenty of practice getting it right. Fill your own pita with toppings of your choice. Falafel $

Stalls on the corner of **Dizengoff and Frishman streets** are open all day, some selling *sabich* while others have stuck to the traditional falafel.

dance fever will have overtaken most bars and there will be people packed into every space bopping away. Bars tend to get going late and stay open until the last person staggers out.

♀ **Armadillo** 51 Ahad Haam St; ☏ 03 6205503; ⏱ 18.00–02.00 Sun–Thu, 20.00–03.00 Fri, 19.00–03.00 Sat. Casual, neighbourhood bar. This is the place to go for a few drinks, some good, unpretentious food & chat with friends.

♀ **Erlich** Tel Aviv Port; ☏ 03 5466728; ⏱ 21.30–late daily. Chic, trendy bar, this is the place where young Israelis strut their stuff & the barmen are straight off the pages of *GQ* magazine.

♀ **Friends** 186 Ben Yehuda St; ☏ 054 8035757; ⏱ 20.00–late daily. One of the most popular places to go to meet members of the opposite sex. Dark & noisy it resembles more of a club but is a great late-night alternative to one.

♀ **Helen and Morti Bar** 196 Ben Yehuda St; ☏ 0772177766 (no area code); ⏱ 19.00–late daily. The new kid on the block, this is a comfortable, neighbourhood-type bar where anything goes. Lively music, a friendly atmosphere & plenty

of flowing drinks make it a good option.

♀ **MASH** 275 Dizengoff St; ☏ 03 6051007; www.mash.co.il; ⏱ 17.00–04.00 daily. MASH has been attracting sports buffs & expats for over 25 years & while it can get decidedly rowdy during televised sporting events is a far cry from the rest of the city's glitzy, chrome-decorated bars. Check their website for upcoming sporting fixtures.

♀ **Mike's Place** 86 Herbert Samuel St; ☏ 054 9292551; ⏱ 16.00–late daily. Although from the outside it may look better suited to a Costa del Sol holiday resort, the inside actually has quite a lot of charisma. It hit international headlines when it was the target of a suicide bombing in 2003 but was subsequently rebuilt. It is a great place to see live sporting events & they have live music most nights of the week.

♀ **Molly Bloom's** 32 Mendele St; ☏ 03 5221558; www.molly-blooms.com; ⏱ 16.00–late Sat–Thu,

12.00–late Fri. Eternally popular, Tel Aviv's first Irish pub is a little rough around the edges but manages it in a charming kind of way. Not a lot of seating room on weekends. Beers include draught Guinness & Kilkenny. Selection of good, simple pub foods.

♀ **Pola Bar** 22 Ben Gurion Bd; ✆ 054 2992227; ⊕ 21.00–late daily. Dark, 2-storey, 'pick-up' style bar that has been a constant on the Tel Aviv bar scene for years now (you might even spot the odd Israeli celebrity). Music tends to lean more towards rock & grunge than pop.

♀ **Silon** 89 King George St; ✆ 03 6200053; ⊕ 18.00–04.00 Sun–Thu, 20.00–05.00 Fri/Sat. Small, friendly bar at the northern end of King George St. Better suited to drinking than dancing (there isn't room anyway), it is unpretentious, welcoming & fun.

NIGHTCLUBS AND LIVE MUSIC Israelis have a penchant for hardcore trance music, and raves and one-off parties are big business, although in the city centre you're more likely to find a mixture of rock, techno, dance and plenty of 1980s hits. Tel Avivians have a lot of partying stamina (mainly because of the small amount of alcohol they consume) and go out late, so don't even consider a nightclub before midnight. Live music clubs range from rock to alternative to South American drums to jazz and R&B. Admission charges tend to vary depending on who's playing.

☆ **Café Barzilay** 13 HaRachav St; ✆ 03 6878090; ⊕ 21.00–late daily; admission 20–80NIS. Small, alternative club featuring live performances of Israeli rock & international DJs. More comfortable than some of the big beasts of the nightclub scene.

☆ **Goldstar Zappa** 24 Raul Wallenberg St; ✆ 03 7674646; ⊕ daily for evening performances; admission 50–150NIS. One of the city's leading live music venues, it hosts Israeli & international artists covering a wide spectrum of music genres.

☆ **HaOman** 15 Abarbanel St; ✆ 03 6813636; ⊕ 23.00–late daily; admission 70–140NIS. This is the younger sibling of the immensely popular HaOman club in Jerusalem. Equally popular in Tel Aviv, this is the place to blow your budget in one evening (drinks are exorbitant) & have a hell of a time doing it.

☆ **Shablul Jazz** Hangar 13, Tel Aviv Port; ✆ 03 5461891; ⊕ 20.00–late daily; admission free–80NIS. Swanky jazz bar with regular jam sessions & open mic nights as well as an impressive wine list & gourmet menu.

☆ **The Barbie** 40 Salame Rd; ✆ 03 5188123; admission varies on performer. This is the place to see big-name rock musicians & bands in concert. The bunker-like club is generally packed with crowds of eccentrically dressed youngsters spilling onto the street.

☆ **The Fifth Dimension** Tel Aviv Port; ✆ 03 6024559; www.mimad.co.il; ⊕ 22.00–late daily; admission 50NIS. Aptly located in one of the port's big hangars, this is a sweaty, noisy, pumping club that has been host to bands such as The Prodigy. The nearby **Hangar 11** is also home to big names when they come to town.

CINEMAS The **Tel Aviv Cinematheque** (*Ha'arba'a St;* ✆ *03 6060800; admission 35NIS*) shows an arty selection of films, ranging from classics to avant-garde to experimental pieces. Annual film festivals are shown so check at the box office for upcoming events. The cinema is often at the centre of Israeli debate thanks to its decision to show politically sensitive films. For new releases and blockbusters (subtitled in Hebrew) try the **Dizengoff Cinema** (*Ground Floor, Dizengoff Centre;* ✆ *03 6200485; admission 35NIS*) or **Ravhen Movie Theatre** (*Dizengoff Sq;* ✆ *03 5282288; admission 35NIS*).

PERFORMING ARTS Theatre has had a long and rich history in Tel Aviv and even today still enjoys regular sell-out performances. The **Habima Theatre** (*Habima Sq, Tarshat Av;* ✆ *03 6295555; www.habima.co.il*) is not only Israel's national theatre but the one that has made the greatest contribution to Israeli and Jewish theatrical culture over the past century. It was founded in 1918 in Moscow and relocated to Tel Aviv in 1931 and today comprises 80 actors who perform four plays daily.

Plays are in Hebrew but there is simultaneous English translation available. The **Cameri Theatre** (*Golda Meir Centre, 19 Shaul HaMelech Av;* ✆ *03 6060900;* e *ifat@cameri.co.il; www.cameri.co.il*) also offers English translation and has a good website for upcoming events. The smaller **Beit Lessin** (*101 Dizengoff St;* ✆ *03 7255333; www.lessin.co.il*) has performances most weeks although mostly in Hebrew, while the **Tzavta** (*30 Ibn Gvirol St;* ✆ *03 6950156*) swings between avant-garde theatre performances, Israeli folk music nights and classical performances (Hebrew only). **Tmuna** (*8 Shontzino St;* ✆ *03 5611211;* e *kupa@tmu-na.org.il; www.tmu-na.org.il*) is a small performing arts centre, where you can sit back with a drink and watch up-and-coming young musicians, actors, dancers and singers. In Jaffa, the **Arab-Hebrew Theatre** (*10 Mifratz Shlomo St;* ✆ *03 5185563;* e *info@arab-hebrew-theatre.org.il; www.arab-hebrew.theatre.org.il*) is housed inside an ancient stone building and comprises two groups that that produce plays in both Hebrew and Arabic.

The **Suzanne Dellal Centre** (*6 Yehi'eli St;* ✆ *03 5105656; www.suzannedellal.org.il*) is the country's foremost dance centre and home of the nationally acclaimed Bat-Sheva Dance Group. Check their website for upcoming shows and ticket booking. The **Israel Ballet** (✆ *03 6046610; www.iballet.co.il*) company also has regular performances of the great classics.

For classical music the **Mann Auditorium** (*1 Huberman St;* ✆ *03 6211777; www.hatarbut.co.il*) is home to the world-renowned **Israeli Philarmonic Orchestra** while the **New Israel Opera** now performs at the **Tel Aviv Performing Arts Centre** (*19 Shaul Hamelech Bd;* ✆ *03 6927777; www.israel-opera.co.il*). There are also regular classical music performances at the **Felicja Blumental Music Centre and Library** (*26 Bialik St;* ✆ *03 6201185; www.fbmc.co.il*).

SHOPPING

Tel Aviv is a shopper's paradise and pretty much anything you're looking for can be found in the city's malls, shopping streets, boutiques and markets. For more mainstream shops, the huge **Dizengoff** and **Azrieli centres** (see page 113) are the places to head to, while the funky **Sheikin Street** (see page 118) offers a range of one-of-a-kind boutiques and a variety of shoe shops. And if it's shoes and boots you're after, **Dizengoff Street** is teeming with a rather strange combination of cheap and expensive shoe shops and a gaudy selection of wedding dresses. At the other end of town, **Allenby Street** is a fun, if rather shabby street of cheap shoes and clothes although you might have to look a bit harder for the good stuff. Where Allenby Street meets the seafront is the plush **Opera Tower Shopping Centre** (*1 Allenby St;* ✆ *03 510796;* ⊕ *10.00–22.00 daily*). For a totally different experience, the **Carmel Market** (see page 119) is a feast of super-cheap clothes, home wares, fresh produce and sweets and is a must-see in the city. Souvenir shopping can be slightly harder in Tel Aviv and one of the best places to visit is the small **Spring** shop (*65 Ben Yehuda St;* ✆ *03 5223759*) which sells a good selection of AHAVA Dead Sea products as well as nice gift ideas, souvenirs, novelty T-shirts and postcards. Alternatively, the twice-weekly **Nahalat Binyamin Market** (see page 119) has a great selection of arts and crafts and it is always possible to pick up a bargain or two at Jaffa's **flea market** (see page 123).

BOOKSHOPS There are plenty of big chain stores and small secondhand shops selling Hebrew and English books as well as books in French, German and Russian.

Bibliophile 87 Allenby St; ☎ 03 6299710;
⊕ 09.00–19.00 Sun–Thu, 09.00–14.00 Fri. This
warren-like used bookstore has a big selection of
tatty books in a variety of languages.
Sipur Pashut Book Shop 31 Shabazi St; ☎ 03
5107040; ⊕ 10.00–20.00 Sun–Thu, 09.30–14.00
Fri. Small, stylish bookshop, worth a visit for

something a bit different.
Steimatzky 101 Dizengoff St; ☎ 03 5233415;
⊕ 08.00–21.00 Sun–Thu, 08.00–14.00 Fri. Has a
big English-language section including the Carta
map series. There is also a smaller branch in the
Dizengoff Centre.

CAMPING SHOPS

LaMetayel 3rd floor, Dizengoff Centre; ☎ 03
5286894; ⊕ 10.00–20.30 Sun–Thu, 10.00–14.00
Fri. Big selection of camping gear at reasonable
prices.

Maslool Traveler's Equipment Center 47 Bograshov St;
☎ 03 6203508; ⊕ 09.00–22.00 Sun–Thu,
09.00–16.00 Fri, 07.30–22.30 Sat. Huge variety of
camping, backpacking & outdoor equipment.
Sleeping bags & boots downstairs.

OTHER PRACTICALITIES

EMERGENCIES

Ambulance ☎ 101
Fire ☎ 102
Police 221 Dizengoff St; ☎ 03 5454210 & 14

HaRakevet St; ☎ 100 or 03 5644458
Tourist police Corner of Herbert Samuel St & Ge'ula
St; ☎ 03 5165382

MONEY There are countless currency-exchange booths around the city centre that
offer commission-free money exchange. While some of them may look a little
shifty they all offer pretty much the same rate, are above board and have shorter
queues than in the post office and banks, and are open later. There are several
branches along Hayarkon and Ben Yehuda streets and King George Street near the
Dizengoff Centre and some offer Moneygram or Western Union facilities, as does
the post office. Travellers' cheques can be changed at most banks and at the post
office for no commission. There are branches of all the major banks dotted around
the city but the following are the most convenient.

$ **Bank Hapoalim** 71 Ibn Gvirol St; ☎ 03 6532407;
⊕ 08.30–14.00 Sun, Tue/Wed, 08.30–14.00 &
16.00–17.00 Mon & Thu. Other useful branches can
be found at 5 Dizengoff Sq; 205 Dizengoff St; 19
Ben Yehuda St; 19th Floor, Round Bldg, Azrieli
Centre; 104 HaYarkon St. Only the branch on

HaYarkon St is open on Fri between 08.30–12.30.
$ **Bank Leumi** 55 Dizengoff St; ☎ 03 9544555/
landline*5522; ⊕ 08.30–17.00 Mon–Thu, 08.30–
12.00 Fri. This is the only branch open on Fri. Other
useful branches are on 1 Jerusalem St, Jaffa; 87a Ben
Yehuda St; 71 Ibn Gvirol St; 94 Allenby St.

POST

✉ **Post office** 108 Ibn Gvirol St; ☎ 03 5227609;
⊕ 08.00–18.00 Sun–Thu, 08.00–12.00 Fri. This is
the main branch but there are also useful branches

on 60 King George St; 286 Dizengoff St; 12
Jerusalem St, Jaffa.

MEDICAL

✚ **Assuta Hospital** 58–60 Jabotinsky St; ☎ 03
5201515
✚ **Ichilov Hospital** 6 Weizmann St; ☎ 03 6974444

✚ **Superpharm** Ground floor, Dizengoff Centre; ☎ 03
6203798; ⊕ 09.30–22.00 Sun–Thu, 09.00–15.30
Fri, 06.30–23.00 Sat

INTERNET Internet cafés can be found strewn all over the city and most offer new
computers and fast internet connection plus hot and cold drinks. Many larger
hotels also offer internet facilities as well as in-room wireless connection.

Interfun 20 Allenby St; ☎ 03 5171448; ④ 10.00–midnight daily; 15NIS/hr.

Private Link Tel Aviv 78 Ben Yehuda St; ☎ 03 5299889; ④ 24hrs daily. 10NIS/30mins, 28NIS/2hrs.

LAUNDRY Almost all automatic laundries are open 24 hours and cost around 12NIS to wash and dry one load. **Hamahbesa** has branches at 102 Ben Yehuda St; 95 Yehuda Halevi St; 109 Ibn Gvirol St; 88 Frishman St and 6 Dizengoff Sq.

TRAVEL AGENCIES

ISSTA Dizengoff Centre, 50 Dizengoff St; ☎ 03 6216100; e customerserv.issta@issta.co.il; www.issta.co.il; ④ 09.00–20.00 Sun–Thu, 09.00–13.00 Fri. Part of Israel's biggest travel agency chain. Staff can be decidedly officious so try not to take it personally.

Ophir Tours Tel Aviv University, Music Academy Bldg; ☎ 03 6429001; e s@ophirtours.co.il; www.ophirtours.co.il ④ 09.00–18.00 Sun–Thu, 09.00–13.00 Fri. Friendly, budget-oriented agency.

BOX OFFICES To find out what's on in the city's theatres, galleries and concert halls and to buy tickets for upcoming events visit the box offices below or visit their websites (note that some are in Hebrew only).

Hadran 90 Ibn Gvirol St; ☎ 03 5279797; www.hadran.co.il

Kastel 153 Ibn Gvirol St; ☎ 03 6045000; www.tkts.co.il (Hebrew)

Lean 101 Dizengoff St; ☎ 03 5247373; www.leaan.co.il (Hebrew)

Rococco 93 Dizengoff St; ☎ 03 5276677

MEDIA The *Jerusalem Post* is an English-language newspaper that has lots of practical information and entertainment listings about Jerusalem and Tel Aviv for tourists and foreign residents. *Haaretz*, Israel's leading newspaper, is also printed in English daily. The monthly *Time Out Tel Aviv* which is produced in English and Hebrew also lists what's on in the city.

WHAT TO SEE

CITY CENTRE

Rabin Square Few around the world will have escaped seeing Rabin Square on the news at some time in its 40-year history. For it is in Tel Aviv's largest public square that celebrations, festivals, rallies, protests and exhibitions are held. The most shocking event to take place here, however, was the assassination of Israeli prime minister Yitzhak Rabin in 1995 by a Jewish student, Yigal Amir. Today a small memorial to the right of the rather unsightly City Hall (when facing it) marks the spot upon which he was killed. Following his assassination the square, then known as Kings of Israel Square, was renamed in his memory (see page 13). Yitzhak Rabin is buried in the Mount Herzl Cemetery in Jerusalem and his funeral was attended by over 80 heads of state. At the time of writing Yigal Amir was serving his life sentence in Ayalon Prison which, from 2006, included conjugal visits with his wife, something seen by most Israelis as a sore and angering decision.

While there isn't an awful lot to see when there isn't an event taking place the square can nonetheless be a good people-watching place where people come out to play frisbee, walk their designer dogs or just sit and chat. During events, however, this is the place to see some real Israeli patriotism, memorial and mourning, gay pride, artistic flair or political aggression.

Dizengoff Dizengoff is the name given to both central Tel Aviv's main thoroughfare and the country's first **shopping mall** (*corner of Dizengoff & King George sts;* ☏ *03 6212416;* ⏰ *09.00–midnight Sun–Thu, 09.00–16.00 Fri, 20.00–midnight Sat*). Spread across both sides of the constantly busy **Dizengoff Street**, the mall is a throwback to the early 1970s when it was built. The maze-like centre seems to be designed to provide shoppers with the maximum amount of walking, and is decidedly confusing. It is still, however, one of the busiest shopping spots in the city and is home to most of Tel Aviv's big-name stores and countless food outlets. The weekend **food market** (⏰ *16.00–22.00 Thu, 10.30–16.00 Fri*) sees the walkways of the mall fill with stalls selling home-cooked, reasonably priced food, including meatballs, couscous, stuffed peppers, cakes, pies and a whole host of traditional fare.

The long, narrow Dizengoff Street that stretches from the Azrieli buildings to the Hayarkon Park is one of the main arteries of central Tel Aviv. From the mall northwards once ultra-trendy shops line the pavements, today selling mainly shoes and gaudy, Cinderella-style wedding dresses. Just north of the mall is **Dizengoff Square** with its kitsch, all-singing, all-dancing water fountain, decidedly unattractive but something the locals are strangely proud of. The square is home to several new boutique hotels (see page 103), a few cafés, a cinema and plays host to an **antique market** (⏰ *14.00–16.00 Tue, 09.00–16.00 Fri*).

Azrieli Centre (*123 Menachem Begin St;* ☏ *03 6081179; www.azrielicenter.co.il;* ⏰ *10.00–22.00 Sun–Thu, 10.00–16.00 Fri, 20.00–midnight Sat*) The recently completed Azrieli buildings have quickly become one of Tel Aviv's most recognisable landmarks. The round, square and triangular buildings are home to not only one of the Middle East's biggest business centres but also the country's largest mall. The Disneyland of shopaholics, the centre is home to an enormous selection of moderate and expensively priced stores. One of its key attractions is the **Azrieli Observatory** (*49th floor, Round building;* ☏ *03 6081179;* ⏰ *winter 09.30–18.00 daily; summer 09.30–20.00 Sat–Thu, 09.30–18.00 Fri; admission adult/child 22/17NIS*) which offers, without a shadow of doubt, the best view of the city. A 3D movie on Tel Aviv and an audio guide to help you pinpoint the major sites on the horizon will certainly aid you in getting your bearings. For a real treat the gourmet **'2C' Restaurant** (see page 105) on the same floor is all about location, location, location.

Helena Rubenstein Pavilion (*6 Tarsat Bd;* ☏ *03 5287196;* ⏰ *10.00–16.00 Mon, Wed & Sat, 10.00–22.00 Tue & Thu*) Part of the Habima Theatre complex, the pavilion displays works by well-known Israeli artists who have made their niche in both the international and national art scenes. The gallery was established in 1959 to serve as an overflow of the Tel Aviv Museum of Art (see below), but has developed into a highly reputable space in its own right. Exhibitions change regularly, some of which are free while others can be accessed using the Tel Aviv Museum entrance ticket.

Tel Aviv Museum of Art (*27 Shaul Hamelech Bd;* ☏ *03 6077020; www.tamuseum.com;* ⏰ *08.00–16.00 Sun–Thu; admission adult/child 42/12NIS*) Having been in its current location since 1971, the museum started its humble beginnings in 1932 in the home of Tel Aviv's first mayor Meir Dizengoff, several years before the State of Israel was founded. It was in that first building that the signing of the Declaration of Independence took place and is today known as **Independence Hall**. The museum's collection is impressive even to an art novice, its permanent collection proudly displaying pieces by Picasso, Miro, Monet, Renoir, Cezanne, Matisse and Chagal to name but a few. Standing as one of the world's foremost art museums, it is the *pièce de résistance* of Israel's art scene and an integral part of the country's cultural heritage. Be sure not to miss the photography department which has some beautiful photographs of 19th-century Palestine, and the temporary exhibitions which often display works based upon contemporary Israeli issues such as the disengagement of Gaza in 2005.

Rubin Gallery (*14 Bialik St;* ☎ *03 5255961;* ✆ *10.00–15.00 Mon, Wed & Thu, 10.00–20.00 Tue, 11.00–14.00 Sat; admission adult/child 20NIS/free*) Renowned as one Israel's most acclaimed artists, Reuven Rubin (1893–1974) bequeathed his house to the city upon his death and it has now been converted into a gallery displaying many of his famous works. His pieces stand alongside other works by Israeli artists and there is an audio-visual presentation on his life.

Bauhaus architecture In 2003, Tel Aviv was awarded UNESCO World Heritage status based upon its abundance of buildings built in the Bauhaus architectural style. Today, the more than 4,000 Bauhaus buildings are the pride and joy of an otherwise architecturally drab, grey city and have awarded Tel Aviv the nickname 'the White City'.

The pre-Nazi Germany school of Bauhaus architecture produced several renowned architects who later settled in Tel Aviv before the founding of the State of Israel and who put their names to the buildings that many years later have come to define the city. As an architectural form, Bauhaus is simple, striking and unadorned and is based on functionality rather than glamour. Signature features of the style are its small, elongated balconies and rounded corners. While Bauhaus buildings can be found dotted all over the city centre, there are well-preserved concentrations along the length of **Rothschild Boulevard**, **Dizengoff Square**, **Bialik Street** and **Kalisher Street** as well as some buildings around the **Sheikin Street** area. The Tel Aviv Municipality organises a free **walking tour** in English (*11.00 Sat, starting from 46 Rothschild Bd*). Alternatively, the **Bauhaus Centre** (*99 Dizengoff St;* ☎ *03 5220249;* ✆ *10.00–19.30 Sun–Thu, 10.00–14.30 Fri*) offers a weekly two-hour guided walking tour (*10.00 Fri; cost 50NIS*). They also have MP3 recordings of the tour if you prefer to go on your own. For more information on Tel Aviv's Bauhaus buildings visit the municipality's website (*www.white-city.co.il*).

Ben-Gurion House (*17 Ben Gurion St;* ☎ *03 5221010; www.ben-gurion-house.org.il;* ✆ *08.00–15.00 Sun & Tue–Thu, 08.00–17.00 Mon, 08.00–13.00 Fri; admission free*) Israel's first prime minister once stated 'I bequeath to the State of Israel my home in Tel Aviv', and to this day that home stands as it did when David and Paula Ben Gurion lived there. They alternated between this abode and their later home in Sde Boker (see page 236) which is also a museum. In the house adjacent are exhibitions about the life, history and achievements of Ben-Gurion.

NORTH CITY CENTRE
HaYarkon Park Tel Aviv's biggest park spreads out from the HaYarkon River that pours into the Mediterranean at the northern end of the city. The park is, in effect, divided into two sections, the larger and more developed being to the east of the Ayalon Highway where, in addition to the river, a manmade lake has been dug and the grounds nicely landscaped. It is a lovely place to go and escape the urban buzz, especially in the warmer months, but be warned – half of Tel Aviv will also have the same idea. For children in particular the park has a wealth of activities including **boating** (**150NIS/hour**) or **canoeing** (**70NIS/hour**) on the lake, countless playgrounds and activity parks and sprawling lawns on which to set up an afternoon picnic. If it's sports you're after head down to the area directly to the

east of the Ayalon Highway bridge where locals will be happy to let you join in with football, basketball, table tennis or tennis; a great way to see real Tel Avivian life and a step off the tourist trail. Alternatively, on the northern side of the river in the west of the park is the **Sportek**. A **climbing wall** (*42 Rokach Av;* ✆ *03 6990910; www.kir.co.il;* ⊕ *17.00–22.00 Sun–Thu, 14.00–20.00 Fri, 11.00–21.00 Sat; admission 50NIS*), **skateboard park** (⊕ *16.00–20.00 Sun–Thu, 11.00–20.00 Fri/Sat; admission 28NIS*) and **mini golf course** (✆ *03 6990229; www.minigolf.co.il;* ⊕ *16.00–20.00 Sun–Thu, 10.00–20.00 Fri/Sat; 26NIS/round*) can all be found in the area as well as plenty of packed grassy areas to throw a ball or frisbee around in.

Eretz Israel Museum (*2 Hayim Levanon St;* ✆ *03 6415244; www.eretzmuseum.org.il;* ⊕ *10.00–16.00 Sun–Wed, 10.00–20.00 Thu, 10.00–14.00 Fri/Sat; admission adult/child 38/26NIS*) Spread across the greenery of the **HaYarkon Park**, the museum is a tell-all of Israel's history and culture. Permanent and temporary exhibits range from archaeology and ethnography to Judaica, folklore and traditional crafts and are presented in a multitude of different ways. Impressive collections of ancient glass, coins and metallurgical pieces can be found in the permanent collection as well as the highly interesting Ethnography and Folklore Pavilion at the southern end of the museum complex.

Old Port Long since closed to sea traffic, the Old Port has been remodelled and reshaped into a hub of recreation, good food, nightclubs, wooden promenades and great views. Located in the north of the city near the HaYarkon River estuary, the area benefits from being situated away from urban areas, its pumping clubs able to make as much noise as they wish all night long. During the daytime the port is a pleasant place to come for a stroll, light lunch or relaxing afternoon in one of the countless cafés. A nice walk starts in the centre of the port and heads southwards past the old warehouses and workshops to the old pier where there is a lovely view south. Likewise, views from the stone pier are worth seeing. For something a bit different, the **Antique Fair and Organic Market** (⊕ *10.00–20.00 Fri (the market closes at 18.00)*) makes for a pleasant couple of hours perusing through old knick-knacks and a whole range of organic foods. At night the area really comes into its own, with more bars and clubs than you can shake a cocktail stick at (see pages 108–109). While there is a good selection of music genres and types of bar, the majority tend to be 'pick-up' bars attracting the young and good-looking in all their lycra finery.

Diaspora Museum (*Beit Hatefusot*) (*Tel Aviv University;* ✆ *03 6408000;* ⊕ *10.00–16.00 Sun–Tue & Thu, 10.00–18.00 Wed, 10.00–13.00 Fri; admission adult/child 35.24NIS*) Located in the southeast corner of the university grounds, the museum has risen to international renown as the first and largest museum dedicated to Jewish history. The permanent exhibition depicts the story of the Jewish people through video clips, drawings, reconstructions, models and computer generations. Exhibits include 'The Jews', 'The community', 'Faith' and 'The return to Zion'.

SOUTH CITY CENTRE
Great Synagogue (*110 Allenby St;* ✆ *03 5604905; modest dress*) Just east of the Shalom Tower on Allenby Street is the Great Synagogue, which, as its name implies, is the largest of Tel Aviv's 350-odd synagogues. Built in 1926, it underwent a major overhaul in the 1970s in an attempt to recreate the former glory of the ornate pre-Holocaust synagogues of Europe. Relative to the distinctly unadorned, plain synagogues that are a feature of Judaism, a huge domed roof and stained-glass windows have given some beauty to the building. Shabbat services are open to the public but appropriate modest dress must be worn for both men and women.

Entertainment
venues

🎭 Mann Auditorium
Helena Rubenstein
Pavilion

GRASHOV

Habima Theatre

MARMOREK

AHAD HA'AM

Cinematheque

HA'ARBA'A

HAHASHMONA'IM

CARLEBACH

JAFFA ROAD

HAMASGER

SHONTZINO ST

MELCHETT

Tika

HEINKIN

ROTHSCHILD BOULEVARD

HALEVI

LINCOLN

Tmuna
(Theatre)

YITZAKH SADEH

AZEH

HA'AM

Pastis ✕

Cantina ✕

MAZEH

Laundry

BEZALEL YAFFE

AHAD

YEHUDA

NAHMANI

el 🛏
renner

HARAKEVET

HARAKEVET

HAMASGER

JAFFA ROAD

SALOMON

Old Central
Bus Station 🚌

HASHOMRON

BNEI BRAK

ROSH PINA

Y L PERETZ

LEWINSKY

MATALON

TCHLENOV

LEWINSKY

ISRAEL MISALANT

HEIL HASHIRON RD

AYALON SOUTH

AYALON NORTH

MATALON

WOLFFSOHN

Tel Aviv
Mall

Central Bus Station 🚌

BEN GUVIN

SCHLOMO ROAD

HAYIM

Hahaganah
Railway Station

see page 102

Tel Aviv-Jaffa WHAT TO SEE

4

Sheinkin Tel Aviv has many areas frequented by those who think they're a cut above the rest and there is nowhere more so than Sheinkin Street. This ultra-trendy, yet slightly bohemian street is the place to go during the week to buy your boutique fashion that you will then wear on a Friday whilst sunning yourself outside one of its countless cafés. Many Israeli designers have set up shop here selling pricey but highly individual outfits and there are more shoe shops than you could shake a stiletto at.

Neve Tzedek This is one of Tel Aviv's most delightful neighbourhoods and unfortunately often overlooked in favour of more commercial areas. The neighbourhood was the first to appear outside the Old Jaffa walls in 1887 and formed the centre of Tel Aviv as the city grew up around it. It eventually fell into decline and became a dilapidated and tired area full of run-down, shabby buildings. A major overhaul in the 1980s however put Neve Tzedek back in the fashionista limelight and it is now one of the city's trendiest and most enchanting areas. It was originally settled by many Jewish artists and today its heritage has been honoured by the artists' galleries that line the main streets as well as the famous **Suzanne Dellal Centre** (see page 110). The small streets that weave through the area are packed with a fascinating selection of shops selling art, designer clothes, pottery and jewellery as well as countless cafés and restaurants when you feel the need to recharge your batteries. On your wanderings look out for the **Rokach House** (*36 Shimon Rokach St*), which was one of the first houses built in the area.

Rothschild Boulevard Running from the Habima Theatre in the north to the Neve Tzedek neighbourhood in the south, the leafy, tree-lined Rothschild Boulevard is Tel Aviv's pride and joy and rightly so. It forms not only the heart of Bauhaus architecture but the heart of weekend recreation and leisure. The long, wide boulevard with its central pedestrian walkway and bicycle lane is dotted with sandwich bars that have formed an unlikely super trend. Come Friday young, chic Tel Avivians come to strut their stuff (and their designer dogs), lounge on the grass or pull up a chair at one of the street's innumerable open-air cafés. The entire length of the street is in fact a hub of restaurants and cafés (see pages 105–107) ranging from the moderately pricey to the downright extortionate, but then you pay for the location.

Located at number 16 is **Independence Hall** (✆ *03 5173942;* ⊕ *09.00–14.00 Sun–Thu; admission adult/child 17/14NIS*), the site where Israel's declaration of independence was signed. The museum hall has been left as it was on 14 May 1948 with cameras, flags and broadcasting equipment *in situ* and is a poignant and stirring dedication to Israel's heritage. On the wall is the famous photograph of Ben-Gurion reading the declaration to a large crowd above which is a photograph of Theodor Herzl, the grandfather of Zionism. The building later became the home of Tel Aviv's first mayor, Meir Dizengoff, and the first site of the **Tel Aviv Museum of Art** (see page 113). The small, one room-museum is surprisingly simple for a country so fiercely proud of its ancestry but worth a visit if you're passing by.

There are several Bauhaus walking tours that operate in this area (see page 99) but if you want to just take a stroll and enjoy the relaxed, care-free atmosphere and do some Bauhaus spotting of your own look out for the following building numbers: 61, 66, 67, 73, 83, 84, 87, 89–91, 93, 99, 100, 117, 118, 119, 121, 123 and 126–128.

Yemenite Vineyard (Kerem Hateimanim) The tiny web of streets that form the Yemenite Vineyard (which actually isn't a vineyard in any shape or form) is one of the most rustically charming neighbourhoods in the city. It was established at the turn of the last century by immigrants from Yemen and until its huge facelift in the early 1990s was little more than yet another run-down neighbourhood. After its major cosmetic surgery, however, it has become one of trendiest places to live and its restored houses are now much sought after (and increasing in price by the day). The narrow streets are laid out in a grid-iron pattern unusual to the city and houses are small and low-rise. Its proximity to the seafront and the HaCarmel Market makes it the ideal place to set up home while for visitors to the city the neighbourhood offers a pleasant stroll and a selection of small, traditional Yemenite restaurants.

HaCarmel Market (⊕ *08.00–17.00 daily*) On the southern side of the junction where Sheinkin, Allenby and King George streets converge is the northern entrance to the tunnel-like HaCarmel Market. This is the city's busiest fruit and vegetable (and everything else you can think of) market and is a bustling, noisy and lively part of traditional Tel Avivian life. All and sundry come to buy their weekly fresh produce, shop for cheap trinkets and stock up on socks and it is a delightful insight into the less chic side of the city. Apart from food, homeware and cheap clothes it is a good place to buy Dead Sea products for discounted prices, but be prepared to haggle. Hidden behind the clothes stores that are found at the Allenby Street end of the market are some fantastic *burekas* and *baklava* shops so look carefully so as not to miss out.

Nahalat Binyamin Market (*10.00–17.00 Tue & Fri*) On market days artists and artisans come to display their handmade works on small stalls set up along the paved section of Nahalat Binyamin Street near Allenby Street. To make it even more special, the market's council handpicks the artists allowed to partake in an attempt to keep away the mass-produced, money-making pieces and retain the cultural diversity of the market. In addition to the stalls, clowns, fortune tellers and performers often show up to entertain the crowds, creating a lively and bohemian atmosphere.

Bet Bialik Museum (*22 Bialik St; ☏ 03 5254530; ⊕ 09.00–16.30 Sun–Thu, 11.00–14.00 Sat; admission free*) Chaim Bialik is regarded as Israel's first great modern poet and the house that he lived in between 1925 and 1933 has been turned into a museum where his 94 famous books are displayed. English information is fairly limited but the museum displays and collection of British Mandate-era paintings are worth the trip.

BEACHES Tel Aviv's beaches are wonderful. Wide and sandy, they are clean, relaxed and, thanks to coastal barriers, much calmer than some of the wild stretches further up the coast. If there is a downside it is the sheer number of people who flock to the beaches on summer weekends where you will be hard pushed to find a square metre of sand on which to lay your towel.

Tel Baruch Beach This is Tel Aviv's most northerly beach and is actually well beyond the urban areas. Located just north of Dov Airport it is a bit of a schlep from the city centre but worth it for the wild sands, natural feel and isolation. Once notorious for its prostitution scene, it has been cleaned up in recent years and is now a wholesome family beach. Plans to extend the nearby airport may scupper the tranquillity of the area in the future but for now it is a great expanse of soft white sand and rolling waves.

The Tayelet (promenade) that runs the length of Tel Aviv's coastline (whose official name is **Herbert Samuel Promenade**) is one of the best additions to the city and the wide, paved pedestrian walkway is one of the best spots in the country to witness the true cross-section of Israeli culture. In the hot and humid height of summer the beach is standing room only, where Tel Avivians and tourists take refuge from the smoggy heat and congestion of the day. From the young groups of teenagers to families and the old, the white sands lining the clean waters of the Mediterranean are bursting at the seams. Probably the most prominent group, however, is the young twenty-somethings. This is where Israeli men come to strut their stuff and girls revel in watching them do it. *Matkot* (bat and ball) has become a very popular, highly competitive game where egos are made and destroyed. Young bronzed Israeli girls wearing next to nothing parade the promenade in a catwalk fashion to rival the south of France. But somehow Tel Aviv has almost managed to escape the arrogance of other cities with such a strong beach culture. Here 'each to their own' seems to be the motto, a place where people from all walks of life converge. From the glamorous and fashionable, the large gay population, the religious and the Orthodox, to families, tourists and businesspeople, foreign immigrants and students, they curiously and surprisingly live harmoniously in a city they have grown to love for its freedom and tolerance.

Metzizim Beach While it would be difficult to call the view from Metzizim Beach beautiful, it is in fact one of the funkiest places to hang out both during the day and at night (when it's even harder to see the power station and old port works). The wide beach, chilled bars and relaxed atmosphere are a refreshing change from some of the younger, more raucous beaches further south.

Hilton Beach Named unsurprisingly after the nearby Hilton Hotel, this beach is frequented predominantly by three very different groups of sun-seekers. The northernmost end is the only section of Tel Aviv's coastline where dogs can run free. While it is a heart-warming sight to see over-excited pups chasing each other and crashing in and out of the waves, it isn't as much fun if you're lying on a beach towel as they do it. Further down from the doggy area is a patch of sand that has become the unofficial gay beach of the city, mainly with men. Tight swim shorts, hunky bodies and a lively atmosphere are its key characteristics. The Hilton Beach is also famed as being the city's best **surfing** beach. An offshore reef causes waves to break nicely on their way towards the coast and surfers of all ages flock to the seas. The **Sea Centre** surfing club (✆ *03 6503000*) operates from here.

Nordau Beach Known as The Religious Beach, this is Tel Aviv's contribution to single-sex swimming. The beach is surrounded by a high wall and is more often than not near deserted. Women looking for that all-over tan have been known to come on women's days without the fear of being leered at, something that doesn't seem to bother the conservatively dressed religious women. Women's days are on Sunday, Tuesday and Thursday while men's days are Monday, Wednesday and Friday.

Gordon and Frishman beaches These are the quintessential Tel Avivian beaches, where muscular bronzed soldiers, tiny tots in rubber rings, sunburnt foreigners and everyone in between come to enjoy the summer sun and refreshing

Mediterranean waters. Their central location means they are never empty, but midweek is certainly less crowded than summer weekends. Lifeguards, shower and bathroom facilities, huge beach bars and cafés and plenty of shade add to their appeal. At the northern end of Gordon Beach is the city's marina, a small, rather quaint area that incorporates the delightful **Gordon Swimming Pool Marina**, at the time of writing this extremely pleasant salt-water swimming pool was under renovation but is worth checking out, especially if you have children.

Jerusalem Beach This is another wide, pleasant beach with several cafés, plenty of space to throw a frisbee around and shallow, clean water. Across Herbert Samuel Street are countless ice-cream parlours, fast-food joints and the beginning of the enigmatic Allenby Street.

Ge'ula Beach Unofficially and more commonly known as Banana Beach after the highly popular bar/restaurant/café located here, this is one of the funkiest and most bohemian beaches along the coast. The **Banana Beach** (✆ *03 5107958;* ⊕ *24hrs*) is a great (if overpriced) place to enjoy a meal at any time of the day or simply cool off with an iced coffee or fruit smoothie. The food is relatively simple but does the trick if your budget runs to it – you're paying for the location and experience anyway. During the summer, big screens often show live sporting events or movies which is a fun and chilled-out evening's entertainment in true Tel Aviv style.

Dolphinarium Beach Named after the old dolphin tank that used to reside here (now a nightclub), the beach attracts the hippy set who come to smoke *nargilah*, juggle fire balls, play the guitar or meditate. Friday afternoons see the beach turned into the setting for a huge jam session where budding musicians come to drum out a beat in the open air. There is also a watersports club where you can rent windsurfing, surfing and parasailing equipment.

> ## BRESLOV
>
> As the sound of loud, pumping music permeates the relaxed, summery atmosphere of Tel Aviv's seafront you would be forgiven for rolling your eyes and looking around for the local boy-racer, his small hatchback and oversized stereo interrupting everyone's leisurely day. Yet, upon turning around you will find that the noise culprit is not a testosterone-fuelled youngster but in fact a minivan full of bearded, white-robed Hassidic Jews. These fun-loving men of God are members of an Orthodox Hassidic group known as Breslov, who originated from the Ukraine and are today a fun and joyous addition to Israeli life. Founded by Rebbe Nachman of Breslov (1772–1810), their ethos is to create an intense relationship with God through happiness, joy and living life to its fullest. Equipped with loud stereo systems, groups of Breslov drive around the streets in white vans, some sitting cross-legged on the roof, their long hair and beards blowing in the wind. As the van comes to a halt at traffic lights, the back doors swing open in a style reminiscent of the A-Team and out burst Breslov men, who proceed to dance enthusiastically until the lights change and they tumble back in and move on. The Breslov are received in Israel with amusement and affection, their contagious happiness bringing smiles to the face of those around. While Breslov reside in many places around the country, Tel Aviv's 'anything goes' attitude seems to complement their fun-loving way of life and they make a delightful addition to the city's eclectic family.

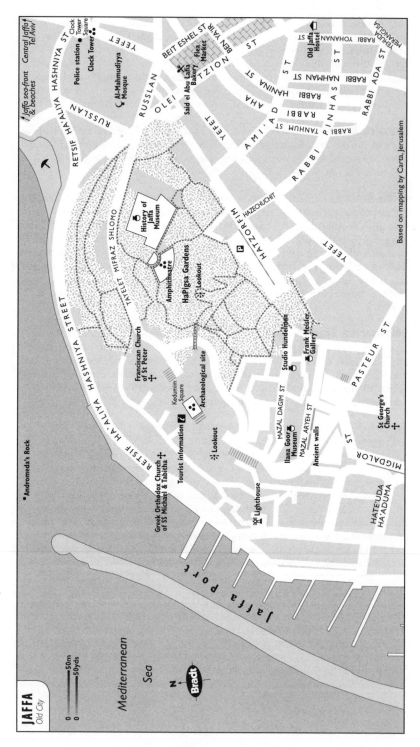

CLOCK TOWER Jaffa's clock tower is the centrepiece of the Old City. It was built at the beginning of the 20th century to commemorate the reign of the Ottoman sultan Abd al-Hamid II and returned to its former glory after a major overhaul in 2006. A free guided tour leaves every Wednesday at 09.30 (see page 99) from **Clock Tower Square** which borders the **al-Mahmudiyya Mosque**, Jaffa's principal mosque erected in 1812 (only Muslims may enter).

FLEA MARKET (SHUK HAPISHPESHIM) Although the name conjures images of cheap tack, Jaffa's flea market (*between Olei Tzion and Beit Eshel streets*) is, in fact, a great place to find yourself an antique bargain (and a lot of cheap tack). Wandering amongst the mountains of furniture, cloth, knick-knacks, Judaica, brassware, carpets and *nargilah* pipes and enjoying the lively, Middle Eastern ambience and noisy chatter, is a world away from the chic cafés in Tel Aviv. Haggling is a must and you're more likely to get a good deal on a Friday when the place is at its busiest.

KEDUMIM SQUARE This is the central square of Old Jaffa and marks the starting point for the labyrinth of cobbled lanes and alleys that snake through the old buildings. The wide square is surrounded by artists' galleries, expensive restaurants and craft and jewellery shops and is one of the most charming and delightful places in all Tel Aviv-Jaffa. The alleys weave their way through the maze of houses downhill to the **port** and the best way to explore is to simply get lost amongst them. You'll end up in the port one way or another.

HISTORY OF JAFFA MUSEUM AND VISITORS CENTRE (⊕ *10.00–18.00 daily; admission adult/child 8/6NIS*) The museum and centre are located in the archaeological site under the square and depict the history of Jaffa through displays and audio-visual presentations. They also hand out free maps. On your way into the square you will pass the imposing, but sadly deteriorating **Franciscan Church of St Peter** (⊕ *08.00–11.45 & 15.00–17.00 daily; modest dress*), said to have been visited by Napoleon during its years as a hostel. Just off to the right of the square a small alley leads to the **Greek Orthodox Church of St Michael and St Tabitha** (⊕ *08.00–11.45 & 15.00–17.00 daily; modest dress*) displaying the traditional bright colours and architecture of Greek ecclesiastical buildings.

HAPIGSA GARDENS The gardens form the summit of the hill upon which Jaffa's Old City sits and countless small paths weave their way through the greenery and rockeries. A small wooden bridge leads from the square to the gardens within which is an amphitheatre where summer concerts are held, a beautiful viewpoint northwards along the coast of Tel Aviv (worth visiting once during the day and again at night) and a monument depicting scenes from the Bible.

ARTISTS' QUARTER Mazal Dagim Street forms the heart of the artists' quarter along which you will find several art galleries including the **Ilana Goor Museum** (*4 Mazal Dagim St;* ☎ *03 6837676; www.ilanagoor.com;* ⊕ *10.00–16.00 Sun–Fri, 10.00–18.00 Sat; admission adult/child 24/14NIS*). The museum and gallery have been created in a space within Goor's beautiful home and is worth a visit, partly for the artwork and partly to appreciate the classic architecture of the building. A little further along is the **Studio Hundelman** (*14 Mazal Dagim St;* ☎ *03 6834593;* ⊕ *10.30–22.30 Sun–Thu, 10.30–Shabbat Fri, end of Shabbat–22.30 Sat*) which designs and sells silk paintings, while the **Frank Meisler Gallery** (*25 Mazal Arie St;* ☎ *03 6813502;* ⊕ *09.00–23.00 Sun–Thu, 09.00–16.00 Fri, 18.00–23.00 Sat*) displays a memorable, expensive selection of metalwork figurines.

PORT As the waves gently lap against the ancient rock walls and old men stand patiently fishing rods in hand it is hard to imagine that this was once one of the busiest ports in the country. The fact that fishing boats still chug in and out of the port on a regular basis has awarded it the distinction of being one of the oldest active ports in the world. Just beyond the sea wall are several rocks, the darkest said to be **Andromeda's Rock**. According to Greek mythology Andromeda was chained to this rock by her father King Cepheus as a sacrifice to Poseidon's sea monster. As the legend goes she was saved by the hero Perseus who slayed the monster and took her hand in marriage.

AROUND TEL AVIV

SAFARI PARK (ZOOLOGICAL CENTRE) (*Ramat Gan;* ✆ *03 6313531; www.safari.co.il;* ☉ *09.00–16.00 Sun–Thu, 09.00–13.00 Fri; admission adult/child 45.35NIS*) On the outskirts of the city is this zoo in a safari park. Visitors (who in summer arrive in their thousands) drive through the African savanna-like lands past big herds of animals and then park up and enter the main part of the zoo. There is a safari bus if you don't have your own transport. The admission charges are used to promote and develop new conservation techniques and the safari park is involved with several programmes that aim to reintroduce endangered species back into the wild. The area outside the zoo is a big weekend favourite with hundreds of barbecuing Israeli families which has a nice, if extremely crowded, ambience. Buses 30 and 35 from central Tel Aviv stop near the park.

HERZLIYA A short 20 minutes away from Tel Aviv's city centre is the town of Herzliya which, over recent years has become one of the major night-owl hotspots. In fact, all bars, restaurants and clubs centre on the expensive, oh-so-trendy area known as Herzliya Pituach, the strip running along the seafront to the left of the highway (the other part of town purely residential). In contrast to Tel Aviv's Old Port area, Herzliya's marina is still very much active, being home to small, private yachts around which has appeared the **Arena Mall** (☉ *10.00–22.00 Sun–Thu, 09.30–16.00 Fri, 11.00–23.00 Sat (although the cinema stays open later)*), as well as dozens of cafés, restaurants and pubs. A wide, sandy beach 100m from the marina has a young, laidback atmosphere, with beach volleyball, a relaxed bar and plenty of towel space, while the strip 0.5km back from the seafront is packed with good restaurants, swanky bars and pubs and, come the small hours, pumping nightclubs.

Getting there Buses 501 and 601 leave from Tel Aviv Central Bus Station (the 601 also stops at Arlozorov Bus Station) stop at the big junction by the highway. From there it is a ten-minute walk to central Herzliya Pituach but to get to the beach and marina you will need to find a taxi.

Where to eat

✘ **Black Steer** 3 Yohanan HaSandlar St; ✆ 09 9557464; ☉ 12.00–midnight daily. Sizzling South African grill house. Unpretentious, rustic steaks in an unpretentious, rustic atmosphere. $$$$$
✘ **Kyoto Bar** 7 Arie Shenkar St; ✆ 09 9587770; ☉ 12.00–01.00 Sun–Thu, 13.00–01.00 Fri/Sat. If budget isn't an issue then this is a real Japanese treat. The fresh & artistic dishes of sushi, sashimi, tapanyaki, tempura & noodles are considered some

of the best in the country. $$$$$
✘ **Tavola** 75 HaNassi St; ✆ 09 9573818; ☉ 12.00–midnight daily. Delightfully wide Italian menu including exotic pasta dishes, meats & seafood & a big selection of starters. $$$
✘ **Tavola** 75 HaNassi St; ✆ 09 9573818; ☉ 12.00–midnight daily. Delightfully wide Italian menu including exotic pasta dishes, meats & seafood & a big selection of starters. $$$

Bars

♀ **Douglas** 4 HaSadnaot St; ☎ 09 9506660; ⊕ 21.00–late daily. Enormous, chrome-plated, ultra-modern late-night bar. Live Israeli rock on Wed from a selection of well-known artists (free entry). Women must be 23 years of age or over, while it's over 25 for men.

♀ **Hattori Hanzo** I Sapir St; ☎ 09 9514045; ⊕ 21.00–late daily. A 3-year veteran of raucous, pumping party nights, this bar-cum-nightclub is the ultimate 'pick-up' place.

♀ **Murphy's** Marina; ☎ 09 9569495; ⊕ 16.00–late Sun–Thu, 12.00–late Fri/Sat.

Irish-style pub that's a bit softer around the edges than those in Tel Aviv. Live music on Tue & Wed & live sporting events on big screens. Big portions of nice bar food. Outdoor seating opposite the marina.

MEDITERRANEAN COAST

5

Mediterranean Coast

Israel's western coastline marks the end of the shimmering Mediterranean waters that stretch from the border with Lebanon to the Gaza Strip and Egyptian border. Great port cities have flourished along these shores for centuries, ancient Caesarea and Akko's Old City gracing the history books and providing a glimpse into the turbulent, magnificent and dramatic past, where empires were won and lost. In modern times Haifa, Israel's third-largest city, has bloomed into a decoupage of charismatic neighbourhoods that tumble down Mount Carmel's northern slopes. The undulating hills of the Carmel mountain range are blanketed with a carpet of green, as they roll alongside the coast. Upon these hills the Prophet Elijah battled the priests of Baal, ancient biblical deer once again roam freely and the irrepressibly picturesque town of Zichron Yaakov stands as a living memorial to Edmond de Rothschild, the grandfather of Zionism.

For visitors to the country the Mediterranean coast offers sweeping sandy beaches, majestic archaeological sites and a mesh of Jewish, Druze, Baha'i, Christian and Muslim traditions. Combine this with a wealth of tourist facilities and the best of the country's public transport and you get Israel's most relaxed, sun-soaked and culturally rich region.

NAHARIYA

The northern coastal town of Nahariya holds claim to a rich history. On these soils Canaanites stamped their mark, Byzantine finds were unearthed, Romans marched along their paved roads, and it marked a crucial stop along the great Via Maris highway. Unfortunately, little of Nahariya's ancient glamour has managed to find a place in the modern version of the town and today this rather gaudy seaside resort is characterised by neon-lit eateries and cafés, a developed beach front and groups of holidaying families. Outside the summer season there is not a lot to entice anyone to Nahariya, but the warmer weather allows for plenty of sporting and water activities, hotels and decent restaurants. A long seaside promenade stretches to the fringes of Akko and makes for some lovely cycling or walking opportunities while the clean, sandy but often overcrowded Municipal Beach forms the hub of summer activities, where beach volleyball, a large playground and a whole host of standard seaside activities operate.

Most facilities in Nahariya can be found along the main **Sderot HaGa'aton** Street which runs from north to south. The train station, the last stop along the Tel Aviv line, is at the northernmost end of the street alongside the central bus station.

GETTING THERE
Train
Nahariya Train Station (*1 HaGa'aton St;* ✆ *04 8564446*) runs services to Tel Aviv (1hr 45mins/36NIS), Akko (15mins/7NIS) and Haifa (40mins/15NIS) and is the final stop on the line. Trains leave approximately every hour 05.20–20.20 Sunday–Thursday, 06.10–14.10 Friday and 09.15–12.00 Saturday. In winter, a more limited service operates 07.20–12.00 Sun–Fri.

Bus
Nahariya Central Bus Station (*3 HaGa'aton St;* ✆ *04 9923434*). Buses leave every 15 minutes to Akko (15mins/7.60NIS) and Haifa (1hr/14.80NIS).

Car rental
🚗 **Avis** 31 HaGa'aton St; ✆ 04 9511880; www.avis.co.il; ◷ 08.00–17.00 Sun–Thu, 08.00–14.00 Fri. Cars from 130NIS per day.

Tourist information
ℹ **Tourist information centre** 19 HaGa'aton St; ✆ 04 9879800; ◷ 08.00–13.00 & 16.00–19.00 Sun–Wed, 08.00–13.00 Thu/Fri. Located on the square near the Municipal Bldg. Most of the big hotels offer tours to surrounding areas so it is worth enquiring at their receptions.

🏠 **WHERE TO STAY** Nahariya doesn't have a lot in the way of mid-range accommodation so it's a choice between the four-star complexes or the family-run, shabby guesthouses. Prices tend to be inflated, especially during the peak seasons and the surrounding moshav and kibbutz offer lovely zimmer which are much better value for money.

🏠 **Carlton Nahariya** (200 rooms) 23 HaGa'aton St; ✆ 04 9005511; www.carlton-hotel.co.il. Good range of services & amenities include a large swimming pool, sun terrace, spa, restaurant, bar & children's club. 4x4 & boat tours can be arranged through their travel service. $$$

🏠 **Hotel Rosenblatt** (14 rooms) 59 Weizmann St; ✆ 04 9920051; e jael@walla.co.il. While in dire need of a makeover, the hotel is clean, well located, & even has an outdoor swimming pool (in summer only). Rooms have AC, TV & extremely outdated, patterned bedding. The best of a rather pricey selection of budget accommodation. $

✖ **WHERE TO EAT** HaGa'aton Street is teeming with eateries, cafés and bars. Pizza joints and shawarma stands are your best budget options.

✖ **El Puncho** 33 HaGa'aton St; ✆ 04 9928635; ◷ 12.00–midnight daily. This Argentinian meat restaurant is decked out in traditional gaucho-style décor, mimicking the cowboy saloons of the rural homeland. $$$$

✖ **Penguin Restaurant** 21 HaGa'aton St; ✆ 04 9928855; ◷ 08.00–23.00 daily. The ever-popular Penguin Restaurant & attached Penguin Café serve a rather theme-less selection of meals, but all are well cooked & portions are generous. Salads, hamburgers, chicken, soups, pasta & Chinese dishes can be followed by a great choice of shakes & ice creams. $$$

OTHER PRACTICALITIES
Emergencies
Police station 5 Ben Zvi St; ✆ 04 9920344.
Ambulance 101

Fire 102

right Basilica of the Annunciation in Nazareth — where tradition states that the Virgin Mary received news of Jesus's birth (PZ) page 167

below A baptism in the Jordan River at Yardenit (IGTO) page 182

bottom The Mount of Beatitudes is a site of commemoration and pilgrimage for Jesus's Sermon on the Mount (PZ) page 180

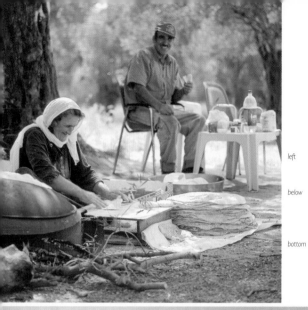

left **The Golan Heights are home to Druze people** (IGTO) page 20

below **Nimrod Fortress sits high on the slopes of Mount Hermon** (PZ) page 227

bottom **Tzfat: 'The Mystical City'** (IGTO) page 189

above **The Hula Valley is an important stop on the great north–south bird migration** (PZ) page 209

right **An Eurasian griffon vulture soaring over the Golan Heights** (PZ) page 5

below **Mount Hermon is Israel's highest point** (PZ) page 225

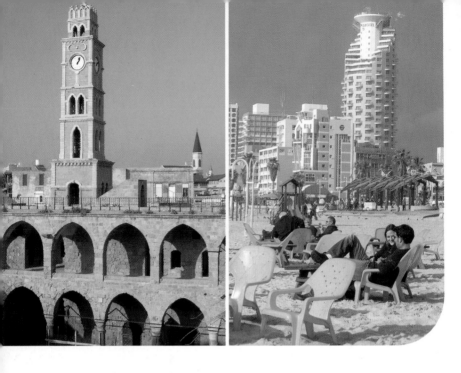

above left **Akko's Old City remains sheltered from modernisation** (PZ) page 131

above right **Tel Aviv's bustling seafront** (PZ) pages 119–21

below **Baha'i Shrine and Persian Gardens, Haifa** (PZ) page 146

right **Old Jaffa has one of the oldest active ports in the world**
(IGTO) page 124

below **Carmel winery at Zichron Ya'akov**
(IGTO) page 157

bottom **Caesarea Maritime National Park**
(IGTO) page 159

left   **Ramon Crater Nature Reserve** (PZ) page 242

below left   **Salt formations at the Dead Sea** (PZ) page 249

below   **Nubian Ibex by the Dead Sea** (PZ) page 5

above	**Bedouin woman and donkey in the Negev Desert** (PZ) page 20
above right	**Solomon's Pillars, Timna Park** (SW) page 259
right	**Camel** (IGTO)
below	**The Ein Gedi Nature Reserve is a true tropical oasis** (PZ) page 248

above   **A lionfish and coral** (PZ) page 6

below   **Watersports in the Red Sea resort of Eilat** (IGTO) page 260

Money HaGa'aton Street is teeming with branches of all Israel's major banks, all offering ATMs.

$ Bank Hapoalim 37 HaGa'aton St; ☎ landline*2407; ⊕ 08.30–13.15 Tue/Wed, 08.30–13.00 & 16.00–18.30 Mon & Thu, 08.15–12.30 Fri

$ Change Spot 36 HaGa'aton St; ☎ 04 9921079; ⊕ 09.00–19.00 Sun–Thu, 09.00–14.00 Fri

Post

✉ Post office 40 HaGa'aton St; ☎ 04 9920180; ⊕ 08.00–12.30 & 15.30–18.00 Sun–Tue & Thu,

08.00–13.30 Wed, 08.00–12.00 Fri

Medical

✚ Hospital Ben Zvi St; ☎ 04 9850505

✚ Szabo pharmacy 3 HaGa'aton St; ☎ 04 9920454;

⊕ 08.00–13.30 & 16.00–19.30 Sun–Thu, 08.00–14.30 Fri

WHAT TO SEE AND DO

Municipal Museum (*Floors 5, 6 & 7, Municipal Bldg, Ha Iriya Sq;* ☎ *04 9879863;* ⊕ *10.00–12.00 Sun–Fri, 16.00–18.00 Sun & Wed; admission free*) The simple Municipal Museum contains several displays including a substantial collection of locally discovered fossils and shells. An art exhibit is housed on the 5th floor while the 7th floor is dedicated to the history of the town.

Canaanite temple (*Ha Ma'apilim St; admission free*) Located a few metres from the Municipal Beach are the remains of a Cannanite temple. It is believed the temple was dedicated to the Goddess Astarte, goddess of the sea, and dates to around 1500BCE. The ruins form part of the Municipal Museum, so ask at the reception if you wish to have a look around.

Byzantine church (*Bielefeld St;* ☎ *04 9879800; admission free; call ahead to arrange entry*) Beautifully preserved mosaics make visiting the church a worthwhile activity. The 4th- to 7th-century mosaic floors are some of the best examples of their kind in the country discovered to date.

Scuba diving As far as Mediterranean dive sites go there are a few interesting ones around Nahariya. The most well-known is the intentionally sunk **Ahi Kidon Military Craft**, which acts as a memorial site for members of the IDF water commando unit. Dive trips to the **Rosh Hanikra Grottoes** and **Ahziv Cave** can also be arranged through the dive centres. A good choice is the **Diving Centre Nahariya** (*5 HaMa'apilim St;* ☎ *04 9511503/9929334;* e *club@putsker.co.il; www.putsker.co.il* ⊕ *08.00–13.00 & 16.00–19.00 Sun–Thu, 08.00–17.00 Fri/Sat; 2-tank dive 170NIS, equipment rental 130NIS per dive*).

Galei-Galil Beach (⊕ *May–Oct 08.00–18.00 daily; admission 20NIS*) Renowned for its cleanliness and safety it offers a plethora of sporting activities, eateries and cafés. The outdoor and indoor pools are included in the entry price.

AROUND NAHARIYA

ROSH HANIKRA At the northernmost point of Israel's Mediterranean coast, the large chalk grottoes and emerald waters of Rosh Hanikra (☎ *04 9857108/09/10; www.rosh-hanikra.com;* ⊕ *summer 08.30–18.00 daily; winter 08.30–16.00 daily; admission adult/child 42/34NIS*) are today a top tourist destination. As the crashing waves eroded away the soft rock over thousands of years, they formed a series of large, watery caves at the base of the high cliff. Today, the site has been developed, allowing visitors to experience these unusual geomorphological structures. A short, steep cable car leads down to the entrance of the grottoes providing magnificent views over the sea and along the jagged coastline towards Haifa Bay.

Historically, Rosh Hanikra's prime location straddling the border with Lebanon made it an important strategic thoroughfare. During the 3rd and 4th centuries BCE, it marked the extent of the Israelite tribes and later became a crucial point along the trade route between Lebanon and Syria, and Palestine, Egypt and north Africa. In 333BCE, Alexander the Great entered the country through Rosh Hanikra, supposedly leading his Greek army through tunnels dug out of the chalk. During the world wars, the British army invaded Lebanon from here, digging a railway tunnel between Haifa and Europe via Beirut and Turkey. The 250m-long tunnel and connecting bridges provided a means of transport for supplies and troops, and also created access for the Ha'apala (Immigration) of Jews fleeing Nazi Europe. During the 1948 Arab–Israeli War, Israeli forces destroyed the bridges, fearing an insurgence from Arab forces through Lebanon.

Today, the southern tunnel and half of the middle tunnel reside in Israeli territory, the remainder in Lebanon. The 'Little Train' (*operating on Sat & holidays*), follows the route taken by British Mandate trains, and connects Rosh Hanikra with Ahziv Nature Reserve (see below).

Getting there From Nahariya, buses 27, 20, 32 and 23 go to Rosh Hanikra and back several times a day (20mins/7NIS).

AHZIV NATIONAL PARK (✆ 04 9823263; ⊕ Apr–Jun & Sep/Oct 08.00–17.00 daily; Jul/Aug 08.00–19.00 daily; admission adult/child 33/20NIS) The ancient town of Ahziv has had a long and prosperous past. An Old Testament settlement, it belonged to the tribe of Asher, and was also mentioned in the **Talmud** and **Mishnah**. The Phoenicians produced a vibrant and much sought-after purple dye from the marine snails that inhabit the coast, and enjoyed a flourishing economy. During the Crusader period, Ahziv was known as Castle Imbert after the Crusader knight Hombertus de Pacci, until it was conquered by the Mamluk sultan Baibars in 1271.

Today, however, the park is loved not for its historical distinction, but for its shimmering turquoise waters that attract bathers and sea turtles alike. From the rocky coast, wide sandy beaches lead towards the sheltered bays and deep natural pools that have formed along the length of the coast. Sweeping manicured lawns are bordered by colourful flowers and plants, in the midst of which sit the remains of part of the ancient city. Needless to say this is a big favourite with families of summering Israelis and in holidays, loud and rambunctious sums it up fairly accurately. During the week, however, you're likely to have this little coastal paradise all to yourself.

The nearby **Moshav Liman** provides the best food and zimmer accommodation in the area. Although prices are a little steep compared with nearby Nahariya, you certainly get what you pay for and are a much nicer alternative to the rather shabby choices in the city. **Biktat HaKarnaf Zimmer** (*3 cabins; Moshav Liman;* ✆ 04 9823359; e maxkarnaf1@bezeqint.net; www.karnaf.net; weekdays 150NIS less ($$); cabin $$$), located in the quiet, peaceful little moshav has extremely hospitable owners who have taken great pride in their luxury zimmer cabins, set within tropical foliage and easily identified by the two rather unusual rhinoceroses painted on the gates. The owners can organise tours and local guides for the area.

At the northern end of the moshav is the **Morgenfeld Steak House** (✆ 04

9524333; kosher; ☺ *12.00–23.00 Sun–Thu, 12.00–15.00 Fri, end of Shabbat–23.00 Sat;* **$$$$**) which combines hearty chunks of prime meat with à la carte fine dining. Entrecôte, Argentinian *asado*, juicy ribs and a mouthwatering selection of desserts are just some of the treats on offer amidst a candlelit, romantic atmosphere.

Getting there The park is located on route 4 between Nahariya and Rosh Hanikra. From Nahariya buses 27, 20, 32 and 23 go to Rosh Hanikra and back several times a day and will stop on request outside the park. Alternatively the little 'noddy' train at Rosh Hanikra trundles backwards and forwards to Ahziv during peak seasons.

AKKO

Within the ancient walls, sheltered from modernisation, development and change, Akko's Old City remains today as it has done throughout its long years of existence. The Old City is undoubtedly one of Israel's most picturesque and historically fascinating places to visit, and a must-see on any itinerary. A woven jumble of cobbled lanes snake around, through and past ancient stone buildings, piled one upon another; majestic, vibrant mosques and churches stream with devout worshippers; immaculately preserved relics remain, left by the city's passionate invaders; people crowd into the aromatic souks and the tranquil waters of the ancient sea port lap against the old sea walls. It was on this small peninsula where empires were battled over, where religions clashed and where cultures merged. Akko was once one of the most crucial cities of ancient times on a par with Alexandria and Troy, a fact difficult to envisage whilst wandering the lively yet peaceful alleys that today house large Muslim, Christian, Druze and Baha'i populations. The UNESCO-designated Old City is a proverbial maze, and while maps are handy, your time would be better spent relaxing into the ambience around you than trying to follow one. Be sure not to miss the wonderful bazaars and souks, where one would be forgiven for thinking they had arrived in the heart of Marrakesh's Medina.

HISTORY It was on these shores that west met east, and few towns can attest to the turbulence and passion that passed inside Akko's walls. The Canaanites, Greeks, Romans, Byzantines, Crusaders, Mamluks, Turks and the British have all left their fingerprints, however large or small, on this stretch of land. The city's most impressive and prominent relics date to the Hellenistic–Roman periods and Crusader and Ottoman rules and it will for ever be remembered as the furthest extent and subsequent demise of Napoleon's Middle Eastern campaign.

Akko is one of the world's oldest continuously inhabited cities, dating back as far as 1504–1450BCE. It was mentioned only once in the Old Testament as one of the few places where the Israelites did not succeed in ousting the Canaanites and suffered three centuries of torment in the years leading up to the Christian era. Akko, at the time a part of the Kingdom of Israel, was incorporated into Alexander the Great's empire following his conquest in 332BCE. In CE638, the Arabs captured Akko and ruled until the Crusaders arrived. The crucial port city was named the Crusaders' headquarters in Palestine and was witness to violent and devastating battles. In 1187, Saladin managed to take Akko, only to be ousted by Richard the Lionheart's troops in 1191. Under his rule, the city became the capital of the Kingdom of Jerusalem and was placed under the directorship of the Knights Hospitaller.

In 1291, the Mamluks embarked on their bloody invasion of Akko, killing every last remaining Crusader and thus putting an end to the Latin Kingdom. The once-

↑Akko
New City

HAHAGANAH STREET

WEIZMANN STREET

CAFARELLI STREET

Burj el Commander

NAPOLEON BONAPARTE ST

Al Jazzar Wall

Land Wall Promenade

Orders Center La-Galil

Steps

Burj al Karim

Underground Prisoners Museum

Visitors Centre

Police stn

P

P

Land Wall Promenade

Citadel

Money Change $

AL-JAZZAR ST

Shuk Al Abiad (White Market)

Walied's Gate Hostel

Land Gate

Malkat Akko Cruises

SALADIN ST

YONATAN HAHASHIMONAI STREET

Al Basha Hammam

Al-Jazzar Mosque

Turkish Bazaar

RICHARD THE LIONHEART ST

(Market Street) MARCO POLO ST

SIGURD STREET

Khan a-Shawarda

The Wall Beach

Humus Saeid

Western Sea Wall

HAHAGANAH STREET

St George's Church

Ramhal Synagogue

S. B. METUDELA ST (Market St)

AL HARIZI ST STREET

Khan al Efranj

Akko Bay

Baha'i House

Genoa Square

ZALMAN HAZOREF STREET

PHILLIPE AUGUST STREET

Khan el Umdan

Venice Square

Sinan Basha Mosque

Ramban Wharf

Uri Buri

Templar tunnel

Pisa Square

Khan a-Shuna

Marina

N

Bradt

Abu Christo

Doniana

Lighthouse Observation Point

P

SALAH AL BASRI

Pisan Port

0   100m
0   100yds

Sea Wall Promenade
Lighthouse

M e d i t e r r a n e a n   S e a

powerful city fell into disrepair and remained virtually ruinous for the following 500 years. It wasn't until the Bedouin sheikh Daher el-Omar made Akko his capital in the 18th century that the city once again began to breathe with life. Between the years 1775 and 1804, the Turkish governor Ahmad Pasha al-Jazzar fortified the city, the great Al-Jazzar Mosque that has become the symbol of Akko owing its origins to this time. Crusader remains became the foundations for the new phase of construction and Muslim buildings still rest on top of the near-perfect relics. Napoleon landed in Akko in 1799 as part of his widespread conquest but Akko was to be the beginning of his Middle Eastern demise, and after two months of heavy and unsuccessful battling he withdrew to France.

Akko fell under Ottoman rule until their defeat by the British in 1918, thus placing the city under the British Mandate. Akko's Citadel fortress became a prison to house and execute political prisoners, mainly from Jewish underground organisations. Akko was captured by Jewish forces on 17 May 1948 during the Arab–Israeli War. Almost 75% of its Arab inhabitants fled the city.

GETTING THERE The **central bus station** is on HaArba'a Street in the New City adjacent to the **train station**. While buses serve Tel Aviv, Haifa and Nahariya regularly, trains are considerably faster and more convenient. Buses 251, 271 and 272 leave every 15 minutes to Haifa's Lev HaMifratz Bus Station (30mins/11.70NIS). Trains depart to Haifa Carmel Station (33mins/16NIS) and Tel Aviv (1hr 22mins/34NIS) every 30 minutes, and to Nahariya (8mins/7.50NIS) hourly.

GETTING AROUND Akko Old City is extremely small and almost wholly pedestrianised so the only way to navigate the labyrinthine alleys is by foot. From the New City and bus station taxis can drop you at the visitor's centre (approximately 10NIS).

TOURIST INFORMATION

Akko Old City Visitors Centre | Weizmann St; 04 9956706; e visitorc@bezeqint.net; www.akko.org.il; ⊕ 08.30–18.00 Sun–Thu & Sat, 08.30–17.00 Fri. This very well-run centre is located on the right as you enter the Citadel (through the visitors' car park). They sell combination tickets to all of Akko's sites, can arrange tour guides, book hotels & arrange full-day excursions to attractions in the area. This should be your first port of call in the Old City. They also show an hourly film about Akko between 09.30 and 15.30 in a variety of languages.

LOCAL TOUR OPERATORS

Orders Centre La-Galil (*Weizmann St;* 04 9916614; e *info@la-galil.co.il; www.la-galil.co.il*) is located near the entrance to the Citadel in the visitors car park. They can book hotels, zimmers & tours to surrounding attractions including 4x4 jeep tours.

WHERE TO STAY

Palm Beach Hotel (127 rooms) 1.5km south of the Old City on the coastal road to Haifa; 04 9877777; f 04 9910434; www.palmbeach.co.il. Modern, beachfront hotel with sports club, health & spa centre, 4 restaurants, 2 swimming pools & a plethora of sporting activities. Rooms are uninspiring but certainly comfortable & well equipped. **$$$**

Walied's Gate Hostel (6 rooms) 13 Saladin St; 04 9911982; f 04 9815530. Not exactly the most swish-looking hostel, it is simple but does the trick. The double rooms with en-suite bathroom are considerably better than the dorms & some have AC. There is a nice rooftop terrace, pool table & kitchen. Good location near the Walls Beach. *Dorms (40NIS).* **$$**

WHERE TO EAT Fish and seafood play a big part in the menus of the more upmarket restaurants while hearty, traditional Middle Eastern food dominates the cheaper eateries. Plastic-chaired, reasonably priced restaurants along **Al-Jazzar Street** are good for a quick bite of *shawarma*, hummus, French fries and salads and there are some fabulous bakeries, sweet cakes, spices and nuts in the **souk**.

Abu Christo South Sea Promenade; 04 9910065; www.abu-christo.co.il; ⊕ 10.00–midnight daily. Well-established & well-respected fish & meat restaurant that boasts the best view in the Old City. The menu includes plenty of Greek- & Arabic- style salads, seafood & steaks. **$$$$**

Doniana Restaurant South Sea Promenade; 04 9910001; ⊕ 12.00–late daily. Sitting high on the sea wall Doniana's offers elegant dining, a picturesque setting & fish so fresh it's almost still wriggling. A big selection of seafood & grilled meats make this an all-round good choice. $$$$

✗ **Humus Saeid** Market St; ☎ 04 9913945; www.humus-saeid.com; ◷ 06.00 Sun–Fri until the food runs out, usually around 14.30. Queues down the street attest to the incredible popularity of this tiny hummus bar. Known across the country, this is normally the first port of call for any visitor to Old Akko. But don't expect a leisurely meal, as you'll have the eyes of the next customer in line

boring into the back of your neck willing you to hurry up. $$

✗ **Uri Buri** HaHaganah St; ☎ 04 9552212; ◷ 12.00–midnight daily. Often considered one of the best fish & seafood restaurants in the country. Although the fruits of the deep sea will burn a deep hole in your pocket, it is money well spent – the food is fabulous. Informal, classy atmosphere & a great location next to the lighthouse. $$$$$

ENTERTAINMENT AND NIGHTLIFE In July, the Crusader Hall plays host to concerts performed by the renowned **Haifa Symphony Orchestra**, the echoing hall providing the perfect accompanying acoustics and a unique setting. Around the Jewish holiday of Sukkot (the Harvest Festival which falls around October) is the **Acco Festival of Alternative Israeli Theatre** (*www.accofestival.co.il*) consisting of theatre performances by national theatre groups. These are mainly in Hebrew but there are some productions in English. Ask at the tourist information centre (see above) for a list.

OTHER PRACTICALITIES
Emergencies
Police (Weizmann St; ☎ 04 9876736/056 273261) 100

Ambulance 101
Fire 102

Money
$ **Bank Hapoalim** 6/8 Ben Ami St; ☎ 03 6532407/ landline*2407; ◷ 08.30–13.15 Sun & Tue/Wed, 08.30–13.00 & 16.00–18.30 Mon & Thu. Located in the New City.

$ **Money Change** Corner Weizmann & Al-Jazzar Sts; ☎ 04 9915097; ◷ 09.30–18.30 daily. Changes euros & US dollars & has an ATM outside.

Post
✉ **Old City post office** 13 Al-Jazzar St; ☎ 04 9910171; ◷ 08.00–12.30 & 16.00–18.00 Sun/Mon & Wed/Thu, 08.00–13.30 Tue, 08.00–13.00 Fri.
✉ **Central post office** 11 Ha'atzma'ut St; ☎ 04

3066666; ◷ 08.00–18.00 Sun & Thurs, 08.00–12.30 & 15.30–18.00 Mon & Tues, 08.00–13.30 Wed, 08.00–12.00 Fri. Located in the New City.

Medical
✚ **Mizra Hospital** ☎ 04 9959595. Located north of the New City.

WHAT TO SEE
Underground Crusader City (☎ *04 9956706;* ◷ *08.30–18.00 Sun–Thu & Sat, 08.30–17.00 Fri (closes 1hr earlier in winter); admission adult/child combination tickets from 25/22NIS)* Today resting under the foundations of al-Jazzar's Citadel, this was the headquarters of the Knights Hospitaller during the Crusades. Excavated in the 1950s to reveal a maze of rooms, the subterranean city is a fascinating place to explore. A vast hall, believed to be a refectory, leads to what was once a secret tunnel that emerged 350m later in Akko's harbour. The tunnel has only partially been excavated and now leads to the Bosta, a large room used by the Knights as a refuge for pilgrims. The crypt of St John, displaying a poignant and telling fleur-de-lys that dated the room to Louis VII's era, was once used as the Knights' banqueting hall.

The Citadel Looming over the submerged Crusader City below, the Ottoman Citadel has been engraved in history books mainly through its role as a high-security prison during the British Mandate. It was in this supposedly impenetrable fortress that members of Jewish Zionist underground organisations were held and several executed. On 4 May 1947, it became the scene of one of the most famous prison escapes in history, when members of the Irgun militant Zionist group broke through the defences in an attempt to free the prisoners. While few escaped alive, it was seen as a major failure on the part of the British and marked a significant downfall in their control. Today the Citadel holds a wealth of sights, most notably the **The Underground Prisoner's Museum** (\ *04 9918264/5/6*; ⊕ *09.00–16.00 Sun–Thu, 09.00–13.00 Fri; admission adult/child 8/4NIS.* \ *049911375*; ⊕ *08.30–16.30 Sun–Thu, 08.30–13.30 Fri; admission 10NIS*). The prison has been left in its original daunting and oppressive state and huge, high ceilings and thick walls make it easy to imagine the horror of being locked up here. The Gallows Room contains the noose from which the nine Jewish resistance fighters were hanged, and photographs and documents commemorating the prisoners who were kept here, including the first prisoner and Israeli hero Z Jabotinsky, are on display. In addition, the **Prison Cell of Baha'u'llah**, the Baha'i faith's founder, can be visited. He was imprisoned by the Ottoman government and spent the best part of his adult life within the walls. Outside is the **Enchanted Garden**, a replica of the one believed to have existed during the Crusader era.

Al-Jazzar Mosque (⊕ *08.00–18.00 Sat–Thu, 08.00–11.00 & 13.00–18.00 Fri; admission 6NIS (closes 1hr earlier in winter); modest dress*) The beautiful, green-domed Al-Jazzar Mosque is hard to miss. Built on the site of Akko's Crusader Cathedral, it is the largest of the city's four mosques, and the third-largest in the country. The submerged cathedral was later flooded and served as a reservoir, which is today accessible from a door at the end of the compound (signposted). Many of the building materials, notably the ornate Roman columns in the courtyard, were taken from the ancient coastal city of Caesarea (see page 158) while inside the mosque there is said to be a strand of hair from the Prophet Muhammad's beard. The entrance to the courtyard is up a flight of stone steps and through a small gate on the lively Al-Jazzar Street just behind the Citadel. Visitors are welcome outside prayer times provided they dress appropriately and respect Muslim religious traditions. A small, simple domed building on the right of the entrance contains the sarcophagi of Ahmed al-Jazzar and his successor Suleiman Pasha.

Al Basha Hammam (Municipal Museum) The *hammam* was built in the 1780s by al-Jazzar as part of his vast mosque complex, and was modelled on Roman bathhouse styles. There are three rooms: one a dressing room, one functioning like that of a Roman *tepidarium* (warm room) and the last a hot steam room. The *baths* (\ *04 9551088*; ⊕ *winter 08.30–17.00 Sun–Thu, 08.30–14.00 Fri, 08.00–15.00 Sat; summer 08.30–19.00 Sun–Thu, 08.30–14.00 Fri, 08.00–17.00 Sat; admission adult/child 25/21NIS (can be included in combination tickets)*) served as more than a place of religious purification, forming an important social centre where meetings were conducted and people came to relax. Colourful lighting, intricate ceramic tiling and marble statues combine with trickling water sounds and **The Story of the Last Bath Attendant** (a rather soapy bath attendant who regales lively tales of the history of Akko) making it an enjoyable and unique museum experience. The entrance to the baths is along Al-Jazzar Street opposite the Citadel a little way up from the Al-Jazzar Mosque.

Khan el Umdan Translating as 'Pillar's Inn', the first glimpse of Akko's most impressive ancient merchants' inn will reveal why it was named thus. Built in the late 18th century, the Khan was placed on a series of large granite columns and acted as storeroom and hotel for merchants arriving at Akko's thriving port. The tiny entrance to this vast courtyard is easily missed. Look for the minaret of the Sinan Basha Mosque on the harbour's edge and the entrance is opposite. The Khan is open to visitors all day and is certainly worth ferreting out.

The city walls The sturdy, pentagon-shaped wall that today surrounds Akko was built in 1750 by Daher el-Omar upon the remains of the Crusader structures, and later fortified by al-Jazzar. When completed it encircled Akko on both land and sea perimeters. From the Weizmann Street entrance, steps on the left lead up onto the **Land Wall Promenade** and on to the **Land Gate**. The **Burj el Commander**, located on the northeast corner of the wall, was the tower said to have defeated Napoleon in 1799 and offers a fabulous view southwest over the rambling buildings of the Old City. The **Sea Wall Promenade** is accessed by steps located a few metres along from Abu Christo Restaurant in the south of the Old City and leads to the **Lighthouse Observation Point**. To see the walls from the invaders' eyes, **Malkat Akko Cruises** (*14 Saladin St;* ☎ *04 9913890;* f *04 9913889;* e *info@nakhourly.co.il; www.nakhourly.co.il; cost adult/child 20/15NIS*) operates boat tours around the walls (40mins) as well as trips along to Rosh Hanikra, Ahziv and Haifa if there are enough people. Boats leave from the marina every hour on Saturdays and tickets can be bought at the dock.

Templars Tunnel (⊕ *08.30–17.30 daily; admission adult/child 10/7NIS*) The tunnel, which was opened to the public in 1999, was built in the 12th century by the Knights Templar and leads from the port in the east to their long-since destroyed and submerged fortress in the southwest of the Old City. The arched tunnels are well lit and not especially narrow making this little-known-about attraction a worthwhile detour. There are two entrances to the tunnel: one through the rather dilapidated **Khan e-Shuna** opposite the Khan el-Umdan, and the second near the lighthouse car park.

Market Street (Benjamin Metudela Street) (⊕ *until 17.00 daily*) Running from north to south, Market Street is noisy, busy and crowded. It is also, however, one of the most fascinating parts of the present-day Old City, where stalls selling sweet pastries, dried fruit, fish, spices and household items squeeze together, the sights, sounds and smells accentuated in the narrow tunnel-like maze. At the end of the street and up a small lane on the right is the **Ramhal Synagogue** (⊕ *08.30–18.00 Sun–Thu & Sat, 08.30–15.00 Fri*), named after the Italian sage Rabbi Moshe Haim Luzatto (the Ramhal), who is best known for his moral guide *Mesilat Yesharim.*

AROUND AKKO

SHRINE OF BAHA'U'LLAH (*gardens* ⊕ *09.00–16.00 daily, shrine* ⊕ *09.00–12.00 Sun–Fri; admission free; modest dress*) The Shrine of Baha'u'llah is the holiest site for members of the Baha'i faith, topping even the vast Shrine of Bab, Haifa's most recognisable landmark. This is the final resting place of Baha'u'llah, founder of the Baha'i faith and the principal pilgrimage site for members of the religion. Following his death on 29 May 1892, Baha'u'llah was interred in the ornate shrine erected next to the **Mansion of Bahji**, where he spent his final days. It is in the direction of the shrine (*Qiblih*), that worshippers face when reciting daily prayers.

The shrine is surrounded by immaculately kept, manicured gardens where not a blade of grass can be found out of place.

GHETTO FIGHTER'S HOUSE (BEIT LOHAMEI HAGETA'OT) (*Kibbutz Lohamei HaGeta'ot;* ❦ *04 9958080;* ⊕ *09.00–16.00 Sun–Thu, Yad LaYeled 10.00–17.00 Sun–Thu; admission adult/child 20/10NIS*) The vast museum complex was established by a group of Holocaust survivors who aimed to tell the story of the Jewish people throughout the 20th century and in particular remember those who died and suffered in the Holocaust. It focuses on Jewish resistance throughout World War II, exhibitions including 'The Warsaw Ghetto Fights Back' and 'Ghettos and Deportations'. The incredibly moving Yad LaYeled (Children's Museum) focuses on the children of the Holocaust, and is a beautiful combination of informative displays, symbolic objects and audio-visual presentations.

Getting there Both the aforementioned sights are located along route 4 between Akko and Nahariya. The Shrine of Baha'u'llah North Gate entrance is approximately 2km from Akko, located within walking distance from the Bustan Hagalil bus stop. Take the side road on the left a few metres from the bus stop in the direction of Akko from where the entrance is a further 450m. The Ghetto Fighter's House is in Kibbutz Lohamei HaGeta'ot. Bus 271 from Haifa to Nahariya stops opposite the museum regularly.

HAIFA

Cascading down the slopes of Mount Carmel towards the sandy beaches of the Mediterranean, Israel's third-largest city is often overlooked as a tourist destination. Yet the city has a lot going for it, and is a great place to spend a few days.

Haifa is probably most well-known for its harmonious interaction among its different faiths, where Jews, Muslims, Druze, Christians and Baha'i exist contentedly alongside one another. The vast, landscaped gardens of the Shrine of Bab, the centre of the Baha'i faith, form the unexpected centrepiece of the city while its thriving port is the largest in the country. Prosperous industries, a large hilltop university, countless religious and historic sights, neighbourhoods old and new, a fascinating collection of museums and a lively restaurant and bar scene make Haifa a firm favourite amongst Israelis and a pleasant contrast to Jerusalem and Tel Aviv.

HISTORY Finds discovered across the city date from the Stone Age to the Ottoman period, while Roman and Greek finds attest to occupation, although by no means comparable to the thriving port city at Caesarea. While not mentioned in the Bible, Haifa appears in the Talmud as an established Jewish settlement which, during the Middle Ages, grew into a shipping centre.

The Crusaders and the Carmelites In 1099, Haifa was conquered by the Crusaders who slaughtered the Jewish residents almost in their entirety. During their occupation of the region, groups of religious hermits began to live in caves dotted across the Carmel area in honour of Elijah the Prophet. Over the next 100 years they formed the Carmelite Order, which spread as far as Europe. While the Order continued to thrive in Europe, the founders on Mount Carmel were exiled when, in 1265, the city fell to the Mamluk sultan Baibars. From 1750 until the beginning of World War I, Haifa remained under Turkish rule following its conquest and refortification by the Bedouin sheikh Dahar el-Omar. The Turks were ousted in 1799 by Napoleon, but this was short-lived following his poignant defeat at Akko.

M e d i t e r r a n e a n   S e a

Bradt

N

0 _____ 600m
0 _____ 600yds

Haifa Port

Shikmona Beach

Bat Galim ✈ HaShaket Beach
Surfer's Beach ✈
**BAT
GALIM**
Rambam Hospital ✚
Bat Galim
(Railway station) 🚉
National
Maritime Museum 🏛
Clandestine Museum 🏛

Cable Car
(Lower station) 🚡
Elijah's Cave
Cable Car
(Upper station)
Stella Maris ✚

Kishon
Port

Kishon

Hutzot HaMifratz
(Railway station) 🚉

Halfa Airport ✈

Lev HaMifratz
(Railway station) 🚉

HAHISTADRUT BD

HAATZMAUT ST

Grand Canyon Mall
(Shopping centre) ●

Maritime Passenger Terminal ●
Merkaz HaShmona
(Railway station) 🚉

see page 143

HA'ATZMAUT ST

HAMEGINIM AV

BEN GURION AV

ALLENBY RD

**GERMAN
COLONY**

Bahai
Shrine ●

HAZIYONUT BD

HANASSI AV

DOWNTOWN

**WADI
NISNAS**

**CENTRAL
CARMEL**

RD

HADAR ST

Carmelit
Subway ●

**HADAR
HACARMEL**

HERZL ST

ARLOSOROV ST

GOLOMB ST

Shulamit Hotel 🏨

MORIAH BD

↓ Haifa University

STELLA MARIS RD

TCHERNIKOVSKY ST

ZA'FAT ST

H A H A G A N A H   A V

H A Y A M   R D

Carmel Beach
(Camel) ✈

Meridien Hotel 🏨
Student's Beach ✈
Hof HaCarmel
Railway station 🚉
Hof HaCarmel
Bus station 🚌

HAHAGANAH AV

Based on mapping by Carra, Jerusalem

138

The German Templars In 1868, the German Templars established a colony in Haifa which today remains one of the city's most picturesque areas (see page 146). The German Templars have been credited with the rapid development of the small, insignificant town they founded. It was, however, at around the same time that the Baha'u'llah, founder of the Baha'i faith, arrived in Haifa, a factor contributing to its development boom at the time. The Templar Society was founded in Germany in 1861 as a result of the severe socio-economic conditions in southwest Germany, and was formed under the aspirations of promoting Messianic ideas as a path to salvation. They purchased lands in Haifa and set up an agricultural community, constructing a beautiful, wide boulevard. The Templars' contribution to the development of Haifa was dramatic: they were the first to use horse-drawn carriages to transport goods and people to Akko; they built modern buildings; a road up to the Carmel; brought with them tools and introduced new agricultural techniques.

The British Mandate During the British Mandate the city renewed its development, with the construction of Jewish neighbourhoods, factories (including the oil refinery) and the Technion College. After World War II, the port at Haifa became the site of several notorious confrontations between the British, and Jews attempting to enter Palestine. The Haganah Zionist organisation operated fervently in the area, smuggling in immigrants and Holocaust survivors. The *Af-Al-Pi-Chen*, a ship used by the British in their blockades, today resides as a lasting reminder outside the Clandestine Immigration and Naval Museum.

ORIENTATION Haifa is divided into three distinct zones ranked one above another both in terms of geography and wealth. The **downtown area (Ir Ha-Tahitt)** with its Old City, harbour and coastal areas is the lowest zone; the central zone is made up of the **Hadar HaCarmel district**, the city's main shopping and commercial centre and home to some of the older neighbourhoods; and **Central Carmel** in the upper reaches of the city, which comprises the richest residential neighbourhoods and luxury hotels and restaurants. The **Universty of Haifa** occupies the highest point and furthest reaches of the city where buildings turn into the sweeping greenery of the Carmel National Park.

Walking around the city is possible, but tough going. The steep slopes are linked by thousands of steps that make a nice downhill tour (see page 142) and a cable car operates from **Bat Galim** to just below the **Carmelite Monastery**. The city is also home to Israel's only subway system, the **Carmelit Underground Railway**. The unmistakable gardens of the **Shrine of Bab** lead down to the **German Colony** at its base, where countless restaurants and cafés line the main **Ben Gurion Avenue**. The major downtown roads are **Ha'atzma'ut Street** and nearby **Jaffa Road**, both running along the coast, while the **Old City** is located one block back. Life in the Central Carmel district centres on **HaNassi Avenue** with its pricey restaurants and trendy bars. In between these, **Herzl Street** forms the hub of activity in the Hadar HaCarmel, an area in serious need of a makeover. While it is the busiest shopping district in the city, it doesn't have an awful lot else going for it. Cheap eateries and budget hotels often attract those on a tighter budget, while **Nordau Pedestrian Precinct** has become the Russian centre of the city, inhabited by scores of immigrants who have added their stamp onto the area.

GETTING THERE
Bus Buses from Nahariya, Akko and the Galilee terminate in the Lev HaMifratz Bus Station while buses coming from the south and Jerusalem stop at the Hof HaCarmel Bus Station (next to the Carmel Train Station). Inter-city buses head in and out of the old central bus station on HaHaganah Avenue. To Tel Aviv, express

buses 910 and 900 (90mins/23NIS), and the slower 921 bus (3hrs/25NIS) depart every 20 minutes. Direct buses 940 and 960 leave every 30 minutes to Jerusalem (2hrs/39NIS), while bus 947 (2hrs 45mins/39NIS) stops at Ben Gurion Airport along the way. To Nahariya, bus 271 leaves every 20 minutes (1hr/14.80NIS) and to Akko buses leave every ten minutes (35mins/11.70NIS). To Nazareth, bus 332 departs every 15 minutes (45mins/18NIS) and to Tiberias, bus 430 every 30 minutes (1hr 10mins/25NIS).

Train Haifa has five train stations: Hof HaCarmel, BatGalim, Merkaz HaShmona, Lev HaMifratz and Hutzot HaMifratz. Lev HaMifratz in the eastern part of the city is useful for connecting to buses heading northwards and to the Galilee as it is adjacent to the bus station of the same name. Lev HaMifratz and Hof HaCarmel are the most convenient for trains to Tel Aviv, the latter being close to the Carmel Bus Station for buses to Jerusalem. Trains depart to Tel Aviv about once an hour (1hr 30mins/31.5NIS). From Hof HaCarmel and Lev HaMifratz trains head north to Nahariya hourly (45mins/16NIS) via Akko (30mins/12.50NIS).

Air Haifa Airport (✆ 04 8476100) ranks as Israel's third-busiest airport after Ben Gurion and Eilat and offers decently priced domestic flights to both cities. **Arkia** (✆ 03 6902222; www.arkia.co.il) offers flights only to and from Eilat for approximately 250NIS one way. **Israir** (✆ 03 7955777; www.israirairlines.com) runs regular flights to both Tel Aviv and Eilat for between 180NIS and 375NIS one way. Alternatively, **Golden Wings Air Tours** (Haifa Airport; ✆ 04 8476188; e goldenwg@netvision. net.il; www.canfeipaz.co.il) offers private-hire small planes to any landing strip in Israel, as well as several destinations abroad. A return flight for five people to Larnaka, Cyprus, for example, costs approximately 7,000NIS. Public transport to the airport is limited but bus 58 from Lev HaMifratz Bus Station runs hourly. **Monitax taxis** (✆ 04 8664343) also serve the airport and wait outside the terminal building.

Sea Cruises to Turkey, the Greek Islands and Italy can be arranged through **Mano Tours** (2 HaPalyam St; ✆ 04 8606666; f 04 8667666; www.mano.co.il) or **Caspi Shipping** (76 Ha'atzma'ut St; ✆ 04 8674444; e lea@caspi-sapanut.co.il; www.caspitours.co.il) and leave from the rather nice **Maritime Passenger Terminal** (✆ 04 8518245; www.haifaport.co.il).

GETTING AROUND Haifa's city centre cascades down Mount Carmel's northern slope making for some interesting, but tiring, topography. Walking downhill is always an option but you'll soon run out of steam if you try and navigate by foot. Thankfully Haifa has several good public transport options to combat foot fatigue. Haifa is also the only city in Israel where public transport runs on Shabbat (albeit limited services).

Bus Intra-city buses operate 05.00–23.30 Sunday–Thursday, 05.00–16.30 Friday, and a limited service runs 09.00–midnight Saturday. Fares within Haifa are usually 5NIS. For more information, call 04 8549131. The following bus routes run along most major streets and stop at the main attractions:

#3 Runs from Hof HaCarmel Bus Station along Hayam Road and onto Arlosorov Street. From there it makes its way down HeHalutz Street, Bialik Street, onto Ma'ale Hashihrur Street and then down HaMeginim Boulevard.
#43 Begins at Hof HaCarmel Bus Station and runs along HaHaganah Boulevard down France Road to Ramat Shaul. From there it heads towards Hasionut Boulevard and onto Herzliya Street by way of Herzl Street.

#99 and #99a Begin at Bat Galim Bus Station and run along Rothschild Boulevard and onto Stella Maris Road. From there they make their way to HaNassi Boulevard and along Moriah Boulevard before turning into Froyd Street and finishing at Hof HaCarmel Bus Station.

#24 Runs to the university on the fringes of the city. The route takes buses along Pika Road, past the Grand Canyon Mall, Rupin Road, Ge'ula Street and Arlosorov. It then continues along Balfour Street and HeHalutz Street, onto HaMeginim and Rothschild boulevards and finishes at Bat Galim Bus Station.

#101 Starts in Lev HaMifratz Bus Station and runs along Ha'atzma'ut Street to Bat Galim Bus Station.

Underground The **Carmelit Underground Railway** (*04 8376861; trains run 06.00–22.00 Sun–Thu, 06.00–15.00 Fri; fare 5.50NIS one way*) is Israel's one and only subway system and is a great way of avoiding the steps of central Haifa. The line starts at **Paris Square** in the downtown area and finishes at the **Gan Ha'em Park** in the Carmel Centre. There are four stations in between: **Golomb Street**, **Masada Street**, **Neviim** and **Solel Boneh**.

Cable car The **Haifa Cable Car** (*04 8335970; ⊕ 10.00–18.00 daily; fare one way/return 16/22NIS*) consists of three little red bubbles that zip up and down the steep slope between **Bat Galim** and the **Stella Maris**, and offers lovely views over the harbour.

TOURIST INFORMATION

ℹ Haifa Tourism Development Association 48 Ben Gurion Av; ✆ 04 8356765; e info@tour-haifa.co.il; www.tour-haifa.co.il; ⊕ 09.00–17.00 Sun–Thu, 09.00–13.00 Fri, 10.00–15.00 Sat. They can organise museum tickets, guides & accommodation. They also have a great website. Bus 22 stops at the corner of Ben Gurion and HaGefen streets.

LOCAL TOUR OPERATORS Many of the nationwide tour operators arrange trips to and around the Haifa and Carmel region. For more information see page 33.

Egged Tours 4 Nordau St; ✆ 04 8623131; www.egged.co.il. Operate informative city bus tours that pass Haifa's most interesting sights.
Golden Wings Air Tours Haifa Airport; ✆ 04 8476188; e goldenwg@netvision.net.il; www.canfeipaz.co.il. Arrange tours over the Haifa region. A 30min flight for up to 3 people costs 520NIS. They also offer air taxi services within Israel.
Society for Protection of Nature in Israel (SPNI) 18 Hillel St; ✆ 04 8664135; e bela@spni.org.il; www.teva.org.il. Have good hiking maps & can arrange trips to the Carmel National Park.

WHERE TO STAY

🏠 **Dan Panorama Hotel** (267 rooms) 107 HaNassi Av; ✆ 04 8352222; e T.PanormamaHaifa@DanHotels.com; www.danhotels.com. Modern, contemporary décor, swish rooms & fabulous bird's-eye views over Haifa & the harbour. It is linked to the flashy Panorama Shopping Centre & has 2 restaurants, a café & bar, fitness centre & sauna. Rooms are priced differently depending on the view. $$$$

🏠 **Meridien Hotel** (200 rooms) 10 David Elazar St; ✆ 04 8508888; www.fattal.co.il. While the hotel is irrefutably luxurious, its crowning glory is its seafront location. Large swimming pool, spa, health club, 3 restaurants & a café. $$$$

🏠 **The Gallery Hotel** (40 rooms) 61 Herzl St; ✆ 04 8616161; e gallery@hotelgallery.co.il; www.haifa.hotelgallery.co.il. Exquisite boutique hotel decked out in minimalist elegance in Bauhaus architectural style. Luxury packages from 700NIS include double rooms, gourmet breakfast & massages. Full range of facilities including spa centre, money change & guided tours of the city. $$$

🏠 **Beth Shalom Hotel** (30 rooms) 110 HaNassi Av;

Haifa isn't an easy city to navigate for first-time visitors. With its higgledy-piggledy street pattern and steep topography it can be a virtual maze and often the best parts are the hardest to ferret out. To see the behind-the-scenes Haifa, the tourist board has designed the Path of 1,000 Steps (which is actually 1,100), which weaves in and out of the patchwork of neighbourhoods, alleyways and terraces that make up the city. The tour takes you past the Baha'i Shrine and German Colony, down to Wadi Nisnas.

The tour Start at the Savyonim lookout point – the Gadera steps – Ha Hashmonaim Street – the public gardens – the Koresh steps to the Reuben Buniak steps – the Abu Nedar Institutes – the 'Ezra' hospital – the ha Zionut Avenue – the Shifra steps – Abbas Street – Ha Geffen Street. Maps showing this (and other) routes are available from the tourist information centre (see page 141).

04 8377481; www.beth-shalom.ch. Perched high on Mount Carmel, this simple hotel is well tended, comfortable & good value for money. Rooms are uninspiring but clean & airy & come with TV, AC & telephone. A small, leafy courtyard is a welcome spot to rest after a day of sightseeing. **$$**

⌂ **Haddad Guest House** (7 rooms) 26 Ben Gurion Av; 772010618 (no area code); e reservation@haddadguesthouse.com; www.haddadguesthouse.com. While the décor is rather plain, the fantastic location in the heart of the German Colony more than makes up for it. Rooms have kitchenette, TV, AC & hairdryers. **$$**

⌂ **Pundak HaNamal (Port Inn)** (10 rooms) 34 Jaffa Rd; 04 8524401; e port_inn@yahoo.com; www.portinn.co.il. Big, bright, airy rooms & a lovely port view make this a refreshing budget option. Comfy lounge area with cable TV, fully equipped kitchen & dining room, laundry facilities, internet, tourist information & a shady little sun terrace make it one of the best choices in town. Double rooms are on a B&B basis. For dorm guests, breakfast is 25NIS extra. *Dorms (70NIS).* **$$**

⌂ **Shulamit Hotel** (70 rooms) 15 Kiryat Sefer St; 04 8342811; e shulamithotel@012.net.il. Great location, attentive service, beautiful rooms & a reasonable price. Price includes breakfast. **$$**

⌂ **Eden Hotel** (14 rooms) 8 Shmariyahu Levin St; 04 8664816; f 04 8642633. Great mid-range option with bright, airy rooms & cable TV. Small & cosy. **$**

✕ WHERE TO EAT

✕ **Jacko Seafood** 12 Kehilat Saloniki St; 04 8626639; ⏰ 12.00–midnight Sun–Fri, 12.00–18.00 Sat. First branch of this 30-year-old chain of well-loved fish & seafood restaurants. Countless different fish, shellfish & seafood cooked any way you like it. There is another branch at 11 Moriah St. **$$$$**

✕ **Isabella** 6 Ben Gurion Bd; 04 8552201; ⏰ 10.00–midnight Sun–Thu, 10.00–02.00 Fri/Sat. Well-loved Italian restaurant with a great selection of fresh pastas & meats (although the steak is a bit on the pricey side). **$$$**

✕ **Sinta-Bar** 127 Moriah St; 04 8341170; ⏰ 12.00–late daily. Elegant bistro bar specialising in meat, fish & seafood (although it's their juicy hamburgers that keep their regulars coming back). **$$$**

✕ **Abu Sha** 29 HaMeginim St; ⏰ 06.00–18.30 daily. Tiny hummus joint that is super popular with locals. Squeeze onto one of the 7 tables & enjoy a filling meal of hummus, chips, salad & *mejadra*, a bowl of hot rice & lentils. **$$**

✕ **Ma'ayan Habira (Beer Fountain)** 4 Natanson St; 04 8623193; ⏰ 10.00–17.00 Sun–Fri, 10.00–midnight Tue. Located in the heart of the souk not far from Paris Sq. Simple Romanian & eastern European dishes cooked with traditional flair & years of expertise. Be sure to try their smoked meats & *krepla* (dumplings in soup). Tables must be reserved on Tue. **$$**

HAIFA
City Centre

Bradt

0 ——100m
0 ——100yds

N

German Colony

Cruise liner berth

Maritime Passenger Terminal

Merkaz HaShmona Railway Stn

HA'ATZMA'UT ROAD

YAFO ROAD

Isabella
City Center (Shopping Cntr)

BEN GURION AV

KEHILAT SALONIKI ST

HAMEGINIM AV

DOWNTOWN

Pundak HaNamal (Port Inn)
Police Station

Caspi Shipping
Jacko Seafood

HA'ATZMA'UT ROAD

Bank Leumi $

Haddad Guest House

Ma'ayan Habira (Beer fountain)

HaHaganah Square
Abu Sha

Mano Tours
Paris Square

NATANSON ROAD

ALLENBY ROAD

BEN GURION AV

Paris Square Stn

HAPALYAM BD

SHIVAT ZIYYON ST
Railway

Central PO

Tourism Development Agency

HAGEFEN AV

Bet HaGefen

HATZIONUT AV

DORDAU ST

HASSAN SHUKRI ST

WADI NISNAS

AVENUE

Underground
Carmelit

Solel Boneh Stn

HASSAN SHUKRI ST

MA'ALE HASHIHRUR ST

Haifa Museum

HANEVI'IM

LEVIN STREET

ABBAS STREET

SHABTAI LEVI ST

Eden

Shrine of Bab

Bahai Shrine

HANEVI'IM AV

Bank Hapoalim $

HaNeviim Stn

HERZL ST

Steimatzky

HADAR

BIALIK ST

HACARMEL

ISSTA

SHMARIYAHU LEVIN ST

HATZIONUT AVENUE

BEN YEHUDA STREET

LaMetayel

BALFOUR ST

The Gallery Hotel, Akko

Persian Gardens

HILLEL STREET

MASSADA ST

MASSADA ST

HOREI YOHANAN HA KADOSH ST

Tambayan

YERUSHALAYIM ST

PEVSNER STREET

Railway
Masada St Stn

SPNI office

HILLEL ST

GOLOMB STREET

Mother's Park

Tikotin Museum of Japanese Art

Underground
Carmelit

Golomb St Stn

HESS STREET

BAR GIORA STREET

ARLOSOROV ST

Haifa Municipal Theatre

GOLOMB STREET

HENRIETTA SZOLD ST

Benei Zion (Rothschild) Hospital

HAPO'EL ST

Beth Shalom

HANASSI AVENUE

Dan Panorama
Panorama Center (Shopping Cntr)

HENRIETTA SZOLD STREET

HAPO'EL ST

HESS STREET

Gan Ha'em Park Stn

Morrison

Gan Ha'em Coffee

HAYAM ROAD

Mt Carmel National Park

Based on mapping by Carta, Jerusalem

Mediterranean Coast HAIFA

5

143

ENTERTAINMENT AND NIGHTLIFE
The arts

☺ **Haifa Municipal Theatre** 50 Pevsner St; ☎ 04 8600555; box office, ☎ 04 8605000. Has regular performances, but few are in English.

☺ **The Auditorium** 138 HaNassi Av; ☎ 04 8353580. Seating up to 1,200 people, the auditorium plays host to concerts & events throughout the year. Buses 21, 22, 23, 28 & 37 stop outside or take the Carmelit Railway to Gan Ha'em Station.

☺ **The Cinematheque** 142 HaNassi Av; ☎ 04 8353530/31; ⊕ 18.00–20.00 daily. The Cinematheque is a hub of all things cinematic. Twice-daily showings of non-mainstream films, cinema courses & a huge auditorium are on offer.

Bars Although not comparable with Tel Aviv's pumping nightlife scene, Haifa has come a long way in recent years and now offers plenty of decent and varied bars and pubs. The main cluster of bars is along Moriah Boulevard (which turns into HaNassi Street).

♀ **Barbarossa** 8 HaPika St; ☎ 04 8114010; www.barbarossa.co.il; ⊕ 18.00–late daily. Modern meat & seafood restaurant with a great bar atmosphere. They offer 9 types of beer, 110 types of whisky, some wonderful Italian appetisers & a mean hamburger. Attracts a slightly older crowd. **$$$**

♀ **Brown** 131 Moriah Bd; ☎ 04 8112391; ⊕ 19.00–05.00 daily. Leather-seated booths, wooden tables & cosy lighting make this a good choice for a relaxed beer & light meal. Music ranges from 1980s hits to Israeli & international rock. **$$**

♀ **Duke** 107 Moriah St; ☎ 04 8347282; ⊕ 12.00–late daily. Traditional, wood-panelled Irish pub complete with well-priced Guinness (26NIS) & good pub food. Happy 'hour' is 17.00–20.00 & live sporting events on big screens. **$$**

♀ **Pundak HaDov (The Bear)** 135 HaNassi Bd; ☎ 04 8381703; ⊕ 11.00–late Sun–Fri, 18.00–late Fri. Cosy pub with indoor & outdoor seating, an extensive cocktail menu, decent pub food & a mellow atmosphere. Often shows live sporting events (when the atmosphere is a little less mellow). **$$**

♀ **Morrison** 111 Yefe Nof St; ☎ 04 8383828; ⊕ 20.00–late daily. Highly popular rock/pick-up bar that hosts Mon open mic nights, Tue live performances (starting at 22.00) & Wed student nights. The one-way mirrors in the toilets are novel but rather disconcerting.

SHOPPING The awkward city layout is not conducive to window shopping and, as such, the city has become known for its numerous malls and shopping centres. The gargantuan **Grand Canyon Mall** (*Simcha Golan Way, Neve Sha'anan;* ☎ 04 8121111; ⊕ 10.00–22.00 Sun–Thu, 10.00–15.00 Fri, end of Shabbat–22.30 Sat) is Israel's largest shopping centre with 150 shops, an indoor amusement park, countless food outlets and a spa. Although built in 1986 the **Panorama Centre** (*109 HaNassi Av;* ☎ 04 8375011; ⊕ 09.00–22.00 Sun–Thu), which is located in the Carmel Centre remains a firm favourite and has great variety of shops, cinemas and cafés. The **City Centre** (*6 Ben Gurion Av;* ☎ 04 8531111; ⊕ 10.00–22.00 Sun–Thu, 10.00–15.00 Fri, end of Shabbat–22.30 Sat) is considerably smaller than the others but useful if you're in the area. **Herzl** and **Nordau streets** are your best bet for shopping streets but pale in contrast to the malls and the shopping mecca of Tel Aviv.

Useful shops

🏬 **LaMetayel** 2 Balfour St; ☎ 04 8644244; ⊕ 09.00–19.00 Sun/Mon & Thu, 09.00–18.00 Tue, 09.00–14.00 Wed, 09.00–13.00 Fri. Good selection of camping supplies.

🏬 **Steimatsky** 16 Herzl St; ☎ 04 8665042; ⊕ 08.30–19.00 Sun–Thu, 08.30–14.00 Fri. Part of the international chain. Has a big selection of English books & newspapers.

Downtown With everything from Turkish bakeries to *burekas* stalls, it is one of the best places to get great, cheap food.

Bat Galim The best place in the city if you're after the fruits of the sea. Fresh fish and seafood can be found in the many seafront restaurants.

German Colony Elegant dining, trendy cafés and wonderful ice-cream parlours line the main Ben Gurion Avenue, which provides a stunning night-time view of the illuminated Baha'i Shrine and Persian Gardens.

Wadi Nisnas The souk that forms the core of the neighbourhood abounds with traditional Arabic fare at extremely cheap prices. Stalls serving falafel, hummus, *shawarma*, freshly baked pitas, sweet pastries and spices are squeezed into the hubbub of activity in the thriving market.

Hadar HaCarmel Offers a broad selection of restaurants, cafés, fast-food joints and bars at various prices. Masada and Hillel streets have recently become the new artistic centres of the area, and trendy cafés have sprung up in between art galleries and exhibits. Falafel stands can be found along Herzl and HaHalutz streets, while the Nordau pedestrian street has slightly pricier cafés.

Central Carmel This area is renowned as being the *pièce de résistance* of eating out in Haifa. The best restaurants can be found alongside five-star hotels with breathtaking views over the city and harbour.

OTHER PRACTICALITIES
Emergencies
Ambulance ✆ 101   **Police** 28 Jaffa St; ✆ 100
Fire ✆ 102

Money ATMs are commonplace and you won't have to look far to find one. Likewise, change bureaux are located along all main roads. There are countless branches of Bank Hapoalim and Bank Leumi dotted around the city.

$ **Bank Hapoalim** 18 Hanevi'im St; ✆ 03 6532407/ landline*2407; ⊕ 08.30–13.15 Sun & Tue/Wed, 08.30–13.00 & 16.00–18.30 Mon & Thu. Main branch. Changes money & travellers' cheques.

$ **Bank Leumi** 21 Jaffa St; ✆ 03 9544555/ landline*5522; ⊕ 08.30–14.45 Sun–Thu, 08.30–12.00 Fri. Main branch.

Post
✉ **Central post office** 19 HaPalyam Bd; ✆ 04 8304182; ⊕ 08.00–17.00 Sun–Thu, 08.00–12.00 Fri. Changes money and travellers' cheques. Other

branches can be found at 152 Jaffa Rd, 63 Herzl St & 7 Wedgewood Bd.

Medical
✚ **Benei Zion (Rothschild) Hospital** 47 Golomb St; ✆ 04 8359359
✚ **Rambam Hospital** Bat Galim; ✆ 04 8543111
✚ **Superpharm** 134 HaNassi Bd in Auditorium Haifa

Mall; ✆ 04 8104844; ⊕ 08.30–10.30 Sun–Thu, 08.00–17.00 Fri, 11.00–23.00 Sat; also at 6 Ben Gurion Bd; ✆ 04 8507755; ⊕ 09.00–22.00 Sun–Thu, 09.00–16.00 Fri, 08.00–23.00 Sat

Internet
✉ **Gan Ha'em Coffee** 122 HaNassi Av; ✆ 04 8384692; ⊕ 09.00–midnight Sat–Thu, 09.00–17.00 Fri. 25NIS/hr. Located at street level

just outside the Gan Ha'em subway station.
✉ **Tambayan** 31 Nordau St; ✆ 04 8669996; ⊕ 10.00–22.00 daily. 15NIS/hr.

5

Travel agencies

ISSTA 20 Herzl St; ☏ 04 8682222;
e admin@isstadirect.com; www.isstadirect.com;

⊕ 09.00–19.00 Sun–Tue & Thu. Can book budget air tickets. Several branches around town.

WHAT TO SEE

Baha'i Shrine and Persian Gardens The immense golden dome of the **Shrine of Bab** (⊕ *09.00–12.00; admission free; modest dress*) and Persian gardens (☏ *04 8313131;* ⊕ *09.00–17.00 daily except 9 Jul & 2 May; admission & tour free*) dominate Haifa's skyline and is the world centre and one of the holiest sites of pilgrimage for members of the Baha'i faith. The structure was built in 1953 over the burial place of Said Ali Muhammad 'Bab', who is considered the founder of the Baha'i Faith. Tours around the gardens are given by Baha'i volunteers and while they must be booked in advance are free and informative (note there are no tours on Wednesdays). The northern entrance is located just below Yefe Nof Street where grand marble steps stretch through immaculate gardens and past vibrant flowerbeds. From the Hadar Bus Station bus 23 stops at Yefe Nof Street.

Cave of Elijah (*230 Allenby Rd;* ☏ *04 8527430; www.bahai.bwc.org;* ⊕ *08.00–18.00 Sun–Thu (17.00 in winter), 08.00–13.00 Fri; admission free; modest dress*) According to tradition, Elijah the Prophet spent many years living in a cave nestled into the Carmel Mountain and many significant events in his life are said to have happened here; it was in this cave that he lived and meditated before defeating the Priests of Baal at Muhraka (see page 153); he took refuge here from King Ahab and his wife Jezebel; and he established his school upon his return from exile. It is also said to be the place where the Holy Family took shelter on their return from Egypt. Today the cave is worshipped by Jews, Christians, Druze and Muslims (who had a mosque here until 1948), who all venerate Elijah. Inside the cave is a small altar, illuminated by candles which can be bough for 2NIS by vendors at the base of the steps leading up to the cave. The steps and entrance are located on Allenby Road, 100m from the Maritime Museum but signposted in Hebrew only. Buses 3, 5, 44 and 45 will drop you off at the highway, 50m from the steps.

Stella Maris The 19th-century **Carmelite Monastery** (☏ *04 8337758;* ⊕ *06.20–12.30 & 15.00–18.00 Mon–Sat; admission free; modest dress*) is located high on the slopes of Mount Carmel, offering fabulous views over the bay of Haifa and north towards Lebanon. Members of the 12th-century Carmelite Order (see page 137) were exiled following the conquest by the Mamluk sultan Baibars and didn't return until the 18th century when the monastery was commissioned. During Napoleon's unsuccessful attack on Akko, an earlier monastery on the grounds was used as a hospital for wounded French soldiers who were promptly slaughtered by the Turks upon Napoleon's retreat. In front of the monastery is a **monument** to the soldiers who died. The beautiful church that stands today is constructed of bright white marble and the dome is adorned with paintings depicting stories from the Old Testament. The **cable car** makes its final stop opposite the monastery next to the **lighthouse**. The street opposite the Stella Maris claimed an infamous attribute in 2006 when it became the first place in Haifa to be hit by a Hezbollah Katyusha rocket. Buses 26 from Hadar HaCarmel and 31 from Carmel Central stop outside.

German Colony The main street through the recently renovated colony is **Ben Gurion Boulevard** which begins at the base of the Baha'i Shrine and runs south to HaMeginim Avenue. The 30m-wide boulevard is lined with stone houses, courtyards and large, leafy trees lined with trendy restaurants, outdoor cafés and pricey ice-cream parlours.

In July 2006, Israel once again hit international headlines when military conflict broke out following Hezbollah's firing of Katyusha rockets at northern Israeli towns. The conflict, known as the 2006 Lebanon War, raged for over a month during which time the residents of Haifa and much of the north of the country spent the majority of their time beneath ground in bomb shelters and bunkers. Businesses suffered, the bustling city came to a near halt and the wails of constant air-raid sirens filled the air. The devastation caused by the conflict was massive on both sides and Israel lost 43 civilians and 120 soldiers in the month-long war. A UN ceasefire ended the shelling on 14 August when the residents of Haifa and northern Israel finally emerged from their shelters. Apart from the vast economic and social impact of the conflict, several events caused catastrophic environmental damage that impacted not just Israel but Lebanon, Turkey and Cyprus. The IDF bombing of the Jiyeh Power Station in Lebanon resulted in the largest-ever oil spill in the Mediterranean Sea. Thousands of tons of oil spilled out, causing a slick covering 170km of coastline. The habitat of the endangered sea turtle that thrives in this area was threatened and thousands of fish and marine life killed. Hezbollah rockets caused numerous forest fires in northern Israel, killing acres of forestland that will take decades to recover.

University The university has claim to the some of the prime real estate in the city, with fantastic views over both the harbour and city, and Carmel Mountain range. The 30th floor of the **Eshkol Tower** has been converted into an **observatory** and is unarguably the best viewpoint in the city. The **Hecht Museum** (✆ 04 8257773; ⊕ 10.00–16.00 Sun/Mon & Wed/Thu, 10.00–19.00 Tue, 10.00–13.00 Fri, 10.00–14.00 Sat; admission free) is located within the university grounds and features, apart from archaeological collections, 19th- and 20th-century paintings and sculptures, including works by Monet, Pissaro and Van Gogh.

Wadi Nisnas The neighbourhood of Wadi Nisnas could serve as a model for peaceful co-existence. The area, located just below the Haifa Museum, is home to both Jews and Arabs who live harmoniously, and actively try to demonstrate that religious preferences should be respected. Every year in December, the neighbourhood puts on the **Hag HaHagim** (Festival of all Festivals) in which Jews, Christians and Muslims take part in a celebration of Hanukka, Christmas and Ramadan. The **Bet HaGefen Jewish-Arab Centre** (2 HaGefen St; ✆ 04 8525252; ⊕ 08.00–13.00 & 16.00–20.00 Sun–Thu, 08.00–13.00 Fri, 10.00–13.00 Sat) arranges Saturday tours of Wadi Nisnas in English, but it is best to call in advance. The neighbourhood is a fascinating place to visit, where churches, mosques and synagogues stand side by side, original buildings remain as testament to one of the city's oldest residential areas and colourful shops line the streets. **Horei Yohanan ha Kadosh Street** and the surrounding lanes and alleys form the centre of the neighbourhood and is a good place to start exploring. Buses 21, 28 and 37 stop along Yohanan ha Kadosh Street.

Museums
Haifa Museum (26 Shabtai Levi St; ✆ 04 8523255; ⊕ 10.00–16.00 Mon–Wed, 16.00–21.00 Thu, 10.00–13.00 Fri, 10.00–15.00 Sat; admission adult/child 29/22NIS) The museum incorporates the **Museum of Modern Art** and the **Museum of Ancient Art** and has departments dedicated to ethnography, folklore and Jewish ritual art. There are good archaeological exhibits of finds from Haifa

MEDITERRANEAN COAST

Gordon, Frishman and Bograshov beaches These are the quintessential Tel Avivian beaches, where muscular bronzed soldiers, tiny tots in rubber rings, sunburnt foreigners and everyone in between come to enjoy the summer sun and refreshing Mediterranean waters. A plethora of amenities, cafés, restaurants, lifeguards and beach beds combined with the wide, golden sands makes this the best city beach in the country.

Beit Yannai About 20 minutes north of Netanya is this wild, sweeping stretch of pristine coast which is the pride and joy of the residents who live in the cosy little moshavs nearby. With a definite neighbourhood feel, high rocky cliffs, scampering dogs, a rustic little café and miles of open sand it exemplifies Israeli beach culture.

Ahziv With the crumbling archaeological ruins of ancient Ahziv (see page 130) forming the backdrop, this northern Mediterranean beach is a hidden paradise. Sheltered pools have carved themselves out of the rocky shoreline, their warm, shallow waters glimmering a vibrant turquoise under the summer sun.

SEA OF GALILEE

Ein Gev Resort Village Beach As the biblical waters of the Sea of Galilee lap against the green-grassed shores, an air of tranquillity and spirituality descends over the private resort village. In contrast to its more rambunctious neighbours along the coast, the Ein Gev Beach and those just to the south of it characterise the air of mysticism that most hope to find.

DEAD SEA

Biankini and Siesta Beach At the northern end of the Dead Sea, where great hotels and the infringement of modernisation have yet to impinge on the untamed coast, the Biankini and Siesta Beach provides a mellow, exotic and authentic Dead Sea beach experience.

RED SEA

Coral Beach Reserve The aquatic, fish-laden tropical garden of Eilat's Coral Beach Reserve is the best-preserved stretch of Israel's Red Sea coast. Rainbow-coloured fish, swirling corals and the year-round warm, gentle waters make this one of the prettiest beaches in the country.

and Caesarea and a collection of over 7,000 international and Israeli contemporary art pieces.

National Maritime Museum (*198 Allenby Av;* ✆ *04 8536622;* ☉ *10.30–16.00 Mon & Wed/Thu, 16.00–20.00 Tue, 10.30–13.00 Fri, 10.30–15.00 Sat; admission adult/child 29/22NIS*). The museum depicts the maritime history and development of shipbuilding in the region. Four floors of collections cover a whole spectrum of themes including maritime mythology, piracy, the Greeks and Romans, scientific instruments, naval ships and shipping over the past 5,000 years.

Tikotin Museum of Japanese Art (*89 HaNassi Av;* ✆ *04 8383554;* ☉ *10.30–16.00 Mon–Wed, 16.00–19.00 Thu, 10.30–13.00 Fri, 10.30–15.00 Sat; admission adult/child 29/22NIS*). The museum displays a rather unique collection of ancient and modern Japanese art.

Clandestine Immigration and Naval Museum (*204 Allenby Rd;* ✆ *04 8536249;* ⊕ *08.30–16.00 Sun–Thu; admission adult/child 10/5NIS*). The museum is easily identified by the large British blockade ship the *Af-Al-Pi-Chen* outside, which was the centre of skirmishes between British officials and immigrants attempting to land in the country following World War II. The museum is devoted to Israeli naval history and the clandestine immigration but pales in comparison with the National Maritime Museum.

BEACHES AND ACTIVITIES Beaches in Haifa can be divided into two types: official, with bars, restaurants and the full set of facilities, and unofficial, which have none of these. The younger set tends to enjoy the unofficial beaches, where the wild sands and sea are facilities enough, while families often opt for the official beaches. The **Carmel Beach (Camel)** marks the beginning of the unofficial beaches, from which uninterrupted sand sweeps the length of the coast as far as Atlit naval base. Just south of the **Carmel Beach** is the ever-popular **Student's Beach**. Official beaches are located between Camel Beach and the Meridien Hotel and around Bat Galim. **Bat Galim Surfer's Beach** and **Shikmona Beach** are the most popular with surfers, windsurfers and kite surfers but often too rough for swimming. Opposite the Clandestine Museum is a **windsurfing centre** where equipment can be hired. The religious **HaShaket Beach** is one of the quietest in the city, with pond-like waters and plenty of shade. Men and women have separate swimming days except Saturdays when it is open to all (women: Sunday, Tuesday, Thursday; men: Monday, Wednesday, Friday). The **Ze'ev Hayam Diving Club** (*Kishon Port;* ✆ *04 8323911/8662005;* ⊕ *08.00–17.00 daily*) or **Val Tal Diving Centre** (*Hubert Humphrey St;* ✆ *04 8511523;* ⊕ *09.00–16.00 Mon–Sat*) offers dive trips to sites in and around Haifa, where several wrecks have created reefs. **Harbour cruises** (*Kishon Port,* ✆ *04 8418765; cost adult/child 30/25NIS*) operate tours three times a day during Passover, Sukkot and summer school holidays. There is a possibility of getting on group-booked cruises at other times of year but you need to call ahead. Bus 58 stops at the Kishon Port.

MOUNT CARMEL NATIONAL PARK

✆ *04 8231452; admission 30NIS per car, free on foot*

Proudly standing as Israel's largest national park, Mount Carmel is in fact a 23km-long limestone mountain ridge extending from Haifa in the north to the Galilee in the east as far as the coastal Plain of Sharon in the south. Its rich, fertile soils have long been a draw for settlers, taking advantage of its lush greenery and thriving plant and animal species for as long as 200,000 years. Today the park is wholly dedicated to the preservation of this natural heritage and of maintaining the indigenous habitat of the area.

The Carmel was designated a national park in 1971 and incorporates (among a whole host of picturesque and historically significant sites) the **Hai Bar Wildlife Reserve**, **Ein Hod** artists' village, **Muhraka Monastery** and **Carmel Caves**. You can easily spend days exploring the area and it is certainly a justifiable expenditure of your time.

The Mediterranean scrub forest, with its carob and rare kermes oak trees provides for some wonderful walks, picnic and camping spots, cycling, jeep trips and nature spotting and is a strong favourite with weekending Israelis. Several streams flow through the mountains: Nahal Me'arot (which can be accessed through the Nahal Me'arot (Carmel Caves) Nature Reserve), Nahal Galim and Nahal Kelah, also known as 'Little Switzerland' because of its striking resemblance to the Swiss alpine forests. The last can be accessed from the park's main entrance near Haifa University.

Apart from the labyrinthine hiking trails weaving their way across the mountain ridge, the sumptuous rustic Druze fare and abounding nature, the Carmel offers some more (or less) active pursuits for those in need of something different.

The Riders Experience Kibbutz Beit Oren; ☏ 04 8307242; www.havayat-harochvim.co.il; ⏰ 09.00–16.00 daily. Well-equipped horse ranch located just outside the kibbutz offering guided horse trips in the surrounding landscape (1hr, 110NIS pp or 300NIS for private couple trek with wine). They also offer tomcar tours (1hr guided, self-drive tour, 320NIS per car), jeep tours (1hr, 550NIS per jeep) & mountain biking (40NIS/hr including a map & a helmet). Call in advance to reserve all activities.

Paradive skydiving centre Moshav HaBonim; ☏ 04 6391068; e manifest@paradive.co.il; www.paradive.co.il; ⏰ 08.30–17.30 daily. One of the top skydiving centres in the country offering magnificent jumps over the Carmel Mountains & glittering Mediterranean Sea.

🏠 **Beit Oren Hotel Spa** (36 rooms) Kibbutz Beit Oren; ☏ 04 8307444; e bo_hotel@beit-oren.org.il. Situated in the heart of the Carmel National Park, the hotel sits at 400m above sea level with breathtaking views over the Mediterranean coast & Carmel range. Swimming pool, spa & fitness centre, restaurant & expansive gardens complete the rural retreat atmosphere. Price based on B&B. HB (130NIS more per double) & FB (230NIS more per double) options are also available. **$$$**

HISTORY Sacred to Christians, Jews, Muslims and Baha'is alike, the Carmel region has seen its fair share of triumphs and defeats over the past 200,000 years. From the skeletal remains of a Neanderthal couple that were unearthed from the caves spattered across the landscape, to World War I when the area's strategic prowess was drawn upon, a wealth of stories emerge. The 20th-century Battle of Meggido that took place on the head of the ridge saw British general Allenby lead his troops to victory, a battle considered a turning point in the war against the Ottoman Empire.

Even as early as Canaanite times the region was considered holy and Baal of Canaan was worshipped from the hilltops. According to Jewish, Christian and Islamic belief it was here that Elijah battled the prophets of Baal in a contest to determine the rightful ruler of the Kingdom of Israel and where, upon his victory, fire rained from the skies. The Assyrians conquered the area in 732BCE, restoring the worship of Baal of Canaan, who was associated by the Greeks with the god Zeus, and was known to the Romans as Deus Carmelus. The 12th-century Carmelites, a Catholic religious order, founded a monastery at the site of Elijah's victory which, during the Crusades, was converted into a mosque, hence its present-day name Muhraka, meaning 'place of burning'. It was later restored (see page 153). In some Christian traditions it is celebrated that at this site Mary, mother of Jesus, gave the Scapular of Our Lady of Mount Carmel (a symbolic devotional cloth) to a British Carmelite.

GETTING THERE AND AROUND Buses from Haifa's city centre will drop you at the park's northern entrance near Haifa University (see page 147). The rest of the park runs parallel with the coast and can be entered from any point (see individual sites for more transport directions). Renting a car is by far the best way to get the most out of a trip to the Carmel National Park as public transport runs only along main arteries and does not delve into the heart of the park itself.

🛏 **WHERE TO STAY** The Carmel National Park covers a wide area and as such, accommodation options are found scattered throughout the small settlements within it. Good choices for the quintessential, picturesque, Carmel experience are **Ein Hod** (see page 152), **Dor Beach** (see page 154) and **Zichron Ya'akov** (see page 155).

🍴 **WHERE TO EAT** Druze villages dot the landscape and their hospitality (and food) is well renowned amongst Israelis. Small, makeshift stalls can be found in clearings by the side of the road, huddled between the trees for shade from the beating summer sun. Selling locally made olive oil in rudimentary bottles as well as freshly made *labane* balls, pita and *zatar*, you haven't experienced the Carmel until you've sat on their small plastic stools and wolfed down a traditional Druze meal. Zichron Ya'akov and Ein Hod both have some high-quality meat restaurants as well as funky little cafés.

WHAT TO SEE
Carmel Caves (Nahal Me'arot)
The Nahal Me'arot Nature Reserve (✆ 04 9841750; www.parks.org.il; ⊕ 08.00–17.00 daily (closes 1hr earlier in winter); admission adult/child 18/8NIS) as it is officially known, sits amidst the lush vegetation of the Carmel mountain range and centres on three large caves. The site has proved to be of crucial importance in prehistoric archaeological investigations, finds indicating that the caves were settled continuously for 200,000 years. This almost unprecedented discovery has highlighted three different prehistoric cultures and a great many artefacts, and has contributed greatly to the study of human evolution. The caves are only a ten-minute walk from the visitors centre. The first of the three is the **Oven Cave**, which displays a chronology of the long life of the area, while the smaller **Carmel Cave** has a reconstruction display of life during the Mousterian period (40,000–100,000 years ago). The last and most impressive **Stream Cave** is 70m long and provides visitors with an insight into prehistoric life with the aid of an audio-visual presentation and some resident bats flapping overhead.

A network of signposted trails lead from the centre of the reserve through the surrounding countryside and along the Carmel range. In spring and summer the area is awash with wild flowers whose scents fill the air and it makes for some delightful and undemanding walks. Helpful and knowledgeable guides can take you on hikes or point you in the right direction, and maps are available in the visitors centre.

Suggested walks (starting from the car park)
1 Head eastwards in the direction of Daliat al-Carmel and the Maharal Valley. The walk passes through a gorge and promises sightings of nesting kestrels and lazy hyraxes.
2 The green route heads along the southern side of the wadi, then follows the rolling hills in the direction of Mitzpe Ofer. The Carmel coastal plain and mountains are to the east.
3 A well-signposted geological trail climbs to the tip of the northern riverbank and offers great views of the landscape below.

Getting there Getting there without your own transport is difficult and involves a long walk. Bus 921 heading up and down route 4 between Haifa Merkazit Hof HaCarmel and Tel Aviv Central Bus Station will stop at the Tzerufa Junction every 30 minutes. From there walk about 1km north, cross the road and follow signs to the park (4km).

Ein Hod The tiny artists' village of Ein Hod lies hidden in a sea of deep green, nestled against Carmel Mountain and surrounded by pine forests and olive groves. Whether you're an art lover or not, the picturesque beauty of this unique little village shouldn't be missed. With stunning views over the Mediterranean Sea, visitors can spend from a few hours to several days enveloping themselves in the creativity that emanates from every household. Painting, sculpting, ceramics, acting, stained-glass printing, photography and glass blowing are just some of the artistic styles that visitors can observe, or partake in (workshops are designed for all levels). The **Janco-Dada Museum** (↘ 04 9843152; ⊕ 09.30–14.00 Sun–Fri, 10.00–15.00 Sat) celebrates Marcel Janco, Ein Hod's founder and a member of the 'dada' movement of modern art. Nearby, the **Artists' Gallery** (↘ 04 9841126; ⊕ 10.00–16.30 Mon–Sat) exhibits one of the country's largest collections of Israeli art. There is also the rather unique **Nisco Museum** (↘ 052 4755313; ⊕ 09.30–16.30 Mon–Sat; admission adult/child 25/10NIS) displaying antique music boxes.

Getting there Bus 921 runs between Tel Aviv and Haifa and is the closest to Ein Hod that you can get on public transport. Ask the driver to stop at the small village of Nir Etzion from where it is a 1km walk east.

Tourist information The **Ein Hod Information Centre** (↘ 04 9841126/054 811968) can book **guided tours** and help make reservations for accommodation and workshops. Ein Hod's very good website (*www.ein-hod.israel.net*) provides more information on classes and workshops as well as contact information for booking bed and breakfast establishments.

⌂ **Where to stay** Bed and breakfast accommodation is plentiful, luxurious and pricey.

⌂ **ArtRest** (2 rooms) ↘ 04 9841560/050 6310047; e arma@netvision.net.il. Clearly designed by an artistic hand, these beautiful suites are reminiscent of a royal boudoir, oozing class & minimalist elegance. AC, TV & DVD, fully fitted kitchen, herb garden, private entrance, sea views & a huge mosaic bath. Minimum of 2 nights' reservation on weekends. **$$$$**

⌂ **Yakir Ein Hod Country Accommodation** (3 rooms) ↘ 04 9842656/050 5543982; e yakir_g@aquanet.co.il; www.yakireinhod.co.il. Fully equipped luxury rooms complete with private balcony with sea view & swimming pool. *Weekdays 200NIS less ($$$).* **$$$$**

⌂ **Batia and Claude (cottage 3)** (1 room) ↘ 04 9841648/050 5319266; e batjan@research.haifa.ac.il. The cheapest of 3 rustic stone cottages. Simple & clean with a very pleasant garden, private entrance, AC, shower & TV. **$$**

✗ **Where to eat** The **Art Bar** (↘ 04 9840071; ⊕ 10.00–15.00 Sun & Tue, 10.00–15.00 & 20.00–midnight Mon & Thu/Fri) produces its own locally brewed beer, a perfect accompaniment for lounging under the shade of an ancient olive tree. There are three restaurants in the village: **Doña Rosa** (↘ 04 9543777; ⊕ 12.30–22.30 Mon–Sat; $$$$) serving prime Argentinian meat dishes; **Abu Ya'akov** (↘ 04 9843377; ⊕ 11.00–21.00 Mon–Sat; $$) serving Middle Eastern salads, meats and hummus; and **Café Ein Hod** (↘ 054 4801985; ⊕ 08.30–19.00 Tue–Sun, until late Thu; $$) providing a bohemian caffeine kick with a splash of secondhand arts and crafts blended in. Indian-style food and big breakfasts are also served.

ISFIYA AND DALIYAT AL-CARMEL These once two separate towns merged in 2003 to become what is now officially known as Carmel City (although they are still commonly known by their original names). Located about half an hour from Haifa, the first one you arrive at is Isfiya. The populations are predominantly

Druze and the people's legendary hospitality draws locals and foreigners alike to bargain in the markets, eat in the traditional Middle Eastern restaurants, enjoy the stunning Carmel views and experience the unique atmosphere of their secretive religion. Older men wear the traditional long gowns and headdresses, often sporting a large bushy moustache while the younger set has adopted a more modern style. In keeping with other Druze settlements square, Arabic-style houses characterise the architecture, the affluence and industriousness of its rural inhabitants clearly displayed, while the surrounding hillsides are layered with carefully tended fields.

Isfiya Historically it is possible this settlement, built on the ruins of an earlier Byzantine one, formed the centre of Crusader rule in the area, judging by extensive excavated finds. The 5th-century Jewish settlement of Husifah was excavated, which included a synagogue and mosaic floor bearing the inscription 'Peace be upon Israel', while copious amounts of gold coins dating to the Roman period demonstrate the town's extent at that time. The modern city of Isfiya was founded in the 18th century when residents prospered from a flourishing agricultural economy. Today the population of Isfiya alone is 9,000, 70% being Druze, the remainder Christian and Muslim.

Daliyat al-Carmel This is the largest and most southerly of all Israel's Druze towns. The 13,000 Druze residents have traced their ancestry back to Aleppo (Halab) in Syria, which explains their strong accents and frequency of the surname Halabi. Today, Daliyat al-Carmel, whose name means 'Vine Branches of the Carmel', boasts a large central market selling handmade Druze crafts and products, and streets teeming with rudimentary, yet delectable local eateries. Markets are closed on Fridays.

Getting there Bus 192 leaves Haifa Central Bus Station several times a day. *Sheruts* leave Haifa regularly between 06.00 and 18.00 and leave from the Hadar at the corner of Shemaryahu Levin and Herzl streets.

MUHRAKA Just south of the Druze town of Daliat al-Carmel, a winding mountain road leads through a dense oak and pine forest to Muhraka (✆ 052 8779686; ◷ Apr–Sep 08.00–12.30 daily; Oct–Mar 14.30–17.00 daily; admission 3NIS), today the site of a Carmelite monastery. Tradition states that it was at this site that the Prophet Elijah battled the priests of Baal amidst fire that rained down from the heavens. Elijah then had the priests taken to Tel Kasis (the 'priests' mound' in Arabic) at the foot of Mount Carmel along the Kishon Stream, where they were slaughtered.

The Carmelite monastery that stands on the site today was constructed during the Crusades, and the four monks residing there today tend to the quaint, peaceful gardens. The view from the top of the monastery is unrivalled. It is possible, especially on clear days, to see right across the Galilee to the Jezreel Valley, Nazareth, Mount Tabor and even Mount Hermon. While of obvious biblical significance, the true magic of Muhraka rests in the picturesque landscape and staggering vista, a strong contender for the best in Israel.

The area around Muhraka provides for some fantastic walks, where the only people you are likely to bump into are goat herders and their flocks. The Society for the Protection of Nature in Haifa sells good hiking maps of the Carmel range.

Getting there Bus 192 from downtown Haifa will take you to Daliyat al-Carmel where it is a half-hour walk to the site. By car follow signs from Daliyat al-Carmel and take a right when the forest road forks.

ATLIT The **Atlit Detention Camp for Illegal Immigrants** (☏ 04 9841980; ⏱ 09.00–17.00 Sun–Thu, 09.00–13.00 Fri; admission adult/child 17/14NIS) was set up by British Mandate authorities in 1938 to house immigrants arriving in Palestine. The immigrants included refugees and Holocaust survivors from the Nazi regime as well as people escaping anti-Jewish persecution from Arab countries. The historic site, located on the original grounds of the camp, commemorates those who were kept here and educates people of their plight. The emphasis is on personal stories, and a large archive has been commissioned to record individual tales. Stories of heroism, escape, and a battle for freedom are depicted through the restored barracks. The ship seen from the highway on the approach to the camp belongs to the site and was one of the 130 vessels used to transport the refugees to the country. Guided tours can be arranged but you need to book in advance.

Nearby, perched at the end of Atlit's promontory, is an impressive UNESCO-listed **Crusader fortress**. Built in 1218, its main function was to control the coastal road with the aim of recovering Jerusalem. While the site has roots in prehistoric, Roman and medieval times, it was during the Crusader occupation of the area that the fortress and promontory were strongly fortified and are the remains we see today. While not comparable with the great fortresses of Montfort (see page 202) and Kochav HaYarden (see page 182), its coastal location nonetheless makes it a nice place to explore if you're in the area.

Atlit is also home to some of the area's loveliest **beaches**. The beaches at the southern end of the small town can be easily accessed but the northern stretches are part of a naval base and thus out of bounds. It is, however, possible to walk all the way to Atlit from Haifa along the beach, a walk of 15km.

Getting there The easiest way to get to Atlit is by train from Haifa Lev HaMifratz Train Station. Trains leave every 30 minutes (27mins/16NIS).

DOR BEACH Dor Beach (admission 20–25NIS) is a mighty strong contender for best Mediterranean beach in the country and, out of peak season, makes for an idyllic, tranquil holiday experience. Three sheltered bays have been carved out of the rocks to form shallow natural pools and still, turquoise waters and white sands complete the check list. The **Dor Holiday Village** (☏ 04 6399018/121; ✉ tantura@bezeqint.net; www.dortantura.co.il) is located to the left of the beach as you enter the car park and provides unusual, igloo-shaped huts ($$$–$$$$$ depending on season) dotted like anthills amidst bright-green lawns only a few metres from the beach. A campsite ($) and more pricey bungalows ($$$$$) are also on offer within the complex. The igloos and cottages have air conditioning, kitchenettes and cable television and can sleep two–five people. Two-person igloos have jacuzzi baths. Facilities include restaurants, a bar and watersports. Kayaks can be rented on the beach (20NIS/30mins).

Getting there There are no direct (or indirect) buses to the beach so it is highly recommended to hire your own car for this area. Bus 921 heading up and down route 4 between Haifa Merkazit Hof HaCarmel and Tel Aviv Central Bus Station will stop at the Dor Junction every half an hour from where it is a long 4km walk to the beach.

ZICHRON YA'AKOV

Founded in 1882 by Romanian Jews during the First *aliyah*, Zichron Ya'akov has managed to come a long way without losing its quaint charm and old-worldly atmosphere. In the year following its founding the village came under the patronage of Baron Edmond de Rothschild (see below) who named it Zichron Ya'akov (Memory of Jacob) after his father. Rothschild had extensive vineyards planted, the country's first, which today are considered amongst the top wine producers in the country and recognised internationally (see page 157). Winemaking soon became the primary economy within the moshav, and in the 1950s new immigrants to Israel flocked in great numbers to Zichron Ya'akov to settle.

Zichron Ya'akov boasts a proud pioneering history with attributes including Rothschild's final resting place, home of the renowned botanist and spy Aaron Aaronson and a centre of the secret Nili intelligence organisation.

In recent decades the town has developed a second crucial economy: tourism. Israelis flock to the beautiful leafy, cobbled lanes strewn with outdoor cafés, restaurants and art galleries; traditional gas lamps adorn the pavements and red shingle buildings and blossoming almond trees combine with the modern development to produce a truly unique Israeli town.

GETTING THERE Bus 872 between Tel Aviv and Zichron Ya'akov runs several times a day (1hr 50mins/23NIS) while bus 202 makes the journey to and from Haifa (27mins/13.50NIS).

BARON EDMOND DE ROTHSCHILD

Born into the powerful banking Rothschild family in 1845, Edmond was not interested in financial matters, preferring instead the more artistic side to life. He was an avid and prosperous art collector, with many notable works in his collections, including several Rembrandt pieces later donated to the Louvre Museum in Paris, his home city. But it is his successful endeavours to help the Jews fleeing the pogroms of eastern Europe and establish a haven for them in the Holy Land for which he is most widely and affectionately remembered fin Israel.

His early offers of help soon grew into a desire to create a self-sufficient Jewish homeland and later, state. His financial support of settlements destined for monetary ruin awarded him the nickname the 'Father of the Yishuv', but in the 1890s disagreements with Theodor Herzl and the Zionist organisation Hovevei Zion over the interpretation of 'political zionism' resulted in the creation of 12 settlements under the Rothschild's Jewish Colonization Association (ICA). In 1924, the Palestine Jewish Colonization Association (PICA) was established, under the patronage of his son James Armand de Rothschild, who arrived in Palestine as a British soldier with General Allenby towards the end of World War I.

Rothschild was awarded honorary presidency of the Jewish Agency in 1929 and made countless visits to Palestine during his lifetime. By the time of his death in Paris in 1934, he had purchased 500km^2 of land and funded the creation of almost 30 settlements at an estimated cost of US$50 million. He was interred in Paris until, in 1954, his and his wife's remains were transported to Israel. After a state funeral held by Israel's first prime minister David Ben-Gurion they were reburied in the Ramat Hanadiv Memorial Gardens near Zichron Ya'akov. His famous statement 'the struggle to put an end to the Wandering Jew, could not have as its result, the creation of the Wandering Arab', was perhaps a foresight and warning to future generations of the political turmoil that was to engulf this country and region from his early days to the present.

WHERE TO STAY

Achouzat Zamarin (6 rooms) 16 Hameyasdim St; 04 6397404; e info@zamarin-spa.co.il; www.zamarin-spa.co.il. Elegant, intimate boutique hotel & spa in the heart of Zichron. The spa is open for day guests or can be combined with overnight stays. Their packages include massage treatments, the spa, overnight stay, breakfast & private jacuzzi for a couple for around 1,000NIS. $$$$$

Hotel Beit Maimon (22 rooms) 4 Tzahal St; 04 6290390; f 04 6396547; www.maimon.com. While the hotel is pleasant & offers good value for money it does lack the character that the town itself is famous for. It does however have fabulous views of the sea, AC, breezy, modern rooms, a range of reasonably priced spa treatments & a swimming pool (in summer). *Weekdays 200NIS less ($$).* $$$$

WHERE TO EAT
Hameyasdim Street is lined with delightful cafés and restaurants, each as quaint as the next. Come the weekend the pedestrian street and every seat lining it is packed to the fullest, but this rather adds to the carefree atmosphere in the town. Prices are predictably high so if you're on a tight budget then eat first and then splash out on a coffee whilst sitting on one of the leafy terraces.

Haneshika 37 Hameyasdim St; 04 6390133; 08.30–22.30 Mon–Sat. Situated in the quaint back garden of one of Zichron's old stone houses, this is one of the most prestigious & pricey restaurants around. The menu is changed regularly but can always be counted upon to be the best of the best. Book in advance especially on weekends. $$$$$

Tishbi Coffee House 33 Hameyasdim St; 04 6290280; 09.00–23.30 Sun–Thu, 09.00–16.00 Fri. This is not only a great place to enjoy an Israeli breakfast or a meal of locally produced wine and cheese, but is one of the oldest houses in Zichron. The coffee house is owned by the local winemaking Tishbi family. $$$

WHAT TO SEE
The Wine Road There is plenty to see in Zichron Ya'akov, most of which can be found by taking a very pleasant stroll along Hameyasdim Street (also referred to as The Wine Road). This was the pioneering colony's first street and has undergone heavy but meticulous reconstruction over recent years to return it to its former glory, with Rothschild's characteristic architectural features such as wooden window frames, tiled roofs, stone posts and traditional building façades having been fully restored. The Wine Road starts at the cemetery in the south end of town and finishes at the Carmel Winery in the north.

Cemetery Rothschild expressed a strong desire to be buried in the old cemetery in Zichron Ya'akov, a wish that was fulfilled several years after his death. It wasn't until 1954, 19 years after his passing, that the baron and his wife Adelheid were transported aboard a naval frigate from Paris and reinterred in the Ramat Hanadiv Memorial Cemetery in Zichron Ya'akov. They received a state funeral presided over by former prime minister David Ben-Gurion. Rothschild's simple yet impressive mausoleum can be found in the centre of the cemetery, while a stone-carved map showing the extent of his colonies can be found in the western part of the beautifully tended memorial gardens. The cemetery is part of a large nature reserve and is dotted with manicured gardens, fragrant blossoms and pools and fountains. The Samaria Observation Point is located between the Rose and Palm Gardens and definitely worth the trip.

Founders Memorial This remarkable building is located next to the town's central bus station a little way up from the cemetery. Its construction is unique in that it has been designed to resemble an open scroll. A fascinating ceramic relief decorates the walls and depicts the story of Zichron's founding.

Aaronson House (*40 Hameyasdim St*) Zichron Ya'akov was home to the Nili group, an anti-Turkish spy ring that supplied the British with intelligence during World War I. The name Nili stands for Netzah Yisrael Lo Yishaker, which translates as 'The eternal one of Israel will not be false'. Aaron Aaronson, an internationally reputed agronomist, and his sister Sarah, were at the centre of the group's operations and spent several years living in the house that now acts as their memorial. Sarah Aaronson has become one of the country's most well-loved martyr heroines, a reputation strengthened by her refusal to divulge secret information upon her capture and brutal inquisition. She took her own life while in the captivity of the Turks. Aaron Aaronson was killed in a plane crash at the end of World War I. There is an impressive collection of photographs and documents on display depicting their heroic story.

A BOTTLE OF ISRAEL'S FINEST

When asked to name a top wine-producing locale, most would utter the familiar names of Chile, Italy, Spain or California. But over recent years, Israel has managed to put itself on the prestigious wine map and now competes favourably with the giants of the wine world. Wine has been made in Israel since pre-biblical times, indeed Noah's first task after completing the Ark was to plant vines. Yet only in recent years has it been considered quality wine, a development owed mainly to the creation of the Golan Heights Winery, which opened in 1983. From the outset the winery was a success, with its second wine, a 1984 Cabernet Sauvignon, winning the gold medal at the International Wine and Spirit Competition. Its Yarden Series is considered its most reputable and prestigious, notably the Cabernet Sauvignon and Merlot. Today the country's largest winemaker is the Rothschild-founded Carmel Winery in Zichron Ya'akov (see page 148). It produces in excess of 13 million bottles a year and has three main series: the Selected Series, the Vineyard Series and the prestigious Rothschild Series which includes Merlot, Cabernet Sauvignon, Chardonnay and Emerald Rieslings. Much of the wine purchased in Israel and exported is kosher. While there are several rules that need to be abided by, there is no conflict of interest in the production of good wine and it remaining kosher. For example, grapes may not be used until their fourth year of growth, equipment must be kept kosher clean and only Sabbath-observant male Jews can take part in the wine-producing process.

TOURS

Most of Israel's wineries offer tours, although you may need to book ahead. While the main attraction is the winemaking process and wine tasting, the wineries tend to be located within some of the country's most stunning landscapes and are lovely places to visit. For more information visit www.israelwines.co.il.

Carmel's Zichron Ya'akov Wine Cellars Zichron Ya'akov; ℄ 04 6290977
Golan Heights Winery Katzrin, Golan; ℄ 04 6968420
Galil Mountain Winery Kibbutz Yiron; ℄ 04 6868740
Tabor Winery Kfar Tabor, Lower Galilee; ℄ 04 6760444
Domaine du Castel Ramat Razi'el, between Tel Aviv and Jerusalem; ℄ 02 5342249
Hamasrek Winery (kosher) Beit Me'ir, near Jerusalem; ℄ 02 5701759
Yatir Winery Tel Arad, Judean Desert; ℄ 08 9959090
Sde Boker Winery Sde Boker, Judean Desert; ℄ 050 7579212
Neot Smadar Winery Neot Smadar, Negev Desert; ℄ 08 6358111

Water tower Located on the right as you walk up Hameyasdim Street is the settlement's first water tower, built by Rothschild. Its outer façade has been designed to resemble that of an ornate ancient synagogue. A climb to the top offers a wonderful panoramic view over the green hills and valleys of the Carmel.

First Aliyah Museum (*2 Hanadiv St;* ☏ *04 6294777;* ⏲ *09.00–14.00 Mon & Wed/Thu, 09.00–15.00 Tue, 09.00–14.00 Fri; admission adult/child 15/10NIS*) Dedicated to the groups of pioneering families that arrived between 1882 and 1904, the museum illuminates their role in the founding of the State of Israel. The museum is housed in the 110-year-old council building built by Rothschild, at its time considered the most impressive in the country. Displays depict the history of the early settlers, its most precious relic being that of a short black-and-white video believed to be the oldest film depicting Israel. Long believed lost, it was discovered in 1997 in a Paris film archive and shows, amongst others, Joseph Trumpeldor (see page 206).

Ohel Ya'akov Synagogue Named after Rothschild's father Jacob (Ya'akov) the synagogue was, at the time, the largest and most beautiful synagogue in all of the baron's colonies. It was founded in 1886 and has been carefully restored to its former elegance.

Carmel Winery (see box above, *A bottle of Israel's finest*)

CAESAREA

Resting on the shores of the glittering Mediterranean Sea, Caesarea offers a wealth of attractions and luxury activities. The modern town is small and extremely wealthy, where large, mansion-like houses sit amidst green lawns and expensive cars line the driveways. Home to Israel's elite, Caesarea has been home to VIPs such as the ex-president Ezer Weizman. But the area is best known not for its well-to-do residents, but for the staggering ancient ruins that lie just south of it. The ruins at Caesarea are amongst some of the most valuable and fascinating in the world, where successive phases of occupation have left a treasure trove of archaeological remains, most notably the Crusader city and Roman theatre. Around the national park, Israel's finest golf course, several wide, sandy swimming beaches and a luxury spa make this a five-star stopover.

HISTORY The site at Caesarea was first settled in the 4th century BCE by the Phoenicians, who built a small harbour city named Straton's Tower. After Alexander the Great's conquest of the country in 332BCE, the city flourished under Greek rule. The Roman Conquest in 63BCE saw the city undergo a major phase of construction, and under Herod was renamed Caesarea, in honour of the Roman emperor. The Temple of Augustus, deep sea harbour, hippodrome, theatre, bathhouses, public buildings, wide roads, markets and state-of-the-art water supply all owe their origins to this time. It has been recorded that Roman procurators Pontius Pilate and Felix resided in Caesarea, and it was here where the Apostle Paul was imprisoned and sent to Rome for trial. It was also the site of Paul's baptising of the Roman officer Cornelius. The Jewish uprising of CE66 was repressed by Vespasian who was later declared Emperor of the Roman Empire in Caesarea and the city became one of the most important in the eastern part of the Roman Empire, classified as 'Metropolis of the Province of Syria Palestina'. Following the Bar Kochba revolt, its leader, Ben Akiva was tortured and died in the city in CE135.

Caesarea prospered during the Byzantine Period until the Arab conquest of 637. The Crusaders captured the city during the First Crusade but it wasn't until 1251 that Louis VI fortified the city, constructing high walls and a deep moat. The fortifications were breached shortly after, however, by the Mamluk sultan Baibars, who captured the town. The once-flourishing port had by this time completely silted over. The city fell into ruins and remained desolate until the 19th century when Bosnian refugees were settled on the land. It was later abandoned during the 1948 Arab–Israeli War, only to be resettled in 1940 with the establishment of the nearby Kibbutz Sdot Yam.

GETTING THERE There are no direct buses from Haifa or Tel Aviv so take any of the countless northbound coastal buses to Hadera where you can change to Caesarea. Bus 76 leaves every two hours. Coming from Haifa you will need to ask the driver to drop you at the junction 4km from Caesarea, where you can walk or hitch the final stretch. Trains leave to Binyamina from Tel Aviv and Haifa regularly, which is 7km from Caesarea. Either find a taxi or hop on a bus going to Or Akiva where it is a 2km walk to Caesarea. If you're driving there be aware there is absolutely no continuity with the English spelling of Caesarea on road signs. It can range from Qesariya, to Kesariya, to Quesariyya, so try to be imaginative and keep an eye open.

WHERE TO STAY

Dan Caesarea Hotel (114 rooms) ☎ 1700 505080. Part of the luxury chain of Israeli hotels, the Dan Caesarea represents the country manor member of the Dan family. Located on the fringe of the Caesarea golf course and its velvet lawns, the hotel prides itself on immaculate service and top-quality facilities. $$$$$

WHERE TO EAT

There are several concentrations of places to eat in Caesarea. Apart from **Agenda** (☎ 04 6262092; ⊕ 24hrs Sun–Thu, until Shabbat Fri, from end of Shabbat Sat; $$$$) which, despite its location in the petrol station, serves high-quality sushi, the industrial area has the **Jacko Restaurant** (15 Tarshish St, Industrial Park; ☎ 04 6377715; ⊕ 12.00–midnight daily; $$$), which is part of the famous Haifa chain, serving fresh fish and seafood, and the burger joint **Koya Bar** (13 HaShoam St, Industrial Park; ☎ 04 6273005; ⊕ 11.30–midnight Sun–Thu, 09.00–midnight Fri, 12.00–midnight Sat; $$$). Restaurants in the archaeological park tend to be a bit pricier but are generally of good quality. The **Crusaders Restaurant** (☎ 04 6361679; ⊕ 11.00–midnight daily; $$$$) serves a wide selection of meat, fresh seafood and fish while **Helena's** (☎ 04 6101018; ⊕ 12.00–midnight daily; $$$$) specialises in Middle Eastern cuisine. Afterwards you can stop at the **Aldo at the Port** (☎ 04 6363104; ⊕ 08.30–22.00 Sun–Thu (until 02.00 in summer), 08.30–02.00 Fri, 08.30–22.00 Sat; $$$) with its lovely sea views and rather unusual flavours of ice cream including sweet potato and cucumber.

WHAT TO SEE

Caesarea Maritime National Park (☎ 04 6267080; e galic@caesarea.cc; www.caesarea.org; ⊕ Apr–Sep 09.00–18.00 Sun/Mon & Wed/Thu, 09.00–20.00 Tue, 09.00–17.00 Fri; Oct–Mar 09.00–17.00 Sun–Thu, 09.00–16.00 Fri; admission adult/child 23/12NIS)

Theatre The theatre has become the symbol of Caesarea and has been fully restored to its former grandeur. Seating up to 4,000 people, it once again hosts concerts, operas and summer events and has been designed so that audiences have a view over the Mediterranean Sea behind. At some point after its original construction, the theatre was extended to form a quasi-amphitheatre, where it is likely gladiatorial battles would have taken place. It is located south of the Crusader city near the Herodian south wall.

Promontory Palace Jutting out into the sea, the high promontory located in the south of the Roman city was the site of King Herod's exquisite palace. The excavated complex, 110m by 60m in size, contained a large central salt-water pool and was surrounded by ornate porticoes. On display within the palace is a replica of a stone mentioning Pontius Pilate, the only physical evidence discovered bearing his name. The original is in the Israel Museum in Jerusalem.

Hippodrome A major feature of the Herodian town, it was here that great sporting events were played out and legendary gladiator games were hosted. The arena served up to 15,000 spectators and was 250m long and 80m wide. It has yet to be excavated and is overgrown, but its shape and extent are still clear.

Bathhouses The excavated 4th-century bathhouses are a wonderful example of Roman architecture. A series of courtyards and rooms, many containing exquisite mosaics, made up the large bath complex that formed the core of Roman social life.

Byzantine Street Along the ancient shopping street are two headless statues, located near the entrance. Dated to the 2nd or 3rd centuries, one is made of white marble and the other from reddish, purple-coloured porphyry. It is believed the latter is the figure of an emperor, most likely Hadrian.

Crusader City Entrance to the city is via the imposing East Gate. To the left of the gate are remains of houses while within the fortified area remnants of the ancient water supply and drainage system, the temple of Augustus and the still-standing Crusader cathedral can be found. The cathedral was dedicated to St Paul and built on the site of an earlier Byzantine church. Near the cathedral is the mosque built by Bosnian settlers in the 19th century.

Aqueduct The aqueduct was commissioned by Herod to bring fresh water from Carmel Mountain 15km away and represents an incredible feat of ancient architectural engineering. The aqueduct was built on arches and the gradient precisely measured, allowing for a constant flow of water into the city. It was later extended by Hadrian and the Crusaders. Today part of the aqueduct is inside the national park and sections can be spotted along the entire coastal region to its source.

Underwater Archaeological Park *(Caesarea Dive Club)* (✆ *04 6265898;* e *diving@post.com; www.caesarea-diving.com*) Most of what remains of the deep sea port today lies under the emerald waters of the Mediterranean Sea and has become an underwater park frequented by scuba-diving enthusiasts and archaeology buffs from around the world. Diving here is open to professionals and amateurs and a reputable dive centre operates informative and insightful expeditions to the ruins of the Roman and Crusader naval port, including several ancient shipwrecks.

Harbour Beach (✆ *050 5385365; admission adult/child 25/20NIS*) is a lovely, well-kept beach that boasts shimmering green waters as its view and the ancient buildings of Caesarea as its backdrop. Parking, lifeguards, changing rooms, parasols and sunbeds are available. There is also a pleasant beach bar (complete with grill). The incredibly picturesque **Aqueduct Beach** just outside the national park is free and a lovely and tranquil place to go swimming. Facilities are limited, however, so families with small children are best advised to opt for the Harbour Beach.

Other Park attractions Located within the boundaries of the national park (but not included in the entry price) are **The Caesarea Experience**, **Caesarea's Stars** and the **Time Tower** (*admission adult/child 40/35NIS including park admission*), three state-of-the-art, multi-media experiences aimed at illuminating Caesarea's tumultuous and fascinating past and the people who lived there.

OTHER ATTRACTIONS Many people don't venture too far outside the archaeological park but there are several expensive and luxurious activities to partake in if your budget runs to it. The **Caesarea Golf Club** (✆ *04 6109602*) is Israel's one-and-only 18-hole golf course and is set within beautiful sea-view grounds complete with bird lake. It is located at the entrance to Caesarea in grounds donated by the Rothschild family. The nearby **Ralli Museum** (*Rothschild Bd;* ✆ *04 6261013;* ⊕ *Mar–Dec 10.30–15.00 Mon/Tue & Thu–Sat; Jan/Feb 10.30–15.00 Fri/Sat; admission free*), housed in a vast mansion, displays a selection of modern and ancient paintings including a gallery devoted to Salvador Dali. The **Caesar Spa** (✆ *04 6266669*) set within manicured grounds, takes pampering to a new dimension. For those with deep enough pockets, this luxury complex offers everything one could need to relax and unwind; massages range from mud to Thai, wraps, aromatic peeling and face and body treatments.

LOWER GALILEE

Akko, Haifa,
Nahariya

KARMI'EL

Tzfat, Rush Pina

Tulip Inn
Capernaum NP
Mt of Beatitudes
Luna Gal
Aqua Park
Church of the Loaves
& Fishes (Tabgha)
Church of
the Primacy
of St Peter
Ramot

Sakhnin

Kibbutz
Ginosaur

Sea of
Galilee

Kursi NP

5km

5 miles

Mt Arbel
278m
Arbel
Kfar Hittin

YMCA
TIBERIAS

Ein Gev

Shfaram

Horns of
Hittin

TVERYA
ILIT

Haifa

Ma'agar
Beit Netofa

Zippori
Cana

Porriya Hospital
Porriya

Peace Vista,
Hamat Gader

Haifa

National Trail

Yardenit
Kibbutz
Deganya A

National Trail

Al-Shibli

Kfar Tavor

NAZRAT
ILLIT

Kiryat Tivon

NAZARETH

Mt Tabor
405m

Jordan

Beit She'arim

Migdal

Tavor
Tavor Stream
Nature Reserve

Yokne'am Ilit

Kochav HaYarden
(Belvoir)

Ma'agar
Kfar Baruch

AFULA ILIT

Zichron
Yaakov

AFULA

Jezreel Valley

JORDAN

Tel Meggido

Meggido Junction

Gilboa Mtns

Kibbutz
Nir David

Jordan River
Crossing

BEIT SHE'AN

Based on mapping
by Carta, Jerusalem

Arara,
Pardes Hana

Jenin

Jenin

Kibbutz
Ma'aleh Gilboa

Gan HaShlosha
(Sahne)

Bradt

N

6

Lower Galilee

The 1st-century historian Flavius Josephus once wrote of the Lower Galilee: 'One may call this place the ambition of nature.' Stretching from the sweeping, fertile plains of the Jezreel Valley (or simply 'HaEmek', 'The Valley') in the south to the natural border of the Jordan River in the east, and up to the more rugged terrains of the Upper Galilee, it is a land of true diversity. Agriculturally, the area has been the beating heart of the country for centuries, its fertile valleys seasonally blanketed with crops. The delicate microclimate of the region, coupled with its diverse geography account for its eclectic mix of produce. Almonds, citrus fruits and olive trees grow in the Beit She'an and Herod valleys, cotton and grain prosper in the warm fields of the Jezreel Valley while flowers and herbs blossom alongside the Jordan River. The Sea of Galilee's abundant fish stocks have long been the backbone of agriculture in the vicinity of the sea, called thus through tradition rather than definition. Throughout the time of Jesus up until today a thriving fishing industry has prospered, forming the economy of many of today's kibbutzim that concentrate in the valleys. The country's pioneering kibbutz, **Deganya Alef**, resides on the shores of the sea and the area is now home to most of the country's kibbutz settlements. **Nazareth**, the heart of Arab life and culture in the region, together with the countless Arab villages that dot the landscape, denoted by their minarets and typical jumbled street planning, are home to one million of Israel's Arab residents, whose traditional way of life and close cultural ties flourish.

Historically, nowhere outside Jerusalem can compete with the Lower Galilee for drama, passion and religious tenor. The scene of legendary battles, it was on these soils that empires were won and lost. At the Battle of Hittin in 1187, the revered Arab leader Saladin defeated the Christian Crusader armies, a battle that marked the beginning of the conquest of Jerusalem and prompted the Third Crusade. Under the shadow of Mount Tabor the prophet and heroine Deborah, alongside Barak, defeated the Canaanite captain Sisera, marking the first great Israelite victory since the days of Joshua, and last battle they would ever have with the Canaanites. After this, during the Hasmonean period, the entire Galilee region was controlled by several empires and emerged as a Jewish stronghold, a claim that remained for five centuries after the demise of the Second Temple. The highly contested lands changed hands countless times throughout the succeeding centuries: Arabs, Crusaders, Mamluks and Ottomans all ruled at times throughout the Galilee's colourful past.

Sacred in the heart of Christians and Jews the world over, the region is the destination for thousands of pilgrims. From the magnificent churches and picture-postcard cobbled alleys of Nazareth's Old City where Jesus's life began, to the sites of his numerous miracles that dot the shores of the Sea of Galilee, biblical stories abound. **Tiberias**, one of Judaism's four holy cities and often considered the capital of the Lower Galilee, was once the seat of the Jewish Sanhedrin, school of

Based on mapping
by Carta, Jerusalem

NAZARETH
Old City

Jewish learning, and home to Rabbi Judah HaNassi as he compiled the Talmud.
Tiberias's party-going streets today belie the magnitude of the city in Judaism's
history, the quiet tombs of some of the great philosophers and rabbis scattered
around the city acting as reminders to this secular settlement.

One hour's drive from Jerusalem and Tel Aviv, it is easily accessible and thus
regularly frequented by Israeli holidaymakers and day trippers, who escape the
cities to unwind in the national parks, hot springs and lakeside beaches. Tour buses,
laden with pilgrims and sightseers, trek through the valleys and hills, fuelling the
region's ever-growing tourism economy. Be it by the rich history, spiritual allure or
thriving flora and fauna that abound in the valleys and hills of the Lower Galilee,
few could fail to be enchanted by the magnetism of the region.

NAZARETH

Nazareth – Israel's largest Arab city – rests atop, between and around five round
hills that form the end of the Galilee Mountains presiding over the Jezreel Valley
below. Outside the country, it is probably most well known as being the childhood
home of Jesus and a site for pilgrims over the last 2,000 years. Religious and
historic sites centre on the Old City in the heart of Nazareth, where preconceived
images of quaint cobbled stone alleys and bustling markets are fully realised.
Outside the Old City, however, Nazareth is a hectic, modern and vibrant Arab city

where the aromas of strong coffee, spices and sweets drift along the streets, where women sport traditional *jalabeya* coats, and where the loud chatter and the sounds of car horns dull only marginally at prayer times. With a population of 60,000 – 60% of whom are Muslim – there is an undeniable and refreshing feeling of unity, where two major religions co-exist in relative success. Inconceivably to many other Arab Israelis, and certainly Palestinians living in the West Bank, the people of Nazareth are content with their situation, where Arab life and culture most certainly prevail. Modest dress is highly recommended – particularly for women – both in the Old City and outside.

HISTORY On account of its absence from both the Old Testament and Talmud it is probable Nazareth was a small and insignificant settlement during Jesus's time and it is likely that the city as it is known today flourished and grew alongside the spread of Christianity. Amongst the Christian sites in Israel and across the world, Nazareth holds its claim as being 'where it all began'. It was here that Jesus spent most of his early life and where the Bible states that Mary was told of the annunciation by the angel Gabriel.

From the Muslim Conquest of Palestine in CE637 throughout the First Crusade and long-lasting conflict, power changed hands regularly, which had a great impact on the religious balance of the population. In 1099, the Galilee was captured by the Crusader Tancred, and Nazareth was appointed as capital of the area. Following Saladin's victory at the Battle of Hittin in 1187, Muslim control was once more established in Nazareth where it lasted until – during part of the Sixth Crusade – it was once more returned to Christian hands. In 1263, however, the Mamluk sultan Baibars had all Christian buildings destroyed and its people evicted, their absence lasting until 1620 when the Lebanese leader Fakhr-al Din II allowed their return. Throughout Ottoman rule Nazareth flourished, and it is well documented as a time of affluence for the city. Testament to this are the traditional two-storey mansions built during this period. Constructed at the base of the Nabi Sa'in cliff rising behind the city, they provide an alternative view of the city's life and are well worth a visit. Stone-built with red-roofed tiles and central courtyards, the most beautiful and ornate, dated to the 20th century, are located highest on the ridge where there is a **hilltop promenade**. These include what are today the **St Gabriel Hotel** and **Salesian Monastery**.

During the 1948 Arab–Israeli War the Arab Liberation Army entered Nazareth, which – on 11 June – surrendered to Israeli forces after signing a truce agreement to cease battling in exchange for assurances that no harm would come to the city's population. It is thanks to this that, while many other Arab towns in the area were forcibly evacuated, the Arab population was never evicted.

GETTING THERE Nazareth is fairly accessible by bus from most major cities. Buses and *sheruts* stop at several bus stops along Paulus VI Street, where the **Egged information kiosk** (*98 Paulus VI St*) is located. Make sure the bus is headed for Natzrat Ha-Atika and not Natzrat Illit, the nearby Jewish satellite town. Countless buses head to the nearby city of Afula every day, which serves closer, more rural areas. Bus 823 runs between Tel Aviv and Nazareth (2hrs 40mins/36NIS) every two hours, stopping in the Old City. From Haifa bus 301 runs regularly to and from Afula (55mins/17.70NIS) where you can change to Nazareth (15mins/9.80NIS). Bus 955 leaves at 06.15 and 08.45 to Jerusalem (2hrs 15mins/35NIS). Bus 431 runs hourly between Tiberias and Nazareth (1hr/19NIS).

GETTING AROUND Nazareth suffers from dire congestion problems and weaving your way through the dusty, strangely organised roads is an arduous task. If you're arriving by car, it's recommended to park outside the Old City area and either walk or take a taxi into the centre. The worst of the traffic centres on Paulus VI Street which, during rush hour, is bumper to bumper. Most of Nazareth's sights are within the Old City and within easy walking distance of each other.

CAR RENTAL COMPANIES

🚗 **Europcar** 19 Paulus VI St; ☎ 04 6575313; ⏰ 08.30–18.00 Mon–Fri, 08.30–14.00 Sat. Cars from 175NIS/day. Minimum 3-day rental.

TOURIST INFORMATION

ℹ️ **Tourist information office** 1601 Casanova St; ☎ 04 6750555; www.nazarethboard.org; ⏰ 08.30–17.00 Mon–Fri, 09.00–13.00 Sat. Located on Casanova St, the main government tourist information branch is small & not particularly well equipped. Staff will – somewhat begrudgingly – provide free maps well designed for navigating the maze of alleys that make up the old market area (most of which are unnamed).

LOCAL TOUR OPERATORS The tourist information office can supply contact details for local tour guides, approximately 450NIS for a two–three-hour tour. **Chada Bulos** (☎ 054 5717774) is one of several well-known guides in the city. The **Fauzi Azar Inn** (see *Where to stay* below) can also arrange tours around the city.

🏠 WHERE TO STAY

🏠 **Galilee Hotel** (92 rooms) 65 Paulus VI St; ☎ 04 6571311; e merywell@netvision.net.il; www.b-and-b.co.il/galilee. In a great location within easy walking distance of the Old City, it has a pleasant ambience & nice, if somewhat old-fashioned, rooms. Often caters to large groups. $$$

🏠 **Golden Crown Hotel** (240 rooms) Mount Precipice; ☎ 04 6508000; e res@goldencrown.co.il; www.goldencrown.co.il. Located on the southern entrance to the city near Mount Precipice offering beautiful views of the Jezreel Valley below. Great value for money, although a bit of a hike to the Old City. Large swimming pool, jacuzzi, gym, sauna, restaurants, shops...the list goes on. Rooms are clean & comfortable. $$$

🏠 **Rimonim HaMayaan (Mary's Well)** (226 rooms) Top end of Paulus VI St; ☎ 04 6500000; f 04 6500055; www.rimonim.com. In keeping with other members of the Rimonim chain, the hotel is nicely decorated, comfortable & equipped with absolutely everything (although it doesn't have the character of some of its counterparts). Perfectly situated in the midst of the hustle & bustle of the Old City next to Mary's Well Sq. $$$

🏠 **Fauzi Azar Inn** (10 rooms) ☎ 04 6020469/054 4322328; e info@fauziazarinn.com; www.fauziazarinn.com. By far the best budget option in town. Located in the true heart of the Old City & souk & housed in a 200-year-old Arabic courtyard house, it offers unparalleled comfort, character & ambience. Internet available & organised tours of Nazareth & surrounding areas can be arranged. *Shared rooms sleep up to 5 (120NIS) & have shared bathroom & kitchen.* $$

🏠 **St Gabriel Hotel** (60 rooms) 2 Salesian St; ☎ 04 6572133; f 04 6572133. Perched high on the hill behind the city with fabulous views. Furnished in plush, Middle Eastern design, it once housed a congregation of Catholic nuns & whose exterior has retained its ecclesiastical splendour. $$

🍴 WHERE TO EAT

🍴 **Diana** 51 Paulus VI St; ☎ 04 6572919; ⏰ 12.00–midnight daily. Ask anyone in the country to recommend a restaurant in Nazareth & this is where you'll be sent. And for just reason – it is simply terrific. Don't be put off by the unimpressive exterior or simple decoration, the food is top notch, freshly prepared Middle Eastern cuisine. Ordering the salad (*mezze*) will result in 22 different dishes being piled upon your table – & that's just for starters. The meat kebabs are succulent & just mouthwatering. There are queues down the street at weekends so it's a good idea to book ahead. $$$.

🍴 **Al Rida** Al Bishara St; ☎ 04 6084404; ⏰ 13.00–02.00 Mon–Sat, 19.00–02.00 Sun. Situated in an old Arabic mansion house with an arched roof, heavy wooden furniture & a small garden, this is one of the nicest restaurants in Nazareth. The food combines Arabic style with contemporary flavours. The mushrooms stuffed with sweet potato are particularly recommended, as are the beef dishes. The view of the Old City from the roof terrace is stunning, especially at night. $$

✖ **Casanova Shawarma** Casanova St. Without a doubt the best falafel in the city. Tiny, take-away stall halfway up Casanova St, it is unassuming & easily missed. Serving falafel (10NIS) with an array of varied, fresh salad accompaniments, *shawarma* (15NIS) & freshly squeezed orange juice (10NIS).

OTHER PRACTICALITIES With the exception of Nazareth's three main hospitals, all major post offices, banks and the city's central police station are either inside (or within easy walking distance of) the Old City. The city keeps hours in accordance with Muslim and Christian holy days (Friday to Sunday).

Emergencies
Ambulance ☎ 101
Fire ☎ 102

Police station 6077 St; ☎ 100 or 04 6574444. Located left off 6089 St, which heads northeast to Mary's Well Sq from the souk. Next to the post office.

Money ATMs are commonplace outside banks, and found throughout the city. Paulus VI Street has many money-changing bureaux and branches of most major banks. The post office will also change money, cash travellers' cheques and has a Western Union service.

$ **Bank Hapoalim** Paulus VI St; ☎ 03 6532407/ landline*2407; ⊕ 08.30–13.00 & 16.00–18.00 Mon & Thu, 08.30–13.15 Tue/Wed, 08.15–12.30 Fri

$ **Discount Bank** Paulus VI St; ☎ 04 6089120; ⊕ 08.30–15.00 Tue/Wed, 08.30–13.00 & 15.00–18.15 Mon & Thu

Post
✉ **Post office** 6077 St; ☎ 04 6554019; ⊕ 08.30–14.00 Mon & Wed, 08.00–12.30 &

15.30–18.00 Tue & Thu/Fri, 08.00–13.00 Sat. Next to the police station.

Medical
✚ **French Hospital** ☎ 04 650900
✚ **Holy Family Hospital** ☎ 04 6508900
✚ **Nazareth Hospital** ☎ 04 6571501/02

✚ **Perach pharmacy** 19 Paulus VI St; ☎ 04 6554018; ⊕ 09.00–13.30 Mon–Sat. Not signposted in English; a few metres from the main bus station.

WHAT TO SEE The Old City (El-Balda El-Qadima) provides the backdrop for most of the main religious and historic sites of interest.

Churches
Basilica of the Annunciation (*Casanova St; ⊕ 08.00–11.45 & 14.00–17.00 Mon–Sat, 14.00–17.30 Sun & hols; admission free*) This is the most prominent and easily identifiable site in the Old City, and makes for a good starting and orientation point. The modern Catholic church stands 55m tall, the entrance of which is located up Casanova Street just off the main Paulus VI Street. Today's modern church – designed in the shape of the Madonna lily, a symbol of the Virgin Mary – was built in 1969 over the remains of earlier Byzantine and Crusader churches, and contains the **Cave (or Grotto) of the Annunciation**, where tradition states the Virgin Mary received news from the angel Gabriel of Jesus's birth. Remains of the earlier churches are still visible in the lower stone cave. The unusual geometric design and grey stone walls dotted with stained-glass windows of the basilica – located up the spiral staircase on the right of the main entrance – are eerily impressive.

St Joseph's Church The church is located 50m from the northern exit of the basilica and is the early traditional site of Joseph's carpentry shop, and later the 'House of Joseph'. The current church was built in 1914 on the site of an earlier 12th-century one. In its heyday caves, granaries and wells – which today are located down the stone stairs from within the church – were used by early Nazarene inhabitants. It was later, when Christian pilgrims were appearing in greater numbers that it turned into a site of worship.

Orthodox Church of St Gabriel (⊕ *07.00–12.00 & 13.00–18.00 Mon–Sat, 12.00–14.00 Sun; admission free*) This is another contender as the site where the Annunciation took place when the Virgin Mary received news from the Angel Gabriel of Jesus's conception. The church – the Orthodox equivalent to the Basilica of the Annunciation – was built over the spring said to be where Mary was fetching water from at the time of Gabriel's appearance. The present church – built in 1750 along the south side of the chapel containing the spring – can be visited, although is often overcrowded with large groups of pilgrims. Descending from the small upper church down stairs into the lower chapel, a single, narrow aisle leads to the northern end where it is possible to look over an altar into the running spring.

Greek Catholic Synagogue Church From the top of the main souk street turn left and then take the next right. The small, stone entrance is easily missed. This is said to be the synagogue where Jesus preached to the people of Nazareth. It became a popular place of Christian worship after influxes of pilgrims during which time the church was built. The building is extremely quaint and stands like an old grandfather clock, snuggled into the maze of souk streets.

Other sights
Mary's Well and Ancient Bathhouse (al-Sabil) The well and bathhouse is fed by the spring gushing through the Church of St Gabriel and is a site whose importance in daily life and religious connotations is undeniable. Christian tradition states that it was here, whilst collecting water from the well, that Gabriel appeared to Mary and divulged news of the conception of Jesus. In the 1990s, beneath an adjacent souvenir shop, profoundly impressive remains of a bathhouse were discovered. Believed to be Roman, they would, therefore, have been built at around the time Jesus lived in Nazareth. Tours to the well-preserved remains can be organised through the **Cactus Gift Shop** (*Well Sq;* ✆ *04 6578539;* ⊕ *09.00–19.00 Mon–Sat; 120NIS for up to 4 people*)

Nazareth Souk As one of the largest markets in the country the souk is a well-trodden corner of the city, frequented by people from all over the Galilee. Its entrance is located at the top of Casanova Street where tight, winding cobbled lanes weave through a large part of the Old City, crammed to the hilt with stalls selling pretty much everything. A huge restoration project has seen the market returned to its original glory, where mansion houses, mosques, churches and squares compete for space.

The White Mosque (al-Abiad) The mosque was built between 1799 and 1808 to commemorate the end of the Ottoman governor al-Jazzar's heavy-handed rule. White was chosen to signify purity and the peaceful co-existence of religions in Nazareth. The mosque is located in the heart of the Old City and is easily identifiable by its colour and thin, elegant minaret.

Nazareth Village (✆ 04 6456042; *www.nazarethvillage.com*; ⊕ 09.00–17.00 Mon–Sat; *admission adult/child 50/21NIS*) The village is a reconstruction of Jewish Nazareth as it would have appeared during Jesus's time and provides a kitsch yet entertaining step back in time. Agricultural techniques, food presses, traditional costumes, food and even animals set the time capsule back 2,000 years.

AROUND NAZARETH

TEL MEGGIDO NATIONAL PARK (ARMAGEDDON) (✆ 04 6522167; *www.parks.org.il*; ⊕ 08.00–17.00 Sat–Thu, 08.00–16.00 Fri; admission adult/child 23/12NIS)
According to Christian tradition, Tel Meggido is the site where the battle for the world will take place and, judging by its tumultuous past, it seems a likely enough spot. Destroyed and rebuilt 25 times in its long existence, Meggido was a crucially important strategic site along the great trunk road leading vast trade caravans from Syria and Mesopotamia down to Egypt. Extensive excavations have revealed the remains of 20 phases of occupation through every period in Israel's history dating from 4000–400BCE, while its battle scars continue on into the 20th century and World War I. Perhaps rather poignantly, it was here that Israeli prime minister Levi Eshkol and Pope Paul VI chose to meet on the pope's 1964 visit to Israel.

Meggido's location on the fertile plains of the Jezreel Valley leading to the Mediterranean Sea would have entitled its rulers and occupants free rein and access to the Via Maris trade highway. It would have been here that the often miles-long camel caravans would have made pit stops to trade in the city's abundant and flourishing marketplaces.

Today, the park provides but a mere glimpse into the city's prosperous and ever-changing past, and of the mighty battles that ensued here. Partial reconstructions of some of the major features of the park do aid in putting together what can sometimes be – to the untrained eye – a mass of stones (tours can be arranged from the national park office). A short but insightful video is broadcast at regular intervals in English or Hebrew at the request of the majority.

The **Chariot City and tunnel** remain the most impressive relics in the park. A 30m-long water system built during King Solomon's reign in the 10th century was constructed to enable the fortified city's occupants to gain access to fresh water throughout times of conflict. Today, visitors can enter the tunnel by descending a hefty 183 steps which are located at the southwest corner of the park. The tunnel leads outside the park boundaries, where a 600m walk will bring you back to the car park.

Getting there The park entrance is located approximately 2km from the Meggido Junction on route 66. Bus 823 runs between Nazareth (45mins/14.80NIS) and Tel Aviv (1hr 20mins/26.50NIS) and will stop at the Meggido Junction if hailed. Buses 830 and 835 running between Tel Aviv and Tiberias (1hr 15mins/26NIS) also stop there and take 40 minutes less to get to Tel Aviv.

BEIT SHE'ARIM (*between Hashomrim and Hatishbi junctions*; ✆ 04 9831643; *www.parks.org.il*; ⊕ Apr–Sep 08.00–17.00 daily; Oct–Mar 08.00–16.00 daily; admission adult/child 18/8NIS*) Extensive excavations that began in 1871 and have proceeded up until today have revealed the ancient Jewish settlement of Beit She'arim and, more significantly to Jewish history, the underground cemetery built at its foot. The Sanhedrin – Jewish school of learning – was located here, and at its head was the much-revered Rabbi Yehuda HaNassi. After many years in Beit She'arim,

Rabbi HaNassi relocated to the nearby city of Zippori, only to be returned posthumously in CE220. Word of the rabbi's death spread the length and breadth of the Middle East and a fervent desire to be buried close to his grave became paramount to many. Beit She'arim hence became the holiest Jewish burial site throughout the Mishnaic and Talmudic periods.

The voluminous caves and countless graves shoe-horned into every potential space that we see today are merely the tip of the iceberg of the possible thousands that are buried in the surrounding hills. Large stone sarcophagi, inscribed in Hebrew, Aramaic and Greek depict Jewish symbols as well as secular images of figures and animals, and show families that derived from as far afield as southern Arabia and Syria. The catacombs are impressive and certainly worth visiting. Cut out of the hillside, they contain dozens of sarcophagi, some caves being up to 30m deep and several metres high. Free tours, offered by volunteers from the nearby moshav are certainly instrumental in making sense of the mounds of tombs and the intricate and revelatory messages inscribed on them. (*Tours start at 10.00, 11.00 and 12.00 Sunday–Friday with an extra tour at 13.00 on Saturday.*) Traditional music concerts, performances, Bar Mitzvahs and weddings are often celebrated in the grounds in summer, using the ornately decorated stone arches of the park's three most impressive caves as the backdrop. The gourmet **Tish'rei Restaurant** (↘ *04 9833373;* ◷ *17.00–midnight daily; $$$$*) is located inside the national park next to the main offices. It serves French-style cuisine in the tranquil setting of the park's gardens. Reservations are recommended, especially on weekends.

Getting there The site is located off routes 75 and 722 between Hashomrim and Hatishbi junctions 20km southeast of Haifa, approximately 10 minutes' drive from Kiryat Tivon. There is no direct transport to the park but bus 338 from Haifa Lev HaMifratz stops at Kiryat Tivon where it is a 2km walk to the entrance.

ZIPPORI (SEPPHORI) (↘ *04 6568272; www.parks.org.il;* ◷ *08.00–17.00 Sat–Thu, 08.00–16.00 Fri; admission adult/child 23/12NIS*) Zippori was once a splendid city and a much-contested site throughout the Galilee region's dramatic past. Excavations that began in 1931 unearthed remains dated from the First Temple Period, through the Roman conquest and Herod the Great's reign to the Byzantine period and beyond. Zippori was appointed capital of the Galilee region shortly after the Roman conquest in 63BCE and changed hands many times amidst fierce battles and revolts. It wasn't until the 3rd century CE that the Jews finally retook control of Zippori and it was during this time that textual and archaeological evidence points to the arrival of Rabbi Judah HaNassi and the Sanhedrin Jewish law makers. Rabbi Judah lived out his final 17 years here and it was during this time that, in CE200, he drafted the Mishnah.

The Sanhedrin remained in Zippori until its relocation to Tiberias at the end of the 3rd century CE and the city's frequent appearance in the Talmud testifies to its significance in Jewish history. Zippori was razed to the ground by a violent earthquake in CE363, shortly after the beginning of the Byzantine period and rapid spread of Christianity. The city was rebuilt and flourished as a Christian city – the population of which were still predominantly Jewish – until the beginning of the Arab period. Throughout the Crusader period, Arab revolt of 1936–39 and 1948 Arab–Israeli War Zippori was contested, battled over and conquered.

Today the excavated ruins are fairly scanty. To the untrained eye there is little to be gleaned from the piles of stones and masonry walls, with the exception of the rather impressive mosaic floors and Roman theatre. The remains are best appreciated through an arranged tour which can be organised through the national park office. A circuitous route through the park's antiquities offers panoramic views over the surrounding area and takes you past relics of street patterns, a marketplace, bathhouses, Jewish and Christian ecclesiastical buildings and a Crusader fortress.

Getting there Bus 343 between Nazareth (15mins/8.50NIS) and Akko (1hr 10mins/21.50NIS) stop every 1.5 hours at the Zippori Junction from where you will have a 4km walk to the entrance of the park. To reach the site by car from Nazareth head north out of the city on route 79 and turn right after 4km towards Moshav Zippori. Upon entering the moshav follow signs to the antiquities park.

CANA Today 8,500 people – 83% of whom are Muslim, 17% Christian – call Cana home. The small town (that can also be spelt Kafr Kanna, Kefar Kana, Khirbet Cana) is located approximately 8km north of Nazareth, and is a likely candidate for the biblical site of the same name, where Jesus performed his first miracle of turning water into wine. Jewish tradition also believes this to be the site of the tomb of the sage Rabbi Shimon ben Gamliel.

The town itself is quaint and attractive, characterised by several churches commemorating Jesus's miracle located on Churches Street, a recently renovated pedestrianised promenade running through central Cana. The **Franciscan Wedding Church** (⊕ *08.00–12.00 & 14.00–18.00 Mon–Sat; admission free*), located in the centre of town, was established in 1883, and is the traditional site of the home where Jesus performed his miracle. Next door, in the **Greek Orthodox Church of St George** visitors are proudly shown an ancient-looking glass jar, purportedly – under Orthodox belief – one of the ten water containers involved in the miracle.

Further along Churches Street is the **Nathanael Chapel**, also belonging to the Franciscan order. It was built towards the end of the 19th century in honour of Nathanael – later to become St Bartholomew – one of Jesus's most vocal opposers who later ended up being one of his disciples.

The ruins of the ancient village of Cana rest atop a nearby hill, which is only accessible by foot or 4x4. The hike is hard graft but those who undertake the challenge will be rewarded by panoramic views of the southern Galilee region.

Getting there Bus 431 between Tiberias and Nazareth passes the town and will stop on request. From Nazareth, Nesiot buses 29 and 30 depart every 20 minutes. To reach Cana by car head north on route 754 for approximately 8km. The turning to the town is signposted on the right.

TIBERIAS

Tiberias is the hub of eastern Galilean life and often considered the capital of the region. Named in honour of the Roman emperor Tiberias, the city has seen its share of proverbial ups and downs. In more recent times, an extensive cleanup operation has been underway to create a Tiberias that offers more than tacky seaside attractions, shabby hotels and littered beaches. The project has seen some success and – while Jewish and Christian pilgrims never halted their yearly processions to the city – visitors now seem to want to stick around a little longer. While beaches in the near vicinity of urban areas are still overcrowded and littered in peak summer months, international restaurants, outdoor cafés and an improved standard of accommodation have gradually appeared. Tiberias has long been a top holiday spot with Israeli teenagers in search of a party atmosphere and hence the summer school holiday months are the city's busiest. Yet pilgrims and partygoers have always seemed to co-exist in relative harmony in this city where beer and the Bible are the main attractions for two very different kinds of visitors.

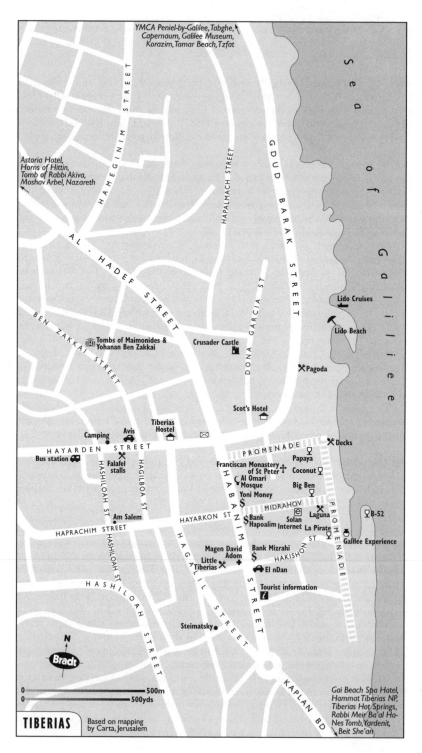

YMCA Peniel-by-Galilee, Tabghe,
Capernaum, Galilee Museum,
Korazim, Tamar Beach, Tzfat

Sea of Galilee

HAMEGINIM STREET

HAPALMACH STREET

GDUD BARAK STREET

Astoria Hotel,
Horns of Hittin,
Tomb of Rabbi Akiva,
Moshav Arbel, Nazareth

AL - HADEF STREET

BEN ZAKKAI STREET

DONA GARCIA ST

Lido Cruises

Lido Beach

Tombs of Maimonides &
Yohanan Ben Zakkai

Crusader Castle

Pagoda

Scot's Hotel

Camping

Avis

Tiberias
Hostel

Decks

HAYARDEN STREET

PROMENADE

Bus station

Falafel
stalls

Papaya

Franciscan Monastery
of St Peter

Coconut

HAGILBOA ST

Al Omari
Mosque

Big Ben

HASHILOAH ST

Yoni Money

HABAZIM

Am Salem

MIDRAHOV

HAYARKON ST

Solan
Internet

Laguna

B-52

HAPRACHIM STREET

Bank
Hapoalim

La Pirate

Galilee Experience

HASHILOAH STREET

PROMENADE

HAGALIL STREET

Magen David
Adom

Bank Mizrahi

Little
Tiberias

HAKISHON ST

El nDan

HASHILOAH STREET

Tourist information

Steimatsky

N

Bradt

0   500m
0   500yds

KAPLAN BD

Gai Beach Spa Hotel,
Hammat Tiberias NP,
Tiberias Hot Springs,
Rabbi Meir Ba'al Ha-
Nes Tomb, Yardenit,
Beit She'an

TIBERIAS

Based on mapping
by Carta, Jerusalem

HISTORY Tiberias was founded in CE20 by Herod Antipas, son of Herod the Great, and the city was soon forcibly populated by reluctant Jews. Over time Tiberias became one of the country's four Holy Cities and was the seat of the Sanhedrin and centre of Jewish learning for many years after the Roman destruction of the Temple of Jerusalem. It was here that the Mishnah, which later grew into the Talmud – dictating Jewish civil and religious laws – was believed to have been complied between the 3rd and 5th centuries CE.

The Jewish community continued to thrive throughout the Byzantine and Arab rule, until the Middle Ages when wars and earthquakes ravaged the city and it fell into rapid decline. Throughout the crusades it was the central city of the Principality of Galilee in the Kingdom of Jerusalem until, in 1187 during the Battle of Hittin on the outskirts of Tiberias, Saladin defeated the Crusaders and the city was all but abandoned. It was at this time that the present-day city was established, just north of its ancestor.

In the 16th century, Suleiman the Magnificent returned Tiberias to the Jews until, in the 18th century, the Arab sheikh Daher el-Omar nominated Tiberias as capital of Galilean territory (which lasted until his assassination in 1775). The two large abandoned mosques, the Al Omari and Al Bahr, which still stand today, owe their origins to this time and are believed to have been built by the city's Jewish inhabitants as a token of gratitude for being allowed to remain. The city prospered thanks to its abundance of fertile agricultural lands and mild climate and today continues to play a pivotal role in Galilean life and Israeli tourism.

GETTING THERE The central bus station is located down a small side road off HaYarden Street just past HaShiloah Street. Buses 961, 962 and 963 depart to and from Jerusalem hourly (3hrs/45NIS) and buses 840 and 841 every 20 minutes to and from Tel Aviv (2hrs 30mins/45NIS) continuing to Kiryat Shmona (1hr 40mins/25NIS). Bus 430 departs hourly to Haifa (1hr 30mins/30NIS) and there are regular services to Tzfat (1hr/20NIS) and Beit Shean (40mins/21.50NIS). Bus 431 runs hourly between Tiberias and Nazareth (40mins/19NIS). Buses 15 and 19 leave Tiberias at 12.00, 13.20, 16.00 and 18.35 going anti-clockwise around the Sea of Galilee to Katzrin (1hr/25NIS) stopping at the Tzemach Junction near Deganya Alef, Lavnun Beach, Kursi Junction, Ramot Junction and Yehudiya Junction.

GETTING AROUND Buses to and from sites and beaches around the Sea of Galilee are few and far between and taxis can be exorbitant if you're using them regularly. There is a taxi rank outside the Rimonim Hotel next to the tourist information centre. The most convenient and economical means of getting around is renting a car from one of the rental agencies in the city. **El Dan** (*HaBanim St;* ☎ *04 6791822;* ⊕ *08.00–17.00 Sun–Thu, 08.00–13.00 Fri*) and **Avis** (*HaYarden St;* ☎ *04 6722766;* ⊕ *08.00–17.00 Sun–Thu, 08.00–14.00 Fri*) rent cars from 150NIS per day. Bicycles can be rented from the **Tiberias Hostel** (see *Where to stay,* page 174).

TOURIST INFORMATION

Tourist information office 9 HaBanim St; ☎ 04 6725666; ⊕ 09.00–16.30 Sun–Thu, 09.00–13.00 Fri. Located in the small archaeological park directly in front of the Sheraton Hotel on HaBanim Street. Certainly worth a trip before embarking on excursions around the city and lake as knowledgeable and welcoming staff will point you in the right direction.

LOCAL TOUR OPERATORS The **tourist information office** has a wealth of knowledge on local tour guides and they also organise a two-hour free walking tour of Tiberias. Tours leave from the tourist information office at 09.00 on Sundays and Mondays and 18.00 on Thursdays.

Am Salem 3 HaPrachim St; ☏ 1800 777 999; ⏱ 08.00–19.00 Sun–Thu, 08.00–13.00 Fri. Can arrange private, English-speaking guided tours to sights in the area.
Lido Cruises Lido Beach; ☏ 04 6721538. Operate

30min cruises around the lake. Schedules change from day to day so call ahead to find out sailing times. During the summer months there are regular sailings so it is possible to just show up at the dock.

🏠 **WHERE TO STAY** While accommodation has been drastically improved over recent years, renovations seem to have started from the top with huge differences between the plusher, pricier establishments and mid-range or budget places. Hostels and cheaper hotels tend to be rather shabby and most could do with a lick of paint. However, come the Jewish and summer holidays all are booked to capacity so if you plan on visiting around those times be sure to book well in advance.

🏠 **Gai Beach Resort Spa Hotel** (200 rooms) Route 90 south; ☏ 04 6700700; e gaibeach@netvision.net.il; www.gaibeachhotel.com. For a good-quality, lively summer resort hotel the Gai Beach offers swimming pools galore, a water park, beach access (see *Beaches* page 171), luxury spa, bars & restaurants & lots of children's entertainment. Prices based on B&B but HB options also available. *Off-season 300NIS less ($$$$).* **$$$$$**

🏠 **Scot's Hotel** (69 rooms) 1 Gdud Barak St; ☏ 04 6710710; f 04 6710711; www.scotshotel.co.il. Standing like a rose amongst weeds, the Scot's Hotel is the jewel in Tiberias's hotel crown. Built as a hospital by Scottish missionary Dr David Torrance in 1894, the castle-like building today acts as a 5-star hotel. While all rooms are faultless, the so-called 'antique rooms' are especially charming (& considerably pricier). Manicured lawns, a swimming pool, staggering lake views & a gourmet restaurant clinch the deal. Prices based on HB. **$$$$$**

🏠 **Astoria** (88 rooms) 13 Ohel Yaacov St; ☏ 04 6722351/2; e hotel@astoria.co.il; www.astoria.co.il. Located at the northern end of town but still within walking distance of the centre. Rooms are clean & functional if a little dowdy & all come

with TV, AC & minibar. Outdoor swimming pool (open in summer), restaurant, bar & exercise room. *Weekdays 100NIS less ($$).* **$$$**

🏠 **YMCA Peniel-by-Galilee** (13 rooms) Route 90 north; ☏ 04 6720685; www.ymca-galilee.co.il. Just 5km up the coast from Tiberias is this wonderful, secluded YMCA, undoubtedly the best budget option in the area. Nestled amidst palm trees & shady gardens, the 1920s stone building (also known as the Harte Villa after its former occupant, the General Secretary of the Jerusalem YMCA) exudes Middle Eastern charm & character. Located right on the shoreline of the Sea of Galilee it has private beach access & a hot spring pool as well as a delightful Middle Eastern terrace restaurant. Rooms are simple but with views like these you won't be looking at them anyway. All northbound buses stop directly outside the YMCA. **$$$**

🏠 **Tiberias Hostel** (18 rooms) Rabin Sq; ☏ 04 6792611. For a hostelling treat both the 4-bed dorm rooms & private rooms come complete with shower, AC, TV & fridge. The hostel is friendly & clean & offers bike rental, travel information, internet access & a bar & lounge area. *Dorms (70NIS).* **$$**

✖ **WHERE TO EAT** Although there has been a marked improvement over recent years, those looking for fine dining are best advised to avoid Tiberias altogether. Most places serve up a pleasant grilled St Peter's fish – the Sea of Galilee's local produce – or grilled meat and salad which are fine once or twice. The pedestrianised **HaKishon Street** is lined with cafés, restaurants and late-night bars and is a good place to soak up the summer resort atmosphere. **Falafel stalls** (*HaYarden St; ⏱ 09.00–20.00 Sun–Thu, 09.00–14.00 Fri; $*) line the road heading towards the bus station while several cheap, plastic-chaired pizzerias and bakeries can be found on the corner of HaKishon and HaBanim streets.

✗ **Scot's Hotel Restaurant** 1 Gdud Barak St; ↘ 04 6710710; www.scotshotel.co.il. Enjoying a sunset dinner on the terrace of the regal Scot's Hotel Restaurant is a true Tiberias treat. With views over the fragrant gardens & still waters of the Sea of Galilee it doesn't get much better than this. The menu changes regularly to incorporate seasonal specialities but expect fresh, homegrown vegetables & herbs, St Peter's fish & a selection of speciality cheeses. To top it off, the wine cellar is first-rate & offers some local boutique bottles. 3-course meal $$$$$

✗ **Decks** Gdud Barak St; ↘ 04 6721538; ⊕ 19.00–late Sun–Thu, end of Shabbat–late Sat; kosher. Picturesque location on a wooden deck jutting out into the lake, this restaurant specialises in expertly prepared meats & fish grilled over wood renowned for its aromatic properties. The lamb, duck & local fish are highly recommended. $$$$

✗ **Little Tiberias** HaKishon St; ↘ 04 6792806; ⊕ 12.00–midnight daily. Cosy, home-style cooking in the middle of the busy pedestrian thoroughfare. Wide selection of meats & seafood & some cheaper pasta dishes if the budget doesn't quite run to the seafood platter. $$$$✗ **Pagoda** Gdud Barak St seafront; ↘ 04 6725513; ⊕ 12.00–late Sun–Thu; kosher. The main reason to come here is undoubtedly the setting, plonked right on the shore of the lake just north of town. This gaudy, Chinese-style restaurant is a big favourite of kosher-keepers who enjoy the somewhat unimaginative Asian food which consists of old Chinese favourites, sushi & some Thai dishes. $$$$

✗ **Laguna Restaurant** Midrahov; ↘ 04 6722321; ⊕ 09.00–02.00 Sun–Thu, after Shabbat–late Sat. One of Tiberias's oldest restaurants, the Laguna offers simple, homemade salads & grilled meats & fish. Not as flashy as some of its neighbours but then it doesn't need to be. $$

ENTERTAINMENT AND NIGHTLIFE Tiberias's nightlife centres on the pedestrianised HaKishon Street leading down to the seafront. Throughout the busy summer months, this is where people congregate to chatter noisily amidst the pumping bar sounds, street vendors and abundance of late-night restaurants.

♀ **Big Ben** Midrahov; ↘ 04 6722248; ⊕ 12.00–late daily. An old Tiberias favourite, Big Ben pulls in the crowds with decently priced beer, a chilled-out atmosphere & plenty of live televised sporting events. Standard pub food fills a hole even if it's not particularly exotic. $$

♀ **Papaya** Promenade; ↘ 054 1241200; ⊕ 17.00–late daily. Although it has a great

lakeside location, this isn't what most people come here for. Cocktails, karaoke, frenetic dancing & an open-air, Hawaiian tropics feel attract hordes of partygoers in summer.

Other good bars to check out in the area include **La Pirate** where Midrahov and the promenade meet, **Coconut** next to Papaya on the promenade and **B-52** next to the Galilee Experience jetty.

SHOPPING

🛖 **Camping** corner of Yohanan Ben Zakkai & HaYarden sts; ↘ 04 6759523⊕ 09.00–19.00 Sun–Thu, 09.00–14.00 Fri. Well-stocked camping & hiking equipment shop.

🛖 **Steimatsky** HaGalil Shopping Centre, HaGalil St; ↘ 04 6791288; ⊕ 08.00–13.00 & 16.30–19.30 Sun–Thu, 08.00–14.00 Fri. Good selection of English books, magazines & newspapers.

OTHER PRACTICALITIES Tiberias is a small and easily navigable city, with an even smaller and more easily navigable centre, which radiates out from the seafront promenade. Parallel to the sea is HaBanim Street where most services and facilities are located.

Emergencies
Fire ↘ 102 or 04 6791222   Police station ↘ 100 or 04 6792444

Money

$ **Bank Hapoalim** 3 HaBanim St; ✆ 03 6532407/
landline*2407; 🕙 08.30–13.15 Sun & Tue/Wed,
08.30–13.00 & 16.00–18.30 Mon & Thu,
08.15–12.30 Fri

$ **Mizrakhi Bank** Corner of HaKishon & HaBanim sts;
✆ landline*5080; 🕙 09.00–13.30 Sun–Thu,
16.00–18.00 Mon–Wed, 08.30–12.00 Fri
$ **Yoni Money Currency Exchange** 2 HaBanim St;
✆ 04 6720017; 🕙 08.30–19.00 Sun–Thu

Post

📭 **Post office** Corner of HaBanim & HaYarden sts;
✆ 04 6790066; 🕙 07.00–18.00 Sun–Thu,

07.00–12.00 Fri. Changes travellers' cheques.

Medical

✚ **Magen David Adom (First Aid)** 1 HaKishon St;
✆ 04 6790101/111
✚ **Porriya Hospital** 7km away from Tiberias centre.

Bus 39 from the central bus station stops outside.
✚ **Superpharm** 42 HaYarden St; ✆ 04 6676663;
🕙 08.30–22.00 Sun–Fri, 10.00–23.00 Sat

Internet

🖥 **Solan Internet** 3 Midrahov; ✆ 04 6726470;
🕙 08.00–midnight Sun–Fri, 16.00–midnight Sat.

20NIS/hr. Internet access, mobile phone &
international telephone cards & fax facilities.

WHAT TO SEE

Tombs As the seat of the Sanhedrin and home to numerous Talmudic scholars, Tiberias's hills are scattered with the tombs of influential men who had a profound impact on Judaism throughout the 2nd and 3rd centuries. Modest dress is required to enter all and *yarmulkes* for men can be obtained at the entrances. About 300m from the northern end of HaGalil Street are several tombs including that of **Maimonides** (also known as Rambam). Born in Spain in 1135, he fled his country from persecution and travelled to Cairo where he worked as Saladin's personal physician. During this time he rose to rabbi and leader of the Jews in Egypt and made significant contributions to the Mishnah. After his death in 1204 his body was taken to Tiberias. There is very little to see except the 14 pillars encircling the tomb which represent the 14 sections of the Mishnah Torah. There are plans to improve the site in an attempt to raise Maimonides's tomb to the status that other, more elaborate tombs enjoy. One such belongs to **Rabbi Meir Ba'al Ha-Nes**, whose grandiose shrine resides on the hill behind the city. Tradition has it that the hot springs adjacent to the tomb have healing qualities. Near the tomb of Maimonides rests the **tomb of Yohanan Ben Zakkai** who was responsible for the relocation of the seat of the Sanhedrin from Jerusalem following its destruction in CE70. The story of his escape from the capital hidden in a coffin, only to emerge in front of Roman general Vespasian is legendary. Upon announcing to Vespasian that he was now the Caesar following the death of the Roman leader, he was granted one wish – he chose to found the Jewish learning centre which was to become the Sanhedrin. In the areas now swallowed up by the modern city's sprawl is the **tomb of Rabbi Ben Akiva**, just off the main road near the police station. Ben Akiva – one of the rabbis who is quoted in the Talmud as being amongst those who carried Rabbi Yohanan Ben Zakkai out of Jerusalem – believed Bar Kochba to be the Messiah and was finally executed after his rising in CE135.

Crusader castle The dilapidated remains of the 12th-century castle are on the northern edge of the Old Town and worth a visit if only for the views over the lake. The Crusader castle, the remains of which are still visible today, was rebuilt in the local black basalt stone in 1738 by Daher el-Omar.

Franciscan Monastery of St Peter The apse of the monastery was designed in the form of a ship's bow, representing Peter's fishing boat. It was built towards the end of the 19th century over remains of the Crusader castle. It is located southeast from the Crusader castle towards the promenade.

Horns of Hittin To put ancient Tiberias into perspective, the somewhat exerting hike of approximately one hour to the top of hill allows for views over the entire Galilee region and beyond into present-day Jordan. It was here that Saladin defeated the Crusaders in 1187, signalling the beginning of the end for the Crusader Kingdom in the Holy Land. It is also an important Druze gathering site (see page 25). The trail starts at the main road leading west out of the city or can be reached by bus 42.

Tiberias Hot Springs (*Eliezer Kaplan Bd;* \ *04 6728500; www.chameytveria.co.il;* ⊕ *08.00–20.00 Sun/Mon & Wed, 08.00–11.00 Tue & Thu, 08.30–20.00 Sat*) This is one of Israel's largest health and spa resorts, offering a whole menu of treatments and massages. There are indoor and outdoor mineral pools, several restaurants and a fitness centre. Opposite the complex is the **Hammat Tiberias National Park** (\ *04 6725287; www.parks.org.il;* ⊕ *Apr–Sep 08.00–17.00 daily; Oct–Mar 08.00–16.00 daily; admission adult/child 12/6NIS*), which pays homage to the 17 natural springs that played a crucial part in the development of Tiberias. Throughout the Roman period thousands of people came to bathe in the therapeutic waters that flowed from the ground, and a large synagogue was built on the site indicating it played a central role in the proceedings of the Sanhedrin. Within the ruins is an ornate mosaic, the oldest in Israel.

The Midrahov (or pedestrian walkway) is the place where it all happens. Tourists can choose to relax in one of the countless bars, cafés or restaurants and soak up the sun, sea and spirituality of the lake, or partake in one of the various activities. Boat trips can sometimes be organised from the dock although there is no set timetable for their departure. Larger groups will have more success in getting the boat to leave the dock, but the tourist information office will be able to tell you what's what with respect to boat-trip departures on specific days. For those of us not able to walk on water, self-drive motor boats can be rented (30mins/120NIS) from **Tiberias Water Sports** (*Midrahov dock;* \ *052 2692664*). Banana boats, water skiing and a range of other watersports are available from the offices on the dock throughout summer.

The Galilee Experience (\ *04 6723620;* ⊕ *08.00–22.00 Sun–Thu, 09.00–16.00 Fri; admission adult/child 25/20NIS*) is located on the second floor of the marina building and has regular showings of its 38-minute-long movie depicting 4,000 years of Galilean history.

BEACHES Tiberias's beaches leave a lot to be desired and those looking for the quintessential Sea of Galilee swimming experience are better off heading to the beaches further along the coast or on the eastern shore (see page 181). If you decide to opt for a beach closer to home then the **Gai Beach** belonging to the **Gai Beach Resort Spa Hotel** (see *Where to stay*, page 174) is your best option. The **Gai Beach Water Park** (\ *04 6700713; Passover–Oct 09.30–17.00 daily; admission 60NIS*) is a big hit with kids and has an assortment of slides and pools as well as beach access. Hotel guests get free entry.

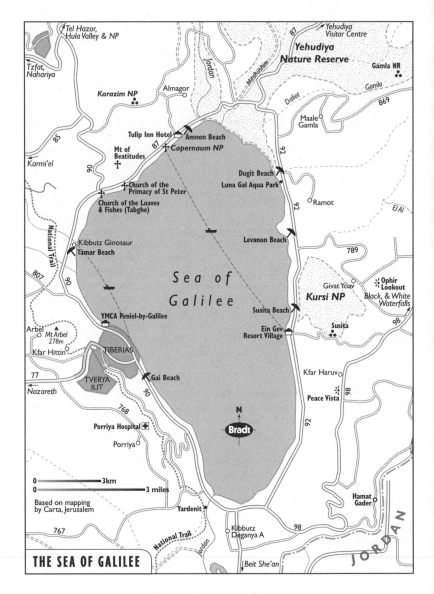

THE SEA OF GALILEE (LAKE KINNERET)

While Tiberias itself is not an unpleasant place to spend a couple of days most visitors use it as a jumping-off point to the sights around the Sea of Galilee. Steeped in Christian biblical history, the sea was the site of many of Jesus's miracles, with small churches dotting the shoreline commemorating these events. For hundreds of years Christian pilgrims have made their way to the gently lapping shores of the Sea of Galilee (known in Israel as 'the Kinneret') to soak up the abounding tranquillity, gaze down at ancient lands and walk in Jesus's footsteps. Today is no different, and despite the scores of tour buses that make regular stops along the sea, it has managed to avoid the mass-produced, over-touristy feel (this, however, doesn't apply to the Sea of Galilee's beaches, which are extremely popular with young Israeli teenagers). The following sights have been arranged in a clockwise direction starting from Tiberias and recommended accommodation has been included under each site where appropriate. Beach campsites (see page 181) are good budget options, especially on weekdays and out of the school holiday season.

Getting there Bus 15 makes an anti-clockwise circuit of the Sea of Galilee stopping at the Tzemach Junction near Deganya Alef, Lavnun Beach and the Kursi Junction before continuing to the Golan Heights. Buses 450, 841 and 963 head north hourly stopping at Ginosaur Junction (for Tamar Beach and the Galilee Museum), Kfar Nahum Junction and Korazim Junction (2km from national park). There are no buses to sites along the north shore so get off northbound buses at the Kfar Nahum Junction and take a delightful walk eastwards to Tabghe (2km), the Church of the Multiplication, Mount of Beatitudes, Capernaum and Amnon Beach.

WHAT TO SEE
The Galilee Museum at Ginosaur (*Kibbutz Ginosaur;* ℡ *04 6727700; www.jesusboat.com;* ⊕ *08.30–17.00 Sat–Thu, 08.30–13.00 Fri; admission adult/child 20/15NIS*) Also known as the Yigal Alon Centre in memory of the founding member of the nearby Kibbutz Ginosaur (and later deputy prime minister), the Galilee Museum comprises several sections. The most interesting – and reason most make the visit – is the Ancient Galilee Boat, a 1st-century wooden ship excavated from the nearby shores. An audio-visual presentation depicts the arduous task of raising and preserving the 8.2m-long ship, often dubbed the Jesus Boat. Upstairs are exhibitions on Galilean culture throughout the Mishnah and Talmud periods, as well as the Yigal Alon remembrance room offering a more personal peek into his life. Head to the roof of the five-storey building for a fabulous view over the lake.

Tabghe and the Church of the Multiplication of the Loaves and the Fishes
(⊕ *08.30–17.00 Mon–Sat, 10.00–17.00 Sun; admission free; modest dress*) The church's rather long-winded title does in fact sum it up pretty nicely. This is the site long believed to be where Jesus performed one of his most well-known miracles: the Multiplication of the Loaves and Fishes and the Feeding of the Five Thousand. The church is located on the northwest shore of the sea in the minute village of Tabghe. The church that stands today was consecrated in 1982 and is a far descendant of the original, built in the 4th century CE. Remains of a large Byzantine monastery – devastated during the Arab Conquest – were discovered when the area was excavated in the 1980s. After restoration to its Byzantine glory (including sections of the original figurative mosaic, the church's highlight) it is now one of the top spots along the sea's pilgrimage route. Tradition has it the block of limestone under the altar is 'the table of the lord', where Jesus performed his multiplication miracle. Located just south of Tabghe is the **Karei Deshe Guest House (HI)** (*65 rooms;* ℡ *04 6720601;* e *kdeshe@iyha.org.il; www.iyha.org.il; weekdays 100NIS less ($$); $$$*) which is perfectly located for exploring the sites along the north shore of the lake. Rooms have two, four or six beds (*dorms $*), air conditioning, television and en-suite bathroom. In keeping with HI standards all rooms are immaculate, if a little uninspiring. A kosher breakfast is included. Sprawling lawns lead down to private beach access.

Church of the Primacy of St Peter
(⊕ *08.00–12.00 & 14.00–17.00; admission free; modest dress*) Just along from Tabghe, the modest Franciscan church marks the site where tradition has it Jesus appeared to his disciples for the third time and where

he confirmed the Apostle Peter. The black basalt chapel is small and simple and pales in contrast to its more elaborate ecclesiastical counterparts along the coast. Aside from its religious connotations there isn't an awful lot to see, but its tranquillity and beachside location make it a worthwhile stop.

Mount of Beatitudes (⊕ *08.00–12.00 & 14.40–17.00; admission free; 5NIS per car to enter car park; modest dress*) While the exact location of Jesus's Sermon on the Mount is a much-contested topic, with potential sites including the Horns of Hittin and Mount Arbel, Mount Eremos, just up from the Church of the Multiplication, has been the site of commemoration and pilgrimage for the past 1,600 years. With funding from Italy – more specifically from Benito Mussolini, whose name plaque was later removed from the doorstep – a beautiful Catholic church was built in 1938. The church oozes numerical symbolism, its octagonal shape representing the eight virtues. Within the church hangs Pope Paul VI's cloak, a memento of his visit to Israel in 1964. Despite the regular stream of tour buses clogging the car park, the church and its shaded, serene gardens remain a quiet and tranquil place of worship.

From the car park, offering a fabulous view southwards over the ancient biblical lands and Sea of Galilee, a somewhat Herculean but worthwhile walk is possible. A steep path leads downhill towards the lake, likely part of the great trunk road coming from Damascus. The road formed an 'N' shape as it swept down and wove its way through the valleys of the Galilee region to the Mediterranean coast and on to the prosperous trade markets of Egypt. Rain makes the path extremely slippery so you will need sturdy walking shoes.

Capernaum A little confusingly, there are two sites along the lakeside that go by the name Capernaum. In fact, the 5km stretch of coast that begins at Tabghe is classified under the umbrella title **Capernaum National Park**. The park's headquarters (⊕ *08.00–16.00 daily; admission free*) form the northern boundary from where there is a beautiful view across the lake towards the Golan Heights. Privately hired boats leave the dock at irregular intervals but if there is space and if you talk nicely to the captain he might let you hop on board. Boats normally head towards Ein Gev Beach on the eastern shore. Alternatively, you can take one of several truly serene and pictur-esque walks along a stretch of lake that remains today as it did hundreds of years ago. The opulent, red-domed **Greek Orthodox Church of the Seven Apostles** (⊕ *08.00–12.00; admission free; modest dress*) can be accessed by the path leading west from the car park. A little further south of the church is the archaeological site of **Capernaum** (⊕ *08.00–17.00 daily; admission 3NIS; modest dress*), best known through the New Testament as the centre of Jesus's Galilean activities after his departure from Nazareth. Today a church stands over an earlier Byzantine one, erected over the spot believed to be the birthplace of St Peter. A little north of this is the remains of a once grand, white limestone synagogue, possibly dating to the 3rd century CE.

Korazim National Park About 5km north of the lake between the villages of Korazim (also spelt Corazim and Chorazim) and Almagor lie some impressive archaeological remains sadly often overlooked by many visitors to the region (☏ *04 6934982; www.parks.org.il; ⊕ Apr–Sep 08.00–17.00 daily; Oct–Mar 08.00–16.00 daily; admission adult/child 18/8NIS*). The ruins are spread over a broad area and include residential buildings, streets, ritual baths, olive presses (some of which have been reconstructed) and the site's *pièce de résistance*, a large, highly ornate synagogue. The city is known of from the Second Temple period and is mentioned in the Mishnah and Talmud as a flourishing agricultural hub. Korazim also appears in the New Testament in conjunction with Capernaum and Bethsaida as the three cities condemned by Jesus for their lack of belief in his preachings.

Kibbutz Deganya Alef Often referred to as the 'mother of kibbutzim', this is Israel's founding collective farm settlement. It was established in 1910 during the Ottoman rule by 12 Jews from surrounding areas.

In 2006, the kibbutz decided to go 'private', relinquishing their long-standing collective system and opting for the increasingly popular style of living that allows people to seek jobs and own property. The small **Deganya Alef Museum and Courtyard** (✆ *04 6608410/053 749102 (for guided tours); ⊕ 09.00–12.00 Sun–Thu; admission free*), built inside what was the original dining room, depicts the life and times of this small but nationally renown kibbutz (ask for an English transcript of the information boards at reception). A destroyed Syrian tank remains in the grounds serving as a reminder of the 1948 Arab–Israeli War.

Several eminent Zionist names crop up in Deganya's past, many of whom are interred in the cemetery. Amongst these are the national poet Rachel, A D Gordon (an early Zionist figure), and General Moshe Dayan (a general, politician and the kibbutz's second-born child). Albert Einstein and his wife also paid Deganya a visit.

Beaches The pebbly beaches around the Sea of Galilee are a top destination for holidaying families and groups of teenagers who come all summer long to pitch their tents, light up a barbecue and soak in the mild waters of the lake. While pollution and plummeting water levels are two of the problems facing the lake, the illegal privatisation of the beaches seems to aggravate Israelis more than anything else, where land squatters charge for entry. Nevertheless, it does often mean a lifeguard, car park, lawns and basic amenities are supplied. There are still public beaches but if there is no lifeguard present it is technically illegal to swim. As a general rule, the beaches on the eastern shore are considerably better than the dirty, litter-strewn ones around Tiberias.

Tamar Beach (✆ *04 6790630; admission adult/child 25/20NIS*) Although swimming is not permitted, the lovely little **Tamar Camping Migdal** (*35NIS pp*) is a great place close to Tiberias to pitch your tent. The on-site **Noni Jino Restaurant** (✆ *050 5468871; ⊕ 12.00–17.00 daily; $$$*) mainly caters to lunchtime tour groups but offers cheap, rustic meat, fish and hummus meals. **Jet ski and yacht lessons** (✆ *1 800 33 30 33*) also operate from here (contact reception for information).

Amnon Beach (✆ *050 6377188; ⊕ Apr–Sep; 80NIS per car*) Lovely swimming area located along the quieter northern strip of the sea. Windsurfing, a lifeguard and toilet and shower facilities are all included in the entry price, and **camping** is also possible (*120NIS per car*). The nearby **Tulip Inn Hotel** (*91 rooms; Amnon Bay;* ✆ *03 5110016; www.fattal.co.il; $$$*) is a large secluded resort village whose pleasant cabins all have air conditioning, private deck and television. Guests enjoy private access to a swimming beach near the Amnon Beach and another designated for watersports. The restaurant serves breakfast, lunch and dinner.

Dugit Beach (✆ *04 6678000; ⊕ Apr–Sep 24hrs; 50NIS per car*) Family-oriented strip of beach next to the **Luna Gal Aqua Park** (*⊕ Apr–Jun & Sep 10.00–16.00 Fri/Sat; Jul 09.30–18.00 daily (until 21.00 Mon & Thu); Aug 09.30–18.00 daily (until 22.00 Mon & Thu); admission adult/child low season 60/50NIS, high season 80/50NIS*). The beach has plenty of watersport activities including kayaking, banana boats, jet skiing and water skiing. **Camping** is permitted along the beach (included in the entry price) and there are clean shower facilities and a small supermarket.

Levanon Beach (Lavnun) (✆ *04 6732044; 80NIS per car*) Popular with big groups of raucous teenagers. Facilities include a small pebbly swimming beach, water sports, grass area for **camping** (included in the entry price), toilet and shower facilities and a snack food kiosk.

Susita Beach (*70NIS per car*) Quieter, more family-oriented beach with plenty of shade for having a picnic or barbecue. **Camping** (included in the entry price) is permitted and there is also a snack bar and clean shower facilities.

Ein Gev Beach If your budget stretches to a night at the **Ein Gev Holiday Resort Village** (*184 rooms;* ➘ *04 6659800;* e *resort@eingev.org.il;* **$$$$**), this is probably the Sea of Galilee's most beautiful, albeit private, beach. The four-star complex is set with green lawns and eucalyptus trees on the edge of the lake, and spacious rooms come with all the trimmings. Just south of the resort village are several kilometres of shady beaches which are particularly pleasant midweek when there are fewer sun seekers (*admission 14NIS pp*).

Yardenit (➘ *04 6759111;* e *yardenit@kinneret.org.il; www.yardenit.com;* ☉ *08.00–18.00 Sat–Thu, 08.00–16.00 Fri (closes 1hr earlier in winter); admission free*) Yardenit is the traditional Christian baptismal site on the Jordan River. The strikingly green, fish-laden waters trickle through the northern valleys only to end up in the over-developed site of Yardenit. While the site has an obvious religious and spiritual draw for many, baptism by bulk seems a more apt description than peaceful confirmation. The site has, however, opened up the surrounding areas, so it is possible – and recommended – to get away from the crowds, gift shops and food outlets and walk along the banks of the river for some getting to one with nature, history and quiet reflection. While the site may be a little on the touristy side, a visit during a service, where up to 1,000 pilgrims clothed in white robes stand knee-deep in the river, is anything from touristy, and is a moving experience whether you're a believer or not. Call in advance for baptismal bookings. Attached to Yardenit is the **Ohalo Manor** (*Kibbutz Kinneret;* ➘ *04 6675538;* e *hotel@ohalo.com; www.ohalo.com;* **$$$**), mainly catering towards pilgrims partaking in baptismal ceremonies. It offers unfussy, clean rooms at reasonable prices. Its lakeside location in the leafy kibbutz is one of its main draws. A favourite of large tour groups so book ahead.

AROUND TIBERIAS AND THE SEA OF GALILEE

KOCHAV HAYARDEN NATIONAL PARK (BELVOIR) (*Yissahar Ridge, 15km north of Beit She'an;* ➘ *04 6581766; www.parks.org.il;* ☉ *08.00–17.00 Sat–Thu, 08.00–16.00 Fri (closes 1hr earlier in winter); admission adult/child 18/8NIS*) It is immediately apparent when climbing the steep, winding road of the Yissahar Ridge up to the Kochav Hayarden crusader castle why such a site was chosen. With breathtaking views over the Jordan Valley, it offered strategic and defence capabilities that surpassed anywhere else in the region and thus became one of the most important fortresses in the country. Today, the heavily moated castle has been fully excavated, the only such example from the Crusader period in Israel.

Though only inhabited for a mere 21 years (1168–89), other residents have called Kochav Hayarden their home for a lot longer. Egyptian vultures, indigenous to the area, have lived in the Galilee and Golan regions for centuries. Problems of farmers illegally poisoning calf carcasses against predators, however, has led to severe decreases in their numbers. A sanctuary, erected 30m left of the castle, has given home and hope to several crippled birds. In 2007, a rare birth was celebrated, the baby chick destined for the wild when strong enough.

Mount Arbel's silhouette is one of the most unmistakable landmarks in the southern Galilee region. Its flat summit and drastically sloping edge is the result of a violent earthquake that shattered it into the two separate mountains we see today. A lookout at its peak proffers views over the Galilee region towards the Golan Heights, but even for seasoned hikers, getting to the top is difficult (but possible). The trail starts in the Valley of Doves at 206m below sea level and ascends directly up the sheer face of the cliff for 384m. Steps and handrails have been erected by the Israel Nature and National Parks Authority, which does ease things somewhat. Vertigo sufferers, however, would be best advised to drive up through Moshav Arbel and walk the short distance to the summit. Many believe that the graves of some of Jacob's children – whose 12 sons comprised the Tribes of Israel – are located here, in the caves that dot the cliff face. The caves – also used as shelter by Jews throughout the Roman and Greek periods – were again inhabited in the 17th century by the Druze. The scanty ruins of an ancient Jewish settlement include what little is left of a 4th-century synagogue dug into the cliff.

Getting there Getting there without a car is not easy. The steep 6km uphill walk from the main road is not for the faint-hearted and hitch-hiking from the bottom is more realistic. Bus 28 from Tiberias to Beit She'an will drop you off on the main road at the small junction. By car from Tiberias head south on route 90 for approx 12km and turn right at the Kochav Hayarden Junction. Follow the road 6km up the ridge turning left at the T-junction at the top.

MOUNT TABOR, AL-SHIBLI AND KFAR TAVOR Mount Tabor is the most easily recognisable feature in the Jezreel Valley landscape. Almost completely symmetrical, the 405m-high domed mountain proffers staggering views of the valley and surrounding areas. The mountain holds importance in both Christian and Jewish biblical history, although the scores of pilgrims who make the regular trip are predominantly Christian. While hotly contested, the **Church of the Transfiguration** (⊕ *08.00–12.00 & 14.00–18.00 Sun–Fri; admission free; modest dress*), holding pride of place on the summit, is the site many believe to be where Jesus was recognised as the Son of God. Jewish tradition places the battle between Deborah and Barak, and Sisera on the slopes of the mountain. For those without their own car, the Tabor Terminal operates shuttle buses up and down the winding mountain (20NIS).

Ascend Mount Tabor through the Bedouin village of **Al-Shibli**, a dusty and rather nondescript place whose friendly residents descend from a nomadic tribe who made Mount Tabor their permanent home. While many have adopted a 21st-century lifestyle, **Tabor's Tent** (⊕ *daily 09.00–midnight; $$*) provides a glimpse into this fascinating culture with demonstrations on making pita, black coffee and herbal medicines. Simple, reasonably priced meals are served under the tent's canopy and it is possible to spend a communal night sleeping on the cushions and mats.

Catering to the abundance of hiking and cycling trails in this area is one of the most popular hostels in the country, located in the pleasant village of **Kfar Tavor** 2km north of the turn-off to Mount Tabor on route 65. The **HooHa Cyclist's House** (*7 rooms; 7 Ha'charuvim St; Kfar Tavor;* ✆ *777080542; www.hooha.co.il; dorms available ($); $$$*) is fully geared towards those arriving on two wheels or two feet and offers a huge pool, bicycle storage, repairs and rental, cycling guides, free internet and spa and massage services. There is also a big garden, fully equipped kitchen and library. It is exceptionally popular so book ahead.

Getting there The village of Kfar Tavor is located just north of the turn-off to Mount Tabor on route 65 between Afula and Golani Junction. From Nazareth or Tiberias make your way to the Golani Junction on route 77 turning south onto route 65. Continue south to the Kfar Tavor Junction. The mountain road will be signposted on the right. The road north of Shibli is steep, narrow and badly paved but traversable with caution. Buses 835, 962, 841 and 442 run regularly between Afula (for Nazareth) and Tiberias, stopping in Kfar Tavor at the base of the mountain. Non-express buses 841 and 442 will drop you at the Kfar Tavor Junction for walking (or hitching) up the mountain, or at the following Gazit Junction for the short walk to Shibli.

BEIT SHE'AN NATIONAL PARK (✆ *04 6587189; www.parks.org.il;* ⊕ *08.00–20.00 Sun–Thu, 08.00–17.00 Fri/Sat (closes 1hr earlier in winter); admission adult/child 23/12NIS)* Beit She'an was put on the ancient map owing to its strategic importance along the great north–south trade route, with the area's abundant fertile lands an added incentive for residents, who first settled in the 5th century BCE. Today the town of Beit She'an is a rather unappealing place. A small, unprosperous settlement, it seems to escape being forgotten only through the extremely impressive national archaeological park situated on its fringes.

The remains are awe-inspiring. Beit She'an's timeline spans 4,500 years, the decades following the Roman conquest truly its glory days when it became one of ten cities that formed the Decapolis – a federated alliance – and the only one west of the Jordan River. It flourished through Hadrian's reign and – after the Bar Kochba revolt – under Antonius Pius and Marcus Aurelius. Rapid and extravagant development saw the construction of statues, governmental buildings and after the adoption of Christianity, the amphitheatre, bathhouses and fountains, which remain Beit She'an's most striking features. The enormity of the amphitheatre is in fact but a fraction of its original size and is today honoured by live summertime concerts held within it. A new evening light show walks visitors through the site, illuminating features with displays on the natural canvas of the hill behind. In daylight hours a trip up the hill's steep steps affords a fabulous view over the ruins.

In the middle of the park, a single standing pillar – the only erect structure unearthed – acts as a poignant reminder of the fateful fall of a once-magnificent city when it was ravaged by a violent earthquake in CE749.

In the town itself is the **Beit She'an Guesthouse (HI)** (*(62 rooms) 126 Menachem Begin Bd;* ✆ *04 6060760;* e *beitshean@iyha.org.il; www.iyha.org.il; $$*). Housed in a vast building of modern, plush architectural design, it even boasts its

---

THE BIG ONE

Both seismologists and the Bible are warning that Israel, sitting precariously on the fault line that stretches the length of the Syrian-African Rift Valley, is due for 'the big one', an earthquake to beat all others. Throughout history, violent earthquakes have devastated great cities and buildings the length and breadth of the country, many of which were never rebuilt. Beit She'an, Capernaum, Tzfat Old City and Jerusalem's Church of the Holy Sepulchre are but some of the casualties of Mother Nature's past power. While Israel feels the effects of dozens of tremors and small quakes every year there is no need to panic yet – we could still be eons away from the devastating quake experts believe is ultimately inevitable.

own swimming pool. Catering to large groups, it does have a rather mass-produced feel but is exceptionally clean (if a little sterile). Single or double rooms have air conditioning, shower and television and include a kosher breakfast.

Getting there Buses heading to and from Jerusalem and Tiberias will pass through Beit She'an. Be sure to ask the driver if he stops there as express services often don't. Buses 948, 961 and 966 depart hourly. Buses 829 and 843 to and from Tel Aviv leave once a day at 14.30 and 14.00 respectively. From Tiberias bus 28 departs every 45 minutes. There are no direct buses from Nazareth or Haifa but bus 412 leaves Afula every 15 minutes where you can connect to both.

GAN HASHLOSHA (*also known as the Sachne;* ✎ *04 6586219; www.parks.org.il;* ⊕ *Apr–Sep 08.00–17.00 daily; Oct–Mar 08.00–16.00 daily; admission adult/child 33/20NIS; combination ticket with Gan Garoo Australian Zoo adult/child 50/40NIS*) Most Israelis would vote Gan HaShlosha one of the most beautiful national parks in the country, and rightly so. The crystal-clear spring waters weave through the park's numerous pools and waterfalls, framed by well-kept lawns and vegetation. The surprisingly impressive, albeit small, **Museum of Regional and Mediterranean Archaeology** (✎ *04 6586352;* ⊕ *10.00–14.00 Sun–Thu & Sat*), barbecue areas, changing rooms, lifeguards and children's play areas have unfortunately meant that the park is also one of the most visited sites in the country, especially in the peak summer months and weekends. Needless to say, it is a different kettle of fish on weekdays and out of the school holiday season, and the constant 27°C waters mean swimming is possible any time of the year (although only one pool is full in the winter months). Early risers will most certainly be rewarded with solitude and tranquillity. An exact replica of the Tel Amal tower and stockade settlement that once stood on this spot is also worth a visit. **The Muse on the Water** (✎ *04 6588097;* ⊕ *11.00–midnight; kosher; $$$*) vegetarian restaurant serves an array of quiches, salads, pasta and fish. They also have a book exchange. Inside the adjacent, and extremely pretty, **Kibbutz Nir David** are plenty of **zimmer** bed and breakfasts, which make a nice choice for a couple of days' stay.

MOUNT GILBOA

The 500m-high Mount Gilboa ridge stretches for 18km across the southeastern part of the Jezreel Valley just south of Beit She'an. Every spring Israelis make their way up the mountain to see the blossoming of the famed purple Gilboa iris and hike in its abounding beauty. Mount Gilboa was the site where King Saul, the first king of Israel and his sons died fighting the Philistines, a tragic event in Jewish history. The well-paved Gilboa scenic route (route 667), which runs the entire length of the ridge, is studded with magnificent views in all directions, as well as countless opportunities for hiking, picnicking and cycling. From here it is possible to see the ancient city of Beit She'an, the hill of Moreh where the Philistines assembled to fight King Saul, Mount Tabor and the Jordan Valley. While the mild year-round weather means visiting at any time is possible, the clearest views are during spring when the whole mountain is alive with blossom. At the eastern end of the Gilboa range is the **Gilboa Herb Farm** (✎ *04 6531093;* ⊕ *12.00–22.00 Mon–Sat; $$$*) a rustic farm building perched atop the mountain. The farm specialises in the growing and exporting of fresh herbs, which their delightful restaurant takes delicious advantage of. Housed in a charmingly simple wood building (if the weather is nice be sure to sit outside) it serves rustic French, Italian and Middle Eastern-style foods.

Getting there The park is located next to Kibbutz Nir David on route 669 next to the petrol station. Bus 412 from Afula to Beit She'an stops every 20 minutes outside the kibbutz.

GAN GAROO AUSTRALIAN ZOO (*adjacent to Kibbutz Nir David;* ✆ *04 6488060;* ⊕ *09.00–20.00 Sun–Thu, 09.00–15.00 Fri, 09.00–17.00 Sat (closes 1hr earlier in winter); admission 35NIS; combination ticket with Gan HaShlosha adult/child 50/40NIS)* This relatively small but well-kept animal park was made possible by contributions from the Australian embassy in Israel and has now joined the ranks of only seven other zoological parks outside Australia to house koala bears. The nearby Kibbutz Nir David grows eucalyptus plants especially for their distinguished guests. Children and animal lovers enjoy the relative freedom the Aussie animals – which include free-hopping kangaroos, kookaburras and flying foxes – receive. The park is recognised by the Australian Wildlife Protection Authority and offers a small education centre (albeit mostly in Hebrew).

Getting there The park is adjacent to Kibbutz Nir David on route 669 just outside the entrance to Gan HaShlosha next to the petrol station. Bus 412 from Afula to Beit She'an stops outside the kibbutz every 20 minutes.

BEIT ALPHA (*Kibbutz Hefzibah;* ✆ *04 6532004; www.parks.org.il;* ⊕ *08.00–17.00 Sat–Thu, 08.00–16.00 Fri; admission adult/child 18NIS/8NIS)* While under the care of the Israel Nature and National Parks Protection Authority, Beit Alpha can't really be described as a park. The site itself houses the ruins of an ancient synagogue dating to the 6th century CE. Its crowning glory and *raison d'être* is the elaborate and well-preserved mosaic floor which can be viewed from raised platforms encircling it. Lights accentuate the significant features of the mosaic throughout a 15-minute video presentation detailing the history of the area and synagogues within Israel. It is a little pricey for the short time it takes to visit the park, but those with a national park combination ticket should definitely make the short detour.

Getting there The park is located next to the Kibbutz Beit Alpha on route 669. Bus 412 from Afula to Beit She'an stops every 20 minutes outside the kibbutz.

UPPER GALILEE

7

Upper Galilee

The landscape of the Upper Galilee provides the biggest surprise to visitors to Israel, who arrive expecting the barrenness of the Negev Desert, the cobbled lanes of Jerusalem's Old City and the white-sand beaches of coastal Tel Aviv. It is difficult to decide where the magic of the Upper Galilee region lies; in its tranquil, rural lifestyle perhaps, or in its abounding natural beauty, with roaring rivers, dense green forests and winding valleys. Yet perhaps its mystical atmosphere arises from the Holy Jewish city of **Tzfat**, from its long-abandoned Crusader fortresses or its impressive archaeological ruins, the ghosts of the past retelling their stories through the remains of once-great sites.

With a landscape reminiscent of the verdant valleys of western Europe the Upper Galilee is perfectly suited to a plethora of activities that you wouldn't necessarily associate with Israel, and plenty that you would. From kayaking down the bubbling Jordan River to inhaling the mysticism that abounds in Tzfat Old City's cobbled alleys, from witnessing the great bird migrations as they rest in the lush **Hula Valley** on their way south to getting swept up in the passionate celebration of Lag Ba'Omer at the tomb of **Rabbi Shimon bar Yohai**, this region is steeped in rural charm. Tiny villages dot the countryside, their family-run guesthouses a far cry from the chain hotels of the Mediterranean coast. A mesh of cultures and religions cohabit a land that has seen its fair share of turmoil, its long border with Lebanon acting as a launch pad for Hezbollah rockets throughout a number of wars and battles. Yet as you watch the sun set over the majestic **Montfort Castle** or listen to the breeze gently whistling through the leaves of **Rosh Pina**'s enigmatic little artists' quarter it is difficult to imagine it in any way other than simply enchanting.

TZFAT

Through all of its countless names and spellings, from Tsfat, Safed, Safad, Tzefat, Zfat, Zefat to Zephath, there is but one name that stands out as the perfect fit: 'The Mystical City'. Perched high on the green, wooded slopes of the Upper Galilee mountains, Tzfat's clean, fresh air seems to whisper the secrets of the past, where Jewish mysticism abounded and whose spirit is still so clearly present. Cobbled stone alleyways, small cottages dotted with blue doors and windows and an abundance of ancient synagogues form the Old City, where today artists show off their talents in open studios.

Tzfat is regarded as one of Judaism's four Holy Cities (along with Jerusalem, Tiberias and Hebron) and was home to some of the religion's true greats. Scholars, spiritual leaders and religious philosophers gathered in the 16th century and together they gave Tzfat its proud status as a world centre for Jewish mysticism, the Kabbalah. Today they rest atop the mountain in the ancient cemetery, whose views befit their status as the 'righteous ones'. With the swift rise in Kabbalah's

TZFAT
Old City

Based on mapping
by Carta, Jerusalem

**Map labels:**

Carmel House
Ascent of Safed

ISRAEL BECK ST

RIDBAZ ST

Tzaddik Educational
Visitor Centre Museum

HAARI STREET

YUD ALEF STREET

ALKEBETZ ST

BAR YOHAI ST

MEGINEI TZFAT ST

JERUSALEM (YERUSHALAYIM) STREET

Beirav Synagogue

Ashkenazi Ari
Synagogue

Tree of Life
HaMaginim
Square

Change
office

Bank
Haolim

Bank Leumi

Livnot TIC

Kabbalah Tour

Abuhav Synagogue

Milk n' Honey
Café

Alsheich Synagogue

Yossi Bana'a
Synagogue

ALSHEICH ST

BET YOSEF ST

TARPAT ST

Yosef Caro Synagogue

Beit Hameiri
Museum

Davidka Memorial

HATIVAT YIFTAH STREET

Sephardic Ari
Synagogue

KEREN HAYESSOD STREET

MA'A'LOT OLEI HAGARDOM ST

Crusader Castle
(Hametzuda)

HATIVAT YIFTAH STREET

HAPALMACH STREET

JERUSALEM (YERUSHALAYIM) ST

ARLOZOROV ST

YUD ALEF ST

TET VAV STREET

HaMa'ayan
Square

HaMifgash

Michael's House

ARTIST'S
COLONY

TET ZAYIN ST

JERUSALEM (YERUSHALAYIM) ST

JERUSALEM (YERUSHALAYIM) ST

Mul Ha'ar
Adler internet Café

California falafel

N

Bradt

Pedestrian Street

0 ——————— 200m
0 ——————— 200yds

Ruth Rimonim

HAPALMACH ST

ALIYAH ST

Hungarian Jewry
Museum

---

popularity across the world, the quiet little town of Tzfat has suddenly found itself the centre of a budding spiritual tourism industry. Followers flock to study in the multitudinous centres of learning, where the substantial Hasidic Orthodox presence lends an air of antiquity, as though time has stood still. But somehow Tzfat's charm and sacred atmosphere have not been weakened (within the Old City at least), and it is an alluring and enchanting place to explore.

HISTORY Although legend has it that Tzfat was founded by one of Noah's sons after the Great Flood, the first textual mention is in the Roman period. The city is

What is Kabbalah? Kabbalah is an aspect of Jewish mysticism that relates to a set of esoteric beliefs and practices that supplement the traditional Jewish interpretations of the Bible. It deals with the nature of divinity, the creation, the origin and the fate of the soul.

What does Kabbalah mean? 'Kabbalah' literally means 'receiving', and is often used synonymously with the word 'tradition'.

Where and when did Kabbalah originate? While many Orthodox Jews date Kabbalah back to a system of interpretations of the scriptures handed down orally from Abraham, the system of Kabbalah seems to have been given its organised form in 11th-century Spain and arrived in Israel when Jews were expelled from the country. It centres on the *Zohar*, the principal source of Kabbalah.

What exactly is the Zohar? The *Zohar* is the principal book of Kabbalah written in the 13th century by Moses de Léon, a Spanish Kabbalist, but attributed to 2nd-century rabbi Shimon bar Yohai. It provides a commentary on the first five books of the Torah and a cosmic-symbolic interpretation of Judaism based on the view of God as the dynamic flow of force through ten *sefirot* (planes or realms). These *sefirot* are symbols for everything in the world of creation.

Who practises Kabbalah? Traditional Kabbalists are generally Hassidic Orthodox Jewish men, many aspects of this mystical practice meaningless outside the realms of Judaism. What are often referred to as Hermetic Kabbalists range from Jews who prefer this form to the traditional practice, as well as non-Jews.

What exactly is Hermetic Kabbalah? Hermetic Kabbalah is a variant on traditional Kabbalah and dates back several hundred years. It is an esoteric, mystical tradition that draws on influences such as traditional Kabbalah, astrology, tarot, alchemy, pagan religions, gnosticism, freemasonry and tantra. It is usually spelt 'Qabbalah' to distinguish it from the traditional form. It has become increasingly popular over recent years because of celebrities such as Madonna and Demi Moore promoting its attributes.

How can I study Kabbalah? This depends on which form of Kabbalah you wish to learn. Traditional Kabbalah is considerably more complicated, a long-standing belief being that when a student is ready, a teacher will appear. However, there are workshops, centres and meetings you can attend (see *Tzfat*, page 183). A good grasp of Hebrew is essential for this and only male Jews may study it (although some women have been allowed). For those wishing to learn more about Hermetic Qabbalah, the internationally known Kabbalah Centre (*www.kabbalah.com*) has centres all over the world (the Los Angeles branch being where high-profile celebrities convene). Within Israel there are branches in Tel Aviv, Jerusalem and Haifa that offer classes, meetings and information.

not mentioned in the Bible and didn't make its mark as one of Judaism's holiest centres until the 16th century. A large Crusader citadel fell to the Muslim conqueror Saladin in the 12th century and in 1266, the Mamluk leader Baibars made Tzfat one of its administrative centres, killing or dispelling much of the population in the process.

In 1492, the same year that Columbus set sail for the Americas, Spanish Jews fled to Palestine escaping persecution. Top Jewish scholars and rabbis congregated, and Tzfat was transformed into a centre for Jewish mysticism, the Kabbalah. Rabbi Isaac Luria, Kabbalah's principal proponent, was a key figure in its creation, along with many other notable sages and Kabbalists. Groups came from many parts of

Europe and north Africa and by 1550 a Jewish population of 10,000 was thriving. Throughout the 18th and 19th centuries Jewish residents suffered plagues, repeated Druze (see page 25) attacks and a severe earthquake that killed 5,000 people. Influxes of Russian Jews and Perushim (disciples of Rabbi Elijah ben Solomon Zalman) did little to maintain the dwindling population.

Amidst the 1929 Arab riots, Tzfat's Jewish quarter was attacked. Many fled and by 1948 the Jewish population numbered just 2,000. Upon the British withdrawal, the Palestinian residents attacked, a move that was successfully countered by divisions of the Palmach (a precursor to the IDF) and resulted in the fleeing of most of the Arab population. Amongst the Arab refugees was the family of Palestinian Authority prime minister Mahmoud Abbas.

ORIENTATION Outside the Old City, with its quaint architecture and charming environment, Tzfat is rather ordinary and there isn't much to see. The main commercial area is **Jerusalem (Yerushalayim) Street**, which separates the artists' quarter to the south and Old Town and ancient synagogues to the north. Accommodation is cheaper in the New City, but if your pocket permits, staying close to the Old City is certainly worth the extra expense. Facilities, hotels and eateries concentrate in the east which also has some of the best views.

GETTING THERE There are two buses daily to and from Tel Aviv leaving Tel Aviv's Merkaz Bus Station at 10.30 and 17.00 (3hrs 20mins/51NIS) and Tzfat at 05.20 and 08.15. From Haifa Lev HaMifratz bus 361 runs every 30 minutes (1hr 40mins/34NIS) and to Tiberias bus 450 runs hourly (1hr/20NIS). There are regular services to and from Jerusalem's central bus station (3hrs 45mins/39NIS). Buses 511 and 501 run hourly between Kiryat Shmona (45min/21.50NIS) and will stop at sights along route 90.

GETTING AROUND All of Tzfat's sights of interest are contained inside the Old City which is easily navigable by foot (and mostly pedestrianised so you don't have a lot of choice). To get to the hospital in the south of the city take bus 6 or 7 from the central bus station. Alternatively there are several taxi companies operating in the city: **Moniot Baruch** (` 04 6999994`), **Moniot Rashbi** (` 04 6822226`) and **Moniot HaAri** (` 04 6922228`).

TOURIST INFORMATION

Israel Extreme ` 052 6478474`; e info@ israelextreme.com; www.israelextreme.com. Tzfat-based tour agency specialising in walking tours around the Old City as well as custom-built adventure excursions to the Upper & Lower Galilee & the Golan Heights.

Kabbalah Tour International Centre for Tzfat Kabbalah; 17 Alkebetz St; ` 04 6821771`; e office@tzfat-kabbalah.org; www.kabbalahtour.com. Kabbalah Tour packages include master classes, workshops, excursions, lectures & performances. Activities & packages range from 1.5hr workshops (500NIS) to 5-day all-inclusive deals.

Livnot Tourist Information Centre 17 Alkebetz St; ` 04 6924427`; ⊕ 08.00–16.00 Sun–Thu. Well-stocked centre that can offer information on attractions & courses. They show a 10min video depicting the history of the city. They also offer internet for 5NIS/15mins.

Richard Woolf ` 04 6935377/505 894647`; e woolfr@netvision.net.il; www.israwebs.com/woolf. A well-known, highly reputable & extremely knowledgeable local tour guide, Richard can tailor-make trips to your preference & time constraints.

WHERE TO STAY

🏠 **Canaan Spa** (102 rooms) Mt Canaan; ☎ 04 6993000; f 04 6993001; www.canaanspa.com. This exceptionally pricey 5-star health luxury spa resort has spectacular views over its private gardens & woodland towards the valleys of the Sea of Galilee. It has a palatial swimming pool, plush rooms, top-of-the-range spa, treatment & sporting facilities, craft workshops & a gourmet health restaurant. The hotel is for over 14s only & mobile phones are not permitted. Minimum of 2 nights on weekends. *Weekdays 300NIS less ($$$$$).* $$$$$

🏠 **Ruth Rimonim Safed** (82 rooms) Tet Zayin St; ☎ 04 6920456/1800 766766; www.rimonim.com. Built on the ruins of a 17th-century Turkish khan, the elegant hotel is one of the most picturesque & well positioned in the city. Luxurious outdoor swimming pool, health club & spa set within spacious grounds with absolutely breathtaking views of the Galilee hills. Ask for a room with balcony. *225NIS more per night in Jul/Aug & on Jewish hols.* $$$$

🏠 **Tzfat Guest House (HI)** (20 rooms) 1 Lohamei Ha'Getaot St; ☎ 04 6921086; e tzfat@iyha.org.il; www.iyha.org.il; reception ☉ 08.00–16.00. Housed in a 2-storey building in the city centre just within walking distance of the Old City. Standard, immaculately clean rooms & dorms ($) with AC,

shower & kosher breakfast but without much atmosphere. To get there take buses 6 or 7 from the central bus station. *Weekdays 260NIS less ($$$).* $$$$

🏠 **Michael's House** (3 rooms) 55 Tet Vav St; ☎ 04 6970470/052 6334532. Located along the stairs leading up to the artists' quarter is this delightful guesthouse. 3 large & beautifully unique rooms have been created within the 150-year-old cottage, each on a different level of the higgledy-piggledy building. The wooden penthouse apartment sleeps 2, the Rose Courtyard sleeps 4 & the family unit can sleep up to 6. $$$

🏠 **Ascent of Safed** (31 rooms) 2 Ari St; ☎ 04 6921364; e ascent@ascentofsafed.com; www.ascentofsafed.com. This large hostel caters to those wanting to delve more deeply into Kabbalah & partake in the plethora of classes & workshops they organise. Trips, excursions & tours can also be arranged. Only married couples may stay in double rooms. *Single-sex dorms available ($) (all beds & rooms are half price weekdays).* $$

🏠 **Carmel Hotel** (12 rooms) 8 Ha'ari St; ☎ 04 6920053. Quaint, old-worldly feeling hotel in the heart of the Old City, with great views & a relaxed & comfortable atmosphere. Room décor is rather spartan but all come with TV & balcony. $$

✗ WHERE TO EAT AND DRINK
Most of Tzfat's restaurants are kosher and abide by Shabbat hours. While many do serve meat, there is an abundance of vegetarian and fish eateries.

Bakeries There are several nice bakeries that provide for an affordable & tasty snack.

✗ **Sheva Daganim** & **Angels** are both located along Jerusalem St & have a wide range of cakes, pastries, bagels & breads.

✗ **Falafel** There are numerous kosher falafel & shawarma stands on Jerusalem Street, the most famous being

✗ **California** where 15NIS will get you a big falafel & a drink.

✗ **Gan Eden** Mt Canaan; ☎ 04 6972434; ☉ 09.00–23.00 Sun–Thu, 08.00–Shabbat Fri, from Shabbat–23.00 Sat. Cosy, romantic Italian-style vegetarian & fish restaurant whose views from Mt Cannan are as exceptional as their food. The couple's breakfast, pasta selection & desserts are recommended. $$$$

✗ **Mul Ha'ar** 70 Jerusalem St; ☎ 04 6920404; ☉ 08.00–01.00 Sun–Thu, 08.00–16.00 Fri, end of Shabbat–01.00 Sat; kosher. Mixed menu that leans

towards Italian-style dishes. The whole grilled fish is particularly good. $$$$

✗ **HaMifgash** 75 Jerusalem St; ☎ 04 6920510; ☉ 08.00–22.00 Sun–Thu, 08.00–Shabbat Fri. Simple eatery selling inexpensive grilled meats, hummus, French fries & salads. Does the job with no frills attached. $$

🍽 **Milk n' Honey Café** 35 Jerusalem St; ☎ 04 6920798; ☉ 08.30–22.00 Sun–Thu, 08.30–Shabbat Fri; kosher. This small, popular, modern-looking café on Jerusalem St sells fresh pizza, sandwiches, pastries & cakes. $$

✗ **Tree of Life** Meginim Sq; ☎ 050 6839110; ☉ 10.00–23.00 Sun–Thu, 10.00–Shabbat Fri; kosher. Ultra-healthy vegetarian restaurant in the heart of the artists' quarter. The inside could do with brightening up a bit but the tables on the square are one of the most picturesque places to have a meal in the city. $$

ENTERTAINMENT AND NIGHTLIFE Having a pumping night out in Tzfat is a distinct impossibility, unless of course you have arrived during the Klezmer Festival in which case concerts go on until the small hours. The alternative to an early bed is a night-time walk around the Old City, which is an extremely pleasant way to while away a few hours.

Clarinet and Klezmer in the Galilee (*www.zhr.org.il*) Normally held in July, this is a week of nightly classical, jazz and klezmer performances held in a variety of venues around town. Some of the world's leading clarinettists join forces to produce this week-long festival which culminates in the Gala Final Concert. **Master classes** (*Hanan Bar-Sela;* ℡ *052 3352797;* **e** *barsela1@bezeqint.net*) in classical and jazz clarinet and klezmer style can be arranged and are romantically set within historical sites and synagogues throughout the Old City. People come from far and wide to appreciate the festival, especially at the weekend, so if you are planning to stay during this time, you will need to book accommodation ahead of time.

OTHER PRACTICALITIES
Emergencies
Ambulance ℡ 101

Fire ℡ 102

Police station ℡ 100

Money
$ **Bank Hapoalim** 72 Jerusalem St; ℡ 03 6532407/ landline*2407; ⏲ 08.30–13.15 Sun & Tue/Wed, 08.30–13.00 & 16.00–18.30 Mon & Thu
$ **Bank Leumi** 35 Jerusalem St; ℡ 04 6994311; ⏲ 08.30–14.00 Sun & Tue/Wed, 08.30–13.00 & 16.00–18.15 Mon & Thu

$ **Change office** Jerusalem St; ℡ 04 6822777; ⏲ 08.30–13.30 Sun–Fri, 16.00–19.00 Sun/Mon & Wed/Thu. Located across the street from Bank Leumi.

Post
✉ **Post office** 37 Jerusalem St; ℡ 04 6920115; ⏲ 08.00–18.00 Sun & Thu, 08.00–12.30 &

15.30–18.00 Mon/Tue, 08.00–13.30 Wed. The main branch is on HaPalmach St.

Medical
✚ **Rivka Zieff Hospital** Ofer Intersection; ℡ 04 6828811

Internet
🌐 **Adler Internet Café** 88 Jerusalem St; ℡ 052 3447766; ⏲ 10.30–02.00 Sun–Thu, 10.30–16.30

Fri, end of Shabbat–late Sat. 15NIS/hr. Sells cold drinks & snacks.

WHAT TO SEE
Synagogues
Yosef Caro Synagogue (*Beit Yosef St*) Named after the great scholar and Kabbalah follower Josef Caro, who is renowned for his authorship of the *Shulchan Aruch* (*The Set Table*), the basis of Jewish law. Upon expulsion from Spain he settled in Tzfat in 1536 serving as the city's Chief Rabbi and Head of the Rabbinic Court.

Yossi Bana'a Synagogue (*Yud Aleph St*) Housing the tomb of Yossi Bana'a in a small chamber at the far end of the building, the synagogue dates to the end of the 15th century and was built by Jewish exiles from Spain. Yossi Bana'a, a 3rd-century Talmudic sage was often referred to as the 'White Zaddik' after his famed miracle where he turned black chickens white on Yom Kippur. Inside the synagogue, an ancient Torah is housed in the Holy Ark, which is removed once a year on the eve of Bag La'omer for the pilgrimage to Meron (see page 199).

Ashkenazi Ari Synagogue (*Guri Ha'ari St*) According to tradition this is the site of one of Tzfat's many miracles where, during the 1948 Arab–Israeli War, people crowded inside seeking shelter. Direct attacks on the synagogue caused much damage, but not a single member of the congregation was injured. It was founded by Spanish exiles in the 16th century and associated with Rabbi Isaac Luri (known as Ari) the revered Kabbalah master. While named after its ties with the Ashkenazi community, it is frequented by the whole spectrum of Jewish worshippers.

Sephardic Ari Synagogue (*Ha'ari Rd*) Built in 1522 by north African Jews, this is the city's oldest synagogue. At the time of writing it was under renovation and was open a few hours a day for Torah lessons only. Throughout the 1948 Arab–Israeli War, the synagogue held an important defensive spot on the border between the Jewish and Arab quarters of the city, and was badly damaged during the conflict.

Abuhav Synagogue (*Alsheich St*) Aesthetically Abuhav Synagogue would probably take first prize, with its large, distinctive white-domed roof, whitewashed walls, blue window frames and elegant interior. Believed to be named after the 15th-century rabbi Yitzhak Abuhav, who is remembered as one of Spain's great sages, he became head of a *yeshiva* in Toledo where he studied philosophy and Kabbalah before moving to Tzfat. The Torah scroll, kept inside the ornate Ark, is not only the oldest scroll in the city, but is the centre of numerous traditions and legends. It is taken out three times a year: on Yom Kippur, Shavuot and Rosh Hashanah.

Alsheich Synagogue (*Alsheich St*) This small synagogue, named after Rabbeinu Moshe Ben Haim Alsheich, is built in the style of 16th-century Sephardic synagogues. Tradition has it that during the severe earthquakes of 1759 and 1837 that ravaged the area, the synagogue remained totally undamaged, and has become a legend handed down through the decades. A large blue door (with a number 10 on the doorpost) marks this rather modest synagogue, whose unkempt exterior somehow adds to its appeal. Note that this synagogue doesn't have a women's section.

Beirav Synagogue (*Meginei Tzfat St;* ✆ *04 6921849; www.beirav.org; services throughout the Sabbath and religious holidays, closed at other times*) Popular with visitors from all over the world thanks to its lively, traditional musical services, it was given a facelift a few years ago when English-speaking members of the Tzfat community renewed activity in the run-down 19th-century building.

Museums
Beit Hameiri Museum (*Keren HaYessod St;* e *yaniv@hameiri-cheese.co.il www.hameiri-cheese.co.il; guided tours 12.00 Fri; admission adult/child 15/20NIS*) Situated in a beautiful stone building, Israel's first dairy has been maintained for over 160 years. Today, the family-run dairy offers weekly tours, offering presentations on cheese and dairy production with some gourmet cheese tasting to finish. This is an interesting and worthwhile detour off the religion trail, and offers the opportunity to buy some traditional Tzfat specialities.

Tzaddik Educational Visitors Centre (*7 Ridbaz St;* ✆ *04 6924556;* e *info@tzaddikcenter.com, www.tzaddikcenter.com;* ⊕ *10.00–15.00 Sun–Wed, 10.00–14.00 Fri; admission 9NIS*) The museum offers a Third Temple multi-media presentation and model exhibit based upon interpretations on the Book of Ezekiel by several top rabbis. It was designed and constructed using advanced computerised architectural programs and a certain degree of prophetic insight.

Hungarian Jewry Museum (*Haazmaut Sq;* ✆/f *04 6923880/1; www.hjm.org.il;* ☉ *09.00–13.00 Sun–Fri; admission free*) Opened in 1986, the museum is still lovingly maintained by two of its original founders. It depicts Jewish life throughout Hungary, Transylvania, Slovakia, Carpathian Russia, Bachka, Banat and Burgenland through a collection of letters, books and personal possessions. Themes touched upon include tradition, culture, World War II and the Holocaust.

Other sights

Artists' colony At the heart of the Old City just off Jerusalem Street, amidst a literal maze of cobbled lanes and ancient stone buildings is Tzfat's artists' quarter. It was established in 1949 in the previously Arab part of the town, following a need to centralise art within the newly formed country. It formed a focal point for artists and attracted big names in the art world, both those from within Israel, and Europe's Holocaust survivors. Today about 60 artists have workshops and galleries here, ranging from paintings to ceramics to sculptures to photography, most in keeping with the underlying theme that abounds in Tzfat: Kabbalah. An amble around the area is one of the city's highlights, where amenable artists show off their works and engage in lively chatter and debate with anyone who wishes to join in. For more information about the galleries visit *www.artists.co.il/safed/safed_e.html*.

Old cemetery According to religious tradition, it is in the ancient cemetery at Tzfat that some of the holiest *Tzaddikim* (righteous people) rest. The custom of praying at the gravesides of these 'righteous ones' is age-old in Judaism, and the cemetery here is comparable only with that of the Mount of Olives in Jerusalem. The beauty of the cemetery only adds to its unquestionable air of peace and spirituality, the unusual blue tombstones and burial caves dotted with brightly coloured flowers resting quietly and majestically upon the hill. Whether you're a believer or not, a mellow stroll around the cemetery to meet some of Judaism's most revered followers is the perfect way to truly feel the Tzfat vibe. In the middle of the cemetery and often crowded with worshippers rests one of the five most important *Tzaddik*, **Rabbi Isaac Luria, R' Yitzchak ben Shlomo** (or 'The Holy Arizal'), the great 16th-century Kabbalah master.

Crusader Castle (Hametzuda) On the top of the hill at the centre of Tzfat stands the scanty remains of a Crusader castle built in CE1140 to control the thoroughfare to Damascus. The castle was built on the site of an ancient citadel, the result of the CE66 Jewish revolt against the Romans. It is a bit of a hike but the views from the top of Israel's highest city and the pleasant park setting are worth the effort.

The Davidka Memorial Located just beyond Jerusalem Street is an old and rather crass cannon which is by tradition said to have driven the last of the Arabs out of the city in the 1948 Arab–Israeli War. The handmade weapon was rather ineffectual with regards to actual firepower but made an almighty blast that had the same end result.

ROSH PINA

According to Jewish Kabbalah tradition, it is in Rosh Pina that the Messiah will appear, and one can certainly see why. Cottages built from local stone perch high on the slopes of Mount Canaan amidst tree-lined cobbled stone lanes. A labyrinth of artists' workshops peek out from behind spring blossoms while gourmet restaurants lay beneath shady leaves. Even the internationally renowned Kabbalah follower Madonna was seen house hunting here, hoping to be one more of the lucky population of 2,400 that call this beautiful little town home. Yet the town is not just a pretty face, holding an honourable place in Jewish history when, in 1883 it became the first Jewish settlement in Palestine to come under the patronage of the Baron Edmond de Rothschild (see page 155).

Rosh Pina has, with the obvious exception of the large and unsightly shopping centre at its foot, preserved its rural heritage, and restored early pioneer houses and a synagogue commissioned by Rothschild can be visited. It was also within this tiny, yet crucially significant settlement that the first Jew to be hanged by the British Mandatory authorities, Shlomo Ben Yosef, is buried. There isn't an awful lot to do here, but that's kind of the idea. Wander through the small lanes of the Old Town, appreciate the beauty of the place, peruse the artists' workshops and sip a cool drink in one of the beautiful cafés and you'll feel it was a job well done.

Over recent years Rosh Pina has adopted a luxury tourism market, so accommodation is pricey but fantastic. Most accommodation is in luxury zimmers and there are plenty to choose from. Guesthouses further from the old part of town are slightly cheaper and lampposts are weighed down with signs advertising zimmers of all shapes and sizes. For all amenities and practicalities, the shopping centre is the place to go.

GETTING THERE AND AROUND Bus 511 leaves every 30 minutes between Rosh Pina and Tzfat (10mins/11.70NIS) continuing to Kiryat Shmona. Rosh Pina is tiny (albeit positioned on a rather steep slope) so walking is your only option if you haven't rented a car.

TOURIST INFORMATION

Tourist information Ground floor of Galil Shopping Centre; ✆ 04 6801465; www.zhr.info. Small and not easy to find so ask around. Not a particularly big English selection. ⊕ *Sun–Thu 09.00–16.00.*

WHERE TO STAY

🏠 **Mitzpe HaYamim** (83 rooms) Old Rosh Pina to Tzfat rd; ✆ 04 6994555; e info@mitzpe-hayamim.com; www.relaischateaux.com/mitzpe. This is one of the most well-known & highly respected hotels & spa resorts in the country & deservedly so. Sprawling landscaped gardens, orchards & a fully operating organic farm envelop the luxury top-of-the-range hotel & spa facilities, whose ethos is to connect its guests with the magic of nature. Designed by Bauhaus architect Yehezkel Rozenberg & commissioned by German homeopath, physician & vegetarian Dr Yaros, this resort is the culmination of decades of fine tuning. Needless to say, you will need to have an accumulation of US$50 bills in your pocket to fully appreciate it. **$$$$$**

🏠 **Auberge Shulamit** (4 rooms) Old Rosh Pina to Tzfat rd; ✆ 04 6931494; f 04 6931495; e shulamit@shulamit.co.il; www.shulamit.co.il. Proffers wonderful views over the surrounding countryside. Classy & elegant, French-style, family-run hotel. Beautifully decorated, luxury rooms are set within a stone lodge that once housed the Israeli–Syrian armistice conference of the 1940s. Breakfast terrace & evening restaurant with wonderful vista. Communal rooftop jacuzzi. In-room massages available. Minimum of 2-night booking on weekends. *Weekdays 160NIS less ($$$).* Dbl **$$$$**

🏠 **Ha Mei'ri Mansion** HaHalutzim St; ✆ 04 6938707; f 04 6936707. Identifiable by its 2 unusual palm trees standing sentry outside, this castle-like zimmer holds pride of place as the very last house at the top of HaHalutzim St. Large, beautifully maintained rooms are like something out of a medieval fairytale. Sun terrace with views over the valley below. *Weekdays 150NIS less ($$$).* **$$$$**

🏠 **Pina Ba'rosh** 8 HaHalutzim St; ✆ 04 6937028/6936582. Exceptionally attractive restaurant & zimmer with spectacular views. Stone cottage swathed in brightly coloured flowers & plants. Bright, airy rooms decorated with elegance & imagination. *W/days 200NIS less ($$$).* $$$$

✘ WHERE TO EAT

For budget eateries there are several inexpensive restaurants and fast-food joints in and around the shopping mall. A busy **falafel kiosk** is located opposite the mall car park which is your best budget option.

✘ **Muscat Restaurant** Old Rosh Pina to Tzfat road; ✆ 04 6994555; e info@mitzpe-hayamim.com; www.relaischateaux.com/mitzpe; ⊕ 13.00–midnight daily. Part of the ultra-deluxe Mitzpe Hayamim (see *Where to stay* above). A unique blend of the most freshly grown produce one could ever hope to find. Using only organic products grown or raised in the resort's farm & wineries as well as quality meats & fish cooked on open grills. $$$$$

✘ **Rafa's House** Artists' quarter; ✆ 04 6936192; ⊕ 12.30–23.30 daily. Located in the picturesque artists' quarter. Selection of claypot dishes & prime steaks. Cool, shaded outdoor area or grotto-style elegant interior. $$$$$

✘ **Auberge Shulamit Restaurant** Old Rosh Pina to Tzfat rd; ✆ 04 6931494; e shulamit@shulamit.co.il; www.shulamit.co.il; ⊕ 12.00–23.00 daily. Fine cuisine specialising in home-smoked fish & meats & terrific views of the Golan Mountains. Delicate hors d'oeuvres & a mouthwatering dessert tray. Pastas or soup of the day make good cheaper-end options. $$$$

✘ **Shiri Gourmet** 8 HaHalutzim St; ✆ 04 6937028; ⊕ 08.30–23.00 daily. French-style cuisine served in a covered patio area surrounded by an abundance of plants & flowers & offering stunning views. Delicate yet unpretentious meals with southern Mediterranean gourmet influence. $$$$

ENTERTAINMENT AND NIGHTLIFE

♀ **Blues Brothers Pub** Erus St; ✆ 04-6935336; www.villa-tehila.co.il; ⊕ 21.00–late Thu–Sat. Attached to the delightful **Villa Tehilla Guest House**, this little watering hole is one of the most pleasant options in town. A leafy beer garden & conservatory make an apt setting for a few relaxing drinks, while the cave-like interior is retro & friendly.

OTHER PRACTICALITIES

All of the following are found in the Galil Shopping Centre at the entrance to Rosh Pina.

Police station ✆ 100. Located just outside the Galil Shopping Centre.
$ **Bank Hapoalim** Galil Shopping Centre; ✆ 03 6532407/ landline*2407; ⊕: 08.30–13.15 Sun & Tue/Wed, 08.30–13.00 & 16.00–18.30 Mon & Thu

✚ **Newpharm pharmacy** Galil Shopping Centre; ✆ 04 6860645; ⊕ 09.00-22.00 Sun–Thu. Look out for a red sign (in Hebrew only).

WHAT TO SEE

Artists' galleries Explore the maze of workshops and watch the artists as they create leather, ceramics, jewellery, pottery, paintings and anything else that takes their fancy. A wonderfully bohemian and almost spiritual atmosphere abounds, where artists happily show off their work and engage in enthusiastic chatter.

Baron Garden Flowers and plants imported from France in 1886 and planted under the care of Baron Rothschild still flourish in the small garden whose design is said to have been based on the gardens at Versailles.

Shlomo Ben Yosef Memorial Follow the main mountain road through Rosh Pina (route 89) until you reach the observation point near his memorial stone. The view across the plains that rest between the Sea of Galilee and the Hula Valley with the Golan mountain range looming behind is utterly spectacular.

MERON

The small moshav of Meron might for the greater part of the year appear to be a quiet and relatively insignificant village, but once a year the entire area fills with pilgrims, here to celebrate the festival of Lag Ba'omer. The moshav and mountain are revered as the site of the final resting place of Rabbi Shimon bar Yohai, a 1st-century rabbi who is attributed by many to having written the *Zohar*, the principal script in Jewish mysticism (Kabbalah) and his grave attracts tens of thousands of Jewish pilgrims every year. It was his request to his students that they should celebrate the anniversary of his death (which fell on Lag Ba'omer) with dancing, singing and feasting.

Lag Ba'omer is celebrated on the 33rd day of the Omer which falls on the 18th day of Iyar on the Jewish calendar (usually in May on the Gregorian calendar). Its origins lie with Rabbi Akiva of whom Rabbi Shimon bar Yohai was a dedicated disciple. According to the Talmud, 24,000 of Rabbi Akiva's students were struck down by a divine plague, punishment for not displaying respect to one another. Lag Ba'omer is today celebrated as the day the plague ended, and of the day upon which it is believed Rabbi Shimon bar Yohai passed.

The festival at Meron is a fascinating mixture of spirituality, celebration, feasting and partying, a religious Woodstock of sorts. The annual pilgrimage centres on bar Yohai's large, domed tomb, where a huge bonfire belches out heat and smoke and male Orthodox members dance fervently around it. Women and children dance and sing traditional songs in the courtyard below. Dozens of sheep and cattle are slaughtered in ritualistic kosher manner, and tents and caravans sprawl across the surrounding countryside, a combination of Hassidic and Sephardim families, many of whom attend with their three-year-old sons. For it is on Lag Ba'omer at Meron that hundreds of toddlers receive their first *upsherin*, Jewish first haircut. The ceremony is a time of great happiness and pride as parents watch as their sons have *peyot* (temple curls) shaped.

Whilst doubtless a happy and celebratory event, it is a sacred and important part of Orthodox belief and sightseers must ensure they adhere to customs. Visiting the impressive tombs of Rabbi Shimon bar Yohai and other early rabbinical figures such as Rabbi Hillel and Rabbi Shammai is, at any time, worthwhile. A little further up the mountain from the tombs is one of the oldest synagogues in the Galilee, whose east wall is carved out of the steep rock cliff.

Mount Meron At 1,200m above sea level, Mount Meron (Har Meron) was Israel's highest mountain until the 1967 Six Day War which saw the Golan Heights and Mount Hermon brought under Israeli rule. The mountain is heavily forested, where dense, green wooded slopes hide caves and sink holes, prime habitat for countless species of rare plants and animals. It is the third contender for the site of Jesus's Transfiguration (along with Mount Hermon and Mount Tabor), both of which are visible from the summit, and proffers staggering views across the Sea of Galilee. Access to the mountain road is through the village of Meron and is a pleasant drive to the summit which is a nature reserve. Several nice trails offer undemanding walks and wonderfully fresh air.

The Story of Rosh Pina (✆ 04 6936913; *showings Fri/Sat 11.00, 12.00 & 13.00; admission adult/child 15/10NIS*) A movie enlightening visitors as to the history of the town is worth the effort, although don't expect the IMAX.

Ancient cemetery Located opposite the artists' quarter, the cemetery rests on the hill, untouched for decades. Here rest the remains of Rosh Pina's founding members, mainly Jewish immigrants from Romania who settled here with the aid of Baron Rothschild. A small path leads to the cemetery from behind the iron gate.

Getting there Bus 361 from Tzfat to Meron leaves every 30 minutes (6mins/9.80NIS). To go up the mountain you will need to have your own vehicle or be prepared for an exerting but beautiful hike.

AROUND TZFAT AND ROSH PINA

TEL HAZOR NATIONAL PARK (↘ *04 6937290; www.parks.org.il;* ⊕ *08.00–17.00 daily; adult/child 18/8NIS*) Covering 1km², Tel Hazor is the largest biblical site in Israel whose population, at its height, reached an estimated 40,000, four-times that of David and Solomon's Jerusalem. Extensive excavations have revealed 22 phases of occupation spanning 2,700 years, stretching from the early Bronze Age (29th century BCE) to the Hellenistic period (2nd century BCE). Hazor comprises two main sections: the acropolis and the fortified enclosure. Its location along the great Via Maris trade route was surely a key factor in its abounding success, and is the only Canaanite site mentioned in the royal documents of Mari, located in modern-day Syria which attest to its importance in trading tin. In its prime, Hazor covered an area twice the size of Meggido (see page 169). In biblical connotations, Hazor didn't pale in importance. It is written that the King of Hazor, Jabin, headed a coalition of Canaanite cities against the encroaching Israelites, led by Joshua. Hazor is described as having been the 'head of all those kingdoms' (Joshua 11.1-5, 11.10). When the Canaanites were defeated, Joshua had Hazor razed to the ground.

Israelite Hazor's rebuilding is attributed to Solomon, who fortified the city in order to control movement along the Via Maris. In the 9th century BCE, presumably under the rule of King Ahab, the city was developed. It was during this time that the massive water system, a major feature of the national park today, was built. Ruins from many of the significant phases of Hazor are visible in the park (a trip to the small archaeological museum in Kibbutz Ayelet Hashahar is recommended before delving into the archaeological ruins). Fortifications from the Canaanite period, a large casement wall and gate believed to be from King Solomon's time and a late-Canaanite altar shed some light onto the tumultuous past of this great city.

Getting there The national park is located along route 90 between Kiryat Shmona (15mins) and Rosh Pina (15mins) 4km from the Mahana'im Junction. Most buses heading to Kiryat Shmona or south will stop there although some express buses coming from Tel Aviv or Haifa don't, so be sure to ask the driver before boarding.

BAR'AM NATIONAL PARK (↘ *04 6989301; www.parks.org.il;* ⊕ *08.00–17.00 daily; admission adult/child 12/6NIS*) A Jewish village in Mishnaic and Talmudic times, Bar'am is now the site of one of the most beautiful ancient synagogues in the country. Many believe the village was built in this remote location because of the legend that Queen Esther was buried here. A biblical figure, Esther rose to Queen of Persia and is famed as having saved the kingdom's Jewish population from persecution. Today, the lively and joyous Festival of Purim is celebrated in her memory, with the *Megillah* (Scroll of Esther) read in Bar'am.

That the village was affluent is indicated to by the presence of two synagogues, only one of which remains today. An inscription discovered at the smaller synagogue reads 'Peace in this place and all of Israel' and is now housed in Paris's Louvre Museum. The larger of the two synagogues is the *raison d'être* of the national park, its majestic façade, large basalt blocks, sculptures and its three gates facing Jerusalem unarguably impressive.

Following the Arab conquest, Christian Arab villagers of the Maronite Church chose to leave the synagogues standing, building their own church – located next to the synagogue – which is today the spiritual centre of the Maronite faith. In 1948, the village was abandoned after the residents were evacuated by the IDF owing to its proximity to the Lebanese border.

The rare kermes oak forest of the **Bar'am Oaks Nature Reserve**, located near the archaeological site, makes a nice conclusion to a visit.

Getting there Bus 43 leaves Tzfat at 06.45, 12.35 and 17.00 (35mins/16NIS) and stops in Kibbutz Bar'am from where it is a short walk to the park entrance. Bus 522 leaving Haifa at 15.15 also stops in the kibbutz (1hr 45mins/34NIS).

PEKI'IN The small, charming village of Peki'in, with its predominantly Druze population (see page 25), is rather unexpectedly one of the most notable sites in Judaism. It claims to be the only place that Jews have lived in continuously for 2,000 years, and evidence of their historic presence can be seen in the form of Jewish symbols embedded into stone houses dotting the village. As the originally large Jewish population dwindled, Jews began to adopt the language and customs of their Arab neighbours, all along retaining their religious beliefs. A restored synagogue dating to the Roman period is located in the centre of the village and is cared for by a member of the Zenati family, whose ancestors were some of the founding Jewish members of Peki'in. The synagogue contains a fragment of an ancient Torah scroll and stone carvings believed to have been brought by fleeing refugees escaping the Roman destruction of Jerusalem.

Peki'in is also the site where it is believed Rabbi Shimon bar Yohai and his son Rabbi Eliezer hid in a cave escaping persecution by the Romans during the Bar-Kochba rebellion. It was during their 13 years in hiding that they compiled the *Zohar*, the foremost book of Kabbalah. According to the village tourist department, Peki'in, with its population of 4,200, receives 60,000 visitors a year, many of whom come to light candles and slip prayer papers into the cracks of the cave.

Besides its obvious historic and religious draw, the village is beautiful in its own right, perched high on the hill overlooking the Bet Kerem Valley below, its ancient stone houses clinging to the slopes. Olive groves and fruit trees fill the surrounding fields, a testament to its rural, agricultural roots, where Druze, Christians and Jews have lived harmoniously for thousands of years.

Getting there Bus 44 to and from Nahariya passes the town every two–three hours (45mins/11.70NIS).

WHERE TO STAY AND EAT There are countless small Druze restaurants in Peki'in serving traditional, hearty meals ($). Pita, hummus, labane cheese, olives, grilled meats and salads are all extremely well priced and one of the most characteristic traits of Druze hospitality and customs.

Peki'in Guest House (50 rooms) ` 04 9574111; e pkiin@iyha.org.il. Geared towards large groups, it is housed in a vast complex & is a good budget option, if not the most visually pleasing choice in town. Kosher breakfast is included & internet & small cinema available. Ask at reception for guided tours or Druze homestay options. Located on the outskirts of the village. $$

MONTFORT CASTLE, NAHAL KEZIV AND GOREN PARK As the sun sets over the Nahal Keziv Valley and the dense pine forests that engulf it, **Montfort Castle** (⊕ *in daylight hrs; admission free*), rising high on a jagged ridge, remains the last thing illuminated, as though left alone on a grand stage. The area here is laden with fantastic hiking opportunities, the Keziv Stream winding its way through the deep valley providing for some Herculean but immensely rewarding walks.

The castle was built by French Crusaders during the late 12th century, but was later bought by the German Teutonic Knights. Following conflicts with the Knights Templar and Knights Hospitaller in Akko, the Teutonic Knights moved to this location, declaring it their Holy Land headquarters. With papal funding, they fortified the castle, turning it into a grand fortress and the largest in the Upper Galilee. The keep that stands in the centre is probably the most indicative of the full extent and magnificence of the structure. In 1271, the Teutonic Knights surrendered to the Mamluk sultan Baibars in exchange for free passage and escaped with their treasury and archives, thus ending the short and turbulent life of Montfort Castle.

Because of its precipitous location the castle can only be reached by a fairly arduous uphill trek. A 1km trail leads from the Hila lookout at the end of the Me'ilia village through road. To avoid the walk, **Goren Forest Park**, with its great picnicking opportunities and population of rather confident jackals, has a lookout terrace. It is located across the valley from the castle. A path can begin or end a lovely hike down into the Keziv Valley and up to the castle, and it offers fabulous views of both, especially at sunset. It is possible to camp unofficially in the park although the ground can be rather rough. There is a small campsite in the **Montfort Ranch** (✆ *057 7336436; 54NIS pp*) which can rent you a tent if you don't have your own and has clean showers and toilets.

An alternative way to approach the castle is to embark on a truly wonderful trek along the Keziv Stream and valley. A 6km circular walk following the black-marked trail starting in Hila leads you through vast pine forests reminiscent of the remote wildernesses of Canada or Scandinavia.

Getting there Goren Park is located between Kibbutz Eilon and Moshav Goren on route 899. From Nahariya, bus 27 stops at Kibbutz Eilon four times a day (09.05, 12.30, 15.10, 17.15). Only bus 28 returns and leaves from the junction on route 899 five times a day (08.35, 12.35, 15.35, 18.05, 20.20). Alternatively there are countless buses leaving every 30 minutes to Ma'a lot Tarshiha from Nahariya where you can hitch to Hila.

 Where to stay

Rotem's Cabins (3 cabins) Hila; ✆ 054 4974286/2074286; e dnyr53@bezeqint.net; www.biktot-rotem.co.il. Beautiful secluded wood cabins in the heart of the Keziv Valley. Even the jacuzzi has a wonderful view over the wooded landscape. Huge, rustic cabins also have TV, DVD (& lots of DVDs to borrow) & kitchenette. *W/days 200NIS less ($$$). Dbl $$$$*

YEHIAM FORTRESS (✆ *04 9856004; www.parks.org.il;* ⊕ *08.00–17.00 daily; admission adult/child 12/6NIS*) This massive fortress is situated within the boundary of Kibbutz Yehiam and holds a tender place in the hearts of all who live there. While the strong walls and imposing buttresses were built centuries ago, the fortress's defensive stature was used in more recent times when, during the 1948 Arab–Israeli War, residents sought refuge and protection from the surrounding conflict.

The exact date of construction is unknown but at some point in its life it, like the nearby Montfort Castle, was sold to the Teutonic Knights upon their departure from Akko. In 1265, it was conquered by the Mamluk sultan Baibars in his rampage through the region. Much of the fortress was destroyed and remained derelict until the Bedouin sheikh Zahir al-Amr returned it to its former glory in the 1760s, constructing the great square defences we see today.

While there is an interesting movie presentation within the national park, the most rousing and worthwhile reason to visit (besides the impressive remains themselves) is the fabulous view of the green peaks and valleys of the Galilee proffered from the top.

Getting there From Nahariya take route 89 heading towards Tzfat and turn onto route 8833 at the Ga'aton Junction. From Nahariya, buses 39 and 42 go to and from Kibbutz Yehiam several times a day.

KIRYAT SHMONA

With a population of approximately 22,000, Kiryat Shmona is the largest city in the Upper Galilee. Sitting amidst the stunning landscape of the region, with its verdant valleys, fresh mountain peaks and its proud religious and Zionist history, it is most certainly the ugly duckling of the area. And Kiryat Shmona is showing no signs of flourishing into a beautiful swan any time soon. The city centre is dilapidated and run-down, seemingly forgotten about in the midst of the tourism boom seen in recent years in the surrounding settlements. While it claims to be the centre of tourism for the region, there really is very little of interest for visitors, and it is highly recommended to stay in one of the countryside zimmers or national park campsites nearby. Large, productive manufacturing plants scar the area directly around the city, their bright lights and incessant noise humming throughout the night. The city is a major transport hub however, and there are buses to and from the otherwise relatively inaccessible northern Golan region. In fairness, the suburbs are marginally better, some parts even passing as quaint, but overall time would best be spent in other areas.

HISTORY The city was founded in 1949 on the site of a ruined Arab village, and was utilised as a camp for farming immigrants slowly developing over the years. The city is named in honour of Joseph Trumpeldor and his seven comrades (*shmona* translates as eight) who died in 1920 defending **Tel Hai** (see page 206). The city regularly makes international headline news as it is a popular target for Hezbollah and PLO rockets, launched from behind the nearby Lebanese border. Throughout countless skirmishes, residents have found themselves packing their bags and temporarily relocating south or spending up to weeks in underground bunkers.

GETTING THERE Kiryat Shmona is the transport hub of the region and can be reached from all major cities across the country. It also has good connections with the more inaccessible parts of the northern Golan and Upper Galilee. Bus routes 840, 841 and 963 run regularly to and from Tiberias stopping at Rosh Pina and the Hula Valley (1hr 40mins/25NIS), the 963 continuing to Jerusalem (4hrs/55NIS). Direct routes 842 and 845 leave hourly to Tel Aviv (3hrs 30mins/53NIS). Route 500 leaves every 45 minutes to Akko (1hr 30mins/34NIS) and Haifa Lev HaMifratz (2hrs/42NIS). Bus 58 leaves at 16.40 and stops at Shear Yashuv (6mins/8.50NIS), Neve Ativ (20mins/18NIS), Majdal Shams (25mins/20NIS), Masade (30mins/21NIS), Merom Golan (45mins/25NIS), Katzrin (1hr 25mins/32NIS) and Gadot (1hr 35mins/34NIS).

GETTING AROUND

Eldan Car Rental Tel Hai St; ℡ 04 6903186;
⊕ 08.00—16.45 Mon—Thurs, 08.00—13.00 Fri.
Cars from 170NIS per day. Minimum age 24.

Sixt Kiryat Shmona South Industrial Area; ℡ 04
6941631 ⊕ 08.00—18.00 Mon—Fri, 08.00—18.00
Sun. Cars from 175NIS per day.

TOURIST INFORMATION

Tourist information centre 70 Tel Hai Bd;
⊕ 08.00—17.00 Sun—Thu, 08.00—13.00 Fri

WHERE TO STAY AND EAT Kiryat Shmona has no major hotels and very few eating options. You are strongly advised to take advantage of the beautiful countryside lodging and restaurants on the doorstep of this unsightly city, notably Kibbutz Manara, She'ar Yashuv, Horshat Tal (see page 208) and Kibbutz HaGroshim (see page 208 Dag al Hadan restaurant).

Nehalim Gan Hatzafon; ℡ 04 6904875;
⊕ 12.00–23.00 Sun–Thu, 12.00–16.30 &
18.00–23.00 Fri, 12.00–23.00 Sat. This is an
extremely pleasant restaurant specialising in meat &
fish dishes with a selection of creative sauces.
Located on a delightful spot near the convergence
of the Banias, Hatzbani and Dan rivers, 2.5km east
of the Hametzudot Junction on the right (look out
for the petrol station). $$$$

Manara Guest House (51 rooms) ℡ 04
6908198, e tayarot@manara.co.il. Simply
decorated but well equipped and roomy. Facilities
include TV, AC, refrigerator, microwave & en-suite
bathroom with bath & separate shower. Guests can
use the swimming pool (in summer) & the price
includes breakfast in the kibbutz cafeteria.
$$$

OTHER PRACTICALITIES There is a small shopping centre opposite the bus station that has all the standard high-street chain stores and is your best bet for getting provisions.

$ **Bank Hapoalim** Tzahal Sq; ℡ 03 6532407/
landline*2407; ⊕ 08.30–13.15 Sun & Tue/Wed,

08.30–13.00 & 16.00–18.30 Mon & Thu

WHAT TO SEE

Shehumit Hill Offers a bird's-eye view of the both Kiryat Shmona and the nearby Hula Valley.

The Golden Park Traversed by the Ein Zahav Stream, this is a rather pleasant escape from the drabness of the city centre. Green lawns, a small wood, an Ottoman-period flour mill and a small, quaint mosque, today housing the **Kiryat Shmona History Museum** (*26 Hayarden St;* ℡ *04 6940135;* ⊕ *08.00–12.00 Sun–Thu*) are all residents of the park.

Manara Cliff and kibbutz These days Manara is most well known for its cable car system leading down Israel's highest cliff (888m). Zimmer have been created by the residents, and the stunning views proffered by being perched high on a cliff edge are one of its key assets (especially if you look beyond Kiryat Shmona at its foot towards the lush greenery of the Hula Valley). The **Galilee Adventure Park** (℡ *04 6905830;* f *04 6905833; www.cliff.co.il;* ⊕ *09.30–16.30 daily; admission weekday/weekend 49/59NIS*) is a little kitsch and clearly aimed mainly towards the younger (or more fearless) set, but the 1,940m-long cable car is a novel way of getting up the cliff to the kibbutz. A 1,200m-long mountain slide that snakes its way back down the cliff hit headline news during the 2006 Lebanon War when Hezbollah rockets destroyed a significant section. Rappelling, a zip line, a trampoline bungee dome and climbing wall give thrill-seekers their choice of extreme activities. For those less disposed to throw themselves off cliffs, a one-hour guided hike can be arranged providing an explanation of the area, land and surrounding sites. Alternatively, the kibbutz's apple orchards are open to summer fruit pickers as is the well-maintained (but often crowded) swimming pool. Price packages can be purchased together with nearby Kibbutz Kfar Blum activities (see page 208).

The entrance to the Manara Cliff cable car is along route 90 just south Kiryat Shmona. Buses heading to and from Kiryat Shmona will drop you at the cable car entrance. To drive to the kibbutz, follow route 90 north and turn left at the Tel Hai turn-off. After 3km, turn left and follow the signs to Manara.

METULLA

Metulla is a small, rural town located at the end of the north–south highway 90, straddling the border with Lebanon. Founded in 1896 as one of Baron Edmond de Rothschild's purchases, the land on which it stands originally belonged to a Druze landowner. Until the 1980s and the construction of the Canada Centre (a vast sporting complex) the local economy depended on agriculture, namely fruit, wine, and cattle. Today, the Canada Centre and the town's surrounding natural and historic attractions have created a prosperous tourist economy, although agriculture still plays a pivotal role. Several waterfalls gush through the orchard-lined valleys on their route from the snow-capped peaks of Mount Hermon to the Hula Valley, visible to the south. The Ayun River, which enters Israel from Lebanon, has carved out a small canyon on its way to the lower lands around the Jordan Valley. The town oozes tranquillity and an appreciation of the nature that surrounds it. The lovely little main street is lined with white limestone houses, restaurants and galleries, and accommodation, mainly in zimmer cabins and bed-and-breakfast accommodation is plentiful. Because of its proximity to the Lebanese border, the town does bustle with soldiers, particularly during times of high alert. But for the most part, it is a quiet, peaceful, rural farming community.

Getting there Buses 20 and 21 leave every two hours between Kiryat Shmona and Metulla (20mins/9.80NIS).

WHERE TO STAY
Beit Shalom Estate (10 rooms) 28 HaRishonim St; ☎ 04 6940767; e miriam@beitshalom.co.il; www.beitshalom.co.il. Refined elegance & antique glamour exude at the luxury Beit Shalom Estate. Exquisitely decorated with no two rooms alike, the family-run guesthouse offers a small spa, gourmet restaurant & a real personal touch. *Suites cost up to 1,200NIS per night and weekday prices up to 200NIS less ($$$).* $$$$

WHERE TO EAT
Bat Ha'Eycar (The Farmer's Daughter) 21 HaRishonim St; ☎ 04 6997177; ⊕ 10.00–midnight daily. Rustic country-style dishes with a taste of the Mediterranean. Housed in a 19th-century stone mansion, this is the place to treat yourself. Mains include lamb kebab on green tahini & chicken liver in plum sauce as well as more simple pasta dishes. $$$$

WHAT TO SEE AND DO
Canada Centre (1 HaRishonim St; ☎ 04 6950370/1; www.canada-centre.co.il; ⊕ 10.00–20.00 Mon–Sat (ice skating 10.00–16.00; admission adult/child 75/60NIS) In

Straddling the border with Lebanon, the site of **Tel Hai** has long since come to represent Zionist heroism, and has become a pilgrimage for scores of Jewish tourists and Israeli schoolchildren. The lands upon which Tel Hai – a modest farming settlement – were built, were originally purchased in 1893 by the wealthy Jewish French baron, Edmond de Rothschild (see page 155). In 1918, members of the Galilee Farmers Union settled here and it became one of only four Jewish settlements in the Galilee (along with Metulla, Hamrah and adjacent Kfar Giladi). The 1916 Sykes–Picot agreement called for the division of large areas of the Middle East, where the Galilee would have been split in half. The secret agreement left the British, French and Arabs in dispute about the future of the area, and although the British conceded to allow the Upper Galilee to be under French control, the Arabs were strongly opposed. A retaliation on 1 March 1920 saw the community of Tel Hai attacked. As the story goes, a group of Arab soldiers demanded to search the premises, believing the Jews to be harbouring French soldiers. The Jewish farmers signalled for reinforcements from nearby Kfar Giladi, who arrived shortly after led by the one-armed Russian Zionist and founder of the Zionist Mule Corps (a British Army battalion formed of Jewish volunteers) Joseph Trumpeldor. A raging conflict ensued and Trumpeldor and his seven comrades were killed. Remaining defenders burned down the courtyard and abandoned Tel Hai. Later the same year, members of Kibbutz Kfar Giladi returned and rebuilt the farm, a move that resulted in Tel Hai (along with Metulla and Kfar Giladi) being included in the British Mandate over Palestine and therefore later, in the State of Israel.

The story of Tel Hai is one that has come to represent Jewish determination and today acts as a poignant symbol of heroism, self-defence and sacrifice told throughout Israeli households. Trumpeldor and his seven soldiers have left a long legacy, notably the city of Kiryat Shmona (City of Eight), which was named in their memory. Claimed to be Trumpeldor's last words, the phrase 'Never mind, it is good to die for our country' became legendary in Israel, although many award the origin of these words to the ancient Latin phrase *Dulce et decorum est pro patria mori* (it is sweet and honourable to die for one's country). Every year, the battle at Tel Hai and the death of Joseph Trumpeldor are honoured in a memorial held on the 11th day of Adar in the Jewish calendar.

The fort that stands today provides visitors with an insight into the historical background of the site, and a monument commemorating the eight heroes stands in the form of a stone lion erected near their graves. Audio-visual presentations in a host of languages and a collection of tools from the time are on display.

rather distinct contrast to the sleepy little town in which it sits, this huge complex is a hub of sport, exercise and leisure facilities. It features the country's largest ice-skating rink, sizeable indoor and outdoor swimming pools, squash courts, table tennis rooms, a fitness centre, bowling alley and basketball court. There is also a shooting range, and a health club offering treatment packages. The entry price includes access to the swimming pools and ice rink.

Nahal Ayun Nature Reserve (✆ *04 6951519;* ⊕ *08.00–17.00 daily; admission adult/child 23/12NIS*) Located on the edge of Metulla is the beautiful Ayun Nature Reserve. As the Ayun Stream sweeps across the border from Lebanon it flows through a canyon, creating in turn four waterfalls. In summer, with water in high demand for agriculture, much of the flow is siphoned off and the bed is normally dry. The rest of the year however sees a raging flow, providing for some lovely hiking opportunities.

One entrance to the reserve is located in Metulla's upper car park (signposted), and is the beginning of the longer of two trails (1hr 30mins). For a lovely hike follow the path downstream, passing all the falls as you go. The *pièce de résistance* of the reserve is the 30m-high Tanur Waterfall, the last of the four. The Tanur Waterfall gushes over the steep canyon shelf, spraying the wild flowers, oleander and honeysuckle with a fine mist of ice-cold water. Note that if you can't arrange for transport to pick you up at the lower car park, there is a rather hefty walk back upstream to the upper car park.

The shorter trail through the reserve forms a circular route, beginning and ending in the lower car park. It incorporates the Tanur Waterfall and a birdwatching post (30mins).

To get to the Tanur Waterfall and lower car park, turn right approximately 1km before Metulla. For the Ayun and Cascade Falls (and upper car park) take the road near the border fence in the north of the town.

AROUND KIRYAT SHMONA AND METULLA

TEL HAI FORT (↘ *04 6951331;* ⊕ *08.00–16.00 Sun–Thu, 10.00–17.00 Fri; adult/child 18/15NIS)* see box opposite.

Bet Ha'Shomer Museum (↘ *04 6941565;* ⊕ *08.00–15.30 Sun–Thu, 08.00–12.00 Fri; admission adult/child 20/15NIS)* On the opposite side of the road at Kibbutz Kfar Giladi, the museum is dedicated to the Ha'Shomer (meaning 'Watchman'), a group of 108 men and women often referred to as the precursor to the IDF, selected to protect Jewish settlements in the country. Until its formation in 1907, settlement protection was outsourced to Circassian and Arab guards. Ha'Shomer was successful in its protection of Jewish interests, to the antagonism of the Arab population. Many, mainly Russians, were exiled by the Ottoman government, yet the group survived until 1920 when it was succeeded by the Haganah, a more organised military organisation. The museum here displays early 20th-century clothing, buildings, photos, weapons and an audio-visual presentation. Batia Lichansky, sister-in-law of Yitzhak Ben Zvi, one of the primary members, also has a sculpture display in one of the rooms.

Getting there Tel Hai is located on route 90 just south of Kiryat Shmona. Head through the city and follow signs to the site and the nearby kibbutz of Kfar Giladi. Bus 21 from Kiryat Shmona runs to and from Metulla every two hours and will drop you off at the kibbutz.

Where to stay

⌂ **Tel-Hai Guest House (HI)** (63 rooms) Kibbutz Tel Hai; ↘ 04 6940043; e tel-hai@iyha.org.il, www.iyha.org.il. In keeping with the hostelling international reputation for exceptionally clean yet uninspiring rooms this hostel provides a good, cheap option in the area. Private rooms & dorms ($) have AC & TV & the price includes kosher breakfast. Located on the opposite side of junction to Kibbutz Kfar Giladi. $$

TEL DAN NATIONAL PARK (↘ *04 6951579; www. parks.org.il;* ⊕ *08.00–17.00 daily; admission adult/child 23/12NIS)* Kill two birds with one proverbial stone at Tel Dan Nature Reserve, combining nature and archaeology. The river Dan is the most crucial source of the Jordan River, fed by melt water from the Hermon Mountains. Countless streams converge in the park's grounds as they pour into the river on their way to the Jordan Valley. Vegetation and wildlife thrive in the abundance of water and the mild climate, forming a shady forest in which to explore. Four trails lead through the park's grounds, providing access to its different attractions. Follow the course of the river through the sometimes 20m-tall Syrian ash trees (1hour 15mins) or head to the remains of the ancient biblical city of Dan (45mins) which, according to the **Book of Judges**, was captured from the Caananites by the Tribe of Dan. It has been associated with Jeroboam, a biblical figure who was the first king of the northern tribe of Israel. Hilltop reconstructions of an arched Caananite gate and Israelite-period city gateway are good accompaniments to the remains.

Getting there Buses 35, 36 and 55 (58 returning) run between Kiryat Shmona and the northern Golan Heights stopping at Kibbutz Dan (1km from the park entrance) six-times daily (8mins/8.50NIS) as well as She'ar Yashuv and Horshat Tal (6mins/8.50NIS) along the way.

Where to stay

Horshat Tal Campsite 04 6942440; www.parks.org.il; 24hrs, last admission 22.30; admission (campsite & national park adult/child 50/35NIS). The Horshat Tal National Park is pleasant, but not really much to write home about. The adjacent campsite, however, provides a fantastic choice of cheap accommodation. Pitch your tent next to the gushing streams flowing through manicured lawns or rent one of the bungalows or cabins Clean showers & toilets & plenty of space under the shade of the ancient oak trees (unless it's a summer weekend in which case it's peg to peg). A night in the campsite grants you access to the park for an early-bird swim in the frosty

waters of the natural pools. Camping $ weekday, $$ weekend up to 4 people; bungalows or cabins $$ weekday, $$$$ weekend up to 4 people
She'ar Yashuv Yashuv The quaint She'ar Yashuv holiday village sits in a prime location, equidistant from the sites of the northern Golan Heights & those in the Upper Galilee. The village is small but chock-full of dainty wooden zimmers as well as a clinic, small gym, grocery store, restaurant & horseriding centre. There is also access to the Banias River from within the village. A map on the right as you enter the village will direct you to the 26 family-run zimmers & other amenities. Between $$$ and $$$$

Where to eat

Dag Al Hadan North of Kibbutz HaGroshim; 04 6950225; www.dagaldan.co.il; 12.00–midnight daily; kosher. Situated on the confluence of the Hatzbani & Dan rivers, this delightful open-air fish restaurant dishes up a fabulous selection of fresh & salt-water fish, as well

offering a lovely riverside location. The local trout is highly recommended. There's a 10% discount for guests taking part in **kayaking & rafting** (04 6950225) activities in the kibbutz. There is also a well-equipped **campsite** (45NIS pp). $$$$

KFAR BLUM

Founded in 1943, Kibbutz Kfar Blum was named after the Jewish socialist and former French president Leon Blum. From its founding until the present day it has survived on an economy formed primarily of agriculture, although of late, tourism seems to have snuck in and taken over, and now the kibbutz offers a rather impressive array of activities, and has become one of the Upper Galilee's top tourist destinations. Its proximity to the Jordan River and surrounding countryside is its biggest draw, attracting those looking for outdoor pursuits and a touch of nature (and a well-deserved rest in the spa, see below).

GETTING THERE Buses 31 and 32 depart Kiryat Shmona (20mins/11.70NIS) at 06.00, 14.00 and 17.30, returning at 04.50, 06.15, 14.20 and 17.50. By car turn east at Gomeh Junction off route 90 and follow the road for 4km before turning left to the kibbutz.

WHERE TO STAY AND EAT

🏠 **Pastoral Hotel Kfar Blum** (125 rooms) ☎ 04 6836611; e pastoral@kbm.org.il; www.kfarblum-hotel.com. Mediterranean-style rustic elegance combines to form this large & exceptionally well-equipped luxury hotel & spa. A range of bright & airy rooms overlook the kibbutz's olive orchards & outdoor Olympic-size swimming pool. Top-of-the-range suites have jacuzzi baths & separate living rooms. Tennis courts, a gym, sports facilities, a European-style restaurant & plush bar are also open to hotel guests. Book well in advance if you plan on visiting in peak seasons & around Jewish holidays. *Off-season rooms are up to 400NIS less ($$$).* $$$$$

🏠 **Kfar Blum Kayaks Camping** Located in the pretty grounds of the kayaking centre (contact see below) next to the Jordan River. Facilities include hot showers, cooking area, picnic tables & kiosk. $

✗ **Pastoral Hotel Restaurant** Pastoral Hotel; ☎ 04 6836611; ⊕ for lunch & dinner; kosher. This European-style buffet restaurant offers good value for money. Good selection of salads & mains served in a rustic, Tuscan-style dining room. Call ahead to reserve on weekends as often full. Buffet $$$$$

WHAT TO SEE AND DO

Voice of Music Festival In summer, the week-long festival, also referred to as the Kfar Blum Festival, marks the centre of all activity in and around the kibbutz. Up to 15,000 music lovers attend the fantastic mix of classical compositions and modern experimental pieces each year.

Kfar Blum Kayaks (☎ 04 6902616; www.kayaks.co.il) Offer two-person kayaks or six-person rafts on trips down the Jordan and Hatzbani rivers. A 1 hour 15 minute circular route costs 70NIS per person while a two hour 30 minute 'adrenaline' trip is 107NIS per person. Children's activities, bicycle tours and a rope park complete with zip line and climbing wall are all offered for around 70NIS per person.

Spa (☎ 04 6836614; e pastoral–spa@kbm.org.il) Open to all, although hotel guests receive free entry to several of the baths and saunas and get 10% off all treatments. This is certainly the place to pamper yourself after days of outdoor activities, but it will come at a rather a hefty price. You do get what you pay for, however, and treatments and facilities are top-notch. The list is extensive and treatment packages can be purchased which are cost effective. A 50-minute Swedish sauna is 250NIS, a 70-minute Ayurveda Indian massage is 370NIS and a Shiatsu session is 170NIS. You will need to make an appointment in advance, especially in busy seasons.

AROUND KFAR BLUM

AGAMON HULA VALLEY BIRDWATCHING RESERVE (☎ 04 6817137; www.kkl.org.il; ⊕ 09.00–1hr before dusk Sun–Thu, 06.30–1hr before dusk Fri/Sat; admission 31NIS (inc shuttle)) The Hula Valley sits tucked into the northern part of the Syrian-African Rift Valley and is one of the most crucial winter stopovers for the 360 species of migratory birds who drop in on their way south. Between the months of October and March, an estimated 500 million birds jostle for space in the skies and waters of the Hula Valley, a large proportion of which is today utilised for agriculture. Up until 1950, when the majority of the area was drained, the Hula Valley was one of the largest wetland areas in the Middle East. Following environmental objections to the drainage, a small swampland was created in 1963 and claimed the honour of being Israel's first nature reserve. Today the area is undoubtedly the single most important wetland in the country for water birds and is graced with the presence of 20 globally threatened species including the imperial eagle, spotted eagle and marbled duck.

Lake Agamon sits at the centre of the Agamon Hula Reserve and is the stage for spotting countless species of wildfowl, including hundreds of thousands of cranes. Wildlife is in abundance too, with water buffalo, once indigenous to the area, having been reintroduced.

A large array of eco-friendly transport methods is on offer to get out into the heart of the park ranging from bicycles, tandems, four-man bicycles, golf carts or the safari wagon, and vary in price from 45NIS to 235NIS. There are two flat and fairly undemanding routes (6km and 10.5km) following a circular route around the lake. A small introduction video is presented at the entrance which can be played in English upon request.

Getting there All Kiryat Shmona-bound buses will stop along route 90 from which it is a hefty 3km walk to the park entrance. Follow directions through agricultural buildings to the large car park. There is a nature reserve run by the Israel Nature and National Parks Protection Authority a little further south along the valley which can be easily mistaken for the birdwatching centre, so look out for signs.

THE GOLAN HEIGHTS

LEBANON

SYRIA

JORDAN

Mt Hermon 2224m

Hermon Forest

Majdal Shams

Neve Ativ

Metulla

Nahal Ayun NR

Tel Dan NP

Kibbutz Dan

Ein Qinya

Nimrod Castle

Birket Ram

Mas'ada

Kibbutz Kfar Giladi

Banias NR

Golani Lookout

Odem Forest Park

Odem

Tel Hai

She'ar Yashuv

El Rom

KIRYAT SHMONA

Kibbutz HaGroshim

Horshat Tal NP

Merom Golan

Quneitra

Manara Cable Car

Kibbutz Kfar Blum

Mt Bental 1170m

National Trail

Hula Valley

Flooded area

TAP Line Road

Hula NP

Gilbon

Gadot Lookout

Tel Hazor

Kibbutz Gadot

Katzrin

Hatzor Haglilit

Rosh Pina

Zavitan Waterfall

Yehudiya

TZFAT (Safad)

Yehudiya campsite

Meshushim Pools

Yehudiya Visitors Centre

Nahariya

Nature

Korazim NP

Reserve

Gamla NR

Daliot Waterfall

Karmi'el, Akko

Almagor

Gamla

Maale Gamla

Tulip Inn

Capernaum NP

Mt of Beatitudes

Church of the Primacy of St Peter

Luna Gal Aqua Park

Ramot

Nahal El Al

Black Waterfall

Church of the Loaves & Fishes (Tabghe)

White Waterfall

Kibbutz Ginosaur

El Al

Sea of Galilee

Kursi Givat Yoav NP

Ophir Lookout

Mt Arbel 278m

YMCA

Ein Gev

Susita

Arbel

Kfar Hittin

TIBERIAS

Nazareth, Haifa

TVERYA ILIT

Kfar Haruv

Peace Vista

Porriya Hospital

Porriya

Based on mapping by Carta, Jerusalem

Beit She'an

Beit She'an

Hamat Gader

N

Bradt

0   5km

0   5 miles

8

The Golan Heights

Please note that the region known as the Golan Heights is, according to UN classification, an Israeli-occupied area of land. Israel's annexation of the Golan Heights in 1981 was not recognised by the UN and as such remains a disputed zone. For the purposes of this guidebook and for ease of use to travellers, however, it has been included under the title of Israel and has no borders or checkpoints, posing few or no problems for visitors to the area.

Conjuring images of war-torn lands, ferocious battles and heavy rocket fire, the Golan Heights is often overlooked by foreign visitors to Israel, its tumultuous existence and remote location acting as deterrents to most. Yet the region is Israel's most misunderstood and in fact exudes a peace, harmony and beauty that few other places can attest to. Culturally and geologically it stands apart from its neighbouring Galilee, its rugged, untamed landscape sparsely inhabited by Druze and Jewish communities. Roaring rivers, jagged mountain peaks, deep canyons and gushing waterfalls have found their place in the wild 55km stretch of land that forms Israel's northern- and easternmost frontiers.

Life in the Golan has for years relied upon agriculture, vineyards, fruit orchards and most significantly cattle rearing. In recent years, however, tourism has started to creep in and now rural pursuits are being offered to those in search of solitude, nature and an escape from all things urban.

Beginning at the Sea of Galilee, the southern Golan plateau exudes a more tranquil environment, where rolling hills dotted with cattle and grazing horses spill into the lake below. Inhabited by Jewish communities, the southern region is characterised by its rich archaeological and historical remains and stunning natural scenery. In contrast is the rugged northern region of the Golan Heights, the towering Mount Hermon range sitting at its northernmost point overlooking Syria and Lebanon. A spattering of Druze communities farm the lower slopes where imposing Roman castles and grand Crusader forts guard the ancient highways.

Oak forests, blossoming wild flowers and alpine meadows combine to form an impressive and unexpected landscape and an environment which supports the country's most varied wildlife species. As a meeting point for fauna arriving from the cold steppes of Asia and Europe and the desert lands of the Syrian-African Rift Valley the variety is immense. Gazelles, hyenas, wild boars, foxes, wolves and millions of species of birds including the breathtaking Bonelli's eagle and Egyptian vultures roam over the lands.

The population of the Golan Heights is approximately 39,000, over half of whom are Druze. Inhabiting the four Druze settlements of the **Majdal Shams**, **Masada**, **Buqata** and **Ein Qinya** they are famed for their hospitality, loyalty and traditional food. The 16,500 Jews who live here are spread across more than 30 tiny villages, their luxury guesthouses, rustic, home-cooked meat restaurants and laidback lifestyle well known across the country.

The Golan Heights

8

ANCIENT HISTORY The melange of historic, archaeological and modern battle sites that are spattered across the Golan Heights lie as a testament to its colourful and turbulent past. Although archaeological evidence dates the Golan's inhabitation as far back as the late Stone Age, permanent settlement didn't arrive until much later. It acted as a buffer zone between the warring Israelites and Arameans, and it was during this time that the city of Golan was founded as an Israelite refuge. The Golan Heights, along with the rest of the region, came under the control of Alexander the Great in 332BCE and in the years following his death was heavily settled, the empire coming to an end when the Golan was conquered by the Romans. During the booming years that followed, cities such as Banias, Gamla, Hippos, Gadera, Seleucia and Sogane became centres of Greco-Roman culture, flourishing until the Jewish revolt against the iron-fisted Roman rule. With the coming of the Byzantine Empire came Christianity and the Golan prospered, new towns, churches and synagogues emerging in great numbers.

After the defeat of the Byzantine Empire in 636BCE, the Golan, and all of Syria, fell into the hands of Muslim Arabs. Over time, the centre of power migrated further east to cities such as Damascus and Baghdad, and the Golan was once again wandered by few more than nomadic Bedouin tribes. That is until the Crusader rule in the Holy Land when the Golan found itself once again a buffer zone, this time between Christian and Muslim forces, each fortifying this no-man's-land with huge castles and forts. Throughout the Golan's long Ottoman rule the region was all but forgotten, inhabited mainly by Bedouins and, in the 19th century, Druze communities who migrated from Lebanon and Syria.

MODERN HISTORY The end of World War I and the signing of the Sykes–Picot Agreement saw the Golan come under French control. The establishment of Syria in 1946 signalled the end of the French mandate, and upon the British departure from Palestine in 1948 (and Israel's subsequent declaration of independence), the Syrians invaded the Golan Heights. They heavily fortified the entire region, converting it into a launch post for attacks against Israel. Bunkers, camps and military towns appeared, the bullet-ridden remnants of which still dot the landscape in the northern highlands.

Years of skirmishes between the Syrians and Israelis over the important water supply in the area culminated in the violent and bloody Six Day and Yom Kippur wars which saw Israel capture and later defend the Golan Heights. During the wars most of the Druze inhabitants fled the area, those who remained cut off from their neighbours on the other side of the border. By the end, Israeli troops were stationed only 35km from Damascus, which eventually resulted in the signing

HITCHHIKING THE ISRAELI WAY

Hitchhiking is standard practice in Israel and you are unlikely to see a bus stop without a small gaggle of youngsters and soldiers pointing at the floor. In contrast to most countries where a smile and a thumbs up is your best hope of getting a free lift from a stranger, in Israel the technique is to look aloof and carefree whilst casually pointing at the ground with one index finger. While it needs to be said that hitchhiking always comes with certain dangers, they are extremely minimal and highly unlikely in Israel and you don't need to worry about giving it a go. Indeed, in some of the more remote places of the country, it may be your only option.

of a disengagement agreement whereby Israel returned 100km² of land to Syria. Military forces on both sides were regulated, leaving a minimal number of troops and a UN observer force installed along the border.

In 1981, the Israeli government made the decision to incorporate the Golan Heights under Israeli law and jurisdiction, a highly controversial move that is to this day not recognised by the UN and much of the international community. Syria has always demanded the return of the pre-Six Day War lands, a factor which, combined with Israel's requirement for the disarmament of the Syrian-backed Hezbollah, stands in the way of any sort of negotiations and peace talks between the two countries. While war is unfortunately never off the table, there have been no battles between the two countries in over 40 years.

ORIENTATION

Travelling in the Golan Heights is somewhat different from other areas of the country and it is a good idea to orientate yourself with the region and what it has to offer before embarking on a trip. Firstly, the region has an extremely limited – if not obsolete – public transport network. Where possible, buses have been included, but the ideal – and sometimes only – way to travel is to rent a car from nearby Galilean towns such as Tiberias or Nazareth. **Dani Aviram** (✆ 052 2616637) has found a niche in the market and runs the only taxi service in the area. As in other parts of Israel, **hitchhiking** is possible, but the sparse communities and lack of traffic on the often near-deserted roads mean you may be waiting around for a long time.

Katzrin is the largest urban centre in the region, and a preliminary glance will tell you that it is not exactly large. For basic services though, this is your best bet. Otherwise, the tiny but hospitable and beautiful moshav, kibbutz and Druze villages that house the rest of the Golan's population provide rural-style accommodation, rustic home cooking and activity centres such as horseriding, bicycle rental and jeep tours. **Ramot** is a good base for these activities in the south and **Merom Golan** or **Neve Ativ** are your best bets in the north. Accommodation in the Golan is expensive; there's no two ways about it. In summer, **campsites** are the only budget options, but come the freezing winter months pricey **zimmer** are your only choice. If your budget stretches to it then you're in for a real treat as the Golan's zimmer are some of the most luxurious in the country. While these can be extremely pricey in peak season and on weekends, weekdays are more reasonable. Several are listed in this section, but it is possible (and recommended) to drive through any of the dozens of moshav or kibbutz and look for vacancy signs outside. In peak seasons it is certainly advisable to book ahead.

MINEFIELDS

Unexploded landmines, unstable, dangerous relics left from the Yom Kippur and Six Day wars, are scattered across the Golan Heights, both in fields and along the sides of roads. Warning signs are everywhere and barbed-wire fences surround 'no entry' zones but be aware, especially when hiking. Always stick to marked trails and heed all warnings. The IDF do extensive training up in the rugged terrain of the northern Golan Heights so be on alert or you might find yourself staring down the barrel of a tank gun. It is important to adhere to 'no entry' signs for both **landmine zones** and **army training areas**. For more information call 04 6977224, but if in doubt, don't enter.

Although rugged and sparsely populated, the Golan Heights is a small region. It is easily navigable, although roads closer to the Syrian border (which is separated by the UN Demilitarized Zone) are sometimes unpaved. Owing to its altitude, most notably in the mountainous zones of the northern Golan, temperatures can plummet and a substantial blanket of snow covers the slopes of Mount Hermon throughout the winter months. Warm clothing is essential, even in the summer months, where the peak of Mount Hermon can still be fairly brisk.

KATZRIN

Katzrin (or Kisrin, Qasrin and Qazrin as various road signs spell it) is the only semi-major settlement in the entire Golan Heights region, and often referred to – rather generously – as the capital. There is no real need to stay in the town, but if you are in search of a post office, supermarket, bank, police station or medical centre then it is the obvious choice. There are, of course, such facilities dotted around the Golan Heights' many moshavs, but Katzrin's concentration of services, centred on its nearby shopping centre, make it the most convenient. While the town itself is not unattractive there isn't an awful lot to do, so if you do choose to stay overnight then expect an early night.

GETTING THERE There is one bus a day to and from Tel Aviv (3hrs 50mins/51NIS) leaving at 16.00 and returning at 05.00. Bus 966 leaves Jerusalem twice a day at 08.45 and 17.15 (4hrs/51NIS) and returns at 06.30 and 13.00. Bus 55 leaves Katzrin at 11.20 (1hr 20mins/32NIS) to Kiryat Shmona stopping at Merom Golan, Masade, Majdal Shams, Neve Ativ and She'ar Yashuv along the way. Bus 58 leaves Kiryat Shmona at 16.40 to Katzrin and makes the same stops. To Tiberias buses 15 and 19 leave at 06.00, 07.00 and 14.00 (1hr/25NIS) taking a clockwise route around the Sea of Galilee. Heading from Tiberias to Katzrin bus 15 leaves at 13.20, 16.00 and 18.30.

TOURIST INFORMATION A new and rather oddly placed **shopping centre** has been built on the outskirts of the town, about 2km from the centre, which contains most of Katzrin's facilities. The industrial centre is located directly behind the shopping centre. The **Golan Heights Tourist Information Centre** (*Katzrin Shopping Centre;* ✆ *04 6962885;* e *tour@golan.org.il;* ⊕ *08.30–16.30 Sun–Thu, 08.30–13.00 Fri*) located in the shopping centre, although tourist information signs still incorrectly direct you into town. Unfortunately the centre is not particularly well equipped and the staff not very knowledgeable.

 WHERE TO STAY, EAT AND DRINK Sleeping options are limited to small bed and breakfasts of which the tourist information centre can provide an updated list. The Golan's magic, however, most certainly isn't in Katzrin and you are well advised to seek refuge in the beautiful rural accommodations in nearby villages. For budget eats there are several fast-food outlets and a supermarket in the shopping mall.

🏠 **SPNI Golan Field School** (36 rooms) Zavitan Rd; ✆ 04 6961234. Has 6-bed rooms that can be rented for 330NIS including breakfast (beds cannot be reserved individually as with dorms). Often full with school groups so best to call ahead. **$$**

♀ **Golan Brewery** Katzrin Shopping Centre; ✆ 04 6961311; ⊕ 11.00–late daily. Offering a cloudy glass of locally brewed ice-cold beer, its location in the shopping centre is rather soulless, but the beer (& lack of alternatives) make it a pleasant choice.

♀ **Safta Pub** Ancient Katzrin Park; ✆ 04 6963033; ⊕ 09.00–late Sat–Thu. Unique pub housed inside an ancient Talmudic building. Has pleasant outside tables in summer & serves simple bar food. **$$**

OTHER PRACTICALITIES
Money
$ **Bank Leumi** Katzrin Shopping Centre; ↘ 03 9544555/ landline*5522; ☺ 08.30–13.00 & 16.00–18.15 Mon & Thu, 08.30–14.30 Tue/Wed, 08.30–12.30 Fri. Has an ATM outside.

Medical
✚ **Emek Pharm** Katzrin Shopping Centre; ↘ 04 6962578; ☺ 08.30–19.00 Sun–Thu, 08.30–13.00 Fri

Laundry
Mayaan Laundry Katzrin Industrial Park; ↘ 04 6964422; ☺ 08.00–17.00 Sun–Thu, 08.00–13.00 Fri. Located just past the Katzrin Winery.

WHAT TO SEE
Golan Archaeological Museum (*Katzrin; tel; 04 6961350; www.museum.golan.org.il; ☺ 09.00–16.00 Sun–Thu, 09.00–15.30 Fri, 10.30–13.30 Sat; admission adult/child 24/16NIS (including entry to Katzrin Ancient Village)*) The museum is located in the town itself, next to the small commercial centre and houses finds from prehistory through to Talmudic times. A reconstruction Chacolithic house is one of the museum's top attractions.

Katzrin Ancient Village (*Katzrin Rd East; ↘ 04 962412; ☺ 09.00–16.00 Sun–Thu, 09.00–14.00 Fri, 10.00–16.00 Sat; admission adult/child 24/16NIS (including entry to the Golan Archaeological Museum)*) Located next to the shopping centre about 2km from town is a large-scale reconstruction of a Talmudic village and synagogue. The village was built here to commemorate the ancient village discovered and excavated nearby, whose synagogue was undoubtedly its crowning glory. After a violent earthquake in CE746, the flourishing town was abandoned and remained deserted until the Mamluk period when it was resettled and a mosque erected inside the synagogue. Reconstruction wine and olive presses, traditional houses, a spring and the synagogue have been built to create an entertaining and informative experience.

Golan Magic (*Katzrin Shopping Centre; ↘ 04 6963625; www.magic-golan.co.il; ☺ 09.00–18.00 Sun–Thu, 09.00–15.00 Fri, 09.00–16.00 Sat; admission adult/child 25/20NIS*) This 180° show features the history and geography of the Golan Heights and incorporates smells, sights and sounds. It is an entertaining, extra-sensory experience and probably the least energetic activity you can do in the Golan region. It is located inside the shopping mall.

Golan Heights Winery (*Katzrin Industrial Park; ↘ 04 6968435; www.golanwines.co.il; ☺ 08.00–17.00 Sun, 08.30–18.30 Mon–Thu, 08.30–13.00 Fri; admission adult/child 17/12NIS*) (See box, *A bottle of Israel's finest*, page 157.)

AROUND KATZRIN

YEHUDIYA NATURE RESERVE (*route 87; ↘ 06 6962817; www.parks.org.il; ☺ Apr–Sep 08.00–17.00 daily; Oct–Mar 08.00–16.00 daily; admission adult/child 18/8NIS*) The Yehudiya Nature Reserve spreads like an outstretched hand across the southern Golan, and is characterised by its five rivers, verdant vegetation, gushing waterfalls, clear pools and steep canyons. The park's 66km² are home to wild boar, jackals, red foxes, Syrian hyrax and porcupines that live amidst the huge variety of tree and plant species. It is also one of the best spots in the region to spy the Bonelli's eagle and Egyptian vulture that are often seen soaring in the skies above. Flowing

8

MESHUSHIM POOLS The hexagonal pools in the west of the park are one of the most famous features in the region, and a dip in the clear waters is an undoubted highlight. Surrounded by eight-sided columns the pools are a geological marvel, formed when mineral-rich molten rock cooled slowly. There are several ways to approach the pools, the shortest and easiest being the 1.5-hour hike from the Meshushim car park. To reach the car park follow route 888 north from the Beit Zaida Junction and turn left just after the village of Had Nes. The trail leads down the canyon, across the river bridge to the pools on the other side. For a longer and considerably tougher hike start at the Yehudiya car park on route 87 and follow the trail westwards to the pools (4hrs). Note that this isn't a circular route so you will need to arrange for transport to pick you up at the end.

UPPER YEHUDIYA CANYON Beginning at either the Yehudiya Campsite or car park on route 87 the trail leads to the ancient village of Yehudiya from where it continues along the top of the canyon before descending steeply to the stream below. At one of the falls, the trail leads across a deep pool so it is important to note that you will need to swim across with all your belongings or turn back at this point. The trail then continues down the canyon where you can either carry on for a further 2km (through some more pools and waterfalls) or follow the green route which will bring you back out at the ancient village of Yehudiya. The circular route takes approximately four hours.

UPPER ZAVITAN CANYON A long but moderately challenging hike leads from kilometre 6.5 on the Katzrin road to the Yehudiya car park (5hrs). The trail follows the Black Gorge southwards, passing the Zavitan Hexagon Pools and Zavitan Waterfall along the way.

through the 'fingers' of the park are the Meshoshim, Zavitan, Yehudiya, Gamla and Daliyot rivers that emerge from deep, rock-cut canyons into the Beit Zaida Valley just north of the Sea of Galilee.

There are innumerable hiking trails in and around the park and the information centre can offer a wealth of advice and recommendations. Trails range from mild, family-oriented walking paths to extremely challenging routes that involve rappelling or swimming so be sure to choose carefully before setting off. While the **Gamla Nature Reserve** is considered part of the Yehudiya Nature Reserve, it has a separate information centre and entrance fee (see below).

The well-equipped **Yehudiya Campsite** (✆ *04 6962817; admission 15NIS on top of the national park entrance fee*) is located next to the information centre midway between the Katzrin road and the Yehudiya Junction on route 87.

Getting there The park entrance is located 5km south of Katzrin on route 87. Bus 15 runs between Tiberias and Katzrin and will stop outside the park entrance. From Tiberias buses leave at 13.20, 16.00 and 18.30 (1hr 45mins/20NIS) and from Katzrin at 06.00 and 07.00 (25mins/13.50NIS).

GAMLA NATURE RESERVE (✆ *04 6822282; www.parks.org.il;* ⊕ *Apr–Sep 08.00–17.00 daily; Oct–Mar 08.00–16.00 daily, although it is best to phone ahead on weekdays as the park is often closed for army training; admission adult/child 23/12NIS*) The dramatic landscape of the Gamla Nature Reserve provides an apt home for both the wildlife and ancient history that reside within its boundaries. The steep sides of the ridge – named after the Arabic word for camel, so called because of its 'humps and saddle' shape – is home to the Israel's largest flock of Griffon vultures which have made their nests on the steep inclines above the ravines. Dozens of pairs of birds fly overhead early in the morning, returning late in the afternoon, a sight certainly worth waiting around for. A birdwatching post has been built a few minutes' walk from the entrance and – if you are lucky enough not to be accompanied by large groups of schoolchildren – offers splendid views over the valleys, and a fine spot from which to watch the vultures on their return (binoculars can be rented from the office).

The 50m-high **Daliyot Waterfall** – the highest in the country – is at the end of one of several trails that cling to the ravine edges. The waterfall is approximately 1.5km down the undemanding 'Dolmen trail'. While nature and wildlife are high on the agenda for most who visit, the park is also home to some fine archaeological remains which play a key role in the Golan's history. The ancient city of Gamla, sitting high on a ridge between two streams, was the capital of Jewish Golan from 87BCE–CE68, and it was here that one of the heroic stories of the Jewish revolt unfolded. Led by Josephus Flavius, Commander of the Galilee, the fortified city of Gamla was the setting for mighty battles between the Jewish army and Vespasian's Roman troops, battles that ultimately resulted in Roman victory. Thousands of Gamla's residents were slaughtered, while others chose to leap from the cliffs

CRASH OUT OR SPLASH OUT IN THE SOUTHERN GOLAN HEIGHTS

Apart from the accommodation recommended in the villages and towns covered in this chapter, there are some other great spots that are worth considering, especially if you're looking for something a bit special, or are travelling on a tight budget.

CRASH OUT
⌂ **Jeep Tours Camping** Ramot; ␇ 04 6732317/050 5209146; $ (see page 212)
⌂ **The Indian Camp (Mapalim)** (see below)

⌂ **Yehudiya Campsite** Yehudiya National Park; ␇ 04 6962817; 15NIS pp (on top of the national park entrance fee) (see page 210)

SPLASH OUT
⌂ **Cnaan Village** (5 rooms) Had Nes; ␇ 04 6822128; e spa@cnaan-village.co.il; www.cnaan-village.co.il. Luxury, intimate spa village in the heart of the lower Golan Heights. The 5 exquisite, romantic suites each reflect a different emotion & include king-size beds, jacuzzis & private terraces with stunning views. The spa boasts a beautiful indoor swimming pool & a range of massages and treatments. *Weekdays 300NIS less ($$$$$).* **$$$$$**
⌂ **Mitzpe HaShalom Country Lodge** (27 rooms) Kfar Haruv; ␇ 04 6761767; f 04 6761771; www.mitzpe-hashalom.co.il. Located next to the Peace Vista (see page216) & set within manicured grounds. While the service is homely & accommodating (they even deliver breakfast hampers to your door), here

it is all about the location. The utterly spectacular views of the Sea of Galilee will take your breath away time and again. Cabins have kitchenette, jacuzzi, AC & living room. Minimum of 2 nights on weekends. *Weekdays 200NIS less ($$$).* **$$$$**
⌂ **Indian Camp (Mapalim)** Avnei Eitan; ␇ 04 6762151; e indiantipi@hotmail.com. This unique campsite offers budget-priced tepee tents or luxury yurts complete with parquet flooring, TVs, kitchenette & AC (although bathroom cabins are outside). Yurt guests can also use the tented jacuzzi & order massages & the price includes a sumptuous picnic breakfast. Tepee tents are basic but a rare good budget option. For 15NIS blankets & pillow can be rented. Tepee $; yurt **$$$$**

rather than surrender. A coin found within the excavated ruins of ancient Gamla reads 'for the redemption of Jerusalem', a poignant reminder of the Jewish revolution against the Romans. Extensive excavations have revealed impressive and substantial remains, including a 2nd-century synagogue, Byzantine church, an aqueduct, ritual bathhouse and several public buildings.

Getting there Follow the Sea of Galilee road until you reach the Gamla Junction and then follow route 869 to the Daliyot Junction. After 2km turn north where a signposted dirt road leads to the park. Buses 15 and 19 leave Tiberias (55mins/22NIS) to Katzrin at 12.50, 13.20, 16.00 and 18.30, and will stop outside the park. From Katzrin the bus leaves at 06.00 and 07.00 to Tiberias.

RAMOT

The tiny moshav of Ramot has developed as a hub of Golan tourism and, if your budget allows, is a beautiful, quaint little place to base yourself for exploring the area. Almost without exception every house has created luxury zimmer accommodation, each competing with its neighbour for novelty, quality and, unfortunately, high prices. Ramot is not a cheap place to stay and those on a budget are limited to camping (see below). During peak times the moshav can get booked up so it is certainly worth making reservations during this time. There is a comprehensive list of zimmer at www.zimmeril.com.

Ramot is perfectly located for exploring the landscape of the lower Golan, with its undulating green hills and views of the Sea of Galilee. Horseriding, jeep tours, cycling and hiking can all be arranged from within the moshav and the weather in the lower lands is generally milder than the highlands of the northern stretches of the Golan Heights. There are several excellent meat restaurants in the village plus two simple supermarkets.

GETTING THERE Public transport is limited to buses 15 (06.30) and 22 (13.40 and 17.25) to Tiberias. Coming in the other direction buses leave Tiberias at 12.50 and 16.45.

TOURIST INFORMATION Ramot is so tiny most establishments don't use street names. A myriad signs as you enter the village will point you to the right hotel, or just ask for directions.

Jeep Tours ↘ 04 6732317/050 5209146. Offer guided jeep tours in the surrounding countryside. 2hr tours cost 550NIS per jeep including drinks & snacks. The well-equipped ranch also has a tidy campsite (or you can sleep on mattresses in the barn), & newly built bathroom block & kitchen (80NIS/night). Located at the far end of town.
Ofan Na'im Bicycle Rental ↘ 04 6732524. Bicycles, helmets & maps are provided which will lead you on several self-guided tours around the area. Prices range from 50NIS for a 2hr tour to 60NIS for a

longer journey down to the Sea of Galilee from where you will be picked up.
Ramot Horse Ranch North Ramot; ↘ 04 6737944/057 7364751; e justuri@hotmail.com. Extremely well-equipped & well-managed horseriding centre located 3km north of Ramot (signposted). Owners Justine & Uri Peleg offer guided treks ranging from a few hours to a few days. At the time of writing plans were underway to build accommodation for riders, so it's worth enquiring about packages.

 WHERE TO STAY
⌂ **Ramot Resort Hotel** (109 rooms) Entrance to Ramot; ↘ 04 6732636; e nramot@bezeqint.net; www.ramot-nofesh.co.il. The most luxurious accommodation in the area with a plush hotel &

cabins overlooking the Sea of Galilee. Facilities include in-room massages, a spa, gym & swimming pool. Cabins have jacuzzi baths, huge-screen TVs & patios while rooms offer breezy balconies. The reception can arrange tours, guides & activities. Minimum 2 nights on weekends. *Weekdays 500NIS less ($$$$$)*. **$$$$$**

🏠 **Barak Guest Rooms** (8 rooms) ☎ 04 6732525/050 2850225. Lovely wood cabins complete with jacuzzi bath, TV, kitchenette, AC & private veranda. Breakfast 30NIS pp extra. *Weekdays 200NIS less ($$$)*. **$$$$**

🏠 **Golan Rooms** (10 rooms) ☎ 04 6731814/052 3393277; e golanrms@ramot-bb.co.il. Stunningly located guest rooms with sweeping views over the Sea of Galilee. Rooms are bright & fresh & have kitchenettes. Large swimming pool, jacuzzi, sauna & restaurant available. Breakfast included. *Weekdays 350NIS less ($$$)*. **$$$$**

Jeep Tours Camping (see previous page)

✗ WHERE TO EAT

✗ **Betty and Nachi Mevashlim** ☎ 04 6732889; ⊕ 18.00–23.00 Sun/Mon & Wed–Fri. Set meal including dozens of small, unique dishes allowing you to sample all the delights of their cooking. Choices include tongue in courgette sauce, oven-baked rack of rib, camembert wrapped in goat's cheese pastry & beef on a bed of rice. Set meal **$$$$$**

✗ **Hava Bakfar** ☎ 04 6797097; ⊕ 18.00–late Mon–Fri, 13.00–late Sat. Well-known meat restaurant specialising in prime Golan-reared beef. Sizzling, rustic & hearty, steak doesn't come much better than this. **$$$$**

AROUND RAMOT

KURSI NATIONAL PARK (☎ *04 6731983; www.parks.org.il;* ⊕ *Apr–Sep 08.00–17.00 daily, Oct–Mar 08.00–16.00 daily; admission adult/child 12/6NIS*) During construction of a road in 1976, construction workers stumbled across what was to be later identified as the largest Byzantine monastery in Israel. Measuring 123m by 145m the church contains large and highly ornate mosaics depicting animals and plants. During the Talmudic and Mishnaic periods, Kursi was a Jewish fishing village, and has long been believed to be the Christian site where Jesus performed his miracle of healing a man possessed by demons. Mark 5: 1–20 tells of Jesus casting the evil spirits from the man into a nearby herd of swine, who then ran down the hill and drowned in the Sea of Galilee. Just south of the monastery and church a small chapel was discovered with an apse covering a cave, considered in Christian tradition to be the place where the miracle occurred. Although the monastery and church suffered vandalism and damage by the Persians in CE614 they were rebuilt, only to be ravaged by an earthquake in the 8th century.

HIKING NAHAL EL AL

Nahal El Al is one of the Golan's most southerly rivers and provides the backdrop to one of the region's most beautiful hikes. Characterised by its two waterfalls, the Black Waterfall and White Waterfall named after the basalt and limestone rocks over which they spill, the area is exceptionally fertile and home to pomegranate, olive and fruit trees. The hike begins from moshav **Avnei Eitan** and follows the course of the river, arriving first at the 8m-high Black Waterfall. From there it continues to the 20m-high White Waterfall, from the top of which is a beautiful view of the area. A small pool at its base is a refreshing welcome in the heat of summer. The entire trek is approximately 4.5km in length (4hrs) and finishes in moshav Eli Ad. For a highly unusual sleeping experience, the **Indian Camp** (☎ 04 6762151; e indiantipi@hotmail.com; tepee 80NIS pp, yurt 500NIS) in Avnei Eitan offers budget tepees and luxury yurts (see page 219).

Getting there The Kursi Junction is located on route 92 that runs along the east side of the Sea of Galilee. Buses leave from Tiberias (20mins/11.70NIS) every two hours and will stop at the junction at request.

HAMAT GADER The hot, mineral-rich waters of the Hamat Gader spa (✆ 04 6659999; www.hamat-gader.com; ⊕ 07.00–16.00 Sun, 07.00–22.00 Mon–Fri, 07.00–21.00 Sat; admission weekday 69NIS, weekend 79NIS) draw thousands of visitors every year in search of a revitalising, youth-enhancing experience. The wafts of sulphur as you enter the park grounds are as unexpected as its **alligator park**, the largest in the Middle East. Parrot shows, baboons and two rather ominous-looking pythons are some of the inmates of the animal park, located on the opposite side of the park to the spa facilities. Hamat Gader's popularity is certainly not new founded. As early as the 2nd century, people were bathing in the spring's hot waters, and the site was frequented through to its abandonment in the 9th century. While the development of the park has seemed to focus on entertainment rather than history, a few structures are worth exploring. A synagogue, built during the Roman–Byzantine period represents the Jewish sages who mention the baths in the Talmud, while the scale of the beautiful Roman bathhouses are testament to its significance in society at the time. The crowds on weekends and holidays – especially in winter, where people look for respite from the cold in the 30°C waters – can unfortunately add grey hairs rather than invigorate the spirit, so it is highly recommended to visit off season or on weekdays. Pools have been created with – for better or worse – a variety of features including fountains and jacuzzi beds. The spa's luxury **hotel village** (✆ 04 6655555; e spa-villagehotel @hamat-gader.com; www.hamat-gader.com; $$$$$) offers cabins, complete with mineral jacuzzi, as well as an extensive range of massages, classes and therapies. The price includes bed and breakfast, a meal in the on-site kosher Thai restaurant **Siam**, massages and the spa facilities. The hotel is for over 16s only and bookings must be for a minimum of two nights on weekends.

Getting there A daily bus leaves Tiberias at 09.15 and returns from Hamat Gader at 14.15. By car heading north from Jerusalem or south from Tiberias along route 90 turn onto route 98 following the Jordanian border fence. The site is signposted from the main road.

MOUNT BENTAL

The slopes of the 1,170m Mount Bental played a key role in the 1973 Yom Kippur War that saw Israel take control of the Golan Heights. Today the summit has been turned into a memorial site for one of the war's bloodiest battles that played out in what has been coined the Valley of Tears, the deserted town of Quneitra sitting in its midst in the stretch of land now patrolled by the UN Disengagement Observer Force (UNDOF). Rather ironically, the view that stretches over the bloodied lands of the Valley of Tears and beyond (Damascus is but 60km away) is one of the region's most stunning, and a must on any visit. An abandoned Israeli bunker has been left as a monument to the 160 Israeli tanks that held off Syria's 1,500-strong force, a win that saw a turning point for Israel in the battle for the Golan Heights. The mountain's facilities are run by Kibbutz Merom Golan at its base, the first kibbutz established in this region following the 1967 Six Day War.

GETTING THERE There are two buses to and from Merom Golan Daily. Bus 55 leaves at 11.45 (45mins/25NIS) to Kiryat Shmona stopping at Masade, Majdal Shams, Neve Ativ and Shear Yeshuv along the way. Bus 58 leaves at 17.30 to Katzrin (25mins/20NIS) and continues to Gadot.

TOURIST INFORMATION The kibbutz is a good choice for somewhere to stay with several eating options and plenty of tourist facilities. Jeep and ATV tours, horseriding treks, a swimming pool and weekend bar make this the ideal place to base yourself for a couple of days. The Merom Golan Tourism Office (✆ *04 6960267*) can help point you in the right direction. **Merom Golan ATV** (✆ *04 6960483/052 8695832;* e *tractoronim_mg@walla.com; www.tractoronim.co.il*) can arrange professional quad-biking trips across the surrounding countryside, ranging from one to three hours. A driving licence is required to be able to drive quad bikes.

🏠 WHERE TO STAY

🏠 **Merom Golan Hotel** (52 rooms) ✆ 04 6960267; e tour_mg@merom-golan.org.il; www.meromgolantourism.co.il. The hotel has 32 very pleasant guest rooms & 20 luxury wood cabins set within the rustic, quiet grounds of the kibbutz. Both the stone-built rooms & enormous cabins have the full range of amenities, the cabins offering an extra veranda & eating area. $$$$

✖ WHERE TO EAT The kibbutz has a kosher dining room that serves simple meals either to the table or in buffet style.

✖ **HaBokrim Restaurant** ✆ 04 6960267; ⊕ 12.00–23.00 daily. The name, which translates as 'the cowboy' gives a pretty good gist of the kind of meals served in this comfortable, ranch-style restaurant. Yes, this is meat heaven. Steak, prime rib & lots of potatoes. $$$$

🍽 **Coffee Anan** ✆ 04 6820664; ⊕ 09.30–18.00 daily. The tongue-in-cheek name not only translates as 'in the clouds', but is a reference to the UN leader who classifies the Golan Heights as military occupied & thus belonging to Syria, not Israel. The café serves an assortment of cakes & vegetarian sandwiches, quiches, pastas & salads. $$

ELI COHEN – A LEGENDARY SPY

In the years following the Six Day War, stories of great bravery and self-sacrifice emerged to a nation reeling in its aftermath. Among these, one man's name stood out, a name that has become legendary in households across the country and whose heroism is unparalleled in Israeli minds: Eli Cohen. An Egyptian-born Jew, Cohen was recruited by Mossad in 1960 after making *aliyah* and serving out his army conscription. He adopted a false Syrian identity under the alias Kamel Amin Tsa'abet, and spent a year in Buenos Aires establishing his cover as a wealthy businessman before moving to Damascus. Over the next few years he managed to infiltrate Syrian ruling circles, gaining the confidence of military and government officials and sending classified information back to Mossad. Information gathered by Cohen on Syrian air force pilots was allegedly used to deter fighter pilots off course to Tel Aviv in 1967. Upon threat to their families, the fighter pilots dropped their bombs into the Mediterranean Sea, reporting back to Damascus that the targets had been hit. In 1965, one of Cohen's radio transmissions to Israel was intercepted and he was sentenced to death, despite protests from several world leaders and Pope Paul VI. He was publicly hanged in Damascus and until this day his remains have never been returned to his family in Israel. Four decades on, negotiations for Eli Cohen's remains continue to be a breaking point in peace talks between Israel and Syria. According to many, at the time of his death Eli Cohen was third in line to the presidency of Syria.

The controversial little stretch of land that forms the Golan Heights bears the scars of its violent and bloody past, where long-forgotten, unexploded landmines lay in their hundreds, bullet-ridden buildings stand abandoned and memorial sites dot the landscape. Yet today there is something peaceful about this beautiful and wild terrain, something that draws visitors in search of rural escape and nature. To help understand the Golan's tumultuous history a stop at some of its most stunning lookouts offers more than a view over the landscape. On the following sites, fierce battles unravelled that shaped this hotly contested little region of the Middle East into what it is today.

Peace Vista Heading north along route 98, the Peace Vista (Mitzpe HaShalom) is signposted on the left just before the small moshav of Kfar Haruv. The view looks north and west across the shimmering waters of the Sea of Galilee edged by the green plantations of the kibbutz that dot its shores.

Ophir Lookout Heading north along route 98 from the Peace Vista, turn left onto route 789 at the Kursi Junction. Signposted on the left just after Givat Yoav an unpaved road follows an olive grove until reaching the car park. At 350m above the level of the Sea of Galilee the view, enjoyed from the shade of the ancient olive trees, is wonderful. A three-hour hike to the ancient ruins of the Jewish settlement of **Bnei Yehuda** can be started from the car park. Blue markers lead the way down the winding path to Kibbutz Ein Gev on the eastern shore of the lake. Getting back to the car park can be problematic, so it is best to either hitch up and leave the car in the kibbutz or arrange to be met at the bottom.

Bental Lookout (Valley of Tears) (see *Mount Bental*, page 222)

Golani Lookout The site is a memorial to the fallen troops of the Golani Brigade in the Tel Fahr battle of the Six Day War. A 650m trail takes visitors past the abandoned Syrian outpost to the lookout point over the Hula Valley. Along the trail memorial plaques tell the story of the battle that resulted in the capture of the Syrian stronghold.

Gadot Lookout Perched on the natural boundary that separates the uplands of the Golan from the verdant valleys of the Upper Galilee, the lookout provides a view not of aesthetic beauty but of historical drama and political consequence. This site marks the spot where the pre-1967 Syrian border stood. As you stand at the lookout, there is a clear and poignant divide between the rocky, once-Syrian lands and the green valleys of Israel behind it. The no-man's-land that you see is in fact remnants of the Syrian front line of defence during the Six Day War, and today thousands of unstable mines remain. The area is heavily fenced off and warning signs are aplenty so be sure not to venture off any paths. Scattered eucalyptus trees grow on the vista, obviously non-native to the region and mark the site of submerged Syrian bunkers, purportedly planted upon the suggestion of the legendary Israeli spy Eli Cohen who used the trees as targets for Israel's air force planes.

Often referred to by Israelis as 'the eyes of the nation', Mount Hermon's strategic location for the military, as it 'peers over the neighbour's walls' into Syria and Lebanon, is a crucial component in the country's early warning system. Heavily patrolled by IDF forces, it is difficult to forget the ever-present animosity that Israel and Syria hold towards each other over this land. But while the military presence is unarguably strong, Mount Hermon's enormity – rising to 2,224m – and sheer beauty, easily overshadow any thoughts of conflict. As Israel's highest point, the climate is significantly cooler than anywhere else in the country, which together with its volcanic basalt rocks and pine forests produces an undoubtedly alpine quality. Summer snowmelts and an abundance of springs feed the rivers that roar their way down to the valleys, its plentiful and influential water source one of the sore points fuelling the region's controversial control. The peak can be snow-capped year round and a drive up the winding, forested road to the summit bestows panoramic views and a temperature drop of up to 15°C (even in the height of summer) that will quite literally take your breath away. Even throughout the stifling hot summers of the lower Golan plains and shores of the Sea of Galilee, the fresh breezes that blow off the mountain demand warmer attire.

Mount Hermon has been a sacred landmark in Hittite, Palestinian and Roman times and stood as the northwestern margin of the Israelite conquest under Moses and Joshua. According to the Gospels, it was the site where Jesus revealed to his disciples his purpose to construct his Church and go to Jerusalem to be resurrected and is another contender to Jesus's site of the Transfiguration.

The throngs of visitors who today make their way to the summit up the steep, snaking mountain pass are not thinking of Mount Hermon's ancestral ghosts or political tensions but are instead heading in the direction of the mountain's very successful – and Israel's only – **ski resort** (❨ 04 6981333; www.skihermon.co.il; admission adult/child 38/32NIS (daily ski pass 200NIS; ski rental 135/120NIS). A vast car park 2km beneath the summit is serviced by shuttle buses, ferrying budding alpinists to and from the resort's range of ski trails and slopes. While not exactly on a par with the Swiss Alps, a ski school, sled riding, cross-country trails, restaurants and emergency Magen David centre have been incorporated to make it an enjoyable experience and a great diversion off the history trail. Out of ski season entry is 10NIS (lift 40/35NIS).

Getting there Bus 55 leaves to Kiryat Shmona at 12.05 (25mins/16.30NIS). Bus 58 leaves at 16.55 to Katzrin (1hr/21.50NIS) stopping at Masade and Merom Golan.

WHERE TO STAY AND EAT
Neve Ativ Located 2km from Majdal Shams and 10km from Mount Hermon, the tiny moshav of Neve Ativ has embraced the tourism trade with open arms and not only runs the Hermon Ski Resort but is also home to countless zimmer, guest rooms and the luxury Rimonim Hermon Hotel. The **Neve Ativ Tourism office** (❨ 04 6981333) can help arrange rafting, trekking, horseriding, cycling, skiing and jeep tours in the area.

Rimonim Hermon Hotel (44 rooms) ❨ 03 6754591; www.rimonim.com. Swiss Alp-style wood cabins, complete with sloping red roofs are nestled amongst pine trees & have great heating for those freezing winter nights. It also has a spa centre, heated swimming pool & restaurant. Minimum of 2-night stay on weekends. *Weekday prices are 200NIS less per night ($$$). $$$$*

Golshei Hahermon Motel (11 rooms) ❨ 04 6981531. This is some of the cheapest accommodation in the moshav. Rooms all have central heating & TV & are clean & cosy. $$$

Located just above Masada, at the base of Mount Hermon, is the volcanic crater pool of Birkat Ram (which translates as the 'ram pool'). According to Talmudic text, the pool opened up during the The Great Flood of Noah, never to close again thereafter. The Talmud speaks of only three such places, the other two being the springs in Hamat Gader and Tiberias. The **Birkat Ram Restaurant** (✆ 04 6981638; ⊕ 09.00–17.00 daily; mains $$) nestled on the shores of the pool is a great place to stop and have some traditional Druze fare with a nice view of Mount Hermon and the pool thrown in for good measure. Specialities include green falafel, *majadra*, *kube* with *sumac*, roast lamb and *makhlube*. The restaurant offers access down to the edge of the lake for a post-meal stroll.

Nimrod The minute moshav of Nimrod (barely more than six families live here) has managed to get itself firmly established on the Golan tourist trail thanks to the acclaimed restaurant **The Witch's Cauldron and The Milkman** (✆ 04 6870049; ⊕ 10.00–late daily; $$$$). From miles around big, witch-shaped signs cast their spell of intrigue, directing motorists to the large rustic cabin on the hilltop village over-looking the Birkat Ram pool. The restaurant developed out of a soaring trade in the owner's homemade goat's cheese and now includes a whole variety of dishes. Winter warmers made from the fruits of the Golan is the general theme with hearty casseroles, creative meat dishes, robust pastries and fresh salads. Under the same ownership is the adjacent, ultra-luxurious **guest house cabins** ($$$$$, *weekdays 300NIS less* ($$$$$)), which are simply indulgent. There are no direct buses to Nimrod and it is a 5km walk from Neve Ativ so your own transport is necessary. Watch out for signs to the Witch's Cauldron and The Milkman Restaurant.

AROUND MOUNT HERMON

MAJDAL SHAMS AND MASADA Of Israel's 104,000 Druze residents, 18,000 live within a small area in the northern Golan Heights, distributed among four main towns: Majdal Shams, Masada, Ein Qinya and Buqata. With 8,000 residents, Majdal Shams is considered the centre of the Druze community in the Golan, with Masada, a short distance south of it, a close second.

While the towns themselves are rather higgledy piggledy, their small, simple restaurants are one of the Golan's true highlights. What these small eateries lack in finesse and elegance (and they do certainly lack it) they make up for in quality, traditional dishes cooked with an expertise you cannot find elsewhere. Hummus, salads, freshly baked pita, olives plucked straight from the surrounding groves, vegetables and meats all washed down with sticky *baklava* and strong coffee combine to form a simple, yet oh-so-memorable meal prepared from the fields of Mount Hermon. The unassuming, rudimentary **Nidal Restaurant** (Route 98, *Masada*; ✆ 04 6981066; ⊕ 07.30–23.00 daily; meal $$) offers hospitality like no other and serves hot, fresh pita, hummus and chips as well as grilled meat dishes and salads.

While one wouldn't call Majdal Shams and Masada beautiful, it is clear from the outset that they, along with most other Druze towns, are comparatively affluent. Modern houses are under constant construction and new cars vie for space on the dusty roads alongside the timeless horse and cart. The towns are a constant buzz of agricultural fervour; tractors chug through from the fields, a shepherd on a mobile phone urges his bleating goats through the town centre while young boys in Nike shirts trot their horses out to pasture.

Following the 1967 Six Day War that left much of the Golan Heights under Israeli control, the unsuspecting Druze village of Majdal Shams found itself quite literally torn apart. The new border meant that many families were suddenly living in separate countries and completely isolated from one another. To date, Syria and Israel have no means of communication, neither telephone nor mail – the borders are completely closed and all ties between its residents severed. As a desperate measure to catch a glimpse of their loved ones, relatives started to gather on a 1,110m-high hill within Syrian-controlled land to shout affections and wave. This hill has become known as the Shouting Hill, and provided the backdrop for the acclaimed Israeli film *The Syrian Bride*. Rising above a narrow, heavily IDF-patrolled valley beginning a few metres from Majdal Shams, it is but a distance of 3km that seems like hundreds, for all know that it is the closest they will ever again get to each other. Today, megaphones and binoculars aid communication, but the air is filled with sadness, weddings, funerals and family occasions shared at a distance that seems nowhere near to ever being closed. A trip to the edge of the village to witness this display of stoicism and family loyalty is certainly a humbling experience and a shocking reminder of the state of affairs within the Middle East.

Finding somewhere to stay in Majdal Shams and Masada isn't difficult, but prices do seem decidedly overinflated for what you get. A simple room in the middle of the town generally costs the same as plusher zimmer cabins in nearby villages such as Nimrod or Neve Ativ.

Getting there Bus 55 leaves to Kiryat Shmona at 12.20 (30mins). Bus 58 leaves to Katzrin at 13.30 (1hr 10mins/23NIS) stopping at Masade and Merom Golan and continuing to Gadot.

NIMROD FORTRESS (✆ *04 6949277; www.parks.org.il; ⊕ 08.00–17.00 daily; admission adult/child 18/8NIS (combined ticket with the Hermon National Park 31/15NIS)*) One of the most striking sights in the northern Golan landscape is the Nimrod Fortress. Sitting high on the slopes of Mount Hermon above the deep valley and ancient road that once connected Damascus and the Galilee, it is an eerily imposing sight.

The early phase of the fortress was built in 1228 by Al-Aziz Uthman, Saladin's nephew, as an attempt to block the march of the Sixth Crusade heading to Damascus from Akko. The fortress was later aggrandised after its capture by the Mamluk sultan Baibars to include the striking towers we see today. Inscriptions, including the carving of a cheetah – Baibars's symbol – are evidence of its ruler at the time. Not long after the Muslim conquest of Akko in the 13th century and subsequent demise of Crusader rule, Nimrod fell into disrepair. Once more brought into commission after the Ottoman Turks conquered the country, it was used as a luxury prison for exiled Ottoman aristocrats from Palestine.

It is possible to spend a few hours exploring the restored sections of the fortress. Of particular interest are the 'secret corridor', large stone brick halls, central keep and towers.

Getting there Bus 55 leaves Neve Ativ to Kiryat Shmona at 12.05 (25mins/16.30NIS) and will stop at the entrance to the fortress.

The Golan Heights AROUND MOUNT HERMON

8

HERMON NATIONAL PARK (BANIAS) (✆ *04 6950272; www.parks.org.il;* ⊕ *08.00–17.00 Sat–Thu, 08.00–16.00 Fri; admission adult/child 23/12NIS (combined ticket with Nimrod Fortress 31/15NIS)*) The Hermon National Park, which is commonly referred to as Banias, sits on the western border with the Upper Galilee and is famed for both its impressive waterfall and dramatic history. The park has two entrances located a few kilometres from each other. Heading from Kiryat Shmona, the first entrance offers an easy ten-minute walk down to the waterfall, while the second entrance a little further along route 99 provides access to the archaeological ruins and springs. Three designated routes of differing length and ardour can be taken, but only one – approximately 90 minutes in length – will lead you from the waterfall to the ruins and springs and vice versa. Be sure not to venture off the designated trail that follows the stream, as the park sits amidst several mined areas. Note that this longer route is not circular so make sure you have enough energy to get you back again.

The Hermon Stream is fed by waters descending from Mount Hermon, with a series of **waterfalls** created as the waters cascade down the steep gradients towards the Hula Valley. The largest of these waterfalls is located here at Banias and is the *pièce de résistance* of the park. The torrent is most impressive throughout the April and May snowmelt (although it flows year round), so be prepared to get a bit wet.

The archaeological park displays phases of the once-prosperous city's tumultuous history. Scanty remnants of Greek culture – brought to the region following Alexander the Great's conquest – can be seen, whilst the extravagant Palace of Agrippa is a lasting legacy of the Agrippa II settlement here. Crusader remains and a steady stream of pilgrims hold testimony to the importance of the site in Christianity. According to tradition, it was here that Jesus gave Peter the 'keys to heaven' and performed the miracle of healing the bleeding woman. The Crusaders viewed Banias as a strategic point between their stronghold in Palestine and the surrounding Muslim regions, and it was strongly defended. Throughout the Crusades, power over Banias changed regularly until eventually Saladin reigned victorious, remains of these mighty battles left as testament across the landscape.

Getting there Bus 55 leaves Kiryat Shmona once a day at 13.00 and will drop you at the springs and archaeological site. From northern Golan the same bus will pass the park entrances at around 12.30 and 12.35 respectively.

NEGEV DESERT

Tel Aviv
6 (under construction)
Jerusalem
Tel Arad
31
31
Dead Sea

Tel Sheva NP
BEER SHEVA
25
25
80
National Trail
258

Hatzerim Air Force Museum
6 (under construction)
25
25
DIMONA
Dead Sea
25

40
222
224
224
Mamshit
206
Little Crater

211
224
YEROHAM
225
227

211
211
Big Crater
National Trail
206

40
Boker Valley Vineyard
Sde Boker
Shivta
Ben Gurion's Grave
Ein Avdat NP
Sde Boker Academy
Carmey Avdat Farm
Avdat NP
0   30km
0   20 miles

N
Bradt

40

171
Desert Ecolodge
Be'erot Camping
Mitzpe Ramon
Alpaca Farm
Saharonim Stronghold
Ramon Crater

171

10
40
National Trail

EGYPT
Based on mapping by Carta, Jerusalem
Eilat

230

9

The Negev Desert

In his book *The Innocents Abroad,* Mark Twain once described the Negev Desert as 'a desolation that not even imagination can grace with the pomp of life and action', an observation that 150 years on remains rather apt. The vast Negev Desert occupies half of the country, and is characterised by the geological phenomena that is the **Ramon Crater** as well as its remarkable landscapes, waterfalls, caves, archaeological sites and rich history. The path of the ancient Nabatean Spice Route once wove its way through the peaks and troughs of the desert mountains, prosperous cities appearing along the way; Abraham built his well in the present-day city of **Beer Sheva**; and Israel's first prime minister settled and died in the remote Kibbutz Sde Boker.

Beer Sheva marks the gateway to the region but is little more than a through route to the wonders of the desert below. Mitzpe Ramon's isolated location teetering on the edge of the crater has awarded it the capital of highland tourism, where nature, active pursuits and ecotourism prevail.

Tourism in the desert is still in its infancy and if you plan on visiting under your own steam – a highly rewarding and recommended experience – then be prepared for the harsh desert elements. While the region is big, this isn't the Sahara Desert and you're never too far from some sort of civilisation, stick to marked roads as the IDF do extensive training in the region and make sure you have plenty of water, petrol and sunscreen. Picnics are recommended as eating options are almost non-existent and it would be a shame to waste the amazing landscape sitting indoors anyway. Beer Sheva is your last port of call for buying provisions, although Mitzpe Ramon (see page 240) does have some basic facilities and a small supermarket. Public transport is extremely limited and independent travellers often have to resort to hitchhiking. Renting a car is undoubtedly the best option to get the most out of your trip and avoid standing in the sweltering desert heat on the side of a dusty road waiting for sporadic buses to pass.

BEER SHEVA

Often referred to as 'the capital of the Negev', Beer Sheva is (with the exception of Eilat), Israel's southernmost city. It sits on the fringes of the desert and acts as a gateway for those delving into the rural depths of the Negev Desert. The city is unsurprisingly rather dusty, run-down and sprawling, new neighbourhoods clearly defined by their white, modern apartment blocks and out-of-place greenery. Yet culturally Beer Sheva is quite a treat. While there is no real need to hang around for too long, it holds claim to an interesting history and ethnographic make-up, acting as a trade centre for surrounding Bedouin settlements. A weekly market is held by these communities and is undoubtedly worth timing your visit to coincide with one. Today Beer Sheva is Israel's sixth-largest city and manages to maintain a certain allure through its highly reputable Ben Gurion University. The university

BEER SHEVA

Based on mapping
by Carta, Jerusalem

Bradt

300m
300yds

N

HEVRON RD
PINHAS HAHOZEV ST
Sixt
Tel Sheva, Arad,
Dead Sea

SHAZAR STREET

HENRIETTA SZOLD ST
Avis
Golden Tulip
in the Negev

Soroka Medical Centre;
Ben Gurion University;
Mango bar, University,
Railway station;
Tel Aviv, Jerusalem

HATIKVA ST

YITZHAK BEN ZVI ST

HEVRON ROAD

Central Railway
Station

Bedouin
Market

Sde Boker,
Mitzpe Ramon

EILAT RD

YITZHAK RAGER BOULEVARD

Central Bus
Station

EILAT ROAD

Bank Leumi $

Hallegev Mall

HEVRON ROAD

Tourist information
& Abraham's Well

Desert Inn
(Ne'ot Midbar)

Baraka

BNEI HAROD ST

SHLOSHET
STREET

Pitput

Hallegev

MORDE HAGETAOT ST

LE'YISRAEL ST

Saban Internet

Bank
Hapoalim

HAHISTADRUT STREET

HERZL STREET

HA'ATZMAUT

Aviv

MORDE HAGETAOT ST

KEREN KAYEMET

OLD CITY

Negev Museum

Shabazi

HERZL STREET

Police station

HA'ATZMAUT STREET

Beit HaFul

Ahuzat
Halperin

HAHISTADRUT

DAVID TUVIYAHU ST

SMILANSKY ST

HAMESHACHRERIM RD
ALON ST
JEO WWI Military
Cemetery

Hatzerim
Air Force
Museum (British)

campus forms the hub of modern life, where bars and nightlife attract the younger set. The run-down old Turkish town (Old City) forms the heart of the ancient city where character, not beauty, is the main charm. In all Beer Sheva can be quite a surprise and not nearly as drab and unappealing as it may appear at first sight.

HISTORY The biblical phrase 'from Dan to Beer Sheva' indicates that the city marked the southern limit of Palestine, and is associated with Abraham, Isaac, Jacob and Elijah. When in 1902 the Ottomans chose Beer Sheva as their administrative centre for the Negev it was but an abandoned site, frequented only by Bedouin groups using the area's water sources. Buildings were erected along with a police and train station and train lines were opened to Ashkelon, Gaza and Damascus.

The city played an important role during the British Mandate period under which it continued to develop, and was at the time home to around 4,000 Muslim Arabs. During the 1936–39 Arab riots, many Jews fled the city, not returning until after the 1948 Arab–Israeli War. Because of the predominantly Arab population, Beer Sheva was given to the Arabs in the 1947 UN Partition Plan of Palestine, only to be taken by Israel the following year. Upon the Israeli conquest, the city was all but abandoned by its Arab inhabitants.

GETTING THERE Beer Sheva acts as the gateway to the south and there are subsequently good bus and rail links with the rest of the country.

Bus To and from Tel Aviv's central bus station bus 370 makes the journey every 15 minutes (90mins/29.50NIS), likewise buses 470 and 446 from Jerusalem (1hr 45mins/39NIS). There are regular buses linking Beer Sheva with Arad (50mins/14.80NIS) from where you can connect to the Dead Sea (bus 385 goes all the way to Ein Gedi). To reach Eilat express buses 394 and 397 makes the journey every two hours (3hrs 20mins/55NIS). Bus 60 hurtles between Mitzpe Ramon and Beer Sheva every 20 minutes and stops at every stop along the way including Sde Boker.

Train The train links Beer Sheva with the rest of the country through Tel Aviv. Trains depart every hour (90mins/25.50NIS).

GETTING AROUND Bus 7 starts at the central bus and train stations, heads down to the market, on to the Old City and then heads north along Yitzhak Rager Boulevard towards the Soroka Hospital and university. Bus 31 from the central station will drop you directly outside the Hatzerim Air Force Museum (10mins).

Car rental companies
🚗 **Avis** 8 Henrietta Szold St; ☎ 08 6271777; ⏰ 08.00–18.00 Sun–Thu, 08.00–14.00 Fri

🚗 **Sixt** I Pinhas HaHozev St; ☎ 08 6282589; ⏰ 08.00–18.00 Mon–Fri, 08.00–18.00 Sun

Tourist information
ℹ️ **Tourist information office** I Hevron St; ☎ 08 6234613; ⏰ 08.30–16.00 Sun–Thu. Located at Abraham's Well. English-speaking staff will help with bus routes, tours of the city & can provide maps.

WHERE TO STAY Beer Sheva is somewhat lacking in hotels as most visitors tend merely to stop in on their way south.

Golden Tulip in the Negev (256 rooms) 4 Henrietta Szold St; ℡ 08 6405444; www.fattal.co.il. Part of the Fattal chain, this is Beer Sheva's plushest hotel option. Centrally located it offers comfortable rooms with kitchenette as well as a swimming pool, health club & business centre. $$$$

Aviv Hotel (21 rooms) 48 Mordei HaGeta'ot St; ℡ 08 6278059. The rather shabby exterior belies the simple yet cared-for rooms inside this 2-star hotel. All come with AC & TV & front-facing rooms have small balconies. $$

Beit Yatziv Hostel (HI) (95 rooms) 79 Ha'Atzmaut St; ℡ 08 6277444; e beit_yatziv@silverbyte.com. Easily recognised by the large HI sign outside, this hostel & guesthouse are the best budget options in town. Located in the Old City they both offer clean rooms with bathroom, AC, kosher breakfast & a swimming pool. *Dorms available ($).* $$

Desert Inn (Ne'ot Midbar) Hotel (135 rooms) 2 David Tuviyahu St; ℡ 08 6424922; e info@neot-midbar.com; www.neot-midbar.com. The hotel prides itself on being eco-friendly & facilities include a health centre with alternative treatments & swimming pool. Rooms are pleasant with TV & AC. $$

HaNegev Hotel (22 rooms) 26 Ha'Atzmaut St; ℡ 08 6277026; e liei5@actcom.co.il. The hotel is in need of a lick of paint but rooms are simple, comfortable & cheap. Good location in the heart of the Old City. Double with or without en-suite bathroom available. $

✖ WHERE TO EAT

While not renowned for its fine dining, Beer Sheva does have a few good options. In the Old City, Smilansky Street has the bulk of the restaurants while in the New City you're best heading to the area around the central train and bus stations, around the university or to the HaNegev Mall. The Thursday Bedouin market offers the chance to try some traditional Bedouin cooking. Israelis also know it as a place to find good hummus and falafel and you can find restaurants almost everywhere, especially around the university dorms.

✖ **Ahuzat Halperin** 23 Smilansky St; ℡ 0507 515154; www.ahuzathalperin.co.il; ⊕ 18.00–23.00 Sun–Fri, 12.00–17.00 Sat. Gourmet-style French cuisine set in a beautiful Old City stone building. Undoubtedly Beer Sheva's finest establishment. $$$$

✖ **Pitput** 122 Herzl St; ℡ 08 6289888; ⊕ 08.00–02.00 daily. Italian-style cuisine with an emphasis on meat & fish. They also do some wonderful, doorstop sandwiches & big breakfasts. In the evening it's also a great place to enjoy a beer.

A changing exhibition inside displays work from artists from the Negev Desert. $$$

✖ **Shabazi** 16 Smilansky St; ℡ 08 6655812; ⊕ 09.00 until the food runs out Sun–Thu. Yemeni-style home-cooked country food. Simple, filling & cheap. $$

✖ **Beit HaFul** 15 HaHistadrut St; ℡ 08 6234253; ⊕ 08.00–midnight Sun–Thu, 08.00–15.00 Fri, end of Shabbat–midnight Sat. Sizzling *shawarma* & fresh falafel that is a big hit with the locals. $

ENTERTAINMENT AND NIGHTLIFE

Thanks to the large number of university students there are many places where you can go out and let your hair down. Big, raucous party nights are frequent but there is also a good selection of quieter, more relaxed places to just sit and enjoy a drink. Alternatively, the HaNegev Mall has plenty of cafés in which to sit and while away the evening over a cappuccino and slice of cake, while the **Rav Chen Cinema** (℡ *08 6235278; admission 31NIS; ⊕ last showing 21.00 daily*) shows mainstream Hollywood flicks.

Baraka 70 Shloshet Bnei Harod St; ℡ 08 6287111; ⊕ 22.30–late daily. One of the most popular clubs in town, it is loud, flashy & fun. Each night sees a different theme ranging from karaoke to student nights to live music.

Manga 85 Yitzhak Rager Bd; ℡ 08 6499951; ⊕ 18.00–late daily. Located near the Teachers' Centre, Manga is the quintessential student pick-up bar: loud, crowded & cheap, however it has a nice covered garden area, comfy sofas & decent sushi. **Pitput** (see *Where to eat* above)

SHOPPING

Bedouin Market The market (⊕ *Thu*) officially opened in 1905, although the area had long been a meeting place for the groups of Bedouins who would come to buy, sell and swap pretty much everything. Today it has become slightly more contemporary, with cheap clothes, shoes and home ware stalls standing alongside authentic Bedouin craft stalls and livestock. It is a fantastic place to buy traditional Bedouin keepsakes such as glassware, jewellery and precious stones, as well as mats, carpets and cushions. It is also a great place to get exceptionally cheap Bedouin food.

OTHER PRACTICALITIES
Emergencies

Ambulance ➲ 101
Fire ➲ 102

Police 30 Herzl St; ➲ 100 or 08 6462744

Money

$ **Bank Hapoalim** 40 Ha'Atzmaut St; ➲ 08 6292662; ⊕ 08.30–13.15 Sun & Tue/Wed, 08.30–13.00 & 16.00–18.30 Mon & Thu, 08.15–12.30 Fri

$ **Bank Leumi** 11 Yitzhak Rager Bd; ➲ 08 6239222; ⊕ 08.30–13.00 Sun & Tue/Wed, 08.30–13.00 & 16.30–19.00 Mon & Thu, 08.30–12.00 Fri

Post

✉ **Post office** Corner of Yitzhak Rager Bd; ➲ 08 6295832; ⊕ 08.00–12.00 & 16.00–17.30 Sun & Tue–Thu, 08.00–13.00 Wed, 08.00–12.30 Fri. Has

Western Union & offers commission-free cash & travellers' cheque exchange & phone. Located opposite the mall just along from Bank Leumi.

Medical

✚ **Soroka Medical Centre** Yitzhak Rager Bd; ➲ 08 6400111
✚ **Superpharm** HaNegev Mall; ➲ 08 6281371 & 70

HaMeshachrerim St; ➲ 08 6424313; ⊕ 08.30–midnight Sun–Thu, 08.30–17.00 Fri, 10.00–midnight Sat

Internet

🖥 **Saban Internet** 21 Joseph Trumpeldor St, ➲ 08 6209823

WHAT TO SEE

Abraham's Well (*1 Hevron St; 08 6234613;* ⊕ *08.00–16.00 Sun–Thurs, 08.00–12.00 Fri; admission 5NIS*) Within the small archaeological site is the stone well believed to have been dug by Abraham. It is recorded in the Bible that at the beginning of 2000BCE, Abraham and Isaac arrived in Beer Sheva where they dug wells and formed alliances with Abimelech, the King of the Philistines. The well itself has been dated to at least the 12th century CE. The site also offers a short but worthwhile guided tour.

Old City The Old City dates to the end of the 19th century and owes its origins to the Turks who designed and constructed it based on a grid pattern. While it has undoubted charm, don't expect the quaint cobbled alleys of Jerusalem, Akko or Nazareth's Old City counterparts. The area is run-down and badly maintained and the local government has done little to restore some of the more impressive Ottoman buildings. Smilansky Street has been partially remodelled and has some restored buildings that provide a glimpse of what the area would have once looked like. Today it forms the centre of the Old City and is home to several good restaurants and cheap shops.

Negev Museum (*60 Ha'Atzmaut St;* ☎ *08 6206570;* ⊕ *08.30–15.30 Mon & Wed/Thu, 08.30–14.00 & 16.00–18.00 Tue, 10.00–13.00 Fri/Sat; admission adult/child 12/10NIS*) The small Negev Museum is housed in a stone Ottoman building dating to 1906 and displays a range of changing exhibitions including contemporary and early Israeli art. The building first acted as Beer Sheva's City Hall until 1953 when it was converted into a museum.

British World War I Military Cemetery (*Ha'Atzamaut St*) A little further up from the Negev Museum is Israel's largest British, Australian and New Zealand military cemetery. Buried beneath the rows of white tombstones are soldiers who died in battles against the Turks during World War I.

Air Force Museum (*Kibbutz Hatzerim;* ☎ *08 9906853;* ⊕ *08.00–17.00 Sun–Thu, 08.00–13.00 Fri; admission adult/child 28/18NIS*) The museum is located 6km west of Beer Sheva, just past Kibbutz Hatzerim adjacent to the IDF's southern air force base. With the roaring drone of fighter jets above, visitors can walk around the large outdoor museum and get up close and personal with air force jets and helicopters from the IDF's past. Guided tours in English can be arranged at the entrance and there is a rather nice audio-visual presentation displayed inside a Boeing plane. Bus 31 from the central bus station stops outside.

Tel Beer Sheva National Park (☎ *08 6467286; www.parks.org.il;* ⊕ *Apr–Sep 08.00–17.00 daily; Oct–Mar 08.00–16.00 daily; admission adult/child 12/6NIS*) Heading east out of the city, near the Bedouin settlement of Tel Sheva, is the national park at the centre of which sits the excavated remains of a fortified city dating from the Israelite period. The city was built atop a *tel* (mound composed of the remains of successive settlements) and much of the ancient city has been restored, which adds a certain humanity and understanding to a visit. Of particular interest are the well, city streets, storehouses, public buildings and private homes, the city wall and gates, and the reservoir.

SDE BOKER

The small isolated kibbutz of Sde Boker resting high in the Negev Mountains is famed across the country as being the later home, and final resting place, of Israel's first Prime Minister David Ben-Gurion and his wife Paula. Ben-Gurion's Zionist vision for the desert lands that occupy half of the country was to cultivate and settle, in his own words stating 'the future of Israel lies in the desert'. In honour of Ben-Gurion's love for this remote region and his passion for creating more land in which Jews from around the world could settle he – and later his wife – were interred on a nearby cliff, adjacent to the *midrasha* (research academy) that was founded from his inspiration. Today the kibbutz acts as a good base for exploring the surrounding Negev, most notably the **Ein Avdat** and **Avdat national parks** (see page 239), and while facilities are fairly limited it does offer a small supermarket and a few guesthouses and hostels.

GETTING THERE AND AROUND Buses 60 and 392 runs along route 40 between Beer Sheva and Mitzpe Ramon (35mins/21.50NIS) several times a day stopping outside the kibbutz entrance which is located 3km north of the entrance to the academy, memorial park and Ein Avdat National Park access road, where the bus will make another stop upon request.

TOURIST INFORMATION

❖ Sde Boker Tourist Information Centre ☏ 08 6554418; ⊕ 08.00–16.00 daily. Located in the

entrance to the research academy.

WHERE TO STAY AND EAT

⌂ Boker Valley Vineyard (I room) ☏ 052 6822930; e hilda@kms.org.il; www.hnbw.net. The family-run winery located 8km north of Kibbutz Sde Boker is rustic Negev at its best. Their luxurious wood cabin is a rural retreat with all the comforts of home. The attached **Vinery Restaurant** serves breakfast, lunch & dinner, & activities, including winemaking & fruit picking, are possible in season. *Weekdays 150NIS less ($$$). $$$$*

⌂ Carmey Avdat Farm (6 rooms) ☏ 08 6535177; e carmey-avdat@bezeqint.net; www.carmey-avdat.co.il. Run by the Izrael family who followed their dream into the desert & established a vineyard on the ancient Nabatean spice route, their luxury cabins take advantage of the natural resources & beauty of the desert & offer peaceful landscape views, natural construction materials & not a TV in sight. Plunge pools & fruit orchards

complete the oasis effect. Breakfast included. Weekends minimum of 2-night stay. $$$$

⌂ Ecological Hamburg Guesthouse (20 rooms) ☏ 08 6532016; www.boker.org.il. The guesthouse forms the higher-end option offered by the field school (reception is in the field school office). Comfortable, modern rooms have TV, AC, refrigerator & nice bathrooms. Often fully booked in summer months so best to reserve ahead. $$

⌂ Sde Boker Field School Hostel (47 rooms) ☏ 08 6532016; e orders@boker.org.il; www.boker.org.il. Divided into 2 separate hostels, they mostly attract teenage school groups so dorms ($) are often fully booked. Rooms are very clean & bright, with en-suite bathrooms, AC & breakfast. Discounted use of academy swimming pool. The field school can also organise jeep & camel tours & recommend hiking routes. $$

WHAT TO SEE

Ben-Gurion's home (☏ 08 6560320; ⊕ 08.30–16.00 Sun–Thu, 08.30–14.00 Fri, 09.00–15.00 Sat; admission adult/child 10/7NIS) The hut in which Ben-Gurion and his wife lived until his death in 1973 stands untouched and is a fascinating insight into the humble home life of the country's first leader. The area around the hut has been converted into a small museum of sorts including displays of his famous statements, photographs of the early kibbutz and an archive of the more than 5,000 books that formed his personal library. The hut is located on the southern edge of the kibbutz.

Ben-Gurion Tombs In honour of his love for the desert Ben-Gurion and his wife are buried on a cliff 3km south of the kibbutz. The tombs form a central space within a beautiful memorial park proffering a staggering view of the sweeping Zin Valley. Picnic tables and public toilets make it a popular lunch spot along the route south.

Sde Boker Academy (☏ 08 6532016; www.boker.org.il; ⊕ 08.00–16.30 Sun–Thu, 08.00–12.00 Fri) Adjacent to the Ben Gurion Tomb Memorial Park is the desert research centre It opened in 1965 and has since established more than 12 scientific

9

When the Nabateans settled in the Negev in the 4th century BCE they took control of the transport of spices, incense, herbs, gems and medicines that were crossing from the Far East and Arabian Peninsula to Gaza Port. What has become known as the 'Spice Route' was the source of the Nabateans' famed affluence and their will and passion to defend it are legendary. With the Roman conquest of Egypt came a struggle for control over the prosperous route, one that ended with the Romans creating alternate routes across the desert. The competition had its effect, however, and as the spice trade started to wane Nabatean inhabitants adopted farming, a practice in which they proved successful. In CE105, however, the Roman emperor Trajan finally annexed the Nabatean kingdom and incorporated it into the Roman Provincia Arabia.

The route itself was paved around the 1st century BCE linking the Nabatean capital of Petra in Jordan to Gaza's port. Along the route appeared great camps, stopovers for the mile-long camel caravans that transported their wealth across the desert. In 2005, UNESCO declared the route and the four great Nabatean cities of Avdat, Mamshit, Shivta and Haluza World Heritage Sites, compounding and protecting their historic importance and allowing visitors to follow in the footsteps of the ancient Nabateans.

Avdat (see opposite)

Mamshit (Memphis) (✆ *08 6556478; www.parks.org.il;* ⊕ *Apr–Sep 08.00–17.00 daily; Oct–Mar 08.00–16.00 daily; admission adult/child 18/8NIS*) The walled Nabatean city of Mamshit is the smallest yet best preserved of the Spice Route cities and the site of one of the biggest ancient treasures ever discovered in Israel, consisting of over 10,000 coins. Well-preserved and restored houses, streets, churches and defensive towers (one of which can be climbed for a great view over the site) provide a true insight into Nabatean culture. Mamshit's two churches, complete with highly ornate mosaics, are a particular highlight of the site and on some Jewish holidays, the city's market street is recreated, providing a kitsch but enjoyable insight into Nabatean life. In the summer months it is possible to live like the ancient Nabateans and camp in the city's ancient *khan* (caravansary).

Shivta (*www.parks.org.il;* ⊕ *Apr–Sep 08.00–17.00 daily; Oct–Mar 08.00–16.00 daily; admission adult/child 12/6NIS*) In the far west of the Negev stands the vast Nabatean city of Shivta whose remains have survived the tests of time beautifully thanks to the region's dramatically low humidity. Although the city started life as a Nabatean caravan stop, most of the remains date to the Byzantine period and include two ornate marble churches and a large baptismal font hewn from rock. A 700-m trail leads north to a modern orchard which utilises ancient methods to grow desert fruits, no mean feat in one of the driest places in the country. At the Telalim Junction along route 40 follow signs to Nitzana along route 211. The site is on the right after approximately 15km.

Haluza Excavated rather hastily, the Nabatean city of Haluza (or Elusa) cannot compete with its Spice Route counterparts for impressively preserved relics. The site, which can be accessed only by 4x4, is covered with sand, only a few of its once-impressive buildings visible above ground. Two churches, a theatre and many inscriptions were discovered, accurately dating the site and putting it firmly on the map as an integral part of the Spice Route.

and educational institutions including a national solar energy centre, school for environmental studies and institute for desert research. The **Desert Sculpture Museum** displays art created from desert materials and tours can be arranged by calling in advance.

Sde Boker Winery (✆ *050 7579212;* e *winery@sde-boker.org.il; www.sde-boker.org.il/winery*) Wine tastings and tours can be arranged by contacting the winery in advance.

EIN AVDAT NATIONAL PARK

(✆ *08 6532016; www.parks.org.il;* ⊕ *Apr–Sep 08.00–17.00 daily; Oct–Mar 08.00–16.00 daily; admission adult/child 23/12NIS*) This highly picturesque national park is often overlooked, not receiving the fame (and subsequent crowds) of other desert oases like the Ein Gedi Nature Reserve on the shore of the Dead Sea. The park runs along both sides of the dramatic **Zin Canyon** through which trickles the Zin Stream. The park's geography is unique, characterised by pools, waterfalls and ice-cold springs while the abundance of water and vegetation has created an oasis for wildlife. A mild one–two-hour circuitous hike takes visitors along the river's edge to the palm-fringed **lower pools** and 15m-high **waterfall**, which form the *pièce de résistance* of the park. A longer two–three-hour hike incorporates the **upper pools**, **En Ma'arif spring**, **poplar grove** and **monks' caves** where clergymen lived during the Byzantine period. The long trail begins in either the upper or lower car park and ends in the other meaning you will either have to walk back or arrange for transport to collect you at the other end. For those wishing to see both the upper and lower pools it is recommended to begin and end your visit from the upper car park accessed from route 40 approx 5km south of the entrance to the field school and Ben-Gurion Tombs. The lower car park entrance is along an access road beginning in the Ben-Gurion Tombs car park.

AVDAT NATIONAL PARK

Driving south along route 90, the ancient hilltop settlement of Avdat is unmistakable. Avdat once stood as one of the most important cities in the Negev, where great Nabatean caravans stopped on their long journeys across the desert's Spice Route (see opposite). The city was named after the Nabatean king Obodas III (Abdah in Arabic) who is believed to have been buried here. The king was revered as a deity and it was under him that the city's temple was built. In CE106, the Romans annexed the Nabatean kingdom and the city moved into another phase of prosperity and prestige. The Romans incorporated Avdat and the Nabatean kingdom into their empire, Provincia Arabia, and created a series of defence fortresses stretching across their empire's southern border. As the spice trade dried up Nabatean inhabitants adopted agriculture as their means of livelihood, in particular the production of wine. At the end of the 3rd century CE, a fortress was built on the eastern half of the acropolis hill, most likely to serve as a defence against threatening Arab tribes. The city reached its peak during the Byzantine period by which time Christianity had taken a firm hold. During this time the acropolis was rebuilt complete with churches, a monastery and citadel. Today, St Theodore's Church, with its Greek-inscribed marble tombstones inserted in the floor, is the most interesting Byzantine relic in Avdat. Early in the 7th century CE, the town was totally destroyed by an earthquake and was never reinhabited.

A visit to the park (✆ *08 6551511;* ⊕ *Apr–Sep 08.00–17.00; Oct–Mar 08.00–16.00; admission adult/child 23/12NIS*) is crucial to the understanding of the fascinating and unique history of the Negev and in particular the Nabatean Spice Route. The remains themselves are incredibly impressive (in particular the churches and reconstructed Roman villa) and the view from the top of the hill unparalleled. The information centre is particularly good and has small displays of artefacts unearthed from the site and an audio-visual presentation detailing its history.

MITZPE RAMON

Few towns can attest to the kind of view that Mitzpe Ramon's residents wake up to on a daily basis. Hovering on the edge of the gargantuan Ramon Crater in the heart of the Negev Desert, Mitzpe Ramon is about as remote as it gets. Small though it is the town makes a good base for exploring the desert and facilities having sprung up over recent years in the area's rural tourism boom. Compared with several other desert towns, Mitzpe Ramon is almost pretty, and certainly clean. Attempts have been made to liven the place up with small gardens and greenery adding a touch of colour to the otherwise brown landscape. Ibex and bicycle-mounted children cruise the quiet, dusty streets unhindered by the lack of traffic. Yet it isn't all roses as the town suffers from intensely hot summers, freezing winters, mass unemployment and a lack of entertainment, but for those looking to partake in true desert adventures and ecotourism and have a choice of places to stay at the end of the day, then Mitzpe Ramon will happily oblige. The town is so small which, compounded with the myriad signs pointing to all tourist attractions and hotels, means street names are rarely used in addresses and it is impossible to get lost.

GETTING THERE Bus 60 to and from Beer Sheva makes the journey every 20 minutes (1hr30mins/23NIS) while express buses 392 and 382 only takes 1hr and continues on to Eilat.

TOURIST INFORMATION Hovering on the precipice of the crater, the **visitors centre** (⊓ *08 6588691/8;* ⊕ *08.00–16.00 Sat–Thu, 08.00–15.00 Fri; admission adult/child 23/12NIS*) offers plenty of local information, particularly about hiking and rappelling, as well as a good bi-lingual map of the town (2NIS) which considering its diminutive size might be a bit of an overkill. An audio-visual presentation depicting the unique history, geology, zoology and archaeology of the crater is shown at intervals inside the centre.

LOCAL TOUR OPERATORS

Desert Ecolodge ⊓ 1599 551111; e deserteco @012.net.il (see *Where to stay* below)
Guide Horizon ⊓ 052 3690805/6595333; e guidmi@netvision.net.il; www.guidehorizon.com. Adrenalin-fuelled buggy tours ranging from half a day to 2 days that end with a sizzling barbecue & soak in the attached spa (see *Where to stay* below).
Karkom Jeep Tours ⊓ 052 8813112; www.negevjeep.co.il; e info@negevjeep.co.il.

Specialists in jeep tours across the Negev & further afield to the Dead Sea, the Spice Route & into Jordan.
Negevland ⊓ 1800 200870; e alengt @bezeqint.net; www.negevland.co.il. All-round adventure masters, the list of activities is exhaustless: jeep tours, mountain biking, rappelling, archery & paintballing. Experienced guides & quality equipment.

WHERE TO STAY

A good variety of accommodation is presented in Mitzpe Ramon, ranging from the most basic communal tents to the luxurious Isrotel Ramon Inn. Family-run zimmer make up the wide choice of mid-range accommodation and the visitors' centre can supply you with a list. When choosing a zimmer or cabin it is worth checking out the kitchen facilities as eating options are sparse. Nights in the desert camps can be a great way of being at one with nature but are a bit rough and ready. Be sure to take some warm clothes, even in summer. There are also several campsites in the crater itself, the best being the **Be'erot Camping Site** (10NIS). Pitch your own tent or sleep in a communal Bedouin one.

🏠 **Isrotel Ramon Inn Hotel** (96 rooms) I Ein Akev St; ☎ 08 6588822; e info@isrotel.co.il; www.isrotel.co.il. Offers luxury package including tours, spiritual workshops, spa, indoor swimming pool, desert activities, top-quality restaurant & of course, immaculate self-catering apartments with staggering views. This is the desert *à la carte*. $$$$

🏠 **Alpaca Farm** (5 rooms) ☎ 08 6588047/ 052 8977010; e alpaca4@gmail.com; www.alpaca.co.il. The bright, spacious cabins sleep 4–7, are great value for money & one of the most unique experiences in the desert. Guests can wander around the farm, get involved in daily tasks & help care for the animals. Cabins have equipped kitchenettes, TVs & big verandas. It is also possible Sleeping on mats in a communal area costs 80NIS per night. Cabin $$$

🏠 **Guide Horizon** (8 rooms) ☎ 052 3690805/ 08 6595333; e guidmi@netvision.net.il;

www.guidehorizon.com. Rustic wood cabin offering lovely private rooms full of character. A funky spa, holistic centre, small pool, sauna & decks scattered with hammocks & cushions are a perfect way to chill out after a rigorous day buggying (see *Local tour operators*, above). $$$

🏠 **Mitzpe Ramon Guest House (HI)** (47 rooms) ☎ 08 6588443; e mitzpe@iyha.org.il; www.iyha.org.il. Obeying the normal standards of perfection expected by Hostelling International, this stands out because of its breathtaking view. Be sure to ask for a room on the crater side. Rooms have TV & AC. $$

🏠 **Desert Ecolodge** ☎ 054 6277413; e deserteco@012.net.il. The lodge works towards their motto of 'social & eco awareness' providing simple, mud lodges ($) or Bedouin-style tent ($) accommodation as well as range of ecologically friendly activities including meditation, traditional food preparation, cultural interaction & hiking. $

✗ **WHERE TO EAT** Food options are rather limited so most visitors opt for self-catering. The small but sufficient **Hyperneto Supermarket** (🕐 *08.00–20.00 Sun–Thu, 08.00–14.00 Fri*) in the main square sells fresh fruit and vegetables and there are some decent bakeries, notably **Cafeneto** (☎ *08 6587777;* 🕐 *08.00–23.00 daily*) near the cliff, which also does good sandwiches.

✗ **Pangea** 5 Har Oded St; ☎ 08 6539222; 🕐 09.00–midnight Sun–Thu, 09.00–16.00 Fri; kosher. Offers big meaty portions including steak, grilled chicken & kebabs. Located just south of town in the Spice Route Quarter. $$$$

✗ **HaHavit Restaurant and Café** ☎ 08 6588226;

🕐 08.00–02.00 daily. Better on the inside than it appears on the outside, it has simple pub food, ice creams, snacks & drinks & what it lacks in culinary finesse it makes up for in the view. $$$

✗ **Pizza Domino** ☎ 08 6595252; 🕐 10.00–02.00 Sun–Thu, 10.00–16.00 Fri. Cheap, cheerful & quick.

OTHER PRACTICALITIES
Emergencies
Fire ☎ 102
Magen David Adom (first aid) ☎ 101

Police ☎ 100. The closest police station is in the town of Dimona 67km away.

Money
$ **Bank** Hapoalim I Ben Gurion Bd; ☎ 03 6532407/ landline*2407; 🕐 08.30–13.15 Sun &

Tue/Wed, 08.30–13.00 & 16.00–18.30 Mon & Thu

Post

📭 **Post office** 4 Tzichor St; ☏ 08 6588416; ☏ 08.00–18.00 Sun & Thu, 08.00–12.30 & 15.30–18.00 Mon/Tue, 08.00–13.30 Wed, 08.00–12.00 Fri. Changes travellers' cheques & offers Western Union.

WHAT TO SEE AND DO The word 'activity' certainly sums up the range of things to do, as most of the unusual selection of tourist attractions involve breaking a sweat. If it's horseriding, bone-shaking jeep tours, hiking, archery, riding a llama or rappelling you're looking for then you're in luck. The town has also discovered the appeal of alternative therapies and massage centres and apart from the Isrotel Ramon Inn spa there are countless independent therapists who work from home or a small clinic. The visitors' centre can provide you with a list and contact details. Therapies include massage, shiatsu, fortune telling, Chinese medicine, acupuncture and reflexology.

Ramon Crater Nature Reserve At 45km long, 8km wide and 500m deep, the Ramon Crater is a vast gash across the Negev Desert. The spectacularly impressive crater holds claim to being the world's largest karst erosion cirque (often referred to internationally by its Hebrew name *machtesh*), and was formed millions of years ago as the ocean that once covered this part of the desert retreated northwards. Around five million years ago, the Arava Rift Valley was formed causing great rivers

---

HIKING IN THE RAMON CRATER

MAKHTESH PROMENADE

A good place to start exploring the crater is from the **HaGamal (Camel) Lookout** which is located south of the visitors' centre along the **Makhtesh Promenade**. While not particularly over-exerting, the trail isn't for the faint-hearted as it skims the edge of the cliff to a suspended platform providing panoramic views of the crater. From the lookout the trail continues on past a **sculpture garden** and takes approximately one hour.

THE PRISM

From a little past the HaGamel Lookout a trail (4km/2hrs) leads down the sharp face of the crater to the **Prism**, a unique sandstone hill. The geological formation was created after the stones were baked in the roasting summer sun only to crystallise as they cooled, leaving prism-like shapes covering the hillside.

SAHARONIM STRONGHOLD

This is one of the most beautiful spots in the crater, a fact that seems compounded by the groups of onagers (wild ass) and ibex, which are often spotted at the natural spring here. From the **Be'erot campground** make your way by car to the Saharonim car park. From this point several trails fan out offering hikes of differing length and difficulty. The simplest (0.5km/1hr) incorporates the Nabatean stronghold at the top of the hill directly in front of the car park and then descends to **Ein Saharonim** (spring) which in winter flows with water. For a longer hike (5.5km/4hrs) continue on from Ein Saharonim across the Saharonim Ridge to the **Wadi Gavanim campsite** (crossing route 40). Continue in a clockwise direction along Nahal Gevanim ending back in the Saharonim car park.

to divert their course, their powerful flows eroding away the land and leaving in their wake a great crater.

The entire crater and its surrounding mountains have been incorporated into the nature reserve and it is one of the few places in the Negev where the IDF do not train. This has resulted in a fantastically open and free area to explore both on foot and by car. Hiking trails are exhaustive and the visitors' centre can sell you a book detailing hiking opportunities, while countless organisations arrange jeep tours around the main sites (see *Local tour operators*, above).

Desert Archery Park (✆ *050 5344598; www.desertarchery.co.il*) The unusual activity that is desert archery is played somewhat like a game of golf, yet instead of clubs you have bows and arrows and instead of a golf green, you have the vast expanse of the Ramon Crater. Courses of between 1km and 4km accommodate fitness levels and a half-hour archery training session is provided before setting off.

Bio Ramon (✆ *08 6588755;* ⊕ *08.00–17.00 Sat–Thu, 08.00–16.00 Fri (closes 1hr earlier in winter); admission adult/child 12/6NIS*) Located near the visitors' centre this small 'live museum' is generally aimed at children but can be fun for all ages wanting to learn about the four-legged residents of the desert.

Alpaca Farm (✆ *08 6588047/052 8977010; www.alpaca.co.il;* ⊕ *summer 08.30–18.30 daily; winter 08.30–16.30 daily*) This lovingly run farm began with the arrival of 190 llamas and alpacas who entered Israel from South America aboard a jet plane. Today the farm raises its more than 400 animals for their fine wool. Activities include touring the farm, feeding the animals, visiting the petting centre, horseriding into the desert and learning wool-making techniques. The farm is located a few km out of town and is well signposted. There is no public transport so you will need to get there under your own steam.

10

The Dead Sea and the Judean Desert

The eerie title of the sea that marks the lowest point on earth couldn't in fact be more apt. Shark-a-phobes be reassured, for in the salty waters of the Dead Sea nothing can live, its extreme salinity meaning all forms of living organism are unable to survive both in the water and on the shores that surround it. Yet in contrast to this rather gloomy picture of a barren and lifeless region, the Dead Sea has had a colourful religious, cultural and geological life and is today one of the country's most alluring and popular places to visit.

Biblical history abounds along the shores of the sea, with names such as John the Baptist, King David, King Herod, Sodom, Gomorrah and Lot intricately connected with its history. With the discovery of the **Dead Sea Scrolls** at Qumran in 1947 the Dead Sea's religious significance became unparalleled. In recent years, the phenomena that spurred King Herod to build his majestic spa on the cliff at **Masada** has been tapped and the sale of Dead Sea products for their therapeutic properties has become a worldwide trade, thrusting Israel into the tourist limelight.

GEOGRAPHY AND GEOLOGY

The Dead Sea is, in fact, a large, saline lake. Fed by the Jordan River that winds its way from the north forming the natural border between Jordan and Israel, the sea lays claim to being the lowest point on earth at 418m below sea level. Its inhospitable environment is due to the fact that the water comprises 30% salinity,

SAFETY

While drowning in water in which you can barely swim let alone fully submerge yourself in may seem ridiculous, the fact that it is difficult to swim in often causes the most problems for bathers. While bobbing around enjoying the newspaper, winds can quickly push you out to sea where you won't stop until reaching Jordan. It is, therefore, imperative (and the law) only to swim in designated areas where there are lifeguards.

The anecdote 'salt is good for healing wounds' couldn't be more apt – or painful – as at the Dead Sea. While it is said to be effective in the treatment of skin problems, the extreme salinity means it can burn excruciatingly if you have any broken skin. If you think you're free of scrapes and scratches, fear not, the sea will find a tiny one you didn't even know existed. Needless to say, splashing or putting your eyes anywhere near the water is painful and dangerous.

Danger signs along the coast that warn of sink holes should be strictly adhered to. The fragile coast is prone to dropping away suddenly and dramatically and leaving a gaping hole in the ground, a geological phenomena not as impressive if you're standing on it at the time.

Jerusalem, Tel Aviv
Jericho
Almog
Kibbutz Kalya
New Kalya Beach
Qumran NP
Biankini & Siesta Beach

Dead Sea

Mineral Beach & Spa

Ein Gedi Guesthouse
Ein Gedi NR
Arugot NR
Ein Gedi Beach
Kibbutz Ein Gedi
Ein Gedi Baths

Based on mapping by Carta, Jerusalem

Masada

ARAD
Tel Arad,
Beer Sheva,
Sde Boker,
Mitzpe Ramon
Ein Bokek
Ein Bokek Beach
Neveh Zohar

Nat'l Trail
Flour Cave
Perazim Gorge
Evaporation Pools
Lot's Wife Pillar (inside cave)
Dead Sea Works
Arava Desert, Eilat

Mt Sodom

0 — 5km
0 — 5 miles

THE DEAD SEA

up to nine-times saltier than other seas and oceans (that's about 300g of salt per kilogram of seawater). Yet this isn't just your ordinary table salt (although it does become that after a trip through the salt works at the southern end of the Dead Sea), the sea is laden with highly concentrated mineral salts. These extremely high concentrations means its density is a lot greater than that of fresh water, which is the underlying cause of both the sea's famed buoyancy and its therapeutic properties.

GETTING THERE

Visiting the Dead Sea is relatively easy either under your own steam or as part of a coach tour. Nothing, however, can beat renting a car and cruising along the coast road at your own pace. Public transport to and from the Dead Sea and desert in general is limited but there are regular services from Jerusalem and Tel Aviv that will drop you at the major sites (see pages 57 and 99).

TOURS

Finding a tour going down to the Dead Sea, Masada and Qumran is about as easy as finding sand in the desert but not always an enjoyable option. Cramming in as much as possible, tours hurtle out of Jerusalem zooming round the sites and heading home again. If time is of the essence and `this is your only option, ask at any hotel or hostel reception and they will book you onto a tour. Flat fees of around 100NIS normally get you on the bus and you then pay for entrance tickets separately.

PRACTICALITIES

The entire coast of the sea is 65km and can be divided into three main sections based on geography and tourist sites. The northern reaches are undoubtedly the most 'wild' where the coast is yet to see the infringement of great hotels and spa resorts and is home to the Qumran Caves where the Dead Sea Scrolls were discovered. The central section incorporates the Ein Gedi region and Masada archaeological site while the ultra-touristy Ein Bokek spa resort can be found at the sea's southern end.

Accommodation, eating options and facilities are in short supply in the area so you're best advised to book ahead, especially in summer when getting a room anywhere is unlikely at the last minute, and stock up on provisions. If you can stand feeling like a roast turkey then camping is also an option.

EIN GEDI

The stretch of coast known as Ein Gedi is one of the most popular and most-visited sections of the Dead Sea. Its proximity to Jerusalem (a mere one hour's drive) and the Masada archaeological site, its abundance of beach facilities, a beautiful valley oasis and a kibbutz spa make it a top spot along the route south. Unfortunately it has become a regular stop for busloads of children on school visits and groups of partying teenagers who pitch their tents and smoke up a *nargilah* at the beach's campsite.

Ein Gedi has a long and unique history and countless excavations in the area have unearthed evidence of settlement here for centuries. Throughout the Chacolithic, Persian and Hasmonean periods settlers concentrated around the springs while biblical references tell us that David sought refuge here from King Saul. During the Bar Kochba revolt (CE132–135), Ein Gedi was an important rebel outpost and it continued to thrive throughout the Roman and Byzantine periods. The antiquities park in the nature reserve delves further into the rich history of the area.

GETTING THERE AND AROUND Buses 486 and 487 from Jerusalem make the journey several times a day (1hr 20mins/32NIS), while bus 421 from Tel Aviv's Arlozorov Bus Station does the journey only once a day at 08.36 (3hrs 20mins/51NIS), returning at 14.30. Bus 384 to and from Beer Sheva and Arad makes the journey four-times daily and will drop you at Masada or Ein Bokek along the way. To get to Eilat make your way to Beer Sheva (see page 231) where there are several express lines a day.

WHERE TO STAY

⌂ **Ein Gedi Guesthouse** (120 rooms) ☏ 08 6594222; e eg@ein-gedi.org.il; www.ein-gedi.co.il. Nestled amongst the green lawns of the kibbutz the clean, spacious rooms feature kitchenettes, AC, TV & are based on HB or FB (kosher). The price includes entry into the Ein Gedi Spa. The **Ein Gedi Country Lodging** offers the same level of comfort but are on a B&B basis & do not include access to the spa. **$$$$**

⌂ **Ein Gedi Youth Hostel (HI)** (51 rooms) ☏ 08 6584165; e eingedy@iyha.org.il; www.iyha.org.il. The fact that it is extremely hard to get a bed in the hostel attests to its popularity & quality for

the money. Located a short walk from the entrance to the nature reserve it is exceptionally clean, offers dorms (**$**) & double rooms, AC & kosher breakfast. **$$**

⌂ **Ein Gedi Campsite** (*free entry*) The desert is hot, so don't expect to get any sleep whatsoever if you pitch your tent at the campsite between May & Sep. Out of season it is much more pleasant although be warned, in winter temperatures drop drastically as the sun goes down & you will need extremely warm attire & good sleeping bags. The campsite uses the beach facilities which are top notch.

WHERE TO EAT Eating options in the Ein Gedi area are as sparse as fish in the Dead Sea. Your best bet is the **Pundak Ein Gedi** (☏ *6594761;* ⏱ *10.00–18.00 daily; mains $$*) a cafeteria-style restaurant near the petrol station. Meals are mediocre but fresh and the air conditioning means it's normally full. Guests at the Ein Gedi Guesthouse get breakfast and lunch and/or dinner so if you're staying a few days you might want to consider this option. There is also a restaurant in the **spa** (see above).

OTHER PRACTICALITIES There is a petrol station near the Ein Gedi campsite and beach, and small supermarket in the kibbutz, but other than this, services are sparse.

WHAT TO SEE
Ein Gedi Beach Ein Gedi Beach is one of the – if not the – most popular beaches along the Dead Sea. The fact that it is free, however, is pretty much all it has going for it. The picnic area is crowded with barbecuing, music-playing families and entry to the water is hindered by sharp rocks and mud. But shower and toilet facilities are top notch and if you don't mind the noise the people-watching opportunities are great. A 24-hour beach snack bar and a petrol station are also on site.

Ein Gedi Nature Reserve (✆ 08 6584285; ☉ open all year Apr–Sep 08.00–17.00; Oct–Mar 08.00–16.00; admission adult/child 23/12NIS plus an extra 23/12NIS for Arugot Nature Reserve) The 25km² Ein Gedi Nature Reserve is a true tropical oasis, providing a lifeline for flora and fauna in an otherwise dry, barren expanse of desert landscape. Situated on the Syrian-African Rift Valley the reserve is fed year round by four springs: David, Arugot, Shulamit and Gedi. Marked trails of varying length and difficulty wind gently uphill, along (and sometimes through) rivers and streams, allowing for fantastic views over the Dead Sea and Jordan Mountains, wildlife spotting and spectacular waterfalls. The **David spring trek** can vary in length between 1.5km and 3km depending on the route chosen, and detours to hidden waterfalls. Allow 90 minutes to three hours, which leaves time for a cooling-off swim in one of the waterfall pools. The longer, 4-km **Arugot trek** is for the slightly more energetic and takes approximately four hours. The extra effort is rewarded by an impressive waterfall. Maps are supplied free of charge from the National Park offices on entry.

Historically the Ein Gedi Nature Reserve was an important area for growing unusual plants. Therapeutic and aromatic plants were grown and dates, a highly sought-after commodity, could be grown successfully. To this day the oasis still boasts an impressive and fundamental array of plant and tree species of east African origin. A large variety of mammals, birds and reptiles are also drawn to the natural oasis, the Nubian ibex and Syrian hyrax being the most noticeable and easily spotted residents. The local celebrities, however, are the small colony of leopards who reside in the nearby hills, but these shy creatures are infrequently seen.

Just outside the reserve, the **Ein Gedi antiquities park** contains the remains of an ancient synagogue and gives a brief insight into the history of the area. Built during the Byzantine period by Jewish residents of the area, this ornate synagogue was an integral part of the flourishing community. After the Arab conquest, however, Ein Gedi was reduced to the small kibbutz settlement it is today. Kibbutz Ein Gedi is situated just above the reserve.

While the reserve and antiquities park are open year round, winter flooding of the David and Arugot rivers often results in the park's closure and hiking is prohibited. The best time to visit is spring or autumn when the summer heat relents and the park is less crowded.

Ein Gedi Kibbutz and spas (✆ 08 6594221/6594726; www.ein-gedi.co.il; e eg@ein-gedi.org.il) The beautiful, palm-fringed kibbutz has successfully cashed in on the rapidly growing international phenomena of Dead Sea treatments. The kibbutz's main economy today centres on tourism and while the flash hotels along the coast at Ein Bokek may have all the mod cons, Ein Gedi has years of experience and the added bonus of its pretty, leafy surroundings and a real family atmosphere. A small supermarket is a good place to stock up on the basics if you are planning picnics or

The incredible buoyancy of the Dead Sea makes for a fun and slightly surreal experience, bobbing up and down like a cork. Beaches have subsequently popped up along the coast ranging from free and crowded to expensive and crowded to private and crowded. In peak seasons finding a place to put your towel is unlikely but out of season (especially midweek) beaches are much quieter. The following beaches run from north to south:

New Kalya Beach (↘ 02 9942391; ⊕ open daily: summer 08.00–18.00; winter 08.00–17.00; admission adult/child 25/15NIS) This stretch of coast marks the northernmost end of the Dead Sea and while it is a big favourite with Jerusalemites (a mere 25 minutes' drive from the capital) it is yet to establish itself on the foreigner trail. Named for the nearby Kibbutz Kalya the beach is a tranquil and relaxing place to enjoy the fruits of the Dead Sea – salt and mud. Facilities: a comfortable beach bar, towel rental, massages, nearby **go-kart track** (↘ 02 942680). For details of how to get there, see page 253.

Biankini and **Siesta Beach** (↘ 02 9400033/9400266; ⊕ 08.00–20.00 daily; admission 30NIS) One of the most authentic-feeling beaches along the sea it has an atmosphere of unpretentious, laidback Moroccan charm, a range of classy facilities and most importantly, a lovely beach. Facilities: traditional, tented **Moroccan Restaurant** (↘ 02 9944111; ⊕ 08:30–19:30 daily; mains $$), luxury cabins (↘ 02 9400266; f 02 9947303; www.biankini.co.il; cabin $$$$) and a great campsite (↘ 02 9944111; 70NIS pp). For details of how to get there, see page 253.

Mineral Beach and Spa (↘ 02 9944888; ⊕ 09.00–17.00 Sun–Thu, 09.00–18.00 Fri/Sat; admission 35NIS) The unflashy Mineral Beach, located 20km south of Qumran, has a wide beach with good sea access, especially for children, with plenty of shaded areas. The spa is simple but enjoyable and there are plenty of mud pools for slathering yourself in. Facilities: warm sulphur pool, spa with massage treatments, freshwater pool and cafeteria.

Ein Gedi Beach (↘ 08 6594433; admission free) (see page 248)

Ein Gedi Spa Beach (↘ 08 6594813; ⊕ summer 08.00–19.00 daily; winter 08.00–17.00 daily; weekday/weekend 90/100NIS) (see page 248)

Ein Bokek Beach (Hordus Beach) (↘ 08 6594433; ⊕ open 08.00–17.00 daily; admission free). This free beach has several pros and unfortunately several cons. The shallow waters of the evaporation pools create white sandy beaches leading down to clear, turquoise waters that gently lap against the sheltered shore. On the downside, behind you is the sprawling and unsightly mass of gigantic hotels and tourist tack. It is also one of the sea's busiest beaches, especially in peak seasons. Facilities: a 24-hour restaurant (see page 253), showers and a plethora of shops, malls and eateries in the resort behind.

self-catering meals but don't expect too much. The kibbutz runs both the on-site **Wellness Centre** and **Ein Gedi Spa** just along the coast. The **Ein Gedi Wellness Centre** offers top-of-the-range holistic treatments including Ayurveda, massages, mud wraps, salt peeling and herbal saunas while the **Ein Gedi Spa** (↘ 08 6594813; ⊕ summer 08.00–19.00 daily; winter 08.00–17.00 daily; weekday/weekend 90/100NIS), 4km south of Ein Gedi Kibbutz, has honed the internationally famed Dead Sea products to the maximum. The spa is a fantastic way to experience the sea's therapeutic properties with a huge array of facilities and treatments. Six thermo-mineral water pools, massages, mud baths and an outdoor freshwater pool will

Renowned worldwide for its purported therapeutic properties, the Dead Sea has become a honeypot for those in search of natural relief from a whole host of ailments. Spa resorts and health clinics along the coast have honed the region's climate, unique conditions and medicinal products into a series of specialist treatments: **climatotherapy**, hich draws on climatic elements such as humidity, pressure and temperature; **balneotherapy**, a treatment that uses the thick black Dead Sea mud; and **thalassotherapy**, which involves bathing in the unique waters of the sea. The following are considered the best Dead Sea spas:

DMZ Medical Spa (Lot Spa Dead Sea Hotel, Ein Bokek; ☎ 08 6689200; www.dmz-medical-spa.com) Treats psoriasis, asthma, orthopaedic and cardiac rehabilitation, cystic fibrosis and skin diseases.
Ein Gedi Spa (see previous page) Renowned for neurological metabolic disorders, traumatic ailments, allergies, bronchial asthma & rheumatic illnesses.
Solarium Spa (Ein Bokek; ☎ 08 6584410; ⏱ 07.00–17.00 daily; admission 50NIS) Specialises in dermatological diseases, particularly psoriasis.

leave you feeling clean, young and healthy. A meal in the spa's restaurant, which serves a healthy selection of meat dishes, salads and desserts, is included in the entry price.

AROUND EIN GEDI

QUMRAN NATIONAL PARK (☎ 02 9942235; www.parks.org.il; ⏱ Apr–Sep 08.00–17.00 daily; Oct–Mar 08.00–16.00 daily; admission adult/child 18/8NIS) The isolated site of Qumran perched on the cliffs at the northernmost end of the Dead Sea was the scene of the discovery of perhaps the world's most significant biblical texts, the **Dead Sea Scrolls**. Today housed inside their very own display hall in Jerusalem's Israel Museum, the scrolls have been dated from between the 3rd century BCE to CE68 and are older than any other surviving biblical manuscripts by almost 1,000 years. Their discovery by a Bedouin shepherd in 1947 gave rise to almost a decade of intensive excavation, archaeologists and historians desperate to discover the authors and age of the thousands of fragments (totaling 800–900 scripts) that were found. It was during this time that they stumbled upon Qumran, a complex of structures located on a barren terrace between the caves and the Dead Sea.

While Qumran had been populated since as far back as the 8th century BCE it was its later inhabitants who put their hand to the scrolls. The Essenes were a sectarian community who lived in this remote region for 200 years, from the Hasmonean period through the Jewish revolt against the Romans. They were breakaways, rejecting the rest of the Jewish people and appeared to have lived a communal life of ritual purity. The scrolls themselves contain versions of the Old Testament as well as texts relating to their sectarian existence. One of the most hotly contested theories that arose from the discovery of the scrolls was that they may have been an early influence on Christianity. Parallels in belief and rules of conduct between the scrolls and the New Testament have sparked heated debate across the world.

The site itself is nowhere near as interesting as its history and the scrolls themselves but is worth a quick stop if you're in the area. The ritualistic and pure life led by the Essenes can be seen in the remains of assembly halls, ritual baths and scriptorium (writing room) as well as a kitchen, dining room and large water cistern.

Getting there All buses heading from Tel Aviv and Jerusalem towards Ein Gedi will drop you at the Kalya Junction for access to the Biankini and Siesta Beach and Qumran Junction for the archaeological park.

MASADA

(↖ *08 6584207/8; www.parks.org.il;* ⊕ *Apr–Sep 08.00–16.00 daily; Oct–Mar 08.00–17.00 daily; admission adult/child cable car & admission 61/34NIS, snake route 23/12NIS*) More than just one of the country's most-visited tourist destinations, the archaeological site of Masada represents Israeli patriotism at its proudest. Upon the protruding rock that towers some 400m above the western shore of the Dead Sea, IDF soldiers come to swear allegiance, repeating the mantra 'Masada shall not fall again'. For it was here, on the precipitous rock shelf that the ancient fortress built by Herod the Great in the 1st century BCE became the 20th-century symbol of Jewish heroism. The fortress was captured by the Zealots, a Jewish sect in CE66 in their revolt against Rome and became the last standing Jewish stronghold. After a long siege, the Romans finally stormed the fortress in CE73, only to find that all 960 Zealots had committed suicide rather than surrender to their forces. Today, it is one of the most important stops on the Jewish pilgrimage route and in 2001 was awarded UNESCO World Heritage status. A new museum complex opened in 2007 now displays some of the most impressive artefacts excavated from the ruins as well as depicting the life, times and history of this fascinating site.

HISTORY Although finds date the origin of the site to the Chacolithic Period 6,000 years ago, it wasn't until Herod got his hands on it that Masada really came into its own. Major fortifications between 37BCE and 31BCE included two beautiful, ornate palaces, heavy defensive walls, state-of-the-art aqueducts and water cisterns and a bathhouse complex. In CE66, following Herod's death, the Jewish revolt against the Romans saw a group of rebels overcome the Roman garrison stationed at Masada. After the fall of Jerusalem in CE70, the rebels were joined by Zealots and families fleeing the devastation only to be stormed by the Romans three years later. They established camps at the base of the fortress and laid a complicated and arduous siege to it, one that would last many months.

GETTING THERE There are two ways to approach Masada: from route 90 that runs along the Dead Sea (5mins off the main road) or along route 3199 from Arad. The youth hostel, visitors centre, cable cars and Snake Path are all accessed from the eastern Dead Sea entrance while visitors arriving for the Sound and Light Show or wishing to ascend the Roman Ramp will need to approach from the direction of Arad. There isn't a through road from the western side to the Dead Sea so be aware that if you come from this direction you will need to take the very long route back to Arad and down past Ein Bokek (1hr drive) to reach the coast and hostel. Buses heading to Ein Gedi from Beer Sheva and Arad will stop at the junction on the way (see *Arad*, page 254) while buses coming from Jerusalem and Tel Aviv will continue on to the archaeological site from Ein Gedi (see *Ein Gedi*, page 247).

WHERE TO STAY AND EAT

Masada Guest House (HI) (88 rooms) ↖ 08 9953222; e massada@iyha.org.il; www.iyha.org.il. Located just off the Dead Sea route 90 sits this huge, immaculate hostel offering more than just staggering views over the Dead Sea. Rooms have AC, TV & minibar & there is a swimming pool in summer. Internet access is available & guests receive a 25% discount off Masada cable-car tickets. Kosher breakfast is included & other meals can be ordered for 45NIS. *Single-sex dorms are 142NIS.* $$$

WHAT TO SEE

The Snake Path The path provides the eastern entrance to the site but the walk uphill is steep and tiring, especially during the blistering summer heat. The alternative option, and one that is adopted by most tour groups, is to take the cable car, which leaves from near the car park and finishes at the top of the Snake Path. Both begin from the Dead Sea road.

The Roman Ramp The ramp that ascends to the fortress from the west side is a third option of entering and exiting the site. The ramp can be accessed only from the Arad road.

Palaces Many of the ancient structures and buildings have been restored, one of the most striking being the wall paintings inside the two Herodian palaces. The three-terraced **Northern Palace** acted as Herod's personal quarters, while the vast complex that comprised the **Western Palace** was home to servants, workshops and storehouses. Inside it is possible to see the remains of Herod's throne room, arranged around a central courtyard. Just to the south of the Western Palace are the remains of Herod's swimming pool, another example of the luxurious lifestyle that he enjoyed at Masada.

Bathhouses Designed in a Romanesque style, the bathhouses have been well restored and show the intricate engineering that went into the creation of Herod's luxurious early spa. The bathhouses are located just south of the Northern Palace.

Roman villa In architectural design reminiscent of the great villas of Rome, the wonderfully restored mansion is a perfect example of the level of luxury and grandeur afforded to those that resided here. After the Zealots took control of the fortress, many of the buildings were divided up to accommodate the substantial population.

Synagogue The incredible discovery of the Masada synagogue has led archaeologists and historians to believe that it may be the oldest Jewish house of prayer in the world. It is the only synagogue to be dated to the time of the Second Temple and contained fragments of scrolls from Ezekiel and Deuteronomy.

Roman camps There are a total of eight Roman camps that surround the lower reaches of the Masada cliff. It was here that Roman garrisons stationed themselves during their long and relentless siege of the fortress. Thanks to the arid climate and soil, the camps are considered the best-preserved Roman army camps ever discovered.

Byzantine church Southeast of the synagogue is another large building complex within which was discovered a 5th-century Byzantine church. A small portion of semi-restored mosaics can be seen at the rear of the building.

Storehouses On the right just through the East Gate are the semi-restored remains of 11 storehouses. Amphorae and jars containing remnants of wine, oil and flour were found in the larger rooms while it is believed valuables and weaponry may have been kept in the smaller ones.

Sound and light show (❧ 08 9959333; Apr–Aug 21.00 Tue & Thu; Sep/Oct 20.00 Tue & Thu; admission 41NIS) Shown against the backdrop of the western side of the mountain (reached from the Arad road), this 40-minute show depicts the history of the site in an impressive light display. The audio is in Hebrew but there are earphones for English, French, German and Spanish visitors. Tickets must be booked in advance through the Arad Visitors' Centre (✆ 08 9954409) who also organise transport there and back (see page 254).

EIN BOKEK

All good things have to come to an end and the natural, rugged beauty of the Dead Sea does so at the Ein Bokek hotel resort. This conglomeration of enormous chain hotels and their attached luxury spas, souvenir shops and food kiosks are an eyesore along the wild stretch of coastline, however, the hotels are expensive and specialist, attracting guests who come to relax and enjoy some pampering and relaxation, not party all night. There is a definite touristy feel to the highly developed strip but a very nice (if overcrowded) free **Hordus Beach** (⊕ 08.00–17.00 daily) can be found nestled amidst the towering buildings. And as a guest, there is no doubt that your Dead Sea therapeutic experience would be a top-of-the-range – if decidedly mass-produced – one. About 3km south of Ein Bokek (but normally clumped under the same title) are the **hot springs** that have been diverted into several five-star hotels that specialise in therapeutic treatments.

GETTING THERE There are four buses a day to and from Arad (45mins) which continue to Ein Gedi, stopping at Masada along the way.

HIKING MOUNT SODOM

Sodom Mountain and Lot's Wife Cave

While there is no proof that this is in fact the biblical site where God unleashed his fury upon the city of Sodom for its 'sins', it has long since been the traditional spot. The 11km by 3km mountain range almost wholly consists of salt and is, according to the Old Testament book of Genesis, the site of the two towns of Sodom and Gomorrah, which were destroyed by God with a rain of fire and brimstone (sulphur) for their wickedness. Before the destruction ensued, God sent two angels to warn all good men to leave the evil town. The angels found only one good man, Lot, who they saved along with his wife and daughters, warning them not to look back. When Lot's wife disobeyed the warning she was turned into a pillar of salt. Tour buses and signposts today point to a pillar above the entrance to a cave just off the main road as that of Lot's Wife and it marks another quick stop along the pilgrimage route.

Nahal Perazim and the Flour Cave

At 3km south of Lot's Wife Cave (or Sodom Cave), a small turn-off on the right between kilometre markers 193 and 194 leads to the Flour Cave. So named because of the fine, white powdery chalk that covers everything it touches (including your hair, clothes and face), the cave is part of Nahal Perazim, a beautiful, narrow, dry gorge. A 15-minute walk through the gorge will bring you to the entrance of the pitch-black cave (torches are advisable) where it is but a short walk to the other end. White floury steps lead up and out of the 18,000–20,000-year-old cave where you can return to the car park along the path above the gorge. Alternatively, more seasoned hikers can follow a blue (then black) marked trail that leads from the exit of the Flour Cave up Mount Sodom.

GETTING AROUND The **Hertz** car-rental office (✆ *08 6584530; –⏰ 08.30–16.00 Sun–Thu, 08.30–13.30 Fri*) is located in the **Petra Shopping Centre**.

WHERE TO STAY Four star is the lowest-ranked hotel you're likely to find at Ein Bokek and all pride themselves on quality, service and top-of-the-range facilities.

⌂ **Crowne Plaza Dead Sea** (304 rooms) ✆ 08 6591919; e ds_gmsec@hiil.co.il; www.ichotelsgroup.com. Luxury compliments of the Crowne Plaza chain of international hotels. Rooms are wood floored, elegant & fresh & have all the mod cons. Facilities include a bistro restaurant, a state-of-the-art fitness & spa centre & indoor and outdoor pools. **$$$$$**

⌂ **Le Meridien Dead Sea Resort** (600 rooms) ✆ 08 6591234; e reservations@fattal-hotels-israel.com;

www.fattal.co.il. Considered the *crème de la crème* of Dead Sea spa resorts, Le Meridien is the place to come for a real pampering session to beat all others. There is not 1, but 2 spa centres, the Mineralia spa, the largest and most luxurious in the area with 25 treatment rooms & 2 indoor and outdoor Dead Sea water pools, & the exclusive Gallery spa. Minimum of 2 nights on weekends. **$$$$$**

WHERE TO EAT For eating options, Ein Bokek is like an oasis of **restaurants**, cheap **kiosks** and **supermarkets**. The 24-hour **On the Beach Restaurant** (✆ *08 6520231; ⏰ open 24 hours daily; mains $$$*) offers standard sandwiches, grilled meats, pizza and pasta while the **Inbar Sandwich and Espresso Bar** (✆ *08 6584671; ⏰ 07.00–02.00 daily; mains $$*) in the **Blue Sky Shopping Centre** has fresh sandwiches, milkshakes and desserts.

OTHER PRACTICALITIES Ein Bokek has countless shops selling the fruits of the Dead Sea (particularly the strip directly in front of Hordus Beach). There is a supermarket, pharmacy and hotel receptions can offer post and internet services.

ARAD

The small, desert city of Arad is most well known for its ancient namesake, today located a few kilometres away at Tel Arad. Yet the city is rather pleasant – if not attractive – in its own right and considerable efforts over recent years to improve its image have been successful. Its altitude and unique, arid climate make it an ideal place for asthma sufferers and plans to develop the city into a centre for medical treatments are underway. Public transport links with the Dead Sea (only 25km away), Jerusalem and Beer Sheva are good in desert terms and there is a modern, ethnically diverse feel to the place. The **Artists' Quarter (Eshet Lot)** in the industrial zone is worth a visit if you're in the area and comprises works by local artists who aim to capture the beauty and ruggedness of the desert in their works.

GETTING THERE Bus 389 from Tel Aviv makes the journey four-times daily (10.00, 13.00, 18.30 and 20:15) (2hrs/34NIS) returning at 06.00, 08.30, 14.00 and 17.00. To Ein Bokek on the Dead Sea there are four buses daily at 06.37, 10.13, 12.58 and 03.43 (45mins) ,which continue to Ein Gedi, stopping at Masada along the way. There are several buses a day to and from Beer Sheva (45mins/14.80NIS) from where you can connect to Jerusalem, Eilat, Sde Boker and Mitzpe Ramon.

TOURIST INFORMATION The **Arad Visitors' Centre** (✆ *08 9954409; ⏰ Apr–Sep 08.00–17.00 daily; Oct–Mar 08.00–16.00 daily; admission adult/child 23/12NIS*) is run by the Israel Nature and National Parks Protection Authority and provides a fun water, light and sound show depicting the history and geology of the region. They also arrange tickets and transport to Masada's sound and light show (see page 243). The centre is located in central Arad near the mall.

WHERE TO STAY

⌂ **Arad Guest House (HI)** (50 rooms) 4 Ha'atad St; ☏ 08 9957150; e arad@iyha.org.il; www.iyha.org.il. Clean, simple dorms with TV, AC, bunks & kosher breakfast. The reception is closed on Shabbat & you need to call ahead if you're arriving in the afternoons & dorm rooms are not available on weekends. *Dorms (104NIS).* **$$$**

⌂ **Margoa Arad Hotel** (146 rooms) ☏ 08

9951222; e gm@margoa.com; www.margoa.com. Posing as a luxury spa hotel the Margoa is better described as an ambitious, mid-range establishment. Unimaginative but tidy, comfortable rooms are good enough while the hotel offers a bar, swimming pool (in summer) & asthma clinic. They can also organise tours to the surrounding areas. Breakfast included. **$$$**

WHAT TO SEE

Tel Arad (☏ *08 7762170; www.parks.org.il;* ⊕ *Apr–Sep 08.00–17.00 daily; Oct–Mar 08.00–16.00 daily; admission adult/child 12/6NIS*) About 10km east of Arad on the road to Beer Sheva are the remains of not one but two ancient settlements. In the 2nd century BCE, a huge Canaanite city was built here, its 1km² area making it the largest excavated Canaanite settlement in the country. Some of the excavated remains of houses have been fully restored, their distinctive shape and layout having coined a new archaeological term 'Aradian house'. Further up the hill, an Israelite settlement dates to about 1000BCE during the reign of King Solomon and came into being some 1,500 years after the abandonment of the Canaanite city. Referred to as a citadel fortress, it lasted throughout the reigns of the kings of Judah until its destruction between 597BCE and 577BCE, during which time Jerusalem was under siege from the Babylonians. Inside the fortress courtyard is an Israelite temple, a smaller version of King Solomon's Temple in Jerusalem.

11

The Arava Desert

As the desert makes its way towards the vibrant city of Eilat there appears to be a lull before the party storm. Civilisation gets sparser, the landscape more remote and facilities fewer and farther between. Yet the Arava Desert is in fact one of the most bewitching regions of Israel's south where Bedouin communities thrive, the Spice Route starts its long trek westwards and where the air is the freshest in the country. Kibbutzim dot the fringes of route 90, their isolated positions and organic farming practices producing an ideal getaway for those seeking the utmost in seclusion and nature. And nature is the name of the game in the southern Arava, the **Yotvata Hai Bar Reserve** (see page 5), **Timna Park** (see page 258) and **International Birding and Research Centre** (see page 268) providing a great insight into the desert's wilder strip of land.

GETTING THERE AND AROUND

This is one of the most inaccessible areas of the country and getting to sights is difficult by public transport. Renting a car in Beer Sheva (see page 231) is by far the best way to get the most out of your time in this remote region. Bus 397 from Beer Sheva stops at the junctions to the kibbutzim and parks along the Arava Desert on its way to Eilat. There are seven buses daily in each direction.

TOURIST INFORMATION

The small **Yotvata Visitors' Centre** (⊕ 08.00–15.00 Sat–Thu, 08.00–13.00 Fri) is located directly outside the mall in Kibbutz Yotvata along route 90. The **Shaharut Camel Riders** (see below) organise camel treks in the wilds of the Arava Desert and there are countless tour operators in Eilat (see page 250) that can arrange 4x4 and birdwatching trips.

WHERE TO STAY

Accommodation is limited to the kibbutz lodgings, which can be rather pricey, although the Timna Park, Yotvata Hai Bar Reserve and **Ye'elim Desert Holiday Village** (✆ 08 6374362; *check in from 10.00 Sun–Fri, 19.00–21.00 Sat*) at **Kibbutz Yotvata** offer camping opportunities if you have your own equipment. For accommodation at **Shaharut Camel Riders** or the **Kibbutz Lotan Guesthouse**, see page 259.

⌂ **Keren Kolot** (22 rooms) Kibbutz Ketura; ✆ 08 6356658; e kerenkolot@ketura.co.il; www.keren-kolot-israel.co.il. If you're not deterred by the smell of cow excrement (& you get used to it rather fast) then the spacious, comfortable rooms offered on the kibbutz are a good base for visiting the area. A communal pool (in summer), simple kosher dining room (25NIS extra), café & bicycle rental

ARAVA DESERT
North

Dead Sea, Jerusalem

Beer Sheva, Tel Aviv

National Trail

Kibbutz Yahel

Ne'ot Smadar Restaurant

Kibbutz Ne'ot Smadar

Birdwatching site

Kibbutz Lotan

Kibbutz Ketura

Biklat Uvda

Yotvata Visitors Centre

Camel Riders (Shaharut)

Kibbutz Yotvata

Yotvata Hai Bar Reserve (wildlife reserve)

National Trail

Timna Park

Solomon's Pillars

0   5km
0   5 miles

Based on mapping by Carta, Jerusalem

are extras as well as tours of the experimental orchards where exotic, hard-to-pronounce fruits are grown. $$

Kibbutz Yahel Hostel (15 rooms) Kibbutz Yahel; ℩ 08 6357967. Simple hostel rooms are offered in the small, pleasant Kibbutz Yahel just off route 90 & they also have fancier cabins with AC. A swimming pool, kosher dining room & sports facilities are available for the guests' use. *Fancier cabins with AC for 200NIS ($$$) more.* $

WHERE TO EAT ✗

Dining options are sparse and often eating in the simple kibbutz dining rooms are the only choice. The **Yotvata Rest Stop** (℩ *08 6357363;* ⊕ *05.30–19.00 Sun–Thu, 05.30–18.00 Fri, 07.00–20.00 Sat; mains $$*) has a buffet-style canteen with OK mains and a really good selection of desserts (be sure to try some of the Choco chocolate milk for which the kibbutz is famous). The wonderful organic farm shop **Ne'ot Smadar** (℩ *08 6358180;* ⊕ *08.30–16.00 Sun–Thu, 08.30–13.00 Fri; mains $$*) at the Ketura Junction offers a few pasta choices which are delicious and oh-so-healthy while the **Shaharut Restaurant** (see *Camel Riders,* page 259) serves freshly baked Bedouin fare in a traditional atmosphere. At the Be'er Menuha Junction on route 90 the **Pundak 101** (℩ *08 6345101;* ⊕ *24hrs; mains $$*) is a gaudy-looking 24-hour park complete with cafeteria-style diner and crocodile and python exhibit.

OTHER PRACTICALITIES

Between Beer Sheva in the Negev Desert and Eilat in the far south of the Arava there is a distinct lack of any kind of facilities. The tiny Kibbutz Yotvata has a small supermarket and petrol station and the kibbutzim dotted along route 90 offer minimal services.

WHAT TO SEE

TIMNA PARK (℩ *08 6316756; www.timna-park.co.il;* ⊕ *summer 07.30–18.00; winter 08.00–17.00; admission* *adult/child 39/34NIS*) The 90km² Timna Valley is home to some of the country's most unique geological formations, a rich and powerful history and a never-ending array of hiking trails. Historically Timna stands alone as the earliest, most technologically advanced and productive copper mining centre in the ancient world. From the 14th to the 12th centuries BCE, the Egyptians operated a vast copper mining centre here. While this was the site's most productive period, evidence has pointed to continued mining communities operating here as far back as the late Neolithic period.

The vast U-shaped valley is surrounded by mountains that hew a myriad colours over the course of a day, hiking trails radiating in every direction over and around them. A car is a prerequisite for visiting the park as there is no public transport and most sites can be driven to. Nevertheless, there are ample opportunities to get away from the road and into the heart of the desert. A hiking map is supplied at the entrance detailing treks of between one and ten hours. Among the park's many attractions are the famous **Solomon's Pillars**, formed by years of erosion of the pink sandstone cliff face from which they protrude. Other notable sites include the rock-cut **Mushroom**, **Valley of Inscriptions** and the **ancient mines**. Camping is possible at the park's entrance but you will need to call ahead to reserve a spot (30NIS).

ARAVA DESERT
South - Eilat Environs

KIBBUTZ LOTAN (☏ *08 6356935;* e *lotan-programs@lotan.ardom.co.il; www. kibbutzlotan.com*) The bohemian kibbutz of Lotan is ideal for hippies-at-heart or weekend hippies in search of some natural living. With the word 'eco' in front of all their activities guests are left in no doubt as to their ethos (and no, you won't be finding TVs inside any of their mud-coated guesthouses). At the kibbutz you can learn how to build your own eco-friendly house, enjoy a *watsu* (water shiatsu) massage in the spa centre, relax in the swimming pool or partake in a spot of birdwatching. Guesthouses (*$$*) are pleasant but simple and somewhat pricey for what you get. The atmosphere on the kibbutz is lovely, however, and you pay for the experience.

CAMEL RIDERS (*Shaharut;* ☏ *08 6373218; www.camel-riders.com*) Camel caravan trips ranging from a few hours up to eight days (75–1,500NIS) are the quintessential desert experience with roaring open fires, sleeping under the stars and a mighty sore rear end being part and parcel of the experience. They also organise jeep tours, have a restaurant and offer Bedouin-style half-board accommodation in a large communal tent or simple, private huts (60/180NIS). If you're arriving by bus (bus 397 between Beer Sheva and Eilat) call ahead to get picked up from the junction.

For a touch of culture, history and Holy Land charm, don't come to Eilat. If, however, you're after some hedonistic, raucous and rather tacky seaside fun, then this is definitely the place. After driving through the serene, staggeringly beautiful landscape of the Negev and Arava deserts, Eilat comes as quite as shock. Perched on the tiny strip of Red Sea coast that Israel lays claim to it is something of a Middle East Las Vegas (without the gambling). Row upon row of big chain hotels line the coast, the glittering Red Sea water swarms with all manner of sea craft and squealing sun-seekers, and the pumping neon-lit pedestrian strip is crammed with restaurants, beach bars and shopping malls. A big favourite with boisterous Israeli teenagers enjoying their first trip away from the folks, Eilat can be rowdy and wild. Nevertheless, it has also managed to maintain a noisy family atmosphere especially on the beaches further along the south coast. The 14km stretch of Israel's Red Sea coast means that day trips to Petra in Jordan and Egypt's Sinai coast are easily accessible, while day trips into the southern Arava Desert are welcome ways to escape the city.

The city enjoys almost 365 days a year of sunshine, a year-round water temperature of 21°C and a winter low of 20°C, making it the country's only beach resort that quite literally never stops. Summer temperatures can reach in excess of 40°C but because of its dry, desert atmosphere and lack of humidity remains rather pleasant and often more bearable than the intense, sticky humidity of the Mediterranean.

GETTING THERE
Bus The central bus station is located on HaTemarin St (✆ 08 6365120) and can be a somewhat disorganised and busy place. Bus 394 from Tel Aviv's central bus station does the journey every 90 minutes (5hrs 15mins/65NIS) but gets booked up in summer by hordes of loud teenagers so reserve a seat in advance. From Jerusalem bus 444 departs Eilat at 07.00, 10.00, 14.15 and 17.00 (5hrs/65NIS)

Air Most commercial flights to Eilat come from Haifa, Tel Aviv's Dov Hoz or Ben Gurion airports with Arkia or Israir airlines. **Arkia** (*Red Canyon Mall;* ✆ 08 6384888) and **Israir** (*Shalom Centre;* ✆ 08 6340666) offer flights to Tel Aviv for between 150NIS and 500NIS, or Haifa for about 450NIS. The airport is in the centre of town and is a five-minute walk to the promenade or city centre.

Land The Taba (see page 37) and Arava (Yitzhak Rabin) (see page 37) border crossings provide overland entry into Egypt's Sinai Peninsula and Jordan respectively..

Car rental
🚗 **Avis** Shalom Centre; ✆ 08 6373164/5; www.avis.co.il; ⏰ 08.00–17.00 Sun–Thu, 08.00–14.00 Fri, 08.00–12.00 Sat. Minimum of 3 days' rental.
🚗 **Europcar** Shalom Centre (Store 1387); ✆ 08 7918014; f 08 6378937; ⏰ 08.00–18.00 Sun–Thu, 08.00–13.00 Fri
🚗 **Sixt** Shalom Centre (Store 1018); ✆ 08 6373511; f 08 6373512; www.sixt.com; ⏰ 08.00–17.00 Sun–Fri. Cars from 160NIS per day.

GETTING AROUND Eilat's city centre is small and so walking is the easiest way to get around. There are taxi's everywhere and fares generally cost around 10NIS. Bus 15 from the town centre makes the 7km journey along the south coast to the Taba border regularly stopping at the beaches, major hotels and Underwater Observatory (see page 267) along the way.

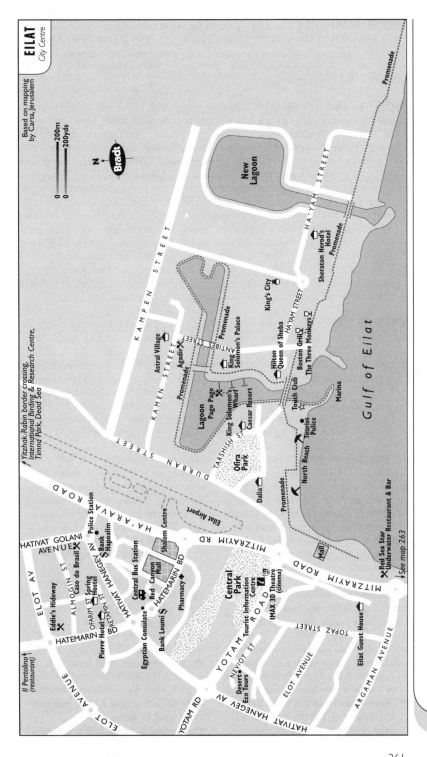

EILAT
City Centre

Based on mapping
by Carta, Jerusalem

0 — 200m
0 — 200yds

N Bradt

Yitzhak Rabin border crossing,
International Birding & Research Centre,
Timnd Park, Dead Sea

KAMPEN STREET

New Lagoon

HA'YAM STREET

Sheraton Herod's Hotel
Promenade

King's City

KAMEN STREET

Astral Village

Agadir

Promenade

ANTIBES STREET

Lagoon

Pago Pago

King Solomon's Wharf

King Solomon's Palace

Promenade

HA'YAM STREET

Hilton
Queen of Sheba

Boston Grill
The Three Monkeys

DURBAN STREET

TARSHISH ST

Caesar Resort

Touch Club

Marina

Ofira Park

Tourist Police

North Beach

Gulf of Eilat

Dalia

Promenade

Red Sea Star
Underwater Restaurant & Bar

See map 263

HA'ARAVA ROAD

Police Station

Bank Hapoalim

Shalom Centre

Eilat Airport

MITZRAYIM RD

Il Pentolino
(restaurant)

ELOT AVENUE

ELOT AV

HATIVAT GOLANI AVENUE

Eddie's Hideway

ALMOGIN ST

Caso do Brasil

Spring Hostel

OFARIM ST

Pierre Hotel

BRETANIN ST

HATEMARIN BD

HATIVAT HANEGEV

Egyptian Consulate

Central Bus Station

Red Canyon Mall

Bank Leumi

HATEMARIN

Pharmacy

Central Park

YOTAM ROAD

NEVIOT ST

Desert Eco Tours

IMAX 3D Theatre
(cinema)

Tourist Information Centre

YOTAM RD

HATIVAT HANEGEV AV

NEVIOT ST

ELOT AVENUE

TOPAZ STREET

Eilat Guest House

ARGAMAN AVENUE

MITZRAYIM ROAD

Mall

The Arava Desert EILAT

11

261

TOURIST INFORMATION The **Eilat Tourist Information Office** (*Bridge Hse, North Beach promenade;* ☎ *08 6309111;* e *jody@tourism.gov.il;* ⊕ *08.00–18.00 Sun–Thu, 08.00–14.00 Fri*) sells tickets for most of Eilat's attractions and can offer help and advice on booking accommodation, particularly budget places which can be difficult to find in peak seasons.

TOURS The **Red Sea Sports Centre** (see page 266) offers one of the best all-round packages of excursions to get you out into the wild desert lands. Jeep safari tours include destinations such as Petra in Jordan, Timna Park and the Red Canyon. **Holit Desert Tours** (*Chan Centre;* ☎ *052 8082020;* f *08 6331210; www.holiteilat.co.il;* ⊕ *09.00–16.00 daily (for bookings 08.00–22.00)*) also has several well-priced tours to sights around southern Israel, Jordan and Sinai. They also arrange cycling tours, rappelling, camel and donkey trips, paintball and archery in the area. **Desert Eco Tours** (*Zofit Centre;* ☎ *052 2765753/3382946;* f *08 6371598;* e *erez@desertecotours.com; www.desertecotours.com*), has an exhaustive list of tours going as far afield as Cairo or as close as Timna Park. Another great way to see the beautiful countryside around Eilat is to partake in a camel safari at the **Camel Ranch** (*Nachal Shlomo;* ☎ *08 6370022;* e *tal-p@actcom.co.il; www.camel-ranch.co.il*). A half-day tour (200NIS) departs morning and afternoon. The ranch is well signposted from the south beach road. There is no public transport so you will need to take a taxi from the centre or walk from Coral Beach.

WHERE TO STAY From first appearances Eilat might look like a mass of hotels but on closer inspection you'll find that, um, indeed you were right. Big, small, cheap, expensive, classy, grubby – you name it, Eilat has it. Yet despite the volume of places to stay the city's continuing tourist boom means that you might have a hard time finding a room in the peak summer months. Budget accommodation isn't as well represented as the mid-range and certainly high-end establishments, and finding a decent, cheap hostel with vacancies is not always an easy task. Mangy mattresses and poky rooms are unfortunately commonplace in many hostels so be sure to see what you'll be getting before handing over any money.

⌂ **Hilton Queen of Sheba Hotel** 8 Antibes St; ☎ 08 6306666; f 08 6306677; www.hilton.com. The US$100 million spectacular that is the Hilton's first theme hotel, the Queen of Sheba has to be seen to be believed. Its jaw-dropping interior design focuses on Solomon & Sheba & the hotel & rooms are decorated in rich, regal colours & style. A spa, swimming pool, massive shopping mall & countless restaurants combine to form Eilat's most impressive hotel. $$$$$

⌂ **The Orchid Hotel and Resort** (178 rooms) South Beach; ☎ 08 6360360; www.orchidhotel.co.il. Standing like a gleaming tropical oasis cascading down the desert hills, the Orchid is a spectacular swirl of palm-fringed pools, luxury oriental cabins & exotic greenery. Facilities include a spa, health resort, gourmet & Thai (kosher) restaurants & access to the beautiful Migdalor Beach opposite. $$$$$

⌂ **Sheraton Herod's Hotel** (468 rooms) Ha'Yam St; ☎ 08 6380000; f 08 6380100; www.herods.co.il. Occupying prime beachfront land, the hotel is something of a tourist attraction in itself as passers-by stop to gawp. It oozes opulence & extravagance in every way & is the ultimate in self-indulgence & glamour. The adjacent, adults-only Vitalis Spa is the icing on the cake for those in search of some 'me' time. *Off-season rooms up to 1,000NIS less ($$$$$)*. $$$$$

⌂ **Caesar Resort Hotel** (241 rooms) North Beach, Tarshish St; ☎ 08 6305555; f 08 6332624; www.caesarhotels.co.il. Great location next to the lagoon, North Beach & promenade, this hotel offers fabulous value for money. Rooms come with AC, TV & wonderfully comfortable beds & the price includes a huge kosher breakfast & use of the swimming pool, jacuzzi & tennis courts. $$$$

⌂ **Astral Village** (184 rooms) Kamen St; ☎ 08 6388888; f 08 6388889; www.eilatinhotels.co.il/en_astral_village. Big resort located behind the lagoon. Kids' entertainment & lots of pools make it a good option for families. $$$

⌂ **Dalia Hotel** (63 rooms) Tarshish St, North

Beach; 08 6334004; f 08 6334072. A great location, cheap prices, comfortable rooms & good service. It offers a bar, lounge, swimming pool, internet access & well-priced Middle Eastern restaurant while bright, comfortable rooms come with TV & AC. **$$$**

🏠 **Eilat Guest House (HI)** (105 rooms) 7 Ha'Arava St; 08 6370088; e eilat@iyha.org.il; www.iyha.org.il. Cosy guest rooms complete with AC & TV. Kosher breakfast is included & extra meals can be ordered in advance. Popular with big groups of youngsters. Lovely roof café with great views over the bay. The huge hostel is located opposite the HaYam Mall. Buses 1 & 15 from the central bus station stop nearby. **$$**

🏠 **Spring Hostel** (40 rooms) 126 Ofarim St; 08 6374660/6326041; e avivhostel88@bezeqint.net; www.avivhostel.co.il. Resembling more of a mini hotel than a hostel you'll be hard pushed to find a room in the incredibly popular Spring Hostel. It's so popular in fact that staff don't feel the need to

be particularly friendly or attentive. Rooms are small but have TV, AC & some have a kitchenette while a small swimming pool, snooker table & lounge area are also available for the guests' use. **$$**

🏠 **Hotel Pierre** (34 rooms) 123 Retamim St; 08 6326601; e pierrehotel@bezeqint.net; www.eilat-guide.com/pierre. This delightful little hotel offers pleasant rooms with TV, AC & minibar. There is a small 24hr bar & continental breakfast courtesy of the French management. **$**

🏠 **Siam Divers** (10 rooms) Coral Beach; 08 6323636; e info@deepdivers.co.il; www.siam.co.il. Attached to the highly reputable diving centre, this newly renovated hostel has one of the best budget locations in the city away from the hubbub of central Eilat. *Dorms available (80NIS).* **$**

Camping Camping on the city's beaches is illegal and often enforced. That being said, just up from the Egyptian border, however, families pitch enormous tents and set up barbecue areas and settle in for the week. It has a fun atmosphere and soft white sand if you can find space. Alternatively the campsite at the **SPNI Field School** (*08 6371127; 40NIS pp*) opposite the **Coral Beach Reserve** (see page 257) has clean amenities and is open year round.

✖ **WHERE TO EAT** Eilat's restaurant options range from the sublime to slime. The city has a restaurant on every inch of space that isn't occupied by a hotel and most are of a very high standard. Unsurprisingly, fresh fish and seafood can be found on most menus and is highly recommended. For something a bit cheaper, there are plenty of fast-food chains and kiosks selling *burekas*, soggy pizza and hamburgers. For something quick and cheap there is **Domino's Pizza** along the promenade, a **Burger Ranch** in the Red Canyon Mall and **McDonald's** and **Burger King** everywhere.

EILAT South

Eilat city centre

MITZRAYIH ROAD

Dolphin Reef

Camel Ranch (camel tour)

Village Beach
Nemo Divers
Last Refuge
Coral Beach
Siam Divers Hostel
Red Sea Sport Centre
Aqua Sports

Coral Beach Reserve

MITZRAYIH ROAD

Orchid
Underwater Observatory

Taba Border Crossing
Princess Beach

Gulf of Eilat

0 ——— 400m
0 ——— 400yds

Based on mapping by Carta, Jerusalem

263

✘ **Caso do Brasil** 3 Hativat Golani St; ☎ 08 6323032; ⊕ 12.00–midnight daily. This is probably the best all you can eat anywhere in the country. It is fantastic value for money as you get the choice of pretty much any kind of meat you can imagine grilled, rotisseried or fried as well as sides of salad, bread, pasta & pizza if you have space. All-you-can-eat lunch/dinner $$$$$

✘ **Pago Pago** North Beach lagoon; ☎ 08 6376660; ⊕ 13.00–late daily. Hop aboard the chic, romantic restaurant-ship docked in the North Beach lagoon for some of the freshest fish & seafood imaginable. Albeit rather pricey, you certainly get what you pay for & the French-style gourmet dishes are superb. Their crowning glory is undoubtedly the mixed seafood platter, big enough for 2. $$$$$

✘ **Eddie's Hideaway** 68 Almogim St; ☎ 08 6371137; ⊕ 18.00–midnight Mon–Fri, 12.00–16.00 Sat. As you approach the building on Almogim St, head round the back to find the entrance. Once inside it is easy to see why this has become one of Eilat's favourite restaurants. The menu is eye popping with treats such as Nairobi shrimp cooked in spicy pineapple sauce or honey barbecued ribs gracing the pages. Comfortable, well priced & deliciously different. $$$$

✘ **Last Refuge** Coral Beach; ☎ 08 6373627; ⊕ 13.00–16.30 & 18.00–23.30 daily. Specialising in locally caught fish & seafood, this restaurant oozes nauticalia. While prices are a bit steep, you do get what you pay for in terms of quality & quantity as well as a pleasant ambience. You can

sit outside on the deck if the weather isn't too stifling. $$$$

✘ **Red Sea Star Underwater Restaurant and Bar** Next to the Meridien Hotel; ☎ 08 6347777; ⊕ 10.00–midnight daily, bar 10.00–01.00 daily. While the continental-style food won't blow you away this sea-themed restaurant & bar has taken it to the extreme & positioned itself 5m below the Red Sea. The décor is a fabulous mesh of all things aquatic while the view out of the observatory windows is the *pièce de résistance*. This is a big favourite for families so book ahead. Diners generally depart by 22.00 & then it becomes a great place to enjoy a cocktail. $$$$

✘ **Agadir** 10 Kamen St, North Beach; ☎ 08 6333777; ⊕ 12.00–03.00 daily. Part of a small nationwide chain of quality meat restaurants. A juicy selection of prime beef burgers come with chunky fries & a choice of creative fillings (& some of the classics too). $$$

✘ **Dolphin Reef Pub** (see page 258 Certainly one of the most tropical & atmospheric-feeling places in the city, you can enjoy grilled meats, fresh fish, hamburgers, salads or lighter bar food snacks as the dolphins splash away in the background. The sandy floor, swinging music (often live) & thatched roof make it a great place to spend an evening. There is a 25NIS cover charge on live music nights. $$$

✘ **Duda Restaurant** North Beach; ☎ 08 6330389; ⊕ 24hrs. Good cheap Israeli staples such as hummus, salads & chips. Located inside the Dahlia Hotel (see page 153). $$

ENTERTAINMENT AND NIGHTLIFE Many of Eilat's nightlife spots can be found around the North Beach area and along the hotel promenade, although there are some lively beach bars further along the coast. It is the city's beach bars that often form the hub of night-time activity, the balmy weather, warm sand and relaxed atmosphere (and wild parties) attracting the younger set. The tourist information centre produces the weekly *Events in Eilat* which is certainly worth picking up when you arrive.

Many of the larger hotels have discos and live music concerts, **Platinum** at the **King Solomon's Palace** being a big favourite with locals and visitors. **The Three Monkeys** (☎ 08 6368800; ⊕ 21.00–03.00 daily) has long been Eilat's flagship boogie bar and forms the centre of the North Beach nightlife. A sandy beachfront location, cheesy dance music, colorful cocktails and lots of beer have ensured its continued popularity. Nearby, **Touch Club** (☎ 08 6339088; ⊕ 23.00–late Wed–Fri) is a new hot-spot. Located inside the Spiral building in front of the marina it is a huge space incorporating an indoor dance floor and bar and outside decking with tons of seating. Thursdays is over 25s night while Friday has a 'party-time' theme. The outdoor seating area of the **Boston Grill** (☎ 08 6333007; ⊕ daily 12.00–00.00) along the promenade in front of the Royal Beach Hotel is another great place to sip a glass of chilled wine and people-watch. For something a little more tropical, the

Dolphin Reef bar and restaurant (see page 267) further south along the coast is another classic Eilat hangout.

For something a bit different there are evening cruises that offer an open bar, dancing and jacuzzis. **Lami Tourism** (*Eilat Marina;* ✆ *08 6333560*) and the **Red Sea Sports Club** (see page 266) both have regular outings in summer.

SHOPPING Israelis love shopping and nowhere more so than in Eilat's glitzy malls where everything is minus the 17% VAT. Eilat has been granted exemption from value-added tax and has subsequently seen a rise in designer and brand-name shops. For foreigners, however, prices in airport duty-free shops are probably still lower. The **Mall HaYam** has the biggest concentration of fashion shops as well as countless cafés, restaurants and sunglasses stores. The **Red Canyon Shopping Centre** on the HaTemarin Boulevard boasts three cinemas, clothes and shoe shops, bookstores and most of the city's administrative offices including Arkia Airlines and the post office, while the nearby **Shalom Centre** has souvenir shops, more clothes and shoes and several car-rental agencies.

ACTIVITIES

Scuba diving Eilat's crystal-clear waters that yield a year-round temperature of 21°C have long been a magnet for scuba divers. Rapid and extreme overdevelopment, however, has led to a serious decline in fish numbers and species and today the area is rather disappointing for seasoned divers and pales in contrast to the great dive resorts along Egypt's Sinai coast. Nevertheless, its shallow, currentless waters are perfect for beginners and still certainly pretty enough to attract scores of divers from around the country.

Diving regulations in Israel are stringent. If you have forgotten your certification card or haven't dived in the last six months expect to be asked to complete a one-hour refresher course or be refused completely. Insurance (175NIS for one year) is a must-have and can be bought from any dive centre. Strict safety rules mean that all Eilat's dive centres now hold a high standard of equipment, tuition and facilities. Needless to say, this comes at a price and you can expect to pay double what you would pay in Egypt. Packages offered by some centres are the most economical option and normally include day trips to the more fish-laden waters of Aqaba, Jordan and Sinai. Diving liveaboards to Sinai and Egypt proper are an amazing experience if your budget runs to·it.

Aqua Sports (*Coral Beach;* ✆ *08 6334404;* e *info@aqua-sport.com; www.aqua-sports.com*) Well-established centre offering the complete diving experience to both beginners and pros. Daily dive and snorkel trips to Sinai are one of their most popular excursions and they also offer liveaboard safaris to Egypt and PADI courses, with a good range of options for snorkellers.

Dolphin Reef (see page 267)

Manta Diving Centre (*Red Sea Sports Centre, Coral Beach;* ✆ *08 6370688;* f *08 6370655; www.redseasports.co.il*) Part of the fantastic **Red Sea Sports Centre** (see page 266), the diving club has probably the best choice of packages and dive excursions. Their three-day dive package (500NIS) is great value for money as is the one-week package (2,220NIS), which includes a dolphin dive, night dive, two days' diving in Aqaba with overnight accommodation and a cruise to Taba or Coral Island.

Nemo Divers (✆ *052 3515808/08 6317616;* e *contact@nemodivers.co.il; www.nemodivers.co.il*) A small, friendly dive shop which offers a comprehensive range of facilities, including PADI dive courses, introductory dives and an array of four- to nine-day liveaboard safaris to Sinai.

Siam Divers (*Coral Beach;* ✆ *08 6323636;* e *info@deepdivers.co.il; www.siam.co.il; 8 dives/with equipment 390/720NIS*) Specialising in technical diving, this big dive resort also caters to beginners and recreational divers. Activities offered include a range of diving courses, more safari liveaboards than you can shake a snorkel at, shore and boat dives and an underwater photography lab (the photographs are underwater, not the lab).

Watersports
Eilat has managed to come up with more ways to get wet than Israelis have found to eat hummus and these days the sea is abuzz with the sound of raucous splashing and the hum of motor boats. No-one does watersports better than the **Red Sea Sports Centre** (*Coral Beach;* ✆ *08 6333666; www.redseasports.co.il*) who operate most of their activities from Jetty C on the King Solomon's Wharf. Canoes, motor boats, water skiing, parasailing and banana boat rides leave regularly and don't need to be booked in advance. Cruises aboard to Coral Island (280NIS/ 1 day) and Taba (160NIS/half day) can be combined with parasailing and scuba diving.

OTHER PRACTICALITIES
Emergencies
Ambulance ✆ 101
Fire ✆ 102
Police station Hativat HaNegev Av; ✆ 100

Tourist police North Beach; ✆ 100; ◷ 10.00–15.00 Sun–Wed, 10.00–18.00 Thu–Sat

Money
$ **Bank Hapoalim** 3 Hativat HaNegev St; tel.03 6532407/landline*2407; ◷ 08.30–13.15 Sun & Tue/Wed, 08.30–12.45 & 16.00–18.00 Mon & Thu
$ **Bank Leumi** HaTemarin Bd; ✆ 03 9544555/landline *5522; ◷ 08.30–13.45 Sun & Tue/Wed, 08.30–13.00 & 16.00–18.15 Mon & Thu

$ **Currency Exchange** There are commission-free currency-exchange booths everywhere and most hotels offer money change (although the commission can often be a little on the steep side). There are countless ATMs, especially in the city centre and malls.

Post
✉ **Post Office** Red Canyon Mall; ✆ 08 6372348; ◷ 08.00–16.00 Sun–Thu. Changes money and travellers' cheques.

Medical
✚ **Yosef Tal Hospital** Yotam Rd; ✆ 08 6358011/6358025
✚ **Superpharm** 9 HaTemarin Blvd; ✆ 08 6383000;

◷ 08.30–22.00 Sun–Thu, 08.00–17.00 Fri, 10.30–23.00 Sat

Internet
@ **Private Link** Central bus station; ✆ 08 6344331; ◷ 09.00–01.00 daily. 15NIS/hr.

WHAT TO SEE
Beaches With such a small claim on the Red Sea coast, pretty much the entire stretch of Israeli land has been developed for beach activities, with the exception of the distinctly unsightly commercial port. In the midst of the city centre is **North**

Beach which forms the hub of all things gaudy and noisy but is often a big hit for youngsters or those wanting to sip a cocktail in the sun. By far the more beautiful and relaxing beaches are found closer to the Egyptian border, namely the **Princess Beach** which is the best place to swim, snorkel and chill out on the sand. Not far from the Princess Beach is the beautiful underwater garden reef of the **Coral Beach Reserve** (↘ 08 6376829; ⊕ 09.00–17.00 daily; admission adult/child 23/17NIS) which is a snorkeller's dream. Over 100 types of stony coral and 650 species of fish have been identified in the reserve and marked buoy trails lead visitors past its highlights. Just north of the reserve are the free **Coral** and **Village Beaches,** which also offer pleasant snorkelling opportunities, shaded sun loungers and waiter-serviced bars. The Village Beach in particular is known for its young atmosphere and if you're slightly self-conscious about your physique then a day here won't help things much. The Coral Beach has a more wholesome, family atmosphere frequented by a whole mishmash of shapes and sizes. For a beach experience with a difference a day at the **Dolphin Reef** (see page 267) will let you share your waters with a family of bottlenosed dolphins.

Underwater Observatory Marine Park (↘ 08 6364200; www.coralworld.com;
⊕ 08.30–16.30 Sat–Thu, 08.30–15.00 Fri; admission adult/child 63/45NIS, with oceanarium 76/58NIS) The futuristic-looking white observatory is an Eilat landmark, jutting out into the reef along the coast. For non-divers and children, the observatory is a lovely way to see life beneath the waves with its 360°, 6m-deep observation deck. For a less natural experience there is a shark tank, aquariums and outdoor turtle and stingray pool while the newly built **oceanarium** is an extremely enjoyable all-moving, all-shaking simulative movie theatre that takes delighted visitors on a tour of the deep-blue seas. The Coral 2000 **semi-submarine**, which has regular departures from the park, is, in fact, no more than a fancy-looking glass-bottomed boat but is, nonetheless, an enjoyable way to see the reef .

Dolphin Reef (↘ 07 6375935; www.dolphinreef.co.il; e info@dolphinreef.co.il; ⊕ 09.00–
17.00 Sun–Thu, 09.00–16.30 Fri/Sat; admission adult/child 53/37NIS) The special relationship between man and dolphin is nowhere more prevalent than at the Dolphin Reef, where a group of bottlenose dolphins, given the choice between human interaction or not, have chosen to stick around. Floating pontoons allow visitors to see the dolphins playing, feeding and interacting, while snorkelling (233NIS/half hour) or diving (280NIS/half hour) encounters provide a once-in-a-lifetime opportunity to get up close and personal. The small beach in the park is separated from the dolphins by a net allowing even swimmers to get close to the dolphins. Snorkelling and diving experiences should be booked up to two weeks in advance in peak seasons. There is no admission fee after 17.00 when the dolphin sessions finish for the day but the lively bar and café remain open until the small hours.

IMAX 3D (4 Yotam Rd; ↘ 08 6361000; e marka@imaxeilat.co.il; www.imaxeilat.co.il;
⊕ 11.00–midnight Sun–Thu, 11.00–Shabbat Fri, 21.00–01.00 Sat; admission 55NIS) Showing a selection of 3D movies ranging from dinosaurs to sea creatures to aliens, this is a fun-for-all-the-family activity.

King's City (Opposite New Lagoon; ↘ 08 6304444; e sales3@kingscity.co.il;
www.kingscity.co.il; ⊕ 09.00–01.00 Sun–Thu, 09.00–Shabbat Fri, end of Shabbat–01.00 Sat; admission adult/child 118/95NIS) This biblical theme park takes visitors (generally those under the age of 15) on a journey through time, using state-of-the-art technology and equipment. Travel from the Egyptian pharaohs to King

Solomon past optical illusions, labyrinths, a water flume ride and into the biblical cave for a 3D movie.

Birdwatching Centre While Eilat's tourism boom has soared over the past decade and people flock to its warm waters and party atmosphere, the city has long since been a holiday destination for visitors of the winged variety. Along with the Galilee's Hula Valley (see page 209), this region is one of the world's best birdwatching spots as they pass on their north–south migration routes from Europe and Africa. The **International Birding and Research Centre** (✆ *050 2112498;* e *ibrce@eilatcity.co.il; www.birdsofeilat.com*) offers expertly guided birdwatching tours in 4x4 jeeps (150NIS/2 hours, 400NIS/full day) as well as the possibility of partaking in the tagging and releasing of birds for research (09.30–11.00, 35NIS). The birdwatching park and centre are located just north of the city near the King Hussein border crossing to Jordan. Turn right at the Eilot Junction (just after the kibbutz), from where it is signposted. The park includes both salty and freshwater pools fringed with different species of vegetation and can be accessed by a variety of picturesque walking trails perfect for wildlife spotting. Binoculars can be rented at the centre for a small charge. In March of every year the **Eilat Spring Migration Festival** (*www.eilatbirdsfestival.com*) is held to coincide with one of the biggest fly-bys of migratory birds. Special all-inclusive flight, transfer, hotel and birding activities packages can be arranged through their website.

Appendix I

LANGUAGE

The Hebrew *alephbet* consists of 27 letters almost all of which are consonants, although there are several letters that can function as vowels. A series of dots and dashes that represent vowels are marked beneath words in children's books and the Bible but are generally omitted from other text. Hebrew words run from right to left and, as such, books, cards, magazines, etc will open in reverse to what is common in many other countries. Pronunciation is generally on the last syllable of the word. Some letters are known in Hebrew as *sofit* or final, and are used at the end of words. They have the same pronunciation but take a different form, for example כ which is ך at the end of words. The Hebrew words below have been spelt phonetically in the alphabet although it is important to note that 'ch' should be pronounced like a throaty 'h', not as in cheese or church.

א *aleph*	Is used either as a silent letter or to make an 'a' sound.
ב *bet*	Can be pronounced as both 'b' or 'v'.
ג *gimel*	Pronounced like the English 'g' as in goat.
ד *dalet*	Pronounced like the English 'd' as in duck.
ה *hey*	Pronounced like the English 'h' as in harp. Takes on a more 'ar' sound when used at the end of words.
ו *vav*	Pronounced like the English 'v' as in volcano. Often used as the vowels 'o' as in octopus or 'u' as in tuna.
ז *zayin*	Pronounced like the English 'z' as in zebra.
ח *chet*	Pronounced like a throaty 'h' (there is no similar sound in the English language).
ט *tet*	Pronounced like the English 't' as in tumble.
י *yud*	Pronounced like the English 'y' as in yak. Can also be as 'i' as in igloo or 'ee' as in sweet.
כ (ך) *kaf*	Pronounced like the English 'k' as in kettle.
ל *lamed*	Pronounced like the English 'l' as in lemon.
מ (ם) *mem*	Pronounced like the English 'm' as in mountain.
נ (ן) *nun*	Pronounced like the English 'n' as in notebook.
ס *samech*	Pronounced like the English 's' as in summer.
ע *ayin*	Pronounced like a throaty 'i' or 'a' as in iron.
פ (ף) *pey*	Can be pronounced as either 'p' or 'f'.
צ (ץ) *tzadik*	Pronounced like 'tz' as in 'pssst' when trying to get someone's attention.
ק *kof*	Pronounced like the English 'k' or 'c' as in coffee.
ר *resh*	Pronounced like a throaty 'r' as in the French *raison d'être*.
ש *sheen*	Can be pronounced as either 'sh' or 's'.
ת *taf*	Pronounced like the English 't' as in tea.

ESSENTIALS

Good morning	boker tov	בוקר טוב
Good evening	erev tov	ערב טוב
Goodnight	layla tov	לילה טוב
Hello/goodbye	shalom	שלום
My name is…	kor-eem li…	קוראים לי
What is your name?	eich kor-eem lecha (m)/lach (f)?	איך קוראים לך?
I am from…England/	ani me…anglia/	אני מאנגליה/מאמריקה/מאוסטרליה
America/Australia	america/ostralia	
How are you?	ma shlomcha (m)/shlomech (f)	מה שלומך?
Pleased to meet you	naim lehakir otcha (m)/othach (f)	נעים להכיר אותך
Thank you	toda	תודה
Please	bevakasha	בבקשה
Don't mention it	al lo davar	על לא דבר
Cheers!	Lechaim!	לחיים
Yes	ken	כן
No	lo	לא
I don't understand	ani lo mevin (m)/mevina (f)	אני לא מבין/מבינה
Please would you	bevakasha daber (m)/	בבקשה דבר/דברי יותר לאט
speak more slowly	dabri (f) yoter le-at	
Do you understand?	ata mevin (m)/at mevina (f)?	אתה מבין/את מבינה

QUESTIONS

How?	eich?	איך?
What?	ma?	מה?
Where?	eifo?	איפה ?
What is it?	ma ze?	מה זה ?
Which?	eize?	איזה ?
When?	matai?	מתי ?
Why?	lama?	למה ?
Who?	mi?	מי ?
How much?	kama?	כמה ?

NUMBERS

1	echad	אחד
2	shtaim	שתים
3	shalosh	שלוש
4	arba	ארבע
5	chamesh	חמש
6	shesh	שש
7	sheva	שבע
8	shmoneh	שמונה
9	teshah	תשע
10	eser	עשר
11	echad esreh	אחד עשרה
12	shteim esreh	שתים עשרה
13	shlosh esreh	שלוש עשרה
14	arba esreh	ארבע עשרה
15	chamesh esreh	חמש עשרה
16	shesh esreh	שש עשרה
17	shvah esreh	שבע עשרה
18	shmona esreh	שמונה עשרה
19	tsha esreh	תשע עשרה

20	esrim	עשרים
21	esrim ve echad	עשרים ואחד
30	shloshim	שלושים
40	arbaim	ארבעים
50	chamishim	חמישים
60	shishim	שישים
70	shivim	שבעים
80	shmonim	שמונים
90	tishim	תשעים
100	meah	מאה
1,000	elef	אלף

TIME

What time is it?	ma hasha'a?	מה השעה
It's...in the morning/at night	Hasha'a...baboker/balayla	השעה ...בבוקר/בלילה
Today	hayom	היום
Tonight	halayla	הלילה
Tomorrow	machar	מחר
Yesterday	etmol	אתמול
Morning	boker	בוקר
Evening	erev	ערב

DAYS

Sunday	yom rishon	יום ראשון
Monday	yom sheni	יום שני
Tuesday	yom shlishi	יום שלישי
Wednesday	yom reviee	יום רביעי
Thursday	yom chamishi	יום חמישי
Friday	yom shishi	יום שישי
Saturday	yom shabbat	יום שבת

MONTHS

January	yanuar	ינואר
February	februar	פברואר
March	mertz	מרץ
April	april	אפריל
May	mai	מאי
June	yuni	יוני
July	yuli	יולי
August	ogust	אוגוסט
September	september	ספטמבר
October	october	אוקטובר
November	november	נובמבר
December	detzember	דצמבר

GETTING AROUND
Public transport

I'd like...	*ani rotzeh (m)/rotzah (f)...*	אני רוצה
...a one-way ticket	*...cartis chad kivuni*	כרטיס חד כיווני
...a return ticket	*...cartis du kivuni*	כרטיס דו כיווני
I want to go to...	*ani rotzeh (m)/rotzah (f) lehagia le...*	אני רוצה להגיע ל...
How much is it?	*kama ze oleh?*	כמה זה עולה?
What time does the...leave?	*be eize sha'a ha...ozev?*	באיזה שעה ה...עוזב?
The train has been delayed/cancelled	*harakevet mitakevet/butlah*	הרכבת מתעכבת/בוטלה
Platform	*ratzif*	רציף
Ticket office	*misrad cartisim*	משרד כרטיסים
Timetable	*luach zmanim*	לוח זמנים
From	*meh*	מ
To	*el*	אל
Bus station	*tachanat otobus*	תחנת אוטובוס
Train station	*tachanat rakevet*	תחנת רכבת
Airport	*namal te'ufah*	נמל תעופה
Port	*namal*	נמל
Bus	*otobus*	אוטובוס
Train	*rakevet*	רכבת
Plane	*matoss*	מטוס
Boat	*oneeyah*	אוניה
Ferry	*ma'aboret*	מעבורת
Car	*mechonit*	מכונית
4x4	*arba al arba*	ארבע על ארבע
Taxi	*monit*	מונית
Minibus	*minibus*	מיניבוס
Motorbike	*ofanoa*	אופנוע
Bicycle	*ofnaim*	אופניים
Arrival/departure	*nichnasim/yotzim*	נכנסים/יוצאים
Here	*po*	פה
There	*sham*	שם
Bon voyage!	*derech tzlecha!*	דרך צלחה!

Private transport

Is this the road to...?	*zot haderech le...?*	זאת הדרך ל...?
Where is the service station?	*eifo hatachanat delek?*	איפה התחנת דלק?
Please fill it up	*bevakasha maleh ad hasof*	בבקשה מלא עד הסוף
I'd like...litres	*ani rotzeh (m)/rotzah (f)...litres*	אני רוצה ...ליטר
Diesel	*diesel*	דיזל
Leaded petrol	*ragil*	רגיל
Unleaded petrol	*netul oferet*	נטול עופרת
I have broken down	*nitkati*	נתקעתי

Road signs

English	Transliteration	Hebrew
Give way	zchut kdima	זכות קדימה
Danger	sakanah	סכנה
Entry	knissah	כניסה
Detour	ma'akaf	מעקף
One way	chad sitri	חד סיטרי
Toll	mass	מס
No entry	ein knissah	אין כניסה
Exit	yetziah	יציאה

Directions

English	Transliteration	Hebrew
Where is it?	eifo?	איפה?
Go straight ahead	lech (m)/lechi (f) yashar	לך/לכי ישר
Turn left	pneh (m)/pni (f) smola	פנה/פני שמאלה
Turn right	pneh (m)/pni (f) yamina	פנה/פני ימינה
...at the traffic lights	...bah ramzor	...ברמזור
...at the roundabout	...bah kikkar	...בכיכר
North	tzafon	צפון
South	darom	דרום
East	mizrach	מזרח
West	ma'arav	מערב
Behind	meachor	מאחור
In front of	lifnei	לפני
Near	leyad	ליד
Opposite	mul	מול

Street signs

English	Transliteration	Hebrew
Entrance	knissah	כניסה
Exit	yetziah	יציאה
Open	patuach	פתוח
Closed	sagur	סגור
Toilets – men/women	sherutim – gvarim/nashim	שרותים גברים/נשים
Information	meidah	מידע

ACCOMMODATION

English	Transliteration	Hebrew
Where is a cheap/good hotel?	eifo yesh malon zol/tov?	איפה יש מלון זול/טוב?
Could you please write me the address?	bevakasha reshom li et haktovet?	בבקשה רשום לי את הכתובת?
Do you have any rooms available?	Yesh haderim pnuim?	יש חדרים פנויים?
I'd like...	ani rotzeh (m)/rotzah (f)...	...אני רוצה
...a single room	...cheder yachid	...חדר יחיד
...a double room	...cheder zugi	...חדר זוגי
...a room with two beds	...cheder im shtei mitot	חדר עם שתי מיטות
...a room with a bathroom	...cheder im miklachat vesherutim	חדר עם מקלחת ושרותים
...to share a dorm	...cheder meshutaf	...חדר משותף
How much is it per night/person?	kama ole lelayla/leadam?	כמה עולה ללילה/לאדם?
Is breakfast included?	haim kolol aruchat boker?	האם כולל ארוחת בוקר?
I am leaving today	ani ozev hayom	אני עוזב היום

FOOD

Do you have a table for…people?	yesh shulchan le…anashim?	יש שולחן ל...אנשים?
…a children's menu?	…tafrit yeladim?	תפריט ילדים?
I am a vegetarian	ani tzimchoni	אני צימחוני
Do you have any vegetarian dishes?	yesh manot tzimchoniot?	יש מנות צימחוניות?
Is this restaurant kosher?	ha'im hamisada ksherah?	האם המסעדה כשרה?
Please may I have…	bevakasha efshar lekabel…	בבקשה אפשר לקבל
…a fork/knife/spoon/the bill	…mazleg/sakin/kaf/cheshbon	מזלג/סכין/כף/חשבון...
Bon appétit!	bete'avon!	בתאבון!

Basics

Bread	lechem	לחם
Butter	chem'a	חמאה
Cheese	gvina	גבינה
Oil	shemen	שמן
Pepper	pilpel	פלפל
Salt	melach	מלח
Sugar	sucar	סוכר

Fruit

Apples	tapuchim	תפוחים
Bananas	bananot	בננות
Grapes	anavim	ענבים
Mangoes	mango	מנגו
Oranges	tapuzim	תפוזים
Pears	agassim	אגסים

Vegetables

Broccoli	broccoli	ברוקולי
Carrots	gzarim	גזרים
Garlic	shum	שום
Onions	btzalim	בצלים
Peppers	pilpelim	פלפלים
Potatoes	tapuchei adama	תפוחי אדמה

Fish

Mackerel	makrel	מקרל
Salmon	salmon	פירות ים
Shellfish	peyrot yam	סלמון
Tuna	tuna	טונה

Meat

Beef	baker	בקר
Chicken	off	עוף
Goat	ez	עז
Lamb	kevess	חזיר
Pork	chazir	כבש
Turkey	tarnegol hodu	תרנגול הודו

DRINKS

Beer	bira	בירה
Coffee	kafeh	קפה
Fruit juice	mitz peyrot	מיץ פירות
Milk	chalav	חלב
Tea	teh	תה
Water	maim	מים
Wine	yain	יין

SHOPPING

English	Transliteration	Hebrew
I'd like to buy...	ani rotzeh (m)/rotzah (f) liknot...	אני רוצה לקנות
How much is it?	kama ze ole?	כמה זה עולה?
I don't like it	ani lo ohev (m)/ohevet (f) et ze	אני לא אוהב/אוהבת את זה
I'm just looking	ani rak mistakel (m)/mistakelet (f?)	אני רק מסתכל/מסתכלת
It's too expensive	ze yakar midai	זה יקר מדי
I'll take it	ani ekach et ze	אני אקח את זה
Please may I have...	bevakasha efshar...	בבקשה אפשר...
Do you accept...?	ata mekabel...?	אתה מקבל...?
Credit cards	cartis ashrai	כרטיס אשראי
Travellers' cheques	hamcha'at noss'im	המחאת נוסעים
More	yotair	יותר
Less	pachot	פחות
Smaller	katan yotair	קטן יותר
Bigger	gadol yotair	גדול יותר

COMMUNICATIONS

I'm looking for...	ani mechapess (m)/mechapesset (f) et ha...	אני מחפש/מחפשת את ה...
Bank	bank	בנק
Post office	sniff hadoar	סניף הדואר
Church	knessiah	כנסיה
Synagogue	bet haknesset	בית הכנסת
Mosque	misgad	מיסגד
...embassy	...shagrirut	שגרירות...
Currency exchange	chalfan ksafim	חלפן כספים
Internet café	internet kafeh	אינטרנט קפה
Tourist information office	merkaz meidah tayarut	מרכז מידע תיירותי

EMERGENCIES

English	Transliteration	Hebrew
Help!	hatzilu!	הצילו!
Call a doctor!	tikre'u le rofeh!	תקראו לרופא!
There's been an accident	haita te'una	היתה תאונה
I'm lost	halachti le'ibud	הלכתי לאיבוד
Go away!	lech (m)/lechi (f) meepo!	לך/לכי מפה!
Police	mishtarah	משטרה
Fire	esh	אש
Ambulance	ambulance	אמבולנס
Thief	ganav	גנב
Hospital	beit cholim	בית חולים
I am ill	ani choleh (m)/cholah (f)	אני חולה

Patience/please wait	joining all fingers and thumb together at the tips
Scepticism	putting one index finger to just under the eye
Hitchhiking	pointing at the ground with an index finger

HEALTH

Diarrhoea	shilshul	שלשול
Nausea	bchilah	בחילה
Doctor	rofeh	רופא
Prescription	nirsham	מרשם
Pharmacy	beit merkachat	בית מרקחת
Paracetamol	paracetamol	פאראסטמול
Antibiotics	antibiotika	אנטיביוטיקה
Antiseptic	chomer mechateh	חומר מחטא
Condom	condom	קונדום
Tampons	tamponim	טמפונים
Contraceptive	glulot neged herayon	גלולות נגד הריון
Sunblock	crem shizuf	קרם שיזוף
I am...	ani...	אני...
...asthmatic	...astmati	...אסטמתי
...epileptic	...epilepti	...אפילפטי
...diabetic	...choleh sokeret	חולה סוכרת
I'm allergic to...	ani elergi le...	...אני אלרגי ל
...penicillin	...penetzilin	פניצילין
...nuts	...egozim	...אגוזים
...bees	...dvorim	...דבורים

TRAVEL WITH CHILDREN

Is there a...?	ha'im yesh...?	?האם יש
...baby changing room	...pinat hachtalah	פינת ההחתלה
...a children's menu	...tafrit le yeladim	תפריט לילדים
Do you have...?	yesh lachem...?	? יש לכם
...infant milk formula	...tachlif chalav letinokot	...תחליף חלב לתינוקות
Nappies	chitulim	חיתולים
Potty	sir layla	סיר לילה
Babysitter	shmartaf	שמרטף
Highchair	kisseh yeladim	כסא ילדים

OTHER

Mine/ours/yours	sheli/shelanu/shelcha	שלי/שלנו/שלך
And/some/but	ve/kama/aval	ו/כמה/אבל
This/that	ze	זה
Expensive/cheap	yakar/zol	יקר/זול
Beautiful/ugly	yaffeh/mecho'ar	יפה/מכוער
Old/new	yashan/chadash	ישן/חדש
Good/bad	tov/ra	טוב/רע
Early/late	mukdam/me'uchar	מוקדם/מאוחר
Hot/cold	cham/kar	חם/קר
Difficult/easy	kasheh/kal	קשה/קל
Boring/interesting	mesha'amem/me'anien	משעמם/מעניין

Appendix 2

BOOKS
Historical and religious

A History of Modern Israel by Colin Shindler. 2008. Cambridge University Press. ISBN 978 0521615389.

Everyman's Talmud by Abraham Cohen. 1995. Schocken Books. ISBN 978 0805210323.

History of Ancient Israel and Judah by J. Maxwell Miller. 2006. SCM Press. ISBN 978 0334041177.

How to Read the Qu'ran by M. Siddiqui. 2008. W.W Norton & Co. ISBN 978 0393330809.

Introducing the Old Testament by John W. Drane. 2000. Lion Hudson Plc. ISBN 978 0745950167.

Israel: A History by Sir Martin Gilbert. 2008. Black Swan. ISBN 978 0552774284.

Israel: the Historical Atlas by The New York Times. 1997. John Wiley & Sons. ISBN 978 0028619873.

Kabbalah for Dummies by Arthur Kurzweil. 2006. John Wiley & Sons. ISBN 978 0471915904.

Lionhearts: Heroes of Israel by Michael Bar-Zohar. 2000. Little, Brown & Co. ISBN 978-0446523585.

Ploughshares into Swords: From Zionism to Israel by Arno Mayer. 2008. Verso Books. ISBN 9781844672356.

Schindler's List by Thomas Keneally. 1994. Hodder and Stoughton. ISBN 9780340606513.

The Politics of Sacred Space: The Old City of Jerusalem in the Middle East Conflict by Michael Dumper. 2001. Lynne Rienner Publishers Inc. ISBN 9781588260161.

The Quest for the Historical Israel: Debating Archaeology and the History of Early Israel by Israel Finkelstein, Amihai Mazar and Brian Schmidt. 2007. Society of Biblical Literature. ISBN 9781589832770.

The Torah: The Five Books of Moses by Sarna. 1992. Jewish Publication Society. ISBN 9780827600157.

Fiction

Light Fell by Evan Fallenberg. 2008. SOHO Press. ISBN 9781569474672.

My Michael by Amos Oz. 1992. Vintage. ISBN 9780099747307.

Guidebooks and General Reference

A Photographic Guide to Birds of Israel and the Middle East by Richard Porter and David Cottridge. 2000. New Holland Publishers Ltd. ISBN 9781859745083.

Israel – A Spiritual Travel Guide, 2nd Ed: A Companion for the Modern Jewish Pilgrim by Rabbi Lawrence Hoffman. 2005. Jewish Lights. ISBN 9781580232616.

Oxford English/Hebrew Hebrew/English Dictionary by Ya'acov Levy. 1999. Kernermann Publishing. ISBN 978-9653070271.

The Millennium Guide for Pilgrims to the Holy Land by Cardinal Edward Cassidy and James H. Charlesworth. 2000. D & F Scott Publishing Inc. ISBN 9780941037938.

WEBSITES

www.jewishencyclopedia.com
www.parks.org.il Israel Nature and National Parks Authority.
www.eyeonisrael.com Interactive map of the country.
www.goisrael.com Israel Ministry of Tourism
www.kabbalah.com Official website of the Kabbalah Centre.
www.kashrut.com Kosher and Jewish prayer time information service.
www.qibla.org Muslim prayer times.
www.jerusalem.muni.il Jerusalem Municipal Tourism department.

WIN £100 CASH!

READER QUESTIONNAIRE

Send in your completed questionnaire for the chance to win £100 cash in our regular draw

All respondents may order a Bradt guide at half the UK retail price – please complete the order form overleaf.

(Entries may be posted or faxed to us, or scanned and emailed.)

We are interested in getting feedback from our readers to help us plan future Bradt guides. Please answer ALL the questions below and return the form to us in order to qualify for an entry in our regular draw.

Have you used any other Bradt guides? If so, which titles? . . . .

. . . .

What other publishers' travel guides do you use regularly? . . . .

. . . .

Where did you buy this guidebook? . . . .

What was the main purpose of your trip to Israel (or for what other reason did you read our guide)? eg: holiday/business/charity etc.. . . . .

. . . .

What other destinations would you like to see covered by a Bradt guide?

. . . .

Would you like to receive our catalogue/newsletters?

YES / NO (If yes, please complete details on reverse)

If yes – by post or email? . . . .

Age (circle relevant category) 16–25   26–45   46–60   60+

Male/Female (delete as appropriate)

Home country . . . .

Please send us any comments about our guide to Israel or other Bradt Travel Guides. . . . .

. . . .

. . . .

. . . .

Bradt Travel Guides
23 High Street, Chalfont St Peter, Bucks SL9 9QE, UK
✆ +44 (0)1753 893444 **f** +44 (0)1753 892333
e info@bradtguides.com
www.bradtguides.com

CLAIM YOUR HALF-PRICE BRADT GUIDE!

Order Form

To order your half-price copy of a Bradt guide, and to enter our prize draw to win £100 (see overleaf), please fill in the order form below, complete the questionnaire overleaf, and send it to Bradt Travel Guides by post, fax or email.

Please send me one copy of the following guide at half the UK retail price

Title	Retail price	Half price
...	....	....	......

Please send the following additional guides at full UK retail price

No	Title	Retail price	Total
...	....	....	......
...	....	....	......
...	....	....	......

Sub total ....
Post & packing ....
(£2 per book UK; £4 per book Europe; £6 per book rest of world)
Total ....

Name . . . .

Address. . . . .

Tel . . . .   Email . . . .

☐ I enclose a cheque for £ . . . . made payable to Bradt Travel Guides Ltd

☐ I would like to pay by credit card. Number: . . . .

Expiry date: . . . / . . .   3-digit security code (on reverse of card) . . . . .

Issue no (debit cards only) . . . . .

☐ Please add my name to your catalogue mailing list.

☐ I would be happy for you to use my name and comments in Bradt marketing material.

Send your order on this form, with the completed questionnaire, to:

Bradt Travel Guides ISR1
23 High Street, Chalfont St Peter, Bucks SL9 9QE
☏ +44 (0)1753 893444   f +44 (0)1753 892333
e info@bradtguides.com   www.bradtguides.com

Bradt Travel Guides

www.bradtguides.com

Africa

Africa Overland	£15.99
Algeria	£15.99
Benin	£14.99
Botswana: Okavango, Chobe, Northern Kalahari	£15.99
Burkina Faso	£14.99
Cameroon	£15.99
Canary Islands	£13.95
Cape Verde Islands	£13.99
Congo	£15.99
Eritrea	£15.99
Ethiopia	£15.99
Gabon, São Tomé, Príncipe	£13.95
Gambia, The	£13.99
Ghana	£15.99
Johannesburg	£6.99
Kenya	£14.95
Madagascar	£15.99
Malawi	£13.99
Mali	£13.95
Mauritius, Rodrigues & Réunion	£13.99
Mozambique	£13.99
Namibia	£15.99
Niger	£14.99
Nigeria	£17.99
Rwanda	£14.99
São Tomé & Príncipe	£14.99
Seychelles	£14.99
Sudan	£13.95
Tanzania, Northern	£13.99
Tanzania	£16.99
Uganda	£15.99
Zambia	£17.99
Zanzibar	£12.99

Britain and Europe

Albania	£15.99
Armenia, Nagorno Karabagh	£14.99
Azores	£13.99
Baltic Capitals: Tallinn, Riga, Vilnius, Kaliningrad	£12.99
Belarus	£14.99
Belgrade	£6.99
Bosnia & Herzegovina	£13.99
Bratislava	£6.99
Budapest	£8.99
Bulgaria	£13.99
Cork	£6.99
Croatia	£13.99

Cyprus see North Cyprus	
Czech Republic	£13.99
Dresden	£7.99
Dubrovnik	£6.99
Estonia	£13.99
Faroe Islands	£15.99
Georgia	£14.99
Helsinki	£7.99
Hungary	£14.99
Iceland	£14.99
Kiev	£7.95
Kosovo	£14.99
Lapland	£13.99
Latvia	£13.99
Lille	£6.99
Lithuania	£14.99
Ljubljana	£7.99
Luxembourg	£13.99
Macedonia	£14.99
Montenegro	£14.99
North Cyprus	£12.99
Paris, Lille & Brussels	£11.95
Riga	£6.95
River Thames, In the Footsteps of the Famous	£10.95
Serbia	£14.99
Slovakia	£14.99
Slovenia	£13.99
Spitsbergen	£15.99
Switzerland: Rail, Road, Lake	£13.99
Tallinn	£6.99
Transylvania	£14.99
Ukraine	£14.99
Vilnius	£6.99
Zagreb	£6.99

Middle East, Asia and Australasia

Borneo	£17.99
China: Yunnan Province	£13.99
Great Wall of China	£13.99
Iran	£14.99
Iraq: Then & Now	£15.99
Kazakhstan	£15.99
Kyrgyzstan	£15.99
Maldives	£13.99
Mongolia	£16.99
North Korea	£14.99
Oman	£13.99
Shangri La	£14.99
Sri Lanka	£13.99
Syria	£14.99
Tibet	£13.99

Turkmenistan	£14.99
Yemen	£14.99

The Americas and the Caribbean

Amazon, The	£14.99
Argentina	£15.99
Bolivia	£14.99
Cayman Islands	£14.99
Chile	£16.95
Chile & Argentina: The Bradt Trekking Guide	£12.95
Colombia	£16.99
Costa Rica	£13.99
Dominica	£14.99
Falkland Islands	£13.95
Guyana	£14.99
Panama	£13.95
Peru & Bolivia: Backpacking & Trekking	£12.95
St Helena	£14.99
USA by Rail	£14.99

Wildlife

100 Animals to See Before They Die	£16.99
Antarctica: Guide to the Wildlife	£14.95
Arctic: Guide to the Wildlife	£15.99
Central & Eastern European Wildlife	£15.99
Chinese Wildlife	£16.99
East African Wildlife	£19.99
Galápagos Wildlife	£15.99
Madagascar Wildlife	£15.99
Peruvian Wildlife	£15.99
Southern African Wildlife	£18.95
Sri Lankan Wildlife	£15.99

Eccentric Guides

Eccentric Australia	£12.99
Eccentric Britain	£13.99
Eccentric California	£13.99
Eccentric Cambridge	£6.99
Eccentric Edinburgh	£5.95
Eccentric France	£12.95
Eccentric London	£13.99
Eccentric Oxford	£5.95

Others

Your Child Abroad: A Travel Health Guide	£10.95
Something Different for the Weekend	£9.99

Index

Page numbers in **bold** indicate major entries; those in *italics* indicate maps